PACIFIC ASIA IN THE 21ST CENTURY
Geographical and Developmental Perspectives

PACIFIC ASIA IN THE 21ST CENTURY
Geographical and Developmental Perspectives

Edited by

Yue-man Yeung

The Chinese University Press

ISBN 962–201–599–9

THE CHINESE UNIVERSITY PRESS
The Chinese University of Hong Kong
SHATIN, N. T., HONG KONG

Printed in Hong Kong by Nam Fung Printing Co., Ltd.

Contents

List of Figures and Tables

Figures

Tables

Preface

The workshop from which this volume has stemmed was jointly sponsored by the Commonwealth Geographical Bureau, the Department of Geography and the Hong Kong Institute of Asia-Pacific Studies at The Chinese University of Hong Kong. It was the first time in its existence of more than twenty years that the Bureau chose Hong Kong as a venue for its workshop. Despite its regional theme, the workshop was attended by representatives from twelve Commonwealth countries, including India, Sri Lanka and Kenya. Sixteen papers were presented in seven sessions, but this volume includes only thirteen of these papers, while two additional papers were received after the workshop was held.

The theme of the workshop, "Geography and Development in Pacific Asia: Towards the 21st century," was chosen with the deliberate purpose of focussing on the broad dimensions of geographical and development issues in a rapidly changing region in physical, economic and social terms. The additional futuristic perspective was embraced because only a few years remain in this century and the likely acceleration of technological and economic changes in the countries in the region, in step with similar changes worldwide, as the 21st century is rapidly dawning on us. This broad canvas on a forward-looking track permits scholars and geographers from different parts of the Commonwealth to draw on experience and vignettes of the region and the countries. In this exercise some valuable lessons of recent development trends are drawn upon in some papers, while exciting vistas of the future are proffered in others. In all, if this volume reveals certain development trends, calls attention to some danger signals, and better prepares policy-makers, scholars and investors to anticipate and perhaps cope with the future, the objectives of this project will have been realized. It is probably the first time that diverse and sweeping human and physical changes in a rapidly growing region are studied with a futuristic orientation.

For a project extending over a long time and involving many individuals in many countries, its successful completion owes to the assistance, goodwill and support of many institutions and people. First of all, the financial support extended by the Commonwealth Foundation towards the workshop held on the 10–14 December 1990 in Hong Kong is gratefully acknowledged. The Commonwealth Geographical Bureau, in particular through Professors John I. Parry, Philip Courtenay and Denis Dwyer, has provided institutional collaboration and personal encouragement. Preparation and the actual running of the workshop relied heavily on an organizing committee consisting of: Yue-man Yeung (Chairman), Kwan-yiu Wong (Vice-Chairman), Ron Neller (Secretary), Fung Tung (Treasurer), and Wing-sing Tang (Activities Convenor). Equally, the Hong Kong Institute of Asia-Pacific Studies provided key secretariat, publicity and logistical support for the workshop. Thanks are due especially to Kin-sheun Louie, Chung-kang Lu and Janet Wong. Chung-kang Lu, of the Urban and Regional Development in Pacific Asia Programme of the Institute, provided able and valuable support to this project, while Janet Wong handled most of the correspondence with the authors. Irene Lai prepared the index and helped with proofreading. From the Department of Geography, Jane Wan and Yuk-mui Yu typed and retyped the manuscript and S. L. Too redrew some of the maps and illustrations. Norton Ginsburg commented helpfully on parts of the manuscript. Last but not least, my sincere appreciation is extended to all participating authors whose valuable contributions, friendly patience and unflagging support have lightened my task of putting this volume together. For any remaining shortcomings in presentation and representation, they are largely mine.

Yue-man Yeung
Hong Kong Institute of Asia-Pacific Studies,
The Chinese University of Hong Kong
April 1993

PART I

Introduction

CHAPTER ONE

Physical and Economic Transformation of Pacific Asia

Yue-man Yeung

*Director, Hong Kong Institute of Asia-Pacific Studies and Professor of
Geography, The Chinese University of Hong Kong, Hong Kong*

Many regions of the world have witnessed momentous material and social
change since the end of World War II, but none can rival the vast and
profound transformation, both physically and economically, that has en-
gulfed the congeries of countries and societies rimming the Western Pacific
Ocean. The transformation is unprecedented in its scale and speed in human
history and, with the globalization trends of late, has increasingly captured
the imagination and attention of politicians, scholars and planners alike. In
identifying the 19th century as the British Century, followed by the
American epoch of eighty years, Weiss (1989) was so sanguine about the
future of the Asian region that he maintained the "Asian Century" had
arrived with the 1980s. Other researchers, noting the shift of gravitation of
economic growth from the Atlantic Rim to the Pacific Rim since the 1970s
and convinced of the positive outlook of the Asia-Pacific region in the future,
have ventured to suggest that the coming century will be the Pacific Century
(Linder, 1986; Ginsburg, 1988). Still other observers temper these en-
thusiasms by underscoring the resurgence of Europe in the late 1980s and
the emergence of a single and expanded European market in 1992 and
presaged a multipolar and borderless global economy (Banfe, 1992).

Whatever might be perceived of the future, there is no disagreement that
the relative importance of that part of Asia comprising East and Southeast
Asia, or simply Pacific Asia, will increase in world affairs. This region would

include all the countries on the Western Pacific Rim stretching from Korea to Indonesia. Thus defined, the term includes the economic superpower of Japan, the four newly industrializing economies of Asia (NIEs, that is, Hong Kong, Singapore, South Korea, and Taiwan), the six countries of the Association of Southeast Asian Nations (ASEAN) of Brunei, Indonesia, Malaysia, Philippines, Singapore, and Thailand, a renascent China, and the countries of Indo-China (Figure 1.1). In 1990 Pacific Asia accounted for 57 percent of Asia's and 34 percent of the world's population; by century-end, these proportions in population will decline to 54 and 32 percent respectively. In contrast to its loss in demographic weight, Pacific Asia is likely to gain greater economic prominence in global terms if recent trends continue.

Lessons of Rapid Growth

The rise of Pacific Asia from poorhouse to powerhouse in the postwar period is a collective success story. This story is the subject of a spate of recent publications (Amsden, 1989; Hughes, 1988; Deyo, 1987; Wade, 1990; Shibusawa, Ahmad and Bridges, 1992; Borthwick, 1992). Japan's economic transformation from a defeated nation in 1945 to its awesome economic strengths is a well-known economic miracle. Japan's economic ascendance has been synonymous with America's relative economic decline. Japan's rapid economic growth may be reflected in its share of the world's gross national product (GNP) from 4.5 percent in the 1960s to 14 percent in 1988, in sharp contrast to the US which experienced a drastic erosion of its share from 50 percent to 23 percent over the same period (Keith, 1989). Japan had already emerged as the biggest creditor country in 1989, with a net credit of approximately $400 billion,[1] versus the US as the largest debtor country with a national debt of $660 billion in the same year (Shi, 1990). Japan has been playing a vital role in launching Pacific Asia as the fastest growth region in the world. Increasingly, new roles are perceived for Japan in a realigned global political economy (Matsui, 1990).

In terms of sustained economic growth, the Asian NIEs are even more impressive in consistently high rates of growth at better than 6 percent per year since 1965 (Table 1.1). As the Asian NIEs are "super-exporters" with growth generated primarily by phenomenal export expansion, some trade figures can bring home the magnitude of change. In respect of industrial products to the US, Taiwanese exports rose over 100-fold during the two

Figure 1.1: The Geopolitical Setting of Pacific Asia

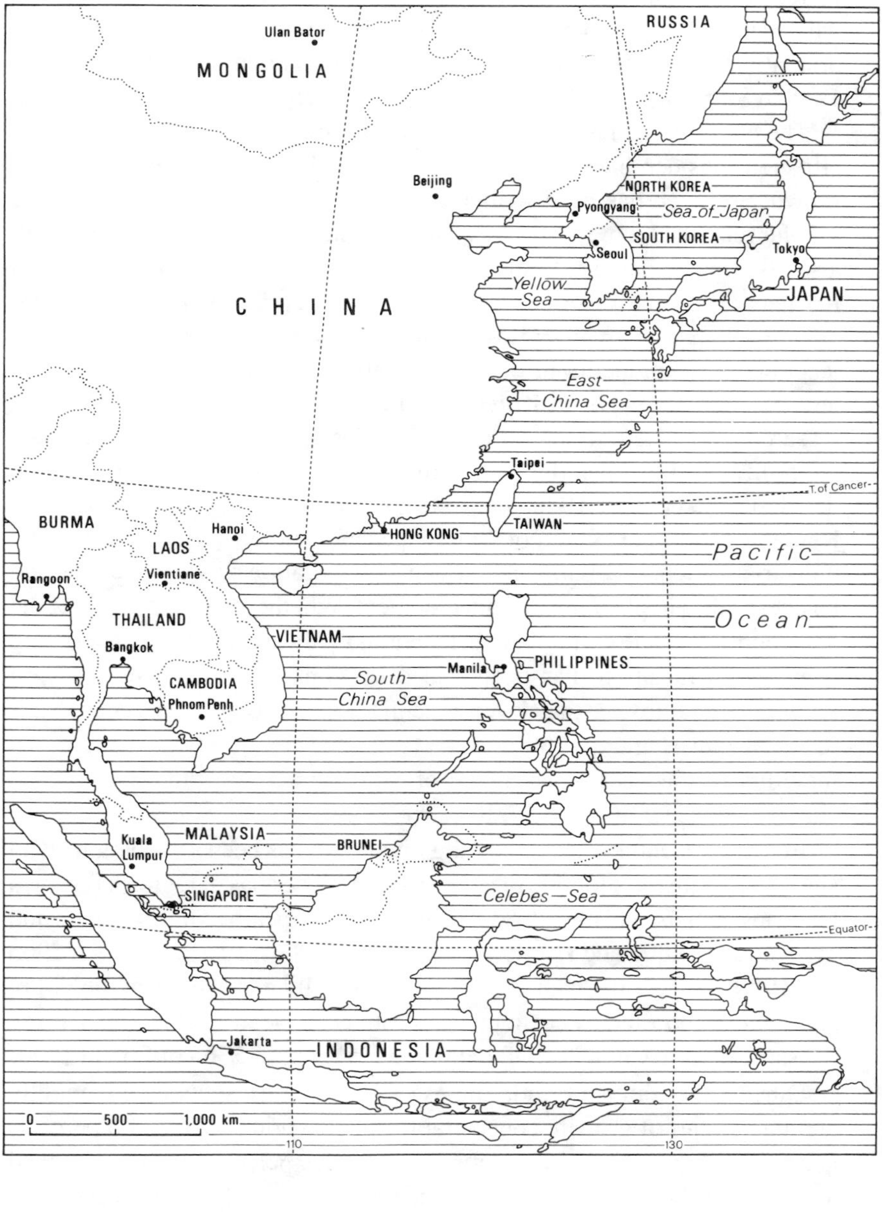

decades ending in 1985, when it reached $8 billion. During the same period, Korea similarly achieved more than a 100-fold increase to over $6 billion, while Hong Kong's exports rose from $310 million to $6 billion. Most dramatic, however, has been Singapore's quantum jump from $8 million in 1965 to $2.5 billion in 1985, a 300-fold increase! (Weiss, 1989:15)

The outstanding development records of Japan and the Asian NIEs have attracted considerable scholarly attention regarding why and how they have grown. So much has been written about their economic success that one scholar remarked, obviously in jest, that the literature was big enough to fill a small airplane hangar (Wade, 1992:270). For Japan, Korea and Taiwan, Kuznets (1988) has ascribed five shared characteristics to their success, namely, high investment ratios, small public sectors, export orientation, labour-market competition, and government intervention in economic matters. Similarities between Korea and Taiwan have been drawn by many researchers, in their structural characteristics, sizeable domestic markets, geopolitical stance, and the Confucian-capitalist brand of economic development (Weiss, 1989; Park, 1990). Amsden (1989) even foresees Korea as Asia's next giant, or "next Japan" and holds it as a model of late industrialization, involving institutional collaboration between the state and business elites in planning and development. Whether the institutions of the developmental state will survive in Korea and Taiwan, which are undergoing democratic transition, has been raised by Onis (1991). There is also a growing literature on the developmental experience of the Asian NIEs (Chen, 1988; Haggard, 1990; Park, 1991) and the question of the transferability of the East Asian model of development has often been posed (Ranis, 1985; Hamilton, 1987; Krueger, 1990).

In China a gentle yet breathtaking revolution has been sweeping its land since 1978 with the adoption of an open policy. The coastal region has grown by leaps and bounds, with the coastal cities spearheading change and innovation (Yeung and Hu, 1992; Linge and Forbes, 1990). Between 1965 and 1990, China's per capita GNP grew annually at 5.8 percent, no doubt significantly boosted by economic gains in recent years (Table 1.1). During the same period, China's GDP increased 5.5 times to $365 billion in 1990.

During the same period, the ASEAN countries achieved equally creditable rates of growth, considerably above world average (1.5 percent) and low-income developing country average (2.9 percent). In fact, Thailand and Malaysia have experienced so rapid a growth recently that they are being

Table 1.1: Selected Geographical and Development Indicators of Pacific Asia, 1990

Countries	Area (thousand sq. km.)	Mid-year Population (million)	% of Urban Population	Annual Growth Rate of GNP per capita (1965–1990)	External Debt (million dollars)	Debt Service Ratio (%)
China	9,561	1,133.9	33	5.8	52,555	9.2
Japan	378	123.5	77	4.1	—	—
NIEs						
Hong Kong	1	5.8	94	6.2	—	—
Korea, Rep. of	99	42.8	72	7.1	34,014	11.0
Singapore	1	3.0	100	6.5	—	—
Taiwan	36	20.2	—	6.8	881	0.9
Southeast Asia						
Indonesia	1,905	178.2	31	4.5	67,908	30.7
Cambodia	181	8.5	12	—	—	—
Lao PDR	237	4.1	19	—	1,063	15.4
Malaysia	330	17.9	43	4.0	19,502	11.4
Philippines	300	61.5	43	1.3	30,456	30.3
Thailand	513	55.8	23	4.4	25,868	15.4
Viet Nam	330	66.3	22	—	14,582	60.0

Sources: The World Bank (1992), *World Development Report 1992*, New York: Oxford University Press; United Nations Development Programme (1991), *Human Development Report 1991*, New York: Oxford University Press, pp. 158–161; Asian Development Bank (1991), *Asian Development Outlook 1991*, Manila: ADB, pp. 283, 300–301; and Hong Kong Government (1991), *Hong Kong 1991*, Hong Kong: Hong Kong Government, p. 55.

touted as the new little dragons of Asia. Between 1970 and 1980 Thailand registered a 6.9 percent annual growth of its GDP. Its economy underwent a dramatic upturn in the late 1980s, when in 1988 its GDP grew at 13.2 percent. Malaysia, too, experienced sharp GDP growth after recovering from the global recession of the early 1980s. Its annual increase of GDP was more than 9.0 percent for three years running from 1988.

Pacific Asia is far from being a homogeneous region. The countries in question vary greatly in terms of size, population, level of urbanization and external debt — some of the selected geographical and development indicators (Table 1.1). Taken together, however, they form a cluster of countries displaying increasing complementarity rather than competition against the backdrop of global restructuring and a new international division of labour. Studies have revealed increasing economic integration among the countries of the region and the operation of shifting comparative advantage, with Japan and the Asian NIEs playing pivotal roles (Shinohara and Lo, 1989).

Rapid economic growth is a desirable development goal that can be translated into improvements in economic and social well-being for citizens of the countries concerned. On the other hand, rapid economic growth also means concomitant change in the economic, social and physical environments. The pace and scale of change certainly have direct ramifications on these environments, some for better, but others for worse. It is therefore necessary to take stock of some of the changes in these environments and ward off any damage through planning and other means. For the purposes of this volume, changes in the geography and development of Pacific Asia are organized along several themes, namely urban and regional change, environmental pressures, transport and communication innovations, and demographic and labour force trends.

Urban and Regional Change

Inasmuch as much of the economic growth in Pacific Asia over the past few decades has been based on export-oriented manufacturing as well as information and technology-intensive services of diverse kinds, it is not surprising that one of the most visible changes has been centred on the cities and their surrounding regions. Cities have grown considerably in size, number, function and complexity. Despite an overall low level of urbanization for countries in Pacific Asia (29.4 percent for East Asia and 29 percent for Southeast Asia in 1990, United Nations, 1989:40–45), there is a sharp variation among individual countries (Table 1.1). Recent studies have conceptualized the cities in the region as the focal interplay between the external process of capitalist expansion and accumulation and the internal process of socioeconomic transformation (Armstrong and McGee, 1985). Other studies stress the need for informed policy making and management techniques to deal with increasingly complex urban functions and challenges (Fuchs et al., 1987); while others highlight the rapidity of urban change (Yeung, 1990), and point out the plight of the urban poor in service provision (Yeung, 1991). In all of these, the centrality of the very large or mega cities has come to the fore.

Of the thirty largest cities in the world in 1985, ten were located in Pacific Asia. The relative prominence of the region in terms of mega-cities will remain in 2000, when Tokyo-Yokohama, Shanghai and Jakarta will be among the first ten largest cities in the world (United Nations, 1989:19). Many of the mega-cities will function as global cities and articulate with a network of similar cities worldwide in the increasing globalization of capital, production and services (King, 1990). In Pacific Asia, urban corridors networking some of these mega-cities and smaller cities have been taking shape, spearheading development and change within the urban and regional environment (Yeung and Lo, 1992). Ginsburg et al. (1991) have observed, as well, the recurring phenomenon of extended metropolitan regions rooted often, but not exclusively, in stable agriculture, with far-reaching policy and development implications in rural-urban migration, land use within the urban region and labour force utilization.

Among the most visible and fascinating urban changes in Pacific Asia is one revolving around the active and booming property market in the broader Pacific region (Rowley, 1987). Goldberg (Chapter 2) demonstrates that the Pacific property market, rather than being highly localized and distinct, as it has been previously viewed, is in fact subject to the same processes of globalization of securities and foreign exchange markets. Massive flows of real estate investment capital occur across regional and national boundaries, forcing urban analysts to reevaluate old truisms about the local nature of property markets and thus of urban development. Goldberg is able to distinguish between the patterns and motivations of Chinese and Japanese property investments in North America and Australasia. It is clear from his analysis that urban property markets in the region cannot escape the global integration processes and that subnational policy-makers will probably have to cope with unprecedented changes in property markets as offshore investments intensify. Goldberg concludes with a look ahead at the durability of present trends and some conjectures about future developments.

Given the growing importance of Asia-Pacific cities, what the future holds for them is an issue of immense theoretical and practical importance. McGee and Yeung (Chapter 3) jointly embark on the task of forecasting urban futures in Pacific Asia towards the early part of the 21st century by reviewing salient urbanization trends in the region and analyzing the determinants of urban futures. In particular, trends in population growth, labour force participation, economic performance, foreign direct investment, technology transfer, energy utilization, and concern about the environment are each touched upon. Taiwan is briefly introduced as a case study from the standpoint of the extended metropolitan region. The authors conclude with several questions for planners and policy-makers as they are challenged to grapple with the future of their cities. In the simplest terms, they must choose between new cities of "spectacle," with an emphasis upon consumption, the built environment and efficient transportation, and attractiveness to both national and foreign investment; and extended metropolitan regions with an accent on much lower densities, more decentralized delivery of services and greater recycling and energy efficiency.

In order to provide a concrete case study of pertinent factors shaping the urban future, Yeh's study (Chapter 4) spotlights urban change in the small territory of Hong Kong from the present to the future. Urban development in Hong Kong, inextricably linked to its rapid economic growth, has been spectacular, especially during the past two decades. It has evolved from an entrepôt into one of Pacific Asia's leading financial, commercial and manufacturing centres. With the implementation of its new town programme, the age-old centralized urban development on either side of the harbour is gradually evolving into a multinodal metropolis. Much of Hong Kong's development has been prescribed in four major policy pronouncements: the Territorial Development Strategy of 1984; the Ports and Airport Development Strategy of 1989; the White Paper on Transport Policy of 1989; and the Metroplan of 1989, which will take Hong Kong's urban and regional planning into the 21st century. There are, of course, many factors that may affect urban change in Hong Kong in the years ahead, such as politics and economic relations with China, its future economy, emigration and labour shortage, and local politics. However, it is almost certain that the current dispersed pattern of urban development will continue and that major development and improvement will occur in the main urban areas through reclamation and urban redevelopment.

On a large scale, the effect of China's open policy and economic reforms on regional development in China is the subject of enquiry by Tang *et al.* (Chapter 5). The traditional phenomenon of regional disparity between the coastal and interior areas through the use of indices of geographic transfers of value and revenue is critically reviewed. The reform measures implemented since 1978 have not ameliorated regional differences; rather, they have been accentuated. Resource-rich interior provinces are kept under strict state control, while the system of subsidies and control has kept coastal manufacturing products and exports artificially low and competitive in the world market. Thus economic reforms have not only failed to minimize uneven development between coastal and interior regions, but also led to a North-South divide as a result of decontrol measures in the period. A dual-space system is predicted to last into the 21st century, barring any drastic political change.

Environmental Pressures

Concerns about the natural environment have been heightened in Pacific Asia, as elsewhere, in recent years, in view of several horrendous environmental disasters that struck the world and the widely perceived notion of the global ecological balance at risk. Among the key dimensions requiring immediate arresting strategies are climate change, ozone depletion and biodiversity (Sanction, 1989). The world experienced its hottest year in 1990 since record taking began 134 years ago and the six hottest years on record in the past nine years; these are statistics that spark a great deal of controversy and speculation about global warming (Lau and Palmer, 1990). With global warming and the thawing of the ice in the polar regions, ocean water would rise with devastating consequences for the low-lying river deltas and floodplains and many of their cities located in Pacific Asia. Across Pacific Asia a tremendous ecological price has been paid for industrialization and economic growth. At least 70,000 chemicals have been used in industry; problems of land subsidence imperil cities such as Tokyo, Shanghai and even Bangkok (Weiss, 1989:20–21).

There is a link between urbanization and global warming for development policy, energy utilization patterns and industrialization strategies pursued by cities; these all have a vital impact on the physical environment (Yeung, 1992). Cities, through their burning of coal and other carbon-based fuels as well as other practices, are responsible for the production of increasing amounts of carbon dioxide, methane, nitrous oxide, and chlorofluorocarbons (CFCs) — "greenhouse" gases — that have allegedly led to alarming warming changes in the earth's climate. Table 1.2 indicates the greenhouse index among countries in Pacific Asia. The index is generally low, but there are some unexpected anomalies, such as Myanmar and Laos. Another contributory factor to the greenhouse effect has been massive deforestation that in the region has proceeded with unprecedented speed and scale. The hardwood forests of Southeast Asia have been rapidly depleted. During the last two decades, the loss of timber stocks in Southeast Asia ranged from 100,000 ha in the Philippines to 550,000 ha in Indonesia. Malaysia lost half of its forested area between 1958 and 1988 (McDowell, 1989). The average annual deforestation as well as other selected environmental indicators are shown in Table 1.2.

Apart from deforestation as one facet of environmental dismanagement, many countries in the region are being increasingly confronted with the dilemma of how simultaneously to protect the physical environment and to pursue economic development. Pollution of the natural environment is a particularly troublesome problem that has escalated to a divisive public issue in some countries in Pacific Asia which narrowly pursue growth and development. Ecological nightmares, such as air pollution and water shortages, for example, are beginning to haunt China, which pays high costs for its economic development (Smil, 1984). Rising ill-health of the residents of Bangkok is manifested by the lead levels of their blood at triple those found in most cities in the West; in Thailand the number of polluting factories skyrocketed from 211 in 1969 to 26,235 in 1989 (Anon., 1991). Japan faces a so-called second environmental crisis, not with companies as the principal culprits, but affluent consumers. However, environmental movements appear to be gaining ground in many countries in Pacific Asia, notably in Japan, South Korea, Hong Kong, Singapore and Taiwan. The little dragons are showing a justifiable concern about pollution of their nests (Hills and Barron, 1990). Throughout most of the region, however, wasted resour-

Table 1.2: Indicators of Environmental Conditions in Pacific Asia

Countries	Production of fuelwood		Average annual deforestation (as % of forest area)	Internal renewable water resources (per capita 1,000 m³ per year)	Greenhouse index:carbon heating equivalents (metric tons per capita)
	Per capita (m³) 1984–1986	Annual percentage increase 1975–1985	1980–1988	1988	1988
High Human Development	0.23	1.7	—	1.6	—
Hong Kong	—	—	—	—	—
Korea, Rep. of	0.15	-1.4	—	1.4	1.2
Singapore	—	—	—	0.2	4.2
Malaysia	0.49	2.3	1.2	28.9	3.2
Medium Human Development	0.31	1.7	1.5	6.3	1.0
Excluding China	0.59	1.1	—	13.6	1.8
Korea, Dem. Rep. of	0.19	1.8	—	—	1.6
China	0.16	2.0	—	2.5	0.6
Philippines	0.53	2.6	1.5	5.4	0.9
Mongolia	0.71	—	—	11.6	1.5
Low Human Development	0.48	2.4	0.8	5.5	0.7
Excluding India	0.61	2.8	0.7	9.1	0.9
Indonesia	0.76	2.1	0.8	14.2	1.3
Vietnam	0.36	2.2	1.7	—	0.8
Myanmar India	0.42	2.0	2.1	27.0	4.3
India	0.29	2.0	2.3	2.3	0.5
Lao People's Dem. Rep.	1.06	1.9	1.0	59.2	12.4
Cambodia	0.65	0.3	0.2	10.9	—
All Developing Countries	0.39	2.1	1.1	6.3	0.9
Least developed	0.63	2.7	0.8	10.4	0.9
Sub-Saharan Africa	0.84	2.9	0.5	3.5	1.0
Industrial Countries	—	—	—	9.4	3.5
World	—	—	—	6.9	1.5

Source: United Nations Development Programme (1991), *Human Development Report 1991*. New York: Oxford University Press, pp. 162–163.

ces and environmental damage threaten growth and life-supporting ecological systems (Greenwood, 1991).

Many of these environmental tension points are beyond the scope of this volume. Nonetheless, Douglas (Chapter 6) deals with the river system and water resources management in Pacific Asia — in its mainland and insular/peninsular parts. Most of the prominent river systems are briefly dealt with and the magnitude of the problems identified varies in both subregions, despite their similarity in characteristics. Attention is called to the environmental consequences of tropical rainforest disturbance through logging operations that cause significant direct and indirect impacts on forestry, agriculture and urban development. Douglas shows clearly the interconnections of such economic exploitation and the changes in geomorphic processes and the environment. Water and land cannot be taken for granted and as key elements of the living environment must be given the highest priority in planning and development. Thus relevant policies should be adopted to maximize economic returns while minimizing the resultant environmental damage.

On a smaller scale, Low (Chapter 7) highlights the need for better water resources management in ASEAN countries in the face of increasing urbanization. The problem is related, on the one hand, to the underdevelopment of water resources and, on the other, to the pollution of available water resources. Water pollution is a common problem faced by cities in the region and is exacerbated by industrialization, deforestation and soil erosion that all take place in and around urban areas. Nevertheless, Low is optimistic about the future, taking her cue from recent regional efforts at improving the management of water resources in the region's urban areas.

Hill (Chapter 8) studies the relatively little-researched subject of upland utilization in southern China and its neighbouring areas. Increased production from the hilly areas in this part of China is important in the light of both the Chinese policy of fostering development *in situ* and the enormous cost of rapid urban growth. Although the societal context of the study differs from other parts of Pacific Asia, more effective utilization of hilly terrain remains a critical dimension of land use in many neighbouring countries. In southern China, in addition to the widely practised shifting cultivation, other utilization strategies include the use of phytomass for fuel and compost, the use of dried grass as feedstuff for animals and pond fish, and the control of burning. A case study of Guizhou illustrates the considerable complexities of devising workable alternatives to existing upland use strategies. Hill concludes with a plea for more research.

Transport and Communication Innovations

One of the key determinants of the pace and scope of the physical and economic transformations of Pacific Asia in recent years and in the future is technological innovation. In this respect the range and speed of innovations in microelectronics and communications since the late 1980s have been astounding. The cluster of new innovations in computers, electronics and telecommunications, new materials, biotechnology and robotics has facilitated rapid changes in the mode and tempo of business transactions, the need for personal contact and the choice of industrial location. A new techno-economic paradigm is widely believed to have been created, with its characteristics in resource saving and knowledge intensity (Lo, 1990). A new era of telecommunications, information technology and space-time collapse is viewed to have arrived. This technological frontier is predicted to expand rapidly in the years ahead into the 21st century, with promising prospects of economic growth and return. Japan and the Asian NIEs are already investing heavily in high technology industries in preparation for the future (Lo and Nakamura, 1991).

Japan and the Asian NIEs have placed utmost importance in technological development in anticipation of future competition. It is recognized that technological leadership may rest in the country that can first develop a fifth-generation computer that can reason like a human being at a capacity that dwarfs today's super-computers. Japan is well placed in this development: a 1987 report by America's National Academy of Engineering revealed that Japan was superior to the US in twenty-five of the thirty-four critical areas of high technology, including fields such as artificial intelligence, optoelectrics, and systems engineering and control. By the latter 1990s, Japan aspires to be the top country in the world in the information industry (Nester, 1990). Korea's development of the semiconductor industry is also spectacular, being the world's third biggest producer of advanced semiconductor memory chips, after Japan and the US. Several other Korean industries, notably computers, automobiles, steel and construction, figure prominently in the world economy (Wade, 1992:278).

From the wide spectrum of technological change, Rimmer (Chapter 9) has assembled a rich array of data and illustrations to forecast, in a comprehensive manner, the development patterns in container ports, air freight, air passengers and telecommunications in the early 21st century, based on recent and present trends. He includes all countries in the Pacific Basin in his analysis, which he terms "the Pacific Economic Zone." In making his forecasts, Rimmer takes into account changing technologies, effects of multinodal arrangements, trade incentives and protectionist tendencies. He predicts major adjustments in market diversification, feeder cargo and information handling by recognized seaports, airports and teleport hubs, with the likely rapprochement involving China, Japan, the two Koreas and the Russian Far East. With Taiwan's reorientation of sea and air trade with China, Kaohsiung will benefit at Hong Kong's expense. The study also predicts a diminished Japanese influence in the zone as China becomes more developed and active.

In contrast, Johnston (Chapter 10) shows, in a more restricted geographical area of Indonesia, how deficient rural transport is in terms of data and service. He advocates an area-based approach to rural transport planning and, despite his focus on one country, the method can be extended to Southeast Asia and beyond. The standard method of analysis of rural transport is, regrettably, volume driven, with funds for infrastructure maintenance or improvement usually going to locations having relatively high traffic volumes. This results in localities already poorly served being further neglected. It should be pointed out that rather than hi-tech transport modes, low-tech transport improvements are of immense importance in isolated and rural areas. Even paved roads, canals, mopeds, trucks, etc. can work wonders. Despite the proposal of a new approach to planning rural transport in Southeast Asia, Johnston is not entirely optimistic of any real improvement in this sector in the foreseeable future.

Demographic and Labour Force Trends

Notwithstanding a small relative decline in its share of the world's total population, Pacific Asia's population will nonetheless increase from 1.77 billion in 1990 to 2.03 billion by century-end (United Nations, 1990:64–69). This huge population is the driving force for physical and socioeconomic change in the region. Thus the size and growth of population, fertility, mortality, migration and urbanization, the population structure and its relation to the labour force are subjects that have wider implications for development and change in the region.

In the two decades leading to 2000, the rate of increase of population in East and Southeast Asia exhibits a secular decline. This is more pronounced in the former than the latter because of significant inroads made on the decline of birth rates and progressively narrowed difference in death rates (Table 1.3). Within countries in Pacific Asia there are massive and sustained movements of population internally and across national boundaries. Internal migration involves primarily rural-urban migration but takes other forms as well, such as the federal land development schemes in Malaysia and the age-old transmigration programmes in Indonesia. International migration may be motivated by employment opportunities as Filipino, Thai and Korean workers are bound for the Middle East or by other reasons as attested to by continued emigration to developed countries outside the region. War and unpopular political ideologies have also driven people from their homes in the search for dreams and opportunities in other countries as refugees, as evidenced by waves of refugees and boat people from Vietnam since the defeat of the US in 1975. Asia-Pacific countries also seek, in their population policies, to alter their current distribution or to reverse the trend (ESCAP, 1990:13). Rondinelli (1991) noted, however, the policy has changed from one of growth control to urban diffusion, in an effort to promote economic development.

Changes in the population structure result from changes in fertility and mortality rates. For example, a fall in fertility would be reflected in a lowering of the proportion of young children in the population and in an

Table 1.3: Indicators of Demographic Trends in Pacific Asia

Regions	1980–1985	1990–1995	2000–2005
Population growth rate (%)			
East Asia	1.18	1.30	0.78
Southeast Asia	2.18	1.94	1.51
Crude birth rate (per 1,000)			
East Asia	18.5	19.7	14.6
Southeast Asia	32.7	27.5	21.9
Crude death rate (per 1,000)			
East Asia	6.6	6.7	6.8
Southeast Asia	10.4	8.0	6.8

Source: United Nations, Population Division, printout of the 1990 revision of its global demographic estimates and projections, medium variant (New York, 1990).

ageing population. For countries that have experienced consistent fertility decline, ageing of their population is already impacting their development policy and social support systems. Japan, China, Hong Kong and Singapore are being confronted with a burgeoning ageing population. China's elderly population of sixty-five and above, for instance, will increase from 72 million in 1990 to 91 million in 2000 (ESCAP, 1990:15).

Labour force participation rates are largely determined by fertility rates fifteen years earlier. In Southeast Asia, where fertility has declined more gradually, the labour force growth rate is projected to remain higher than the population growth rate by 0.4 percent between 1980 and 2010. There is, consequently, a challenge for these governments to provide adequate employment for the growing labour force in the years leading to the end of this century and beyond (ESCAP, 1990:17).

In a recent survey of the demographic trends in six countries of Pacific Asia — the so-called New Demographic Leaders (NDLs), i.e., South Korea, Taiwan, Singapore, Malaysia, Thailand and Indonesia — it was shown that reduced childbearing, increased life expectancy, slower population growth and rapid urbanization were having a pervasive and positive influence on the region's economy. During the past twenty years, the NDLs have experienced particularly rapid improvements in mortality and steep declines in fertility. Pacific Asia's demographic transition is causing a remarkable increase in purchasing power. For the next two decades the trends to watch for include declining fertility rates, an accelerating rate of household formation and ageing populations (Bauer and Mason, 1990).

In the light of the above demographic trends, it is instructive that Neville (Chapter 11) highlights the interim features of the ageing population in ASEAN and selected countries of Pacific Asia, and examines the process from the standpoint of wider societal implications. Taking 1970 as the base year of his analysis, Neville evaluates major population shifts over fifty years, from 1970 to 2020. The age structural shifts towards old populations are under way in almost all countries under review, with Japan, Hong Kong and Singapore characterized by the steepest fertility declines in the vanguard of demographic change in the region. Attention is drawn to varied employment opportunities and purchasing power between the present and future generations of population and the need for families, institutions and, indeed, countries to be prepared for the population change and its attendant implications.

The labour force in Malaysia constitutes a fascinating case study in the light of its fundamental shifts in socioeconomic policies over the past few decades. O'Brien (Chapter 12) examines the history and contemporary development of the Malaysian labour force through an analysis of internal and external factors of the demand for labour. The labour force structure has been analyzed over time from 1957 to 1988. Apart from the forward-looking internal development policies adopted since Independence in 1957, the overriding policy instrument causing basic changes in the labour force has been the extremely successful New Economic Policy adopted since 1971. This effectively reshaped development in education, occupational structure, ethnic balance and geographical distribution of employment opportunities and the proletarianization of the labour force. Favourable external factors related to the new international division of labour coincided with progressive domestic economic policies and enabled Malaysia to transform itself from a post-colonial economy to a second-tier NIE. O'Brien projects the continuation of present trends into the 21st century along trajectories already established since the 1970s.

An uncertainty that looms large for the future of Hong Kong is the return of sovereignty to China in 1997 and, by extension, Hong Kong's role in the regional economy of Pacific Asia. This gives rise to emigration of large proportions, reaching a yearly total of approximately 60,000 since 1990. Nash (Chapter 13) focusses specifically on the impact of Canadian and Australian business migration programmes on Hong Kong's business future, directly related to population outflows. Both Canada and Australia are major recipients of Hong Kong's emigrants, 15–20 percent of whom qualify as business migrants. The outflow of funds from Hong Kong to these two countries amounted to HK$30 billion in 1989, more than half of which accounted for by business migration. It has been projected that, as more business migration programmes are being designed and promoted by other countries as well, the drain on Hong Kong's skilled labour force and financial resources will accelerate. Nash concludes that, for the good of Hong Kong, such programmes should be critically reviewed, if not abandoned.

NOTE

1.   US dollars are referred to unless otherwise indicated in this volume.

REFERENCES

Amsden, Alice H. (1989). *Asia's Next Giant: South Korea and Late Industrialization*. New York: Oxford University Press.

Anonymous (1991). "Pollution: The Dirt on the Dirt." *Business Asia*, 17 June.

Armstrong, Warwick and T. G. McGee (1985). *Theatres of Accumulation: Studies in Asian and Latin American Urbanization*. London and New York: Methuen.

Banfe, Charles (1992). "Asia: The Year 2000 Leader." *Asia Magazine*, 21 August.

Bauer, John and Andrew Mason (1990). "Asia 2010 — The Power of People." *Far East Economic Review*, 17 May, pp. 27–58.

Borthwick, Mark (1992). *Pacific Century: The Emergence of Modern Pacific Asia*. Boulder: Westview.

Chen, Edward K. Y. (1988). "The Economic and Non-Economics of Asia's Four Little Dragons." *Supplement to the Gazette*, 35(1), 21 March, University of Hong Kong.

Deyo, Frederic C. (ed.) (1987). *The Political Economy of the New Asian Industrialization*. Ithaca: Cornell University Press.

Economic and Social Commission for Asia and the Pacific, United Nations (ESCAP) (1990). *Population Research Leads*.

Fuchs, Roland J., Gavin W. Jones and Ernesto M. Pernia (eds.) (1987). *Urbanization and Urban Policies in Pacific Asia*. Boulder and London: Westview Press.

Ginsburg, Norton (1988). "Geography and the Pacific Century." *Asian Geographer*, 7(1), pp. 1–11.

————, Bruce Koppel and T. G. McGee (eds.) (1991). *The Extended Metropolis: Settlement Transition in Asia*. Honolulu: University of Hawaii Press.

Greenwood, Gavin (1991). "Environment in Asia 1991." *Far Eastern Economic Review*, 19 September, pp. 37–57.

Haggard, Stephan (1990). *Pathways from the Periphery: The Politics of Growth in the Newly Industrializing Countries*. Ithaca: Cornell University Press.

Hamilton, Clive (1987). "Can the Rest of Asia Emulate the NIEs?" *Third World Quarterly*, 9(4), pp. 1125–1156.

Hills, Peter and William Barron (1990). "Hong Kong: Can the Dragon Clean Its Nest?" *Environment*, 32(8), pp. 17–20 & 39–45.

Hughes, Helen (ed.) (1988). *Achieving Industrialization in East Asia*. Cambridge: Cambridge University Press.

Keith, Ronald C. (1989). "The Asia-Pacific Area and the 'New International Political Order': The View from Beijing." *China Report*, 25(4), pp. 343–358.

King, Anthony D. (1990). *Global Cities: Post Imperialism and the Internationalization of London*. London and New York: Routledge.

Krueger, Anne O. (1990). "Asian Trade and Growth Lesson." *American Economic Review*, 80(2), pp. 108–112.

Kuznets, Paul W. (1988). "An East Asian Model of Economic Development: Japan,

Taiwan, and South Korea." *Economic Development and Cultural Change*, 36(3), pp. S11–S43.

Lau, Muriel and Richard Palmer (1990). "World's Hottest Year Heats Up Greenhouse Effect Debate." *South China Morning Post*, 31 December.

Linder, Staffan B. (1986). *The Pacific Century: Economic and Political Consequences of Asia-Pacific Dynamism*. Palo Alto: Stanford University Press.

Linge, G.J.R. and D. K. Forbes (eds.) (1990). *China's Spatial Economy: Recent Developments and Reforms*. Oxford: Oxford University Press.

Lo Fu-chen (1990). "Current Global Adjustment and Shifting Techno-economic Paradigm on the World City System." Paper presented at the Symposium on The Mega-City and the Future: Population Growth and Policy Responses, 22–25 October, Tokyo.

Lo Fu-chen and Yoichi Nakamura (1991). "Uneven Growth, the Mega-Trends of Global Change and the Future of the Asia-Pacific Economies." Paper presented at the Conference on the Future of Asia-Pacific Economies, 11–13 March, Delhi.

Matsui, Noriatsu (1990). "The New Roles of Japan in the Global Political Economy." *Asian Economic Journal*, 5(11), pp. 56–75.

McDowell, Mark (1989). "Development and the Environment in ASEAN." *Pacific Affairs*, 62(3), pp. 307–329.

Nester, William R. (1990). *Japan's Growing Power Over East Asia and the World Economy*. Houndmills: Macmillan.

Onis, Ziya (1991). "The Logic of the Developmental State — Review Article." *Comparative Politics*, 24(1), pp. 109–126.

Park, Bon Ho (1991). "East Asian Development in the Global Perspective." *Asian Economic Journal*, 5(11) pp. 1–13.

Park, Yung Chul (1990). "Development Lessons from Asia: The Role of Government in South Korea and Taiwan." *American Economic Review*, 80(2), pp. 118–121.

Ranis, Gustav (1985). "Can the East Asian Model of Development be Generalized? A Comment." *World Development*, 13(4), pp. 543–545.

Rondinelli, Dennis A. (1991). "Asian Urban Development Policies in the 1990s: From Growth Control to Urban Diffusion." *World Development*, 19(7), pp. 791–803.

Rowley, Anthony (1987). "A Concrete Trend: Real-Estate Investment Flows to Financial Capitals." *Far Eastern Economic Review*, 12 March, pp. 39–40.

Sancton, Thomas (1989). "The Fight to Save the Planet." *Time*, 18 December.

Shi Min (1990). "The World Economic Pattern in the 1990s and the Asia-Pacific Economic Cooperation." *Asia-Pacific Studies*, 2, pp. 9–19.

Shibusuwa, Masahide, Zakaria Haji Ahmad and Brian Bridges (1992). *Pacific Asia in the 1990s*. London: Routledge.

Shinohara, Miyohei and Lo Fu-chen (eds.) (1989). *Global Adjustment and the*

Future of Asian-Pacific Economy. Tokyo: Institute of Development Economies.

Smil, Vaclav (1984). *The Bad Earth: Environmental Degradation in China*. New York: M. E. Sharpe.

United Nations, Department of International Economic and Social Affairs (1989). *Prospects of World Urbanization 1988*. Population Studies, No. 112. New York: United Nations.

Wade, Robert (1990). *Governing the Market: Economic Theory and the Role of Government in East Asian Industrialization*. Princeton: Princeton University Press.

——— (1992). "East Asia's Economic Success: Conflicting Perspectives, Partial Insights, Shaking Evidence, Review Article." *World Politics*, 44, pp. 270–320.

Weiss, Julian (1989). *The Asian Century*. New York: Facts on File.

Yeung Yue-man (1990). *Changing Cities of Pacific Asia: A Scholarly Interpretation*. Hong Kong: The Chinese University Press.

——— (1991). "The Urban Poor and Urban Basic Infrastructure Services in Asia: Past Approaches and Emerging Challenges." *Occasional Paper*, No. 7. Hong Kong: Hong Kong Institute of Asia-Pacific Studies, The Chinese University of Hong Kong.

——— (1992). "China and Hong Kong." In *Sustainable Cities: Urbanization and the Environment in International Perspectives*, edited by Richard Stren, Rodney White and Joseph White. Boulder: Westview, pp. 259–280.

——— and Hu Xu-wei (eds.) (1992). *China's Coastal Cities: Catalysts for Modernization*. Honolulu: University of Hawaii Press.

Yeung Yue-man and Lo Fu-chen (1992). "Global Restructuring and Emerging Urban Corridors in Pacific Asia." Paper presented at the Workshop on The Asian Pacific Urban System: Towards the 21st Century, 11–13 February, Hong Kong.

PART II

Urban and Regional Change

CHAPTER TWO

The Evolving Pacific Property Market: A View from North America

Michael A. Goldberg
Dean, Faculty of Commerce and Business Administration,
University of British Columbia, Vancouver, Canada

Introduction: Globalization of Financial and Property Markets

Domestic economic policy can no longer be made independent of global considerations. Private firms are in the same position, especially those in financial services where global integration proceeds at a sometimes worrying pace (Kaufman, 1986; Wachtel, 1986). Much of the integration has occurred among the developed countries of Europe and North America, but considerable and rapid regional integration of financial markets has also occurred in Asia (Tan and Kapur, 1986; Grub *et al.*, 1982). Given such integration there is a growing network of "international financial centres" (IFCs) where the world's financial decisions are increasingly concentrated (Reed, 1981). The evolution of these IFCs is important for the integration of Pacific urban property markets, and will be touched on briefly.

One has only to look at the core of major cities in the Asia-Pacific region to see the symbols of multinational enterprise and international financial firms to get an idea of local impacts of globalization (Daniels, 1986; O'Connor and Edgington, 1987). The integration of global capital flows cannot be separated from other international investment flows even in areas such as urban property markets, long thought to be insulated from global forces (Daly, 1982; Daly and Logan, 1989; McGee, 1984).

To explore the evolving Pacific property market, this chapter begins by discussing the globalization of financial markets that really spawned global real estate markets. The perspective is a North American one as it is becoming part of the Asia-Pacific region at a rapid rate, especially on the west coasts of Canada and the US.

Attention then turns to Southeast Asian ethnic Chinese real estate investment that has attracted so much attention in North America (and Australia), in part because it has been accompanied by the immigration of many investors, and in part because of its scale. Also, this group has long been involved in real estate investment around the region and have truly been pioneers in the field and prime movers in the development of a Pacific property.

Focus next shifts to recent Japanese real estate investment that has been making headlines around the Pacific Rim region. Differences between Japanese and ethnic Chinese real estate investment behaviour are also reviewed.

Discussion continues by examining national, provincial and local policy initiatives that seek to tap into this growing pool of real estate and investment capital. Vancouver, British Columbia serves as a case study since all three levels of government promote Vancouver as a Pacific Rim commercial centre.

The chapter concludes by gazing into the future to suggest emerging trends, opportunities, and pitfalls in the increasingly integrated global economy.

Globalizing Financial Markets

The globalization of financial markets has paralleled that in the real estate sector of the economy. Each has tended to be both the cause and effect of the other in varying degrees.

One of the earliest globalizing forces can be traced to the 1950s when the Soviet Union held US dollar balances outside the US to avoid possible seizure of the assets (Levi, 1989:282). This practice spawned the Euromarket, which is very much the heart of global banking. From about Cdn$110 billion in 1970, to Cdn$450 billion in 1975, the Eurocurrency market is now estimated to be in excess of Cdn$2.5 trillion (Economic Council of Canada, 1989). More broadly, international trade surpluses have been another contributing factor in the growth of international lending. "Petro-dollars" are the most frequently cited example along with recent Japanese trade surpluses.

Recent advances in telecommunications and computing technology have permitted stock, option and commodity exchanges around the world to link with one another to facilitate global trading. They have also enabled new instruments to be developed and marketed globally. For example, since 1984, the Singapore International Monetary Exchange (SIMEX) and the Chicago Mercantile Exchange (CME) have linked, allowing buyers and sellers to take a position on one exchange and liquidate it on the other, creating a twenty-four hour trading day (Hamilton, 1986).

Tax and regulatory regimes also encouraged financial market participants to move funds into, or out of, certain countries. Tax havens like the Cayman and Channel Islands are examples. Similarly, Singapore emerged as an international financial centre (IFC) in the early 1970s primarily through the tax concessions it offered to financial institutions active in the "offshore" Asian dollar market (Skully and Viksnins, 1987). "Offshore" banking centres have subsequently been established in Tokyo, Vancouver and Vanuuatu, providing tax free zones for offshore banking transactions that do not involve domestic residents (Bryant, 1987). In 1987, these centres held $973 billion (21 percent) of the $4.73 trillion of foreign liabilities of banks (IMF, 1988).

Deregulation and liberalization of financial markets in the 1970s and 1980s is a final factor in the globalization of finance. Deregulation has integrated domestic financial systems into a single truly global financial system, allowing no country to regulate its financial sector isolated from developments in the international financial community. Britain's "Big Bang" of 1986 and the improved access of foreigners to Japan's capital markets are testimonies to this fact. So are developments in Thailand, Malaysia, South Korea and Taiwan allowing (eventually) domestic firms and investors to borrow and invest abroad freely, while foreigners have access to their stock and bond markets.

The Globalization of Urban Property Markets

Growing evidence suggests that yield enhancement and portfolio diversification are also driving the globalization of urban property markets. Some of this evidence will be reviewed below.

A. The Global Integration in Urban Property Markets: An Overview

A diversity of indicators point to more global real estate markets. In the US, the real estate professional media have been inundated with features about foreign investment, in particular from Japan, as well as with articles on foreign markets, especially those in Asia (Apgar, 1984; *The Economist*, 1989a, b; Gralla, 1990; Holloway, 1989; *Land Use Digest*, 1987 and 1990a, b; Leventhal, 1987, 1989, and 1990a, b; Mogami, 1987; Rodman, 1989; *Roulac's Strategic Real Estate*, 1988; *Shopping Centers Today*, 1987 and 1990; Tsui, 1987; and *Urban Land*, 1990a, b, c). Globalizing financial markets have also directly affected real estate markets via growing international trading of real estate assets and real estate-backed financial instruments (Hendershott and Van Order, 1989).

The Canadian situation is similar. The mass media and professional magazines carry frequent stories not just about foreign investment in Canada, but also about offshore real estate opportunities for Canadians (Cu-Uy-Gam, 1989; Daniels, 1990; Gates, 1987 and 1990; Horvitch, 1990; Keast, 1988 and 1989; McKenna, 1987; Miller, 1989; Mitchell, 1989; Ohse, 1989; Quint, 1990; Schreiner, 1990; and Stoffman, 1989).

Analogous impressions can be gleaned from reviewing the Asian media (*Asiaweek*, 1990; Dunfee, 1990; *Far Eastern Economic Review*, 1989; Friedland, 1989 and 1990; Tiglao, 1990; and Tsuruoka, 1990). Given the growth in global integrated activities (e.g., multinational firms, international finance) it should be obvious that these firms all need urban space. As global markets develop, more and more market information flows around the world relating to all markets, not just the product and service markets in which firms are directly involved (McLernon, 1989). This global information explosion combines with the needs for space and diversification of investment, to yield a truly global property market.

B. Evidence from North America

In 1985 Cdn$6.5 billion were invested in real estate or 2 percent of total foreign investment in Canada (McKenna, 1987). Americans were the largest investors with the British and Dutch and the Japanese back in the pack but gaining rapidly (Gates, 1987). Canadians are also focussing more on offshore markets (McKenna, 1987), again suggesting a more international property sector.

In Vancouver, it is estimated that ethnic Chinese own about Cdn$5.0 billion in real estate. A problem such numbers pose is that it is often difficult to ascertain whether an ethnic Chinese investment is truly offshore or really a domestic investment on the part of a Canadian family member, given the close ties among Southeast Asian ethnic Chinese and their Canadian relatives.

Turning to the US, Europeans were the largest investors, followed by Europeans and then Asians, particularly the Japanese (Apgar, 1984; Bacow, 1987 and 1988; Leventhal, 1987 and 1989; Regeling *et al.*, 1984). The Japanese have been garnering most of the headlines (as they have been doing elsewhere) with their US holdings expected to exceed US$60 billion by the end of 1990 (Ohse, 1989). In specific US cities like San Francisco, ethnic Chinese and not Japanese are a major focus (Yannie, 1988). Finally, Americans too are taking a broader view with more being written about offshore property markets, particularly those in Asia (Tsui, 1987), reflecting once again the international nature of information on property markets, a necessary condition for a global market in property.

C. Evidence for Australasia

From Australian business and popular media it is clear that Asian investment is in the public eye. Japanese purchases like the Regent Hotel and Gold Coast resorts are examples as is the ethnic Chinese redevelopment of the Queen Victoria Building and Chinatown (Livanes, 1989; Hajdu, 1990). Australian media also keep people abreast of Pacific Rim property markets (e.g., *Triple A*, 1987).

Looking at the Asia Pacific region, there is abundant information available via the annual property reviews done by the *Far Eastern Economic Review*, and high profile treatments by *Asiaweek*, and the *Asian Wall Street Journal* to name the most widely read. With the extensive family and business networks in the region, international real estate investment within the Southeast Asian region has been extremely active for some time.

Given the intraregional property investments generally dominated by the ethnic Chinese of Southeast Asia, it is instructive to examine these flows that may be seen as prototypes for the more general globalization of real estate investment. They are also highly visible and thus deserve closer attention to sort myth from reality. Finally, they are centrally important to the development of a Pacific Rim property market and indeed have long been involved in real estate investment around the region and are pioneers in the field and thus prime movers in shaping the development of a Pacific property market.

Southeast Asian Ethnic Chinese Real Estate Investment Behaviour: Details of a Much Publicized Real Estate Capital Flow

To understand overseas Chinese business behaviour it is useful to review their history and economic roles in Southeast Asia over the past century so that the context within, and from which, the overseas Chinese operate can be gleaned (See Goldberg (1985) for details of what follows).

A. Brief History of the Overseas Chinese and their Evolving Role in the Southeast Asia region

The overseas Chinese comprise between 30 and 40 million people of ethnic Chinese origin living Southeast Asia (often called the "Nanyang" — literally the "southern ocean" for the South China Sea) (Wu and Wu, 1980). The large growth in ethnic Chinese populations in the region began in the 1860s with the series of unequal treaties imposed by Western powers on China. These provided for emigration to provide low cost labour and local commerce for Western colonization of the region. Most emigrants viewed themselves as "sojourners" who would make their fortune abroad and return to ancestral villages, as wealthy respected persons.

Economic success for the ethnic Chinese was both a blessing and a curse leading to discriminatory practices, periodic race riots, restrictions on landholdings, and limitations on economic power as in Malaysia's "New Economic Policy" which promotes *bumiputra* co-ownership of ethnic Chinese business. Thus, the overseas Chinese have faced considerable discrimination and threats over the past 130 years. The uncertainty provided by this unpleasant history is an important motivating factor in their desire to diversify and establish businesses and families in a number of countries, particularly politically stable nations like Canada, the United States, Australia and the United Kingdom.

B. Overseas Chinese Business Culture and Style

Considerable research exists on overseas Chinese culture and business (Chan, 1983; Lim and Gosling, 1983; Limlingan, 1986; Suryadinata, 1989; Willmott, 1972; and Wolf, 1978). Below is a distillation of the salient features.

1. The Family

The Chinese family is quite legitimately a legendary social institution (Baker, 1979). In traditional Chinese society, the family was seen as the basic building block of a stable society. The most relevant characteristics of the family are: the paramountcy of the family over the individual; the necessity to perpetuate the family line; the responsibility held by the current generation to serve as a bridge between past and future generations; the dominance of males over females and of age over youth. The Chinese family extends beyond immediate family to include even rather distant aunts, uncles and cousins.

2. Trust

The concept of trust is absolutely central to the overseas Chinese way of conducting business. One's reputation is everything. On it depends credit-worthiness, business contacts and references, and social acceptance. One just does not do business with someone that one does not know. Trust takes time to establish (thus the often lengthy business courtships that so frustrate hurried Westerners).

3. Friends and Business Associates

In view of the centrality of trust in overseas Chinese business dealings, it is not surprising that friends and longstanding business associates are heavily relied upon to provide information about business opportunities, about prospective clients and customers, and to assist generally with business. They represent extensions of the circle of trust that began within the family and provide an additional network of connections and high quality sources of information.

4. Money and Credit

Sinologist Maurice Freedman (1979) suggests that the single most important overseas Chinese business ability related to money and credit. Starting as merchants in Southeast Asia and being excluded from land ownership, the overseas Chinese quickly had to extend credit to customers and obtain credit from suppliers. The merchant and credit functions were tightly integrated and led to powerful ethnic Chinese banks and financial institutions in Southeast Asia today.

5. Patriarchy

The family, as noted was highly patriarchal in nature with eldest brothers replacing fathers when the older generations died or were no longer able to "rule." In the present context, this suggests that company titles of family members and their formal education may be considerably less important than their age and sex in giving real clues about decision-making power.

6. The Historic and Contemporary Meaning of Land

Historically, land in China was of vital importance (Beattie, 1979; and Chao, 1986). In an agricultural society ownership and control of land was synonymous with wealth and power. Therefore, the family that could acquire land and retain it through time, would be able to perpetuate itself and maintain its status and well-being, both major concerns in light of the previous discussion about the family and the necessity of protecting the family line over time.

7. The Historic and Contemporary Meaning of Business

In Southeast Asia, land ownership was generally closed to ethnic Chinese. Land could not, therefore, be used to sustain the family over time. Business and commercial enterprise replaced land in this function. Business success was more than just economic well-being as a result, being inextricably tied to the need to maintain the family line with all its meaning.

8. Education: Binding Land and Business, Today and Yesterday

China boasts the world's oldest civil service examination dating 2,500 years ago to Confucius. Education was critical for passing these examinations, and in turn a civil service position could lead to power, prestige, land, and family continuity. In the Nanyang, education took on a different meaning in the absence of Imperial Examinations and land ownership: it was a means for perpetuating family business enterprise and a tool for enhancing family position and maintaining the family over time. The great value Chinese placed on education in Imperial China has a contemporary counterpart.

C. Some Findings on Overseas Chinese Real Estate Investment Behaviour

Recent real estate investment activity in North America by Nanyang Chinese illustrates many of the points about trust and informal information and communication networks.

1. The Issue

Over the past two decades, there have been intermittent and almost always overblown headlines, mass media stories and more recently books

(Cannon, 1989; and De Mont and Fennell, 1989) about the pending domination of particular real estate markets by overseas Chinese, particularly those from Hong Kong. Concern about early headlines led to the research described below. The research had two objectives: first to try to discern the extent of ethnic Chinese North American real estate holdings; second, to try to develop an understanding of the motivations behind these investment decisions. The first objective proved very difficult to achieve. The second is our focus below.

2. The Method

After reviewing the literature and finding no data on the nature and magnitude of ethnic Chinese real estate investments, it was decided to use in-depth personal interviews to develop a qualitative understanding of the subject. Interviews took place in May 1983 with some eighty Nanyang Chinese investors and their advisors in Bangkok, Hong Kong, Kuala Lumpur and Singapore and in various cities in North America.

Questions focussed on: origins and destinations of real estate flows; investment criteria; information sources and methods of analysis; and methods of investing.

3. The Findings

(a) Origins and destinations of real estate flows: It becomes apparent at the outset that there is a great deal of diversity in the patterns of real estate investment flows. One general point that can be made is that Western North America is the most frequently cited destination, not surprising given its proximity to the region. Major flows also occurred within the region itself, particularly to Hong Kong when the property market there was booming in the late 1970s and early 1980s. Also, Australia was a common destination. Europe and less developed nations (LDCs) outside Asia were not seen as having sufficient growth potential (Europe) or stability (LDCs).

(b) Investment criteria: Half a dozen criteria were cited. Some were expected, others were surprising. Portfolio diversification was the most cited criterion and has two components: the desire to diversify non-real estate assets by acquiring real estate; and the desire to diversify geographically out of the region. A closely related issue was "capital conservation" that stressed the need for political stability to ensure that the acquired real estate would maintain its value and provide a safe haven for family funds. Reasonable proximity to Southeast Asia was important in this regard as

well since it provided a ready means to check-up on investments and seek
out additional opportunities.

Both of these were anticipated criteria. More surprising was the link
between the location of prospective real estate investment and the location
of family and friends, and especially the place where children and
grandchildren were attending university. This education-investment-
family-wealth-preservation criterion was unexpected and yet consistent
with overseas Chinese cultural views of education and family maintenance
as seen above.

(c) Information sources and methods of analysis: Reinforcing the role of
family and friends, we see the importance here of using existing ties to get
information about potential real estate investments and then relying on
many of these people to help in evaluating the prospects. Little use was
made of organized and widely publicized "real estate fairs" and media
advertising. Private sources such as family, friends, and trusted professionals were relied upon instead.

(d) Methods of investing: Of interest here was the suggestion that many
overseas Chinese used elaborate and convoluted means to transfer funds
and hold real property. This was not found to be case. Investments were
made using existing banking ties in a straightforward way.

D. Conclusions and Extensions Concerning Overseas Chinese Real Estate Investment Behaviour

By putting overseas Chinese real estate investment in an historical, cultural,
and economic context it becomes obvious why these investment flows have
been so large of late and so widely dispersed geographically among the
stable English speaking democracies of North America and Australia. Past
"homelessness" in Southeast Asia and the desire to preserve and protect the
family motivate ethnic Chinese to seek secure investments with longer term
capital appreciation for future generations. Real estate is a logical answer.
It is easy to maintain using local professional managers and it provides
stable cash flows with good potential for long term gain in North America
and Australia.

The future for continued flows of this capital to Australia, Canada and
the United States is excellent (Yannie, 1988). This is independent of such
publicized (and in my view somewhat overrated) events as the expiry of the
lease on Hong Kong in 1997. Rather it is a function of the continued

excellent growth prospects for the Southeast Asia region and the resulting continued accumulation of capital by the ethnic Chinese in the region. As these capital pools grow, there will be greater and greater pressure to diversify out of the region for sound business reasons unrelated to the lingering fears of, and discrimination against, the ethnic Chinese.

Hong Kong is a good example. It is a small territory with fewer than six million inhabitants. Prudence suggests that businesses expand out of such a small base and Australia and North America are good locales given their long term growth potential and political stability. Singapore and Malaysia are in similar positions being rather small with limited markets.

Sound business practice thus calls for continued flows of real estate investment capital to these regions. In addition, given growing unease by ethnic Chinese in Malaysia, in Indonesia and the Philippines, increasing movements of capital can be reasonably expected in the longer term.

Burgeoning Japanese Real Estate Investment: A Brief Review

Up through the 1970s, when one heard of "Asian" offshore real estate investment, such investment was virtually synonymous with ethnic Chinese investment activity. All of this changed abruptly in the early 1980s with the advent of Japanese property acquisition and development around the Pacific Rim. As was the case with the ethnic Chinese, in part this investment is motivated by diversification (geographically, by currency, and by type of asset) given the limited extent of the Japanese land mass (Burton, 1990; *The Economist*, 1989a; Holloway, 1989; Leventhal, 1989; Ohse, 1989; and Rodman, 1989). Offshore property acquisition is also seen as a means for preserving capital and diversifying assets. These rationales suggest long-time horizons as with the Nanyang Chinese. In keeping with this sort of investment horizon, stability of cash flow and high-quality buildings and/or locations are of interest, again similar to much ethnic Chinese real estate investment.

However, there the similarities stop. Japanese offshore property investment is, with few exceptions (notably Hawaiian hotels), a reasonably recent phenomenon related to the exceptional strength of the yen in 1986 and 1987, which in turn is tied to the enormous trade surpluses and foreign cash reserves held by Japanese firms (Edgington, 1988). Two broad types of investments can be identified. The first are recreational resort and hotel properties as typified by investments in Hawaii and the Australian Gold Coast and the recent purchase of a major resort in Whistler, British Columbia (Daniels, 1990). In these acquisitions and developments Japanese tourists and business people represent an important part of the market towards which these investments are being aimed, very different from the ethnic Chinese case. Thus, where recreational and resort real estate is usually seen as a volatile and high risk investment, the Japanese see it differently given the scale of the Japanese domestic market where these developments are often aimed.

The other stream in Japanese real estate investment is prime office space. The much heralded purchase of ARCO Plaza in the centre of Los Angeles for US$620 million and of Rockefeller Center for nearly US$800 typify this sort of purchase. Given the strength of the yen in the late 1980s, the large amount of foreign cash reserves for equity investment, and the Japanese penchant for high quality properties (Mogami, 1987) these sorts of investments are continuing apace into 1988 (Bacow, 1987; Leventhal 1987, 1989 and 1990a; Lindner and Monahan, 1988). Most recently, the Japanese are diversifying these investments by focussing relatively more attention on European and less on the US markets (*Land Use Digest*, 1990a, b; *Pacific Rim Business Journal*, 1990; and Young and Evans, 1990).

One major property type that the Japanese have kept away from to date has been retail. However, there is evidence in the US that this also is about to change. Leventhal (1989: 3–5) estimates that approximately 5 percent of Japanese real estate investment (US$42.88 billion at the end of 1988) was in retail, a very distant fifth behind office (#1 at roughly 50 percent), resort and hotel (#2 at roughly 25 percent), mixed use (#3 at roughly 15 percent), and residential (#4 at roughly 10 percent). With huge Japanese department store chains becoming focussed on international expansion, all this is likely to shift in the next several years (Christman and Smith, 1988; *Shopping Centers Today*, 1990).

Japanese offshore property investment differs from that of the ethnic Chinese in that Japanese investment is overwhelmingly corporate in nature and large in scale with a significant tendency to follow domestic customers abroad as with Japanese hotel and resort development. Leventhal (1989: 13–16) suggests that only 11 percent of the new Japanese investment during 1988 was by individuals and investment companies. Ethnic Chinese real estate purchases have also been tied, as we saw, to the geographically

dispersed extended family often being associated with prospective immigration to the country where the investment is located. In contrast, there
has been little migration from Japan. Japanese global family networks are
also modest compared with those of the Chinese. Finally, where ethnic
Chinese property investments are highly varied, so far Japanese investments have been much more focussed and generally large.

Given the relative newness of Japanese offshore property investments,
there is much still to learn. Japanese investors are still feeling their way and
their behaviours will likely change as they gain experience. Similarly, as
more is known about these behaviours, host country property developers
and agents will doubtless also change their approach to dealing with the
Japanese. It is safe to say that the scale of Japanese Pacific Rim real
estate investment is such as to establish them as very major players in the
international real estate market, further adding to the globalization of local
property markets.

Other Actors in the Globalization of Property Markets

Arguably the largest single private real estate development project is being
undertaken at London's Canary Wharf by Canada's Reichman family
(Garner, 1990). Estimated to cost more than US$7.0 billion, with over 10
million square feet of buildings taking more than a decade to complete, the
project illustrates the scale of impacts that international real estate capital
can have on an urban area, even one as enormous as London, England.

The Reichman's are not alone. Such giant construction and development
firms as Japan's Kumagai Gumi, American Trammel Crow, Australia's
Bond Corporation, and Britain's Grosvenor Estates all have undertaken
large-scale development far from their home base. Recently, a formal
international real estate market started to promote global real estate investment and advance the development of a global real estate market (*Urban
Land*, 1990b).

Aside from large real estate development firms, there are other, and
perhaps even more important, sources of, and forces in, global real estate
investment. Of greatest significance are the massive pools of capital controlled by pension funds, global asset managers, and life insurance companies.
For example, the Japanese Postal Savings System and its life insurance
subsidiary jointly command well over US$1 trillion in assets. Nippon Life

Insurance Company has over US$300 billion in assets. Lastly, global asset managers are responsible for trillions of dollars in assets. These enormous pools of capital are continually scanning the global investment environment to maximize yield, stabilize return, and minimize risk. Increasingly, real estate is forming a central part of their global portfolio management strategy as Nippon Life's purchase of ARCO Plaza in Los Angeles illustrates.

The enormity of these pools of investable funds and the growing sophistication of the people who manage them provide exciting opportunities for the real estate industry all around the world. These managers and the funds for which they are responsible will increasingly be potent forces in the world's major urban property markets. In the process, these funds will heighten and speed the globalization of real property markets.

An Overview of Some Policy Initiatives Designed to Tap into the Growing Global Financial, Commercial and Property Network

McLuhan's notion of the global village goes beyond information about the village to include the global market for village real estate. This globalized property market raises a number of policy issues that we treat before concluding. The policies set out below have one common thread: they illustrate subnational governmental units (cities, provinces or states) being involved in proactive economic policy-making. Previously national governments made economic policy and took international positions with enormous impacts on cities and provinces, while more junior governments were passive observers. This more active role for junior governments is gathering momentum and over the next decade could well rival in total, national policy efforts.

A. Vancouver: Policies to Develop as a Pacific Rim Service Centre

The British Columbia provincial economy has historically been resource-based and cyclical. Vancouver has similarly experienced its own booms and busts. To broaden the province's and city's economic base several activities have been designed to expand the service sector, especially in financial services.

There are several elements in the strategy to make Vancouver a major Asia-Pacific urban centre. First, in late 1970s the city formed the

Vancouver Economic Advisory Commission (VEAC) to help develop an economic development strategy. The strategy evolved and was formally adopted by City Council in 1983, to build on the city's role as retail, business and public services centre for British Columbia and Western Canada (Vancouver Economic Advisory Commission, various years).

Simultaneous with this city strategy, the province began planning and construction of EXPO 86 and its spinoff benefits. International financial services in Vancouver were the key, building on the Vancouver Stock Exchange, university business schools in the region, the existing regional financial infrastructure, and a history of no exchange controls or freezing of foreign assets in Canada. This, plus excellent airline access to Asia, moderate living and office costs, good business services, and a high quality physical environment suggested that the idea was worth pursuing. Thus "IFC Vancouver" began (*Euromoney*, 1987).

The governments of Canada and British Columbia signed a "Memorandum of Understanding" (MOU) to establish Vancouver as a "Pacific Rim centre for trade, tourism and finance," in February 1986. Cdn$6.0 million were allocated to do research, develop policies, and move them to implementation (Asia Pacific Initiative, 1988). Also in February 1986 Canadian Finance Minister Wilson announced he would be designating Vancouver and Montreal as "International Banking Centres" which passed in December 1987. Companion provincial measures passed in October 1988 and a provincially sponsored group created to foster Vancouver as an international financial center (Goldberg, 1990).

The province and city are exploiting specific international financial niches to broaden the provincial and urban economy and capitalize on the city's amenities, infrastructure and Pacific Rim location. The booming East Asian region is leading these initiatives, supporting the present hypothesis that globalization of national and urban economies leads to globalization of local real property markets.

B. Australian Initiatives

Australian cities and states have been active in seeking to provide high-value services in the Asia-Pacific region. Two initiatives come to mind: one from Melbourne and Victoria, and the other from Sydney and New South Wales.

The strategy statements by the State of Victoria are superb examples (Ministry for Planning and Environment, 1987). These volumes map out innovative policies for the State of Victoria and the city of Melbourne to benefit from growth in the Asia-Pacific region. Services dominate these strategies, particularly financial services.

Sydney too has attempted to tap into the international network of financial centres. The push to establish offshore banking units (OBUs) in Australia was pressed particularly hard by Sydney financial interests. The push continued after it was clear that Australian financial system reforms in 1982/1983 would not include OBUs (Carew, 1985). Both these efforts aimed at tying Australian urban economies to the Asia-Pacific regional and global economies. They imply further linking of Australian urban property markets to these larger economic spheres is on the way.

C. Recapitulation

The foregoing illustrates that globalization (particularly of financial and producer service markets) is no longer solely a national policy issue but has become the purview of cities and states/provinces as well. Attendant to this global integration of goods and service markets is a globalization of previously highly localized urban property markets. Thus, just as national economic policy-makers must be concerned increasingly with the international economic promotional activities and policies of subnational governmental units, so must local and provincial (state) authorities be attentive to the international economic marketplace within which their property markets function.

Conclusion and Looking Ahead

This chapter discussion started with a review of the extent to which global markets have developed, not just for goods but especially for capital. From this base that we explored, evidence was marshalled to suggest that urban property markets are following suit rapidly. The international real estate behaviour of the ethnic Chinese of Southeast Asia was especially examined at some depth. A review was also made of booming Japanese global property investment. These groups have invested within Asia for some time. Of interest here is the extent to which they are investing across the Pacific leading to a more tightly integrated Pacific property market.

The previous pages also explored some proactive efforts being made by cities and states-provinces to link into this global network of capital and economic activity. Subnational governments are becoming important international economic actors whose future impacts are likely to be substantial. This will be all the more important given the growing (and likely central) role of huge global institutional real property investors. The result is that a Pacific, indeed a global, property market is already upon us.

The most powerful trend emerging from the above is that local urban property markets cannot escape the global integration process; this trend should continue and increase in future. More urban property development and investment will have an international component so that local land use and development policies will need to evolve in this broader international perspective. This will likely apply not just to the largest cities but also to much smaller ones (e.g., Victoria, B.C). It will be particularly apparent across the Pacific given past and growing family and business links among major cities on both sides of the ocean. Growing affluence can be expected to increase investment in major Pacific property markets by ethnic Chinese, Koreans, and of course by the Japanese.

Local and state (provincial) policy-makers will face a special challenge since this opens up new sources of financial capital, development expertise, and planning ideas that recipient cities can use. Offshore real estate investment also implies closer ties with offshore investors leading to further offshore business investment and offshore sales of local goods and services.

Difficulties also loom. Heightened outside control of local economies implies a growing inability to be truly masters of our own fates. To some extent this has always been the case for cities and globalization just makes it more dramatic. Cities will also have to absorb more people from other cultures as "urban globalization" advances. Finally, subnational policymakers will have to cope increasingly with a pace, scale and diversity of change that they have not likely encountered previously.

REFERENCES

Apgar, Mahlon IV (1984). "The Changing Realities of Foreign Investment." *Urban Land*, 43(11), pp. 6–11.
Asia Pacific Initiative (1988). *Backgrounder*. Vancouver: Asia Pacific Initiative.
Asiaweek (1990). "Hotels: Kings of the Room Boom," 16 February, pp. 24–28.
Bacow, Lawrence S. (1987). "Understanding Foreign Investment in US Real Estate." Working Paper, No. 12. Cambridge, Massachusetts: M.I.T. Center for Real Estate Development.

———— (1988). *The Internationalization of the US Real Estate Industry*, Working Paper, No. 16. Cambridge, Massachusetts: M.I.T. Center for Real Estate Development.

Baker, Hugh D. R. (1979). *Chinese Family and Kinship*. New York: Columbia University Press.

Beattie, Hilary J. (1979). *Land and Lineage in China*. Cambridge, Massachusetts: Harvard University Press.

Bryant, Ralph C. (1987). *International Financial Intermediation*. Washington, D.C.: The Brookings Institution.

Burton, Jonathan (1990). "America up for Auction: Savings and Loan Fiasco Yields Property for Sale." *Far Eastern Economic Review*, 22 February, pp. 40–41.

Cannon, Margaret (1989). *China Tide: The Revealing Story of the Hong Kong Exodus to Canada*. Toronto: Harper and Collins.

Carew, Edna (1985). *Fast Money 2*. Sydney: Allen and Unwin.

Chan, Anthony B. (1983). *The Gold Mountain: The Chinese in the New World*. Vancouver: New Star Books.

Chao Kang (1986). *Man and Land in Chinese History: An Economic Analysis*. Palo Alto: Stanford University Press.

Christman, Edward and Rodney N. Smith (1988). "Japanese Move into Retail: Snap up Hawaii Strips, Buy Equity in US Malls." *Shopping Centers Today*, 1 and 6–7 November.

Cu-Uy-Gam, Miriam (1989). "Offshore Cash Helps Lay Foundation for Property Deals." *The Financial Post*, 6 November, p. 33.

Daly, M. T. (1982). *Sydney Boom, Sydney Bust*. Sydney: Allen and Unwin.

Daly, M. T. and M. I. Logan (1989). *The Brittle Rim: Finance, Business and the Pacific Region*. Sydney: Penguin.

Daniels, Alan (1990). "Tokyo Firm Buys into CP Hotel: 80% of Chateau Whistler Reported Sold for $80 Million." *Vancouver Sun*, 15 March, C1.

Daniels, Peter W. (1986). "Foreign Banks and Metropolitan Development: A Comparison of London and New York." *Journal of Economic and Social Geography*, 77(4), pp. 269–287.

De Mont, John and Thomas Fennell (1989). *Hong Kong Money: How Chinese Families and Fortunes are Changing Canada*. Toronto: Key Porter Books.

Dunfee, E. J. (1990). "Sweet and Sour in 'Van Kong'." *Asia Magazine* (Hong Kong), Weekend 19–21 January, pp. 6–15.

Economic Council of Canada (1989). *A New Frontier: Globalization and Canada's Financial Markets*. Ottawa: Economic Council of Canada.

The Economist (1989a). "Japanese Property: A Glittering Sprawl," 3 October, pp. 25–28.

The Economist (1989b). "Japan's Big Property Grab," 3 October, pp. 85–86.

Edgington, David W. (1988). *Japanese Business Down-Under: Patterns of*

Japanese Investment in Australia, 1957–1985. Sydney: The Transnational Corporations Research Project, University of Sydney.

Euromoney (1987). "Special Supplement on Pacific Rim Financial Centres," May.

Far Eastern Economic Review (1989). "Focus: Property," 143(11), pp. 41–65.

Freedman, Maurice (1979). *The Study of Chinese Society*. Palo Alto: Stanford University Press.

Friedland, Jonathan (1989). "California's New Gold Rush." *Far Eastern Economic Review*, 143(12), pp. 80–82.

———— (1990). "Hong in a Hurry: Malaysian Conglomerate Returns to the Acquisition." *Far Eastern Economic Review*, 144(7), pp. 50–54.

Garner, William (1990). "The Biggest Building Site in Europe." *Telegraph Weekend Magazine*, 24–25 February, pp. 30–40.

Gates, Bruce (1987). "Land Prices Lure Japanese." *The Financial Post*, 3 August, p. 7.

———— (1990). "Study State Laws before Investing in US Property." *The Financial Post*, 19 March, p. 37.

Goldberg, Michael A. (1985). *The Chinese Connection: Getting Plugged in to Pacific Rim Real Estate, Trade and Capital Markets*. Vancouver: The University of British Columbia Press.

———— (1990). "Vancouver As a Pacific Rim International Financial Centre: A Progress Report Two Years Later." *UBC Business Review*.

Gralla, Heidi (1990). "Developers Eye Europe; Simon in Hungary." *Shopping Centers Today*, March, pp. 3 & 26.

Grub, Philip D., Tan Chwee-huat, Kwan Kuen-chor and George H. Root (1982). *East Asia: Dimensions of International Business*. Singapore: Prentice Hall of Southeast Asia.

Hajdu, J. C. (1990). *Recent Cycles of Overseas Property Investment in Central Sydney and Melbourne*. Clayton: Department of Geography, Victoria College.

Hamilton, Adrian (1986). *The Financial Revolution*. New York: The Free Press.

Hendershott, Patric H. and Robert Van Order (1989). "Integration of Mortgage and Capital Markets and the Accumulation of Residential Capital." *Regional Science and Urban Economics*, 19, pp. 189–210.

Holloway, Nigel (1989). "Japanese Funds Inflate Hawaii's Property Bubble." *Far Eastern Economic Review*, 3 August, pp. 48–51.

Horvitch, Sonita (1990). "Prime Toronto Real Estate Draws Foreign Investment." *The Financial Post*, 19 March, p. 44.

International Monetary Fund (IMF) (1988). *International Financial Statistics*. Washington, D.C.: International Monetary Fund.

Kaufman, Henry (1986). *Interest Rates, the Markets, and the New Financial World*. New York: Times Books.

Keast, Gordon (1988). "The World's Longest Commute." *Equity*, March, pp. 22–29.

────── (1989). "The House of the Rising Son." *Equity*, May, pp. 78–79.

Land Use Digest (1987), Vol. 20, No. 11, 15 November, "Land Prices in Tokyo Increased by More Than 85 Percent" (p. 3) and "Japanese Investment in US Real Estate is Expected to Double" (p. 4).

────── (1990a). Vol. 23, No. 6, June, "Japanese Investment Shift" (p. 2).

────── (1990b). Vol. 23, No. 9, September, "Trends in Japanese Real Estate Investment" (p. 2).

Leventhal, Kenneth and Company (1987). *Real Estate Newsline*, Vol. 4, Nos. 7 and 12, July and December.

────── (1989). *1988 Japanese Investment in United States Real Estate*. Los Angeles: Kenneth Leventhal and Company, 1989.

────── (1990a). "Japanese Investment in US Real Estate Declined Nearly 11% in 1989, Mainly Because of Reduced Office Investment." *Real Estate Newsline*, Vol. 7, Nos. 3 and 4, March–April.

────── (1990b). "Golf Course Development Increases to Highest Level since 1960s as US Golf Population Soars to Record Levels." *Real Estate Newsline*, Vol. 7, Nos. 7 and 8, July–August, pp. 4–7.

Levi, Maurice D. (1989). *International Finance*. Revised Edition. New York: McGraw-Hill Book Co.

Lim, Linda Y. C. and L. A. Peter Gosling (ed.) (1983). *The Chinese in Southeast Asia*, Vols. I and II. Singapore: Maruzen Asia.

Limlingan, Victor Simpao (1986). *The Overseas Chinese in ASEAN: Business Strategies and Management Practices*. Manila: Vita Development Corporation.

Lindner, Russell C. with Edward L. Monahan, Jr. (1988). "Observations on Understanding and Working with Japanese Investors." *Real Estate Review*, 17(4), pp. 31–36.

Livanes, George (1989). "A Review of Acquisition of Real Estate by Chinese in the Haymarket Area of Sydney." M.A. Thesis, Department of Geography, University of Sydney.

McGee, Terence G. (1984). "Circuits and Networks of Capital: The Internationalization of the World Economy and National Urbanization." Vancouver: The Institute of Asian Research, University of British Columbia, Mimeo.

McKenna, Barrie (1987). "Foreign Rush to Canada Could Turn to Torrent." *The Financial Post*, Property Post Special Report, 23 November, pp. 43–44.

McLernon, John (1989). "Real Estate Development and Investment Opportunities in a Global Economy." A talk presented at the National Meetings of the Urban Development Institute Canada, Whistler, British Columbia, 7 April.

Miller, Rich (1989). "Japanese Real Estate Group Buys Houston Skyscrapers." *The Financial Post*, 3 November, p. 8.

Ministry for Planning and Environment (1987). *Victoria: The Next Decade*. Melbourne, Australia: Ministry for Planning and Environment, State of Victoria.

Mitchell, Alanna (1989). "Canadian Real Estate Joining Global." *The Financial Post*, 10 April, p. 14.

Mogami, Naohiko (1987). "The Japanese Investment Boom." *Urban Land*, 46(7), p. 28.

O'Connor, Kevin and David Edgington (1987). "Producer Services and Metropolitan Development in Australia." Clayton, Victoria: Department of Geography, Monash University.

Ohse, Hisanobu (1989). "Japanese Investors Buying up Property in Southern California." *The Financial Post*, 1 August, p. 6.

Pacific Rim Business Journal (1990). "Japanese Investment Declines, U.S. Corporations to Benefit," 15–28 May, p. 15.

Quint, Michael (1990). "Japanese Expand Real Estate Lending as U.S. Banks Retreat from Market." *The Globe and Mail*, 19 March, B6.

Reed, Howard Curtis (1981). *The Preeminence of International Financial Centers*. New York: Praeger Publishers.

Regeling, Henry A. A., C. J. Bartram and Takahide Moribe (1984). "Foreign Investors in the United States: A Symposium." *Real Estate Review*, 14(3), pp. 34–42.

Rodman, Jack (1989). "Japanese Investors Expected to Invest More in Residential Development in US." *Real Estate Newsline*, 6(5), pp. 1, 7–8.

Roulac's Strategic Real Estate (1988). "Japanese Lead Foreigners in U.S. Megadeals," 10(1), pp. 6–7.

Schreiner, John (1990). "Japanese Infatuated with Investment in Canada." *The Financial Post*, 20 March, p. 13.

Schwann, G. M. (1989). *When Did You Move to Vancouver? An Analysis of Migration and Migrants into Metropolitan Vancouver*. Vancouver.: Laurier Institute.

Shopping Centers Today (1987). "Japanese Expected to Wield Influence," October, pp. 1–4.

——— (1990). "Japanese Retailer Plans US Centers," 3 January.

Skully, Michael T. and George J. Viksnins (1987). *Financing East Asia's Success: Comparative Financial Development in Eight Asian Countries*. New York: St. Martin's Press.

Stoffman, Daniel (1989). "Asia Comes to Lotusland." *Report on Business*, November.

Suryadinata, Leo (ed.) (1989). *The Ethnic Chinese in the ASEAN States: Bibliographical Essays*. Singapore: Institute of Southeast Asian Studies, National University of Singapore.

Tan, Augustine H. H. and Basant Kapur (eds.) (1986). *Pacific Growth and Financial Interdependence*. Sydney: Allen and Unwin.

Tiglao, Robert (1990). "Gung-ho in Manila: Chinese-Filipinos Create an Economic Power Base." *Far Eastern Economic Review*, 15 February, pp. 68–71.

Triple A. (1987). "Special Survey-Property 1987," August, pp. 88–103.

Tsui, John F. (1987). "Overview of Pacific Rim Property Markets. " *Urban Land*, 46(11), pp. 12–15.

Tsuruoka, Doug (1990). "Kuala Lumpur Flashes Warning for Foreign Investors: Shaky Foundations." *Far Eastern Economic Review*, 22 March, pp. 64–65.

Urban Land (1990a). "Real Estate Capital Flows," 49(1), pp. 32–33.

———— (1990b). "First International Property Market Held in France," 49(7), pp. 21–22.

———— (1990c). "Outlook for European Investment in U.S. Real Estate," September, pp. 28–29.

Vancouver Economic Advisory Commission (various dates, 1984 to present). Selected Task Force reports on "Business and Trade Services" and on "Banking/Finance/Insurance." Vancouver: Vancouver Economic Advisory Commission.

Wachtel, Howard (1986). *The Money Mandarins: The Making of a Supranational Economic Order*. New York: Pantheon Books.

Willmott, William E. (ed.) (1972). *Economic Organization in Chinese Society*. Palo Alto: Stanford University Press.

Wolf, Arthur P. (ed.) (1978). *Studies in Chinese Society*. Palo Alto: Stanford University Press.

Wu Yuan-li and Wu Chun-hsi (1980). *Economic Development in Southeast Asia: The Chinese Dimension*. Palo Alto, California: The Hoover Institution.

Yannie, Vincent J. (1988). "The Effects of Hong Kong's Transfer to China in 1997 on San Francisco Real Estate." Essay prepared as partial requirement for a Master's Degree in Political and Economic Assessment of Pacific Basin Economies, San Rafael, California, Dominican College, 16 August.

Young, Nicholas E. and Michael Evans (1990). "Japanese Real Estate Investment in Europe Accelerated in 1989 as Investors Sought Higher Yields and Diversification." *Real Estate Newsline*, March–April, p. 1.

CHAPTER THREE

Urban Futures for Pacific Asia: Towards the 21st Century

Terry G. McGee
Institute of Asian Research and Professor of Geography,
University of British Columbia, Vancouver, Canada
Yue-man Yeung
Director, Hong Kong Institute of Asia-Pacific Studies and Professor of
Geography, The Chinese University of Hong Kong, Hong Kong

Introduction

The aims of this paper are at least threefold. They are to take stock of the salient urbanization trends, to analyze the determinants of urban futures, and on the basis of these to describe and speculate on the emerging patterns of urbanization in Pacific Asia in the earlier part of the 21st century. Of course, any attempt to predict the future is a hazardous task and it is certainly the case with the urbanization process that is influenced by so many different factors.

In speculating on the urbanization process, the statistical dimension poses particular problems. This is because it is most frequently based upon two assumptions. First, that there is some acceptable definition of urban places and that these will not change over time. Secondly, that the patterns of urban growth which have been exhibited over past periods of growth will be continued along trajectories of urban growth similar to that of Western countries. This involves a rather precarious acceptance of linear progression and of the Western model of economic change that may not necessarily be the case.

For Pacific Asia, this paper refers to all the countries on the Western Pacific Rim, stretching from Korea to Indonesia. For lack of data, the socialist countries of Laos, Kampuchea, the Democratic Republic of Vietnam, Soviet Asia and North Korea are excluded from most of the discussion.

Secondly, for a definition of "urban," in general, we have accepted the country definition of using a threshold size for urban places of 100,000. While this definition undoubtedly leads to the inclusion of populations who are living within urban areas but employed in agricultural production and those living outside urban areas engaged in non-agricultural activity, it is in our view the best working definition that permits comparative analysis.

Structural Changes and Urbanization

Before embarking on the task of predicting urban futures, it is necessary to understand the patterns of economic change occurring in Asia over the last thirty years, for it is now well established that structural change (defined as the shift of employment from agriculture to non-agriculture and the increase in the GDP in a similar manner) are closely related to the urbanization process.

With respect to the level of urbanization, Table 3.1 shows two clear groupings. First, Japan and the so-called newly industrializing countries (NICs), with more than 50 percent of their populations in urban places, are now assuming patterns very similar to the developed countries. Second, there is a group of countries including Thailand and Indonesia, where levels of urbanization remain relatively low (in the 21–27 percent range). China should really belong to this group despite the fact that its level of urbanization is recorded at 50 percent by the World Bank. It does appear that the World Bank figure is a gross over-estimation, and a more realistic estimate based on the 1990 Population Census is 26.3 percent (*Wen Wei Po*, 20 November 1990). The huge difference in estimation is the result of definitional variation.

Finally, there is a third group consisting of Malaysia and the Philippines where the level of urbanization is approximately 41 percent. We are inclined to the view that Thailand may well fall into this group as well in future.

If this threefold division is accepted, then the patterns of structural change revealed in Tables 3.1 and 3.2 are closely related.

First, in the highly urbanized countries there has been very rapid structural change which has seen a growing increase in the role of industry (except in Hong Kong where the industrial contribution to GDP has fallen), which is reflected in the increase in the size of industrial employment. This

Table 3.1: Selected Urban and Structural Change in Pacific Asian Countries, 1965–1988

Countries	Popul. (1988) (mn)	Average Annual Pop. Growth Rate		Urban Pop. as % of Total Pop.		Average Annual Urban Pop. Growth Rate		Proportion of Labour Force in					
								Agriculture		Industry		Service	
		1965–1980	1980–1988	1965	1988	1965–1980	1980–1988	1960	1980	1960	1980	1960	1980
Japan and NICs													
Japan	123	1.2	0.6	67	77	2.1	0.7	33	11	30	34	37	55
Hong Kong	6	2.0	1.5	89	93	2.1	1.7	8	3	52	57	40	40
Singapore	3	1.6	1.1	100	100	1.6	1.1	8	2	23	39	69	59
Taiwan	17	2.7	1.1*	30.4	71*	2.7	—	56	20	11	33	33	47
Korea Rep.	42	2.0	1.4	32	69	5.8	4.2	66	34	9	29	25	37
ASEAN-4													
Malaysia	17	2.5	2.6	26	41	4.5	4.9	63	50	12	16	25	34
Philippines	60	2.9	2.5	32	41	4.2	3.7	61	46	15	17	24	37
Thailand	54	2.9	1.9	13	21	5.1	4.7	84	76	4	9	12	15
Indonesia	175	2.4	2.1	16	27	4.8	4.8	74	58	8	12	17	30
Giant Economy													
China	1,088	2.2	1.3	18	50	2.3	—	75	62	15	25	10	13

* Data for 1981–1988: *Asia 1990 Year Book*. Other Taiwan data from Republic of China, *Statistical Yearbook 1987*.
Sources: The World Bank (1990), *World Development Report 1990*.

Table 3.2: Selected Pacific Asian Economics: Structural Contrasts in Distribution of GDP, Grouped by Urbanization Trajectories, 1960–1988

Countries	Agriculture			Industry			Manufacturing			Service		
	1960	1980	1988	1960	1980	1988	1960	1980	1988	1960	1980	1988
Japan and NICs												
Japan	13	4	3	45	43	41	33	30	29	42	53	57
Hong Kong	4	2	0	39	31	29	26	26	22	57	67	70
Singapore	4	1	0	18	37	38	12	26	30	78	62	61
Taiwan*	28	9	6	29	46	47	22	42	39	43	49	49
Korea Rep.	37	16	11	20	39	43	14	28	32	43	45	46
ASEAN-4												
Malaysia	36	23	—	18	30	—	9	18	—	46	47	—
Philippines	26	22	23	28	36	34	20	24	25	46	42	44
Thailand	40	22	17	19	28	35	13	19	24	41	50	48
Indonesia	54	26	24	14	39	36	8	13	19	32	35	40
Giant Economy												
China	39	33	32	38	47	46	30	37	30	23	20	21

* 1987 data, from the Council for Economic Planning and Development, Republic of China, 1988, *Taiwan Statistical Data Book.*

Sources: The World Bank (1989, 1990), *World Development Report 1989, 1990.*

pattern is not so clear in the service sector, where in the city-states the employment proportion has remained stable or fallen, while in Taiwan and Korea it has increased but changed little with respect to its proportional contribution to the GDP.

With respect to the second group of countries, Malaysia and the Philippines have experienced rapid urbanization with a considerable decline in agricultural employment, limited increase in industrial employment but growing numbers in service. Indonesia, despite its still rather modest level of urbanization of 27 percent in 1988, has witnessed a notable restructuring of its economy so that the relative importance of the main economic sectors is rapidly conforming to the two countries. As yet, Thailand does not appear to fit too well into the group but there are indications that it is transforming itself along lines of the other ASEAN countries (see Greenberg, 1990).

Finally, China is not unlike the majority of Asian countries in which urbanization appears to have progressed slowly and structural change as evidenced by shifts on the industrial contribution to the GDP and employment are comparatively small, particularly if manufacturing is utilized rather than industry (which includes, for instance, the case of Indonesia with substantial oil processing). Generally, the decline in agricultural employment appears to have been largely absorbed into the service sector but unlike the urbanized countries this has been primarily into low productivity service occupations; this is an important fact when looking at the types of future centres that may emerge.

These patterns of urbanization and structural change, while the reflection of national processes such as state and local capital investment and planning, also reflect the influences of international linkages and capital that will be dealt with in the next section.

In summing up, it is possible to argue that only a small proportion of Asian countries have experienced structural change and spatial transformation to an urbanized condition (Yeung, 1976). For most Asian countries, the majority of their populations are still resident in agricultural areas and the urban revolution has hardly begun.

Determinants of Urban Futures

At present the methodology of forecasting urban futures is developed in only a rudimentary manner, given the large number of variables involved.

One method is to employ the technique of exploratory scenarios construction, using a range of techniques to assist forecasting, such as trend extrapolation, cyclical analysis and consensus surveys. Possible or desirable urban futures may be identified and a programme may be designed to achieve any or all of them. It is an exercise in social engineering. Another method available to the forecaster is the use of anticipatory scenarios whose objective is to establish whether a specific normative goal or target might be achieved. The objective set for the planner may result from a national policy. Successive attempts are taken to determine alternative ways by which the objective might be achieved and which of the alternative routes should be followed (Newton and Taylor, 1985). However, neither of these methods are adopted in this paper. What is attempted is a systematic consideration of the relevant factors that bear directly on urbanization to the end of this century, to be followed by speculations on urban futures in Pacific Asia.

From a global perspective, one of the most dominant concerns of Asian urbanization is the huge population base that exists in the region. Between 1950 and 1985, Asia's urban population increased almost fourfold to 480 million at an overall urbanization level of 29.3 percent. This figure is estimated to increase by 72 percent to 827 million, by century-end, when 38.2 percent of Asia's population will be domiciled in urban places (DIESA, United Nations, 1988). This means that in the remaining years of this century, several hundred million new inhabitants will have to be absorbed into the present urban system, displaying the importance of the "tyranny of numbers" in any discussion on the future of urbanization in Asia. Beyond numbers alone, there is a tendency for an increasingly large proportion of urban populations to concentrate in cities of over 500,000 inhabitants, that is, larger cities. If United Nations population projections are accurate, by 2000, thirteen of the thirty largest cities in the world will be located in Asia, many of them will be gargantuan urban conurbations of over 10 million inhabitants each. To be exact, six such mega-cities will be located in Pacific Asia, namely Tokyo, Seoul, Shanghai, Jakarta, Manila, and Beijing.

Already some of the giant cities of Pacific Asia are having to cope with staggering populations in terms of job and service provision. Greater Tokyo is said to contain the highest concentration of both people and wealth on earth, with 32 million people living within a 50-km commuting radius and generating about 3 percent of the world's goods and services. Osaka is not too far behind with about 20 million people living within commuting distance, forming part of Osaka-Kobe-Kyoto megalopolis (*Asiaweek*, 6 July 1990, p. 19). Tokyo and Osaka are not alone in having to face continuing challenges of feeding, housing, servicing, and providing effective governance for ever increasing populations, but they give a foretaste of the mega-cities of the future for other Asian Pacific countries that undoubtedly do not command the same range and size of resources.

Particularly relevant to urban growth is the concern of labour force participation. In the countries under review, the projection of labour force participation, along with overall population growth, is for modest or declining rates in Japan and the NICs. However, for the ASEAN-4, both new entrants to the labour force and their rates of increase are projected to be robust to the end of this century. The implications for urban governments to find jobs for these new entrants to the labour force are as urgent as they are daunting (see Table 3.3). For China, the relevant figures of which are not available in the same source, the total workforce will number 717 million persons by 2000 if current participation patterns are maintained, a 26

Table 3.3: Labour Force Projection and Annual Rates of Growth in Pacific Asia, 1975–2000

Countries	Labour Force (in thousands)			Annual Rate of Growth (%)		
	1975	1990	2000	1975–1980	1985–1990	1995–2000
Japan and NICs						
Japan	57,261	66,458	71,193	1.08	0.93	0.53
Hong Kong	1,872	2,427	2,691	2.46	1.06	1.11
Singapore	853	1,137	1,282	2.86	1.30	1.24
Taiwan	—	—	—	—	—	—
Korea	19,630	28,850	35,839	2.86	2.29	2.13
ASEAN-4						
Malaysia	4,006	6,396	8,639	3.05	2.95	3.01
Thailand	19,195	29,516	38,813	2.91	2.91	2.70
Philippines	15,699	24,278	32,833	2.79	3.05	2.96
Indonesia	47,024	66,967	84,277	2.38	2.36	2.26
Giant Economy						
China	—	—	—	—	—	—

Source: International Labour Office, *Labour Force Estimates and Projection 1950–2000*, 1977, pp. 62–64.

percent increase over 1985 employment level. The greatest increase in employment will take place in urban areas, a perfectly understood trend in view of its open policy adopted since 1978. Urban employment is projected to increase from 208 million people in 1985 to 385 million people by century-end. Approximately 54 percent of all workers will live in cities and towns, compared to 36 percent at present. In China, the pressure on the cities is already being felt by a freer movement of population resulting from the implementation of more liberal economic policies. During the Seventh Five-Year Plan (1986–1990), the planned new urban employment was set at 130 million, 100 million of which was earmarked for rural-urban migration and only 30 million for urban youth entering the workforce (Taylor, 1986:2).

The economic health of a nation is a critical factor that shapes the character of its cities. In the postwar period, the rapid economic growth of Japan and the NICs has thrust Pacific Asia into the world stage of international trade, technological innovations and foreign investment. This group of countries continued with their impressive economic growth, as measured by GDP, in the period 1985–1990. The high rates of growth are anticipated to be maintained in the 1990s, despite a little moderation. Their share of economic importance in the Pacific Basin will also increase towards 2000, bearing in mind this regional grouping includes industrialized market economies of the United States, Canada, Australia and New Zealand (see Table 3.4). On the same theme, the ASEAN-4 countries as well as China are also projected to experience robust growth, with China's growth of GDP and its share in regional importance being the most notable of all Asian Pacific countries.

In carrying forward the national economies of Pacific Asia, foreign direct investments plays a vital role. Within the region, the process was accelerated by Japan in the late 1970s, when the Japanese economy went through industrial adjustment and restructuring and began to relocate some of its "sunset" labour-intensive and resource-processing industries to developing Asian countries. The process was necessitated by shifting comparative advantage and facilitated by what may be called concerns about the greenhouse environment. It included investment in export processing zones and other specially designed locations to accommodate inward foreign direct investment. By the mid-1970s, Japan had already built up the largest foreign direct investment stock in Asia. It further expanded rapidly in the

Table 3.4: GDP and Its Growth in Pacific Asia, 1985–2000

Countries	Growth Rate % 1985–1990	GDP		Growth Rate % 1990–2000	GDP	
		1990 (US$ billion)	Share in PB		2000 (US$ billion)	Share in PB*
Japan and NICs						
Japan	4	1.473	21.2	3–4	2,078	22.9
Singapore	2	21	0.3	2–4	28	0.3
Hong Kong	3	38	0.5	2–4	51	0.6
Taiwan	7	86	1.22	4–6	140	1.5
Korea	7	125	1.8	4–6	204	2.2
ASEAN-4						
Malaysia	4	41	0.6	4–6	64	0.7
Thailand	4	53	0.8	3–4	75	0.8
Philippines	1	34	0.5	3–4	48	0.5
Indonesia	2	94	1.4	3–4	133	1.5
Giant Economy						
China	5	360	5.2	4–6	586	6.5

* Pacific Basin
Source: Shinichi Ichimura (ed.), *Challenge of Asian Developing Countries*. Tokyo: Asian Productivity Council, 1988, p. 59.

1980s, reaching a total of $21.8 billion in 1986, or five times larger than it was in 1975. By comparision, American foreign direct investment stock was valued at $16 billion in 1986. Pacific Asia remained almost the exclusive locus of Japanese foreign direct investment in Asia, although within countries along with Western Pacific Rim, there has been a shifting emphasis away from Indonesia to China. China and Hong Kong together account for 42 percent of Japan's annual inflows of foreign direct investment in 1987 (see Table 3.5).

Following the same logic of shifting comparative advantage, the "second generation" of currently industrializing economies — Hong Kong, Singapore, Taiwan and South Korea — have lost a large part of their location-specific advantage in labour-intensive and, subsequently, light manufacturing exports to the "third generation" countries, such as China, Indonesia, Malaysia, the Philippines and Thailand. They all enter actively into the early stages of industrialization. Owing to Asian Pacific countries' record of high and stable economic growth, they continued to remain attractive and major destinations of foreign direct investment

**Table 3.5: Annual Inflows of Foreign Direct Investment
from Japan to Pacific Asia, 1981–1987**

Countries	Average 1981–1985		Average 1986–1987	
	Amount	Percent	Amount	Percent
NICs	820	42.2	2,055.5	57.1
Hong Kong	367	18.9	787.0	21.9
Singapore	266	13.7	398.0	11.0
Taiwan	78	4.0	329.0	9.1
S. Korea	109	5.6	541.5	15.0
ASEAN-4	1,024	52.6	791.5	22.0
Malaysia	95	4.6	160.5	4.5
Thailand	73	3.8	187.0	5.2
Philippines	56	2.9	46.5	1.3
Indonesia	800	41.2	397.5	11.0
Giant Economy				
China	52	2.7	726.0	20.2
Other Asian Countries	48	2.5	24.5	0.7
Total	1,944	100.0	3,597.5	100.0

Source: United Nations (1988), *Economic and Social Survey of Asia and the Pacific 1988*, p. 84.

flows. In 1985, all the Asian Pacific countries under review accounted for 81 percent of all such investment in the whole of Asia (United Nations, 1988:80–106). Clearly, these patterns of development demonstrate increasing global interdependence and complementarities at work for the mutual benefit of host/home country economies. It is part of the global process of surplus accumulation, in which the Pacific Asia theatre happens to be particularly active (Armstrong and McGee, 1985). Within Asia, the flows of inward foreign indirect investment exhibited three marked characteristics: a heavy degree of geographical concentration in Pacific Asia; a wide range of country sources; and the increasing importance of services-related foreign direct investment.

Hand in hand with foreign direct investment is technology transfer and changes it will introduce into host countries for technological change/innovations and economic development. In this respect, the role played by transnational corporations in transferring technology to local companies and personnel is of utmost importance. The example of Singapore is salutary in illustrating the host government's realization of the process and its active steps to upgrade its technological competence. Towards the end of the 1970s, in order to implement Singapore's second industrialization programme to restructure its economy towards high technology, high value-added and skill-intensive industries, the government undertook a series of measures to facilitate the transition. A high-level committee was appointed to draw up plans for national computerization, in 1980, followed in the next year by the establishment of the National Computer Board. The Institute of Systems Science was set up in 1981 at the National University of Singapore under a four-year partnership programme with the IBM. Enrolment at the university and polytechnics has also increased to provide the manpower needed by economic restructuring. Singapore is now home to 600 international manufacturing companies that operate for the mutual benefit of host/home countries. A complementary development is the implementation of a R&D strategy and the development of a thriving Science Park (Tan and Tan, 1990). China, in a similar, albeit less determined fashion, has actively sought technology transfer and techncial cooperation with the developed world since 1978. However, its success in absorbing new technology and its ability to innovate itself is more dependent on a host of political and cultural factors (Stewart, 1990).

Rapid technological changes occurring in industrialized countries present major challenges as well as opportunities for countries in Pacific Asia. There are implications for technological capability development, for employment and for shifts in the structure of comparative advantage. At present, the most promising technological changes appear to be centred in micro-electronics information technology, biotechnology and new materials technology. The first two mentioned can potentially create profound changes in the economies of the region via increased industrial productivity, whereas biotechnology can open up dramatic increases in agricultural productivity (United Nations, 1988:90). These changes will likely lead to spatial and organizational adjustments within cities in the region. Gilbert (1990:32) sums up the situation well:

> Today, global flows of digital inforamtion are being channelled to restructure industries worldwide, creating opportunities for nations with (and representing a threat for those without) strong information technology infrastructures and capabilities.

There is the other side of the coin in the process of technology transfer and foreign direct investment. Shinohara (1989) has cautioned that the more rapid the increase of direct overseas investment, the greater will be the danger of deindustrialization for Japan. The strengthening of the yen will not only cause Japan's trade surplus to drop sharply by stimulating direct overseas investment, it will also change the inter-industry structure of neighbouring countries that are overly dependent on Japan for the supply of capital goods.

Finally, energy surely is the key not only to economic growth in Pacific Asia in the 1990s but also to the shape and patterning of its cities. In terms of fuel energy requirements in the region, the forecast provides, in relative terms, for decreasing reliance on oil but an increasing relative share of nuclear power and natural gas, with coal and hydro/geothermal power remaining rather stable. Between now and 2005, the total energy demand in developing countries is expected to grow at an average rate of 4.3 percent per annum. The high energy demand can be attributed to three factors: rapid growth in population and economic activity; increasing industrialization and road transportation; and diminishing availability of non-commercial sources of energy (IEA, 1988). For countries in Pacific Asia, there is continued dependence on the Middle East for its oil. Japan, for example, tried to minimize its import of Middle East oil by reducing importation from this region to 76 percent in 1979, a reduction of 9 percent since 1970. Even after the Gulf War, energy supply, in particular oil, will continue to be a critical factor determining the economic health and shaping urban futures in Pacific Asia.

Indeed, the world has become lately much more environmentally con-scious in the light of a series of environmental disasters in recent years and the heightened concerns about global warming and depletion of the ozone layer. The need for evolving ecologically stable cities, with an accent on resource conservation, will be recognized by more planners and policy-makers. Meier (1976) called eloquently for resource-conserving cities in developing countries in the mid-1970s. This obviously is a relevant option for some cities of the future in Pacific Asia.

While the questions of whether or not the urban revolution is an in-evitable and necessary part of the process of economic development and how urban futures will stem from it have been, and are still, heatedly contested, it does seem that there are necessary "spatial shifts" in the location of population and economic activity that accompany economic and structural change. In the case of Japan, Korea and Taiwan this has led to the growth of one large metropolis (Tokyo, Seoul, Taipei) as well as urbanized corridors of smaller cities that stretch between these large metropolitan centres and the next largest city (Tokyo-Osaka; Seoul-Pusan; and Taipei-Kaohsiung). These corridors are linked by fast rail and road transportation that enable the flow of goods and people within the corridors. Today, these urban corridors (including the two centres on which they merge) play major roles of the economic activity and population distribution of these countries.

In the other parts of Pacific Asia, while these urban corridors are developing particularly in China and Malaysia, the main features of the urban pattern are a dominance of the largest urban agglomerations in the urban hierarchy and a much less developed system of secondary and intermediate cities. Some planners and policy-makers have suggested that this offers the opportunity to funnel population who are moving from rural areas away from the large metropolis to these secondary centres thus avoiding costly investment in metropolitan infrastructure. However, given the potential volume of movement in the largest of the Asian Pacific countries (Indonesia and China), this "decentralized" pattern of urban growth is unlikely to avoid these problems completely. It should be emphasized that this prediction does not rule out the possibility of secondary centres growing in size and numbers. It is simply that they will not be able to absorb all the rural-urban shifts that will occur.

New Urban Regions in Asia

Against the factors analyzed earlier, what we are hypothesizing here is the emergence of great extended metropolitan regions in Asia that extend over many hundreds of miles. While such regions will have many features similar to the Megalopolis region outlined by Gottmann in the sense of the interregional specialization and nodal characteristics, they will also have some distinctions, including a very different set of ecological preconditions and a different historical phase of incorporation into the global economy that emphasizes the role of international investment and linkages.

What are the features of these extended metropolitan regions? First and of most important, it must be emphasized that these regions, while they

have different morphologies (corridor including several cities, one dominant city, etc.), are characterized by absorbing an increasing proportion
of their countries' population and economic growth. The historical jux-
taposition of port cities, which remain almost universally the centres upon
which these regions have developed, with the high density regions surrounding them creating the necessary preconditions for global linkage and
readily available surplus labour. These conditions have encouraged both
national and international investors into these regions. This investment
takes the form of direct investment into new industrial estates and free
export zones.

Research undertaken so far on extended metropolitan regions in Asian
Pacific countries shows that the proportion of national population has
increased and that these regions contribute a significant component of
national production. It also reinforces the arguments for the economic
importance of these regions and the critical role they play in the national
economies (McGee, 1989; Ginsburg *et al.*, 1991).

Second, it is important to stress the significant role that infrastructure
investment plays in these regions. Historically, many of these regions have
installed well-developed systems of road and water transportation but the
acceleration of investment in ports, railway and road construction in the
colonial period and in the post-independence period have created the
linkages on which the economic growth of these regions flourishes. For
instance, Taiwan both in the Japanese period and the period since the 1950s,
consistently directed a major part of its public capital investment towards
the transportation sector, improving the port of Keelung, Kaoshiung and
creating the new port of Taichung as well as fast electrified railways,
freeways and airports. This has created a "transactional environment" that
permits a collapse of time and space, eventually greatly reducing transportation costs.

Third, there are intense changes occurring at the demographic and
household level in these regions with declining birthrate, increasing
employment by women and growing household income from a multiplicity
of sources. This means that an increasing number of households that
formerly earned income from agriculture are now earning income from
non-agricultural sources. For instance, in a survey of villages in the extended metropolitan region in Taiwan, up to 60–70 percent of household
income is recorded as coming from non-agricultural sources. This reflects

Table 3.6: Consumption and Education Information in Metropolitan Regions Taiwan (1986)

Regions	Annual Consumption of Electricity million KWH		Automobiles 1,000		Education 1,000		Newspapers 1,000		Radios 1,000		TV Sets 1,000	
	No.	%	No.	%	%*	Index	No.	%	No.	%	No.	%
Taipei M.	2,937	21	297	20	59	148	888	21	940	21	761	16
Keelung C.	248	2	18	1	44	109	64	2	73	2	91	2
Hsinchu C.	222	2	23	2	42	105	71	2	78	2	75	2
Taipei P.	2,162	16	219	15	42	104	618	15	707	7	704	15
Taoyuan P.	784	6	103	7	40	99	268	7	305	7	290	6
Taichung C.	623	5	76	5	50	124	208	5	187	4	192	4
Taichung P.	742	5	107	7	30	75	247	6	251	6	260	6
Kaohsiung M.	1,026	7	120	8	46	115	286	7	335	7	340	7
Kaohsiung P.	668	5	63	4	36	88	188	5	225	5	248	5
1. T.K.	6,354	46	659	45	48	120	1,907	46	2,103	46	1,921	41
2. T.C.	1,364	10	184	12	40	100	455	11	438	10	451	10
3. K.S.	1,694	12	183	12	41	103	474	12	561	12	588	13
Total	9,412	68	1,026	69	46	113	2,837	69	3,101	68	2,960	63
Rest of Taiwan	4,525	32	461	31	33	82	1,284	31	1,459	32	1,759	37
Taiwan	13,936	100	1,487	100	40	100	4,120	100	4,560	100	4,719	100

* Percent of population of senior high school and above in population aged 15 and over.

Sources: *Urban and Regional Development Statistics—Republic of China* (1987). Taipei: Urban and Housing Development Department, Council for Economic Planning and Development, Executive Yuan.

growing opportunities for employment in manufacturing and the service sectors being offered to the inhabitants of these regions. As a result of these economic developments, the lifestyles and consumption practices of the inhabitants of these regions are changing dramatically. Data assembled in Table 3.6 for Taiwan show that in the extended metropolitan region stretching from Taipei to Kaoshiung the ownership of automobiles, TV, radios, etc. is almost double that of the rest of Taiwan, reflecting much higher household incomes. Thus, these regions are becoming major consumption regions for both imported and domestic consumer durables. This is further fostered by international and national marketing strategies that focus on these regions. For example, the "commercial" TV channels recently introduced in Kuala Lumpur and Jakarta were initially beamed to the extended metropolitan region.

Finally, the rapid growth of these regions poses many problems to national governments. The growth of industry causes environmental problems and there are serious difficulties in delivering adequate basic services to the growing population of these regions. The problem of providing basic infrastructure services in the large cities in the region is especially acute, with the urban poor bearing the brunt of inadequacy and the resultant social and economic inequities accentuated (Yeung, 1990).

Policy for Future Urban Pacific Asia

The theme that has been presented here can be regarded as quite challenging for planners and policy-makers concerned with the urban future of their countries. In a very general manner, three questions can be raised about the future of Asian urbanization.

First, what kind of urban system will come to dominate the majority of Asian countries. One school of thought represented by the Richardson hypothesis of polarization reversal argues that the urban systems of Asia will pass through a sequence of concentration in existing urban centres, particularly the largest urban centre, followed by a shift in the proportion of population in the secondary centres as economic development occurs and spreads. In the Asian context we would argue that a different pattern is emerging that indicates a continuing growth of non-agricultural population in large urban corridors or mega-urban regions. As the economy of these Asian countries becomes more developed and shifts to a service economy based on finance capital (as is the case with Hong Kong and Singapore and increasingly Taipei), a growing specialization that emerges in the urban system will lead the Asian mega-urban regions to move to a condition such as that described by Gottmann in *The Megalopolis* of which the best example in Pacific Asia is the Tokyo-Osaka corridor. If these arguments are valid, then from a policy point of view, it behoves the government of these countries to invest particularly in the transportation and service infrastructure of these mega-urban regions. In the case of Japan, Taiwan, Korea, Hong Kong and Singapore, which are quite correctly held out as the examples of the most successful economic development in Asia, it is the success in the conquest of the "space-time" relationships of their cities and countries that has been the essence of their "urban change." Whether or not the other countries of Asia will be able to accomplish such changes will depend upon their ability to accommodate and invest capital in this sector.

Indeed, the investment in transportation is being accompanied by the adoption of high technology and communication innovations. Singapore recently hosted a Singapore 2000 exhibition, in which the Lion City was perceived as a "global technopolis" or a "communications city" well into the next century. Likewise, Hong Kong has ambitious and grandiose infrastructure investment projects, including a replacement airport at Chak Lap Kok on Lantau Island and a "Metroplan" to develop the metropolitan area at an estimated cost of $42 billion. Other large Asian Pacific cities, such as Jakarta, Kuala Lumpur, Seoul, Tokyo, Osaka and Shanghai all have plans for the future but the extent to which positive change can be realized will depend on resource availability and the ability to solve difficult problems. However, glimpses of future Asian cities may be appreciated in some ongoing or completed projects. In Singapore, a study is being mounted to turn 72 ha of the downtown area into a "tropical" metropolis with plants and trees providing "vertical landscaping" on buildings. Enormous "umbrellas" would provide shade for buildings and reduce national energy consumption (*Asiaweek*, 17 August 1990, p. 63). A new generation of sophisticated intelligent buildings is being born, such as the Malaysia National Insurance headquarters in Johore Bahru and the Manila Stock Exchange Centre, to be completed in 1991 and 1992 respectively (*Asiaweek*, 6 July 1990, p. 17).

A second question of considerable importance to the authors is the way that the "political economy of space" generates architectural and urban form which we would argue is related to the historical evolution of the economies of the countries and cities under discussion. It is also related to the particular phase of domination of certain types of capital (merchant, industrial and finance). From this perspective, it is possible to argue that the NICs and Japan are moving into a period where finance capital is increasingly coming to dominate investment. The principal feature of the "political economy" of this form of investment is emphasis upon consumption and "spectacle." Cities are placed directly in competition with one another as locales for tourism and consumption investment; credentials are established through "spectacles" such as the Olympics (Tokyo, Seoul), conferences, and expositions. In order to be competitive, it is necessary for these cities to create a built environment and an efficient transportation environment that is attractive to both national and foreign investment. Thus the urban centres of these countries have been characterized by a rapid growth of housing (financed in a variety of public/private ways) that can be described as functionalist and high density, utilizing economies of scale in the provision of services. A polycentric pattern of commercial centres has developed focussing upon commercial and office development. These cities are also characterized by rapid mass transit systems as well as tourist "zones." The result of these developments is to create a built environment in which the regional identity is dominated by "international images" that mask the rich cultural traditions of the inhabitants of these countries.

At present, throughout the rest of Pacific Asia in countries and cities still dominated by merchant capital, but with a growth of industrial and finance capital, there are continuing debates among policy-makers, architects and planners as to the future form and built environment of their cities. In cities such as Jakarta, Bangkok, Kuala Lumpur, Shanghai and Beijing, elements of the "new cities of spectacle" are emerging in the form of high-rise housing, shopping and commercial centres, but they are combined with the more traditional built environment of the city consisting of squatter and low-income housing, open markets and small shops that still cater to the low-income populations. What one sees in the context is a kind of layering of the built environment in which the modern city is high rise connected by "flyover" for automobile transport that passes over the "lower-order" city, reminding one of the architectural fantasies of the Buck Rodgers science fiction cities of the future. Thus there is a continuing battle for urban space between the two classes that inhabit the city, which, if it is to follow the pattern of the NICs, will see the triumph of the city of consumption and spectacle.

One alternative to this kind of scenario is to encourage a spread out city form linked by very fast communication, of which Tokyo gives hints of possibilities. This is the extended metropolis we have outlined earlier in which a much lower density environment is sustained, and delivery of services (water, sewage, energy) is more decentralized and characterized by greater recycling and energy conservation. Given the very large number of people who will be involved in the urbanization process in Asia, there may be little alternative to this form of development.

This leads us to the third question that relates to the resources that are necessary to sustain the future urban environments in Pacific Asia. These may be briefly summarized as food, energy, and finance. All these sources are closely related to the future types of cities that will emerge in Asia. If the high density cities of "spectacle" are to become the prevailing mode, then there will be increasing demands for imported food, energy and fuel and finance to build these cities. If the low-density extended city with a mode of decentralized form of energy, service provision and collective transportation comes into being, there may be greater opportunities for local food production, local service delivery, etc., as well as the persistence of some of the elements of the "traditional" built environment.

However, it may be too idealistic to imagine that the "decentralized city" will prevail because it is extraordinarily difficult for the governments of the countries to resist global pressures for the high-density city. A salutory example is the case of the Pudong project to create an industrial, commercial and financial zone to the east of the Huangpu River east of Shanghai. This development is envisaged as costing in the first stage $10 billion of which it is hoped foreign investors will provide more than half; the rest will come from the central government and Shanghai sources. While the plans for its development are still somewhat unclear, it is very clear in the minds of the proponents of this scheme that this development would act as the central core for the economic advancement of the rest of the Yangtze River region, pulling a great deal of economic activity away from this region. Whether or not sufficient capital can be found for this development, its advancement is symptomatic of the trends we have been discussing and it seems to suggest that the future Asian Pacific city is already here.

REFERENCES

Armstrong, Warwick and T. G. McGee (1985). *Theatres of Accumulation: Studies in Asian and Latin American Urbanization*. London and New York: Methuen.

Chatterji, Manas (1990). *Technology Transfer in the Developing Countries*. Houndmills: Macmillan.

Gilbert, Arthur Lee (1990). "Information Technology Transfer: The Singapore Strategy." In *Technology Transfer in the Developing Countries*, pp. 320–334.

Ginsburg, N., B. Koppell and T. G. McGee (eds.) (1991). *Extended Metropolis in Asia*. Honolulu: University of Hawaii Press.

Greenberg, Charles (1990). "The Emergence of the Extended Metropolitan Region. Case Study of Bangkok." Unpublished paper, Institute of Asian Research, University of British Columbia.

International Energy Agency (IEA) (1988). *Energy Policies and Programmes of IEA Countries: 1988 Review*.

McGee, T. C. (1989). "Urbanisasi or Kotadesasi? Evolving Patterns of Urbanization in Asia." In *Urbanization in Asia: Spatial Dimensions and Policy Issues*, edited by Frank J. Costa et al, Honolulu: University of Hawaii Press, pp. 93–108.

Meier, Richard (1976). "A Stable Urban Ecosystem: Its Evolution with Densely Populated Societies." *Science*, 192(2334), pp. 962–968.

Newton, P. and M. Taylor (1985). "Probable Urban Futures." In *The Future of Urban Form: The Impact of New Technology*, edited by J. Brotchie, P. Newton, P. Hall and P. Nijkamp. London: Croom Helm, pp. 313–336.

Shinohara, M. (1989). "High Yen, Overseas Direct Investment, and the Industrial Adjustments in the Asia-Pacific Area." In *Trends of Economic Development in East Asia*, edited by Wolfgang Klenner. Berlin: Springer-Verlag, pp. 11–23.

Stewart, Sally (1990). "Technology Transfer and the People's Republic of China." In *Technology Transfer in the Developing Countries*, pp. 345–352.

Tan Thiam-soon and Tan Chwee-huat (1990). "Role of Transnational Corporations in Transfer of Technology to Singapore." In *Technology Transfer in the Developing Countries*, pp. 335–344.

Taylor, Jeffrey R. (1986). *Employment Outlook for China to the Year 2000*. Washington, D.C.: Center for International Research, US Bureau of the Census.

United Nations (1988). *Economic and Social Survey of Asia and the Pacific 1988*. Bangkok: ESCAP.

United Nations (1988). Department of International Economic and Social Affairs (DIESA). *World Demographic Estimates and Projections, 1950–2025*. New York: United Nations.

Yeung Yue-man (1976). "Southeast Asian Cities: Patterns of Growth and Transformation." In *Urbanization and Counterurbanization*, edited by Brian J. L. Berry. Beverly Hills: Sage Publication, pp. 285–309.

———— (1990). "Access by the Poor to Basic Infrastructure Services in Urban Areas in Asia: From Past Experience to the Way Forward." *Occasional Paper*, No. 104. Hong Kong: Department of Geography, The Chinese University of Hong Kong.

CHAPTER FOUR

Urban Development of Hong Kong in the 21st Century: Opportunities and Challenges

Anthony Gar-on Yeh

Reader, Urban Planning and Environmental Management Centre,
University of Hong Kong, Hong Kong

Introduction

Hong Kong, as a British territory with a total land area of 1,068 sq km, is located on the southeastern coast of China, adjoining the Chinese province of Guangdong. It will be returned to China on 1 July 1997, when Hong Kong will become a Special Administrative Region (SAR) of China. Under the spirit of "one country, two systems" of the Joint Declaration, Hong Kong is expected to operate its existing economic system with some minor changes after 1997.

Since the end of World War II, Hong Kong has enjoyed tremendous economic growth. Starting with the postwar entrepôt trade, it became the leading manufacturing centre in Asia in the 1960s. Although manufacturing still remained important to its economy in the 1970s, Hong Kong was further transformed into a major financial centre in the region (Chen, 1984, 1990). In the period 1961–1981, the annual growth rate of its Gross Domestic Product (GDP) at constant price was 10 percent (Youngson, 1982), exceeding not only the average growth rate of the less developed countries but also that of the developed countries. In 1989, it ranked second in GDP per capita in Asia, after Japan. Rapid economic development has led to a general improvement in living standard, education level, and expectations of the people.

Urban development in Hong Kong, which was closely related to its fast pace of economic growth, was spectacular in the past two decades. Property development in the private sector was predominantly in the form of modern high-rises for domestic/commercial/office industrial uses. The spatial structure of Hong Kong has changed from a uni-centre city to a multi-centre city, with development extended to the once rural areas of the New Territories (Lo, 1975, 1986). The long-established urban development pattern on the two sides of the Victoria Harbour — notably Kowloon, New Kowloon and Hong Kong Island — is changing with the population dispersing to the new towns (Figure 4.1). The proportion of population living in new towns increased from 9.8 percent in 1971 to 18.8 percent in 1981 and 28.8 percent in 1986. It is anticipated that approximately 40 percent of the population will be living in the New Territories when the new towns are all completed. The population distribution of Hong Kong is changing rapidly: population in the New Territories has surpassed that of Hong Kong Island and approached that of Kowloon and New Kowloon. The city has extended its development from the traditional main urban areas of Hong Kong Island, Kowloon, and New Kowloon to the New Territories, forming a large metropolitan area.

Hong Kong is generally regarded as one of the cities in Asia that is developing and working very well (Yeung, 1990). This paper attempts to analyze the important factors that influenced Hong Kong's urban development in the last two decades, discuss the pattern of urban development of Hong Kong in the 21st century, and analyze some important factors that will shape its future urban development.

Motivating Forces of Urban Development in Hong Kong in the Last Two Decades

A. Spectacular Economic Development

Hong Kong had a high average annual growth rate of real GDP of 8.6 percent from 1966–1985. Its real GDP and GDP per capita are among the highest in the world. By 1989, the GDP per capita was US$9,732. This remarkable development was mainly the result of the rapid expansion of Hong Kong's export-led industries (Lin et al, 1980). The most significant change in Hong Kong's economy in the 1960s was an increase in the contribution of the manufacturing sector to the total production. Its share in

Figure 4.1: New Towns in Hong Kong

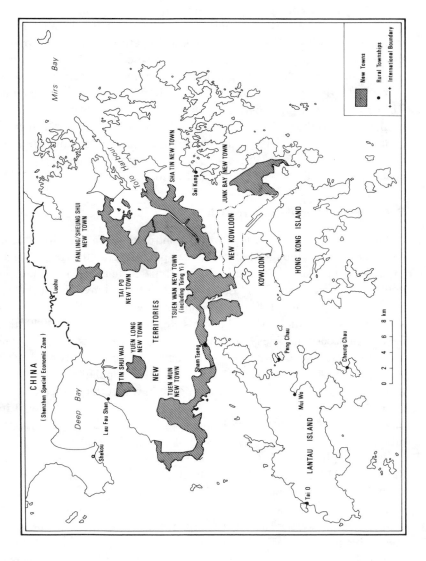

GDP was about 24 percent in 1961 and went up to nearly 31 percent in 1970, reflecting the rapid pace of development of the export processing industries. A major structural change in the economy occurred in the 1970s, with Hong Kong emerging as a fast-growing financial centre in the Asia-Pacific region. There was a decline in the share of GDP in manufacturing, which declined from 31 percent in 1970 to 20 percent in 1988. In contrast, the financial service sector increased from 15 percent in 1970 to 24 percent in 1981, surpassing the contribution of the manufacturing sector. However, it dropped to 19 percent in 1988. The high GDP growth has provided funds for the public housing programme and public projects that are often difficult to find in other cities in the developing countries in Asia. The increase in the financial sector has led to the construction boom of office and commercial buildings in 1981–1983, rapidly changing the landscape of the central business districts of Central and Tsimshatsui.

B. Controlled Population Growth

Natural increase in Hong Kong is under control with a falling birth rate and a stable death rate, though Hong Kong's population growth is often inflated by sudden influxes of migrants from China. China has been the pre-dominant source of legal and illegal immigrants to Hong Kong (Skeldon, 1986). Although immigration from China has been generally under control since the establishment of the People's Republic of China in 1949, there have been occasional tides of migrants from China as a result of its changing political climate. The recent tide occurred after the downfall of the "Gang of Four" in 1976, which led to much freer population movement in and out of China. The pressure of immigration was further exacerbated by Hong Kong's philanthropic "touch base" policy that allowed illegal immigrants from China to stay in Hong Kong if they were able to reach the urban areas (Lui, 1983). The number of captured illegal immigrants increased sharply from 1,800 in 1977 to 82,000 in 1978 and a record high of 89,000 in 1979. Although the "touch base" policy was abandoned in October 1980 and a policy of immediate repatriation of illegal Chinese immigrants was adopted to discourage further illegal immigration from China, Hong Kong experienced a sudden sharp increase in population in the 1980s due to this tide of illegal immigration. In 1979 alone, there were 170,000 legal and illegal immigrants from China, who caused a 3.5 percent increase in population, a growth rate that is much higher than the average annual growth rate of 1.6 percent. The sudden increase in population, although it increased the supply of skilled and semi-skilled labour, upset the plans for the provision of social facilities, especially public housing. This can be reflected, to some extent, by the increase of the squatter population from 300,000 in 1978 to 750,000 in 1980 (Hong Kong Housing Authority, 1981). Such an unpredicted wave of immigration was one of the reasons given by the Governor for not achieving the objective of improving the housing conditions in Hong Kong (Fong and Yeh, 1987). Fortunately, the influx of illegal immigrants from China is now largely under control with the co-operation of China.

The ability of Hong Kong to achieve a high level of economic development in the 1960s was mostly attributed to the population growth of the 1950s that provided cheap labour to support the export-led industries, which at that time were mainly labour intensive. Population growth was largely under control after the economy had taken off in the 1970s. Otherwise, like other Asian cities, which were affected by large inflows of rural-urban migrants, the living conditions and urban environment of Hong Kong could not have been improved.

C. Public Housing Development

The public housing programme in Hong Kong was gradually developed to cope with changing housing conditions and the socio-economic environment (Fong and Yeh, 1987). It has gone through *ad hoc* planning in the early years of public housing provision to more comprehensive planning in recent years.

Public housing development in Hong Kong was triggered mainly by the great squatter fire on Christmas eve of 1953 in Shek Kip Mei. It initiated an emergency housing programme and established the Resettlement Department in early 1954 to resettle the fire victims. The initial resettlement estates were built to an extremely low standard of 2.2 sq m of usable floor space per adult.

There was no overall public housing policy in the 1960s: the public housing programme was fragmented and uncoordinated. It was estimated that in 1972, over 1.6 million people had been housed in various types of government subsidized housing (Hong Kong Housing Authority, 1974). In the early 1970s the Government became aware of the need for a comprehensive approach and an integrated housing agency. Eventually in 1972, the then newly appointed Governor, Sir Murray MacLehose, announced a Ten-Year Housing Programme with the aim of tackling the problems of slum and squatter areas, as well as the resettlement estates built earlier. The target was to house 1.8 million people over the next ten years in permanent, self-contained homes with good amenities and a decent environment at a standard of 3.3 sq m per person. A new Housing Authority was set up to consolidate government efforts in attaining this goal.

The restructured Housing Authority was formed in April 1973, under the new Housing Ordinance of 1973. It was responsible for policy formulation and the Housing Department, being its executive arm, would be responsible for implementing and managing housing programmes. The implementation of the Ten-Year Housing Programme required lots of land, which consequently called for the development of new towns and market towns in the New Territories. The programme was later extended to incorporate home ownership and private sector participation schemes that produced flats for sale to lower-middle and middle-income families in both the public and private sectors.

Housing policy, like other public policies, is influenced by the changing political, social and economic environment. There were major changes in the political and social environment in Hong Kong in the 1980s that have affected housing policy and made the government reassess its 1973's housing policy. First, Hong Kong's political structure began to change dramatically following the introduction of the District Administration Scheme in 1982 and indirect election to the Legislative Council in 1985. More public participation was allowed in the reformed political system. Second, there were increasing impacts of pressure groups on public policies, particularly on the public housing allocation policy. Third, there had been a change in the democratic structure, especially an increase in the number of low income small one and two-person households living in substandard tenement buildings or squatter areas that were not eligible for permanent public housing under the pre-1984 policies. Fourth, the substandard living conditions in the old resettlement estates, the management problems arising from their poor planning and internal layout and the financial costs involved in improving and maintaining them eventually led to the government's decision to redevelop some of the older public housing estates, particularly the resettlement estates.

As a result of these internal and external pressures, the Housing

Authority had to review its public housing allocation policies (Hong Kong Housing Authority, 1984), housing subsidy policy (Hong Kong Housing Authority, 1985a, 1985b, 1986b), and rental policy (Hong Kong Housing Authority, 1986a). Consequently, two-person households were eligible to apply for rental and home ownership flats. The housing needs of singles were also taken care of by providing hostel rooms in permanent public housing. A policy for public housing tenants who lived in public housing for over ten years and who exceeded a subsidy income limit was adopted in 1986 so that they would pay double the normal rent (Yeh, 1990a). It was recommended that the tenants' ability to pay, as well as the comparable estate value, be used as major factors in setting rents. It was proposed that the median rent-income ratio for new estates should not exceed 15 percent.

To keep pace with changing socio-economic development, the Housing Authority undertook a major review of the housing policy in 1986 in order to devise a strategy that could satisfy identified housing needs and demand in the most effective manner. As a result of the comprehensive review of previous housing policies, the Long Term Housing Strategy (LTHS), which aimed at a more demand-led approach in the provision of public housing and covered the years between 1987 and 2001, was approved by the government in April 1987. The Strategy aims to satisfy the projected public housing demand till 2001 with 960,000 housing units. A total of 380,000 units will be for outstanding demand in 1985, 550,000 for net households formation, and 30,000 due to private sector demolitions. The strategy will improve opportunities for public housing tenants to move to assisted home purchase flats, extend existing renewal of former resettlement estates and Government Low Cost Housing in order to improve the housing quality, and to fully utilize private housing by the introduction of a Home Purchase Loan Scheme to assist low-middle income families to purchase private sector flats. To increase the flexibility in coordinating the efforts and resources of the private and public sector to meet the new housing objectives, the Housing Authority was administratively reorganized in 1 April 1988 to be headed by a non-official member. The reorganized Housing Authority is given the task of co-ordinating its housing production with that of the private sector to meet public needs and is given the financial flexibility to channel its resources to its priorities. It aims to provide accommodation at affordable and realistic rents and prices.

The formulation of housing policies in recent years has undergone significant changes in response to the changing socio-economic and political environment. With rapid economic development, Hong Kong is able to afford significant improvements in administration and management, space standards, quality and design of its public housing. There is a major increase in the proportion of people living in public housing. In 1988, around 2.5 million people, constituting 45 percent of the total population, are benefiting from subsidized public housing either through public rental housing, home ownership public housing, or the purchase of private housing with the assistance from the Home Purchase Loan Scheme (Hong Kong Government, 1989a).

Public housing has contributed greatly to urban development in Hong Kong. It is both an instrument for clearing land for urban expansion and a motivating force for the new town development that dispersed population into the New Territories. The relationship between public housing development and new town development will be examined in the next section.

D. New Town Development

New town development in Hong Kong can be dated back as early as 1953 when the first industrial satellite town was developed in Kwun Tong. Located at the urban fringe of that time, Kwun Tong was, of course, not planned to be self-contained. The first self-contained new town, Tsuen Wan (including Kwai Chung), was designated in 1959. The development of Kwun Tong and Tsuen Wan was an attempt to alleviate the congestion problem in main urban areas as a result of an unprecedently rapid population growth due to a large influx of refugees from China after the revolution in 1949, and to provide land for industrial growth. Since both new towns were developed in haste, their planning and development were *ad hoc* and chaotic.

In 1965, the Government decided to proceed with the planning and development of two other new towns at Castle Peak (renamed Tuen Mun in 1973) and Sha Tin. However, because of the slump in the property market after the bank crisis in 1965 and the riots in 1967, the new towns programme lost its momentum (Leung, 1983). The major boost to the new towns programme in Hong Kong came from the Government's Ten-Year Housing Programme introduced in 1972, the aim of which was to provide 1.8 million people with permanent, self-contained accommodation in a decent environment (Wang and Yeh, 1987).

The development in the New Territories in the early 1970s can be identified on three distinct levels: (i) new towns of Tsuen Wan, Sha Tin, and Tuen Mun; (ii) market towns of Tai Po, Fanling/Sheung Shui, and Yuen Long and; (iii) smaller rural townships, such as Sham Tseng, Lau Fau Shan, Sai Kung, Tai O, Mui Wo, Cheung Chau, and Peng Chau in the outlying islands (see p. 71 Figure 4.1). Development plans and population targets for new towns were constantly revised with a view to meeting the requirement of the Ten-year Housing Programme. The second generation new towns developed in the 1980s are smaller in scale compared with the first generation new towns developed in the 1970s.

The concepts of "self-containment" and "balanced development" of British new town planning were adopted aiming to reduce the need of commuting to main urban areas. In achieving this objective, adequate provision of working opportunities, shopping, recreation, and community facilities was necessary (Lands and Works Branch, 1984). There were also plans to provide an optimal split between public/private, ownership/rental, and high/low density developments. New towns developed after 1973 were more comprehensively planned than the early ones such as Tsuen Wan New Town. Segregation of land uses was advocated and made possible under comprehensive planning. Land in new towns was largely obtained by reclamation, which is cheaper than resuming privately owned agricultural land. The costly development of Fanling/Sheung Shui New Town, where land is extensively agricultural, attests to this.

The impact of new towns development in Hong Kong is phenomenal (Yeh, 1987). It helps to decentralize population from main urban areas to the basically rural New Territories. The development of new towns proceeded at an unprecedented rate in Hong Kong: between 1976 and 1981, their average annual population growth rate was about 11 percent, which was much higher than the Hong Kong average of 3 percent and main urban areas of 2 percent. Considering that one of the major objectives of developing new towns was to provide land for massive public housing programme, it is not too surprising to find that 70 percent of the population increase in new towns was in public housing in 1981 (Yeh and Fong, 1984).

One of the most important aspects of new towns development is the large scale movement of population to the New Territories in the following ten to twenty years, which is necessary if they are to be successful (Wigglesworth, 1971:67). This has not been a great problem as it can be seen that

50 percent of the total population increase in Hong Kong during the period 1971 to 1981 has been successfully directed to new towns. This was mainly a result of massive "quasi-voluntary" migration accompanied with the public housing programme and an inadequate public housing supply in main urban areas. The average waiting time for allocating a public housing unit is nine years in urban areas, but only four years in remote new towns such as Tuen Mun. In a study of the main reasons for living in Tuen Mun New Town, 80 percent of the public housing residents gave the reason of easier access to public housing (Leung, 1980).

Although new towns in general have no problems in building up their public housing population as programmed, they are not very successful in attracting private housing and investment. Most of the private housing built is found in main urban areas and the vacancy rate of private housing in new towns is much higher than that in main urban areas (Yeh and Fong, 1984). The lack of job opportunities in new towns makes it necessary for the residents to commute to work, which consequently increases the traffic load on the existing transportation network. Although a substantial number of manufacturing jobs have been attracted to new towns, decentralization of wholesale, retail and office jobs has not been very successful (Yeh, 1985a).

The structural change in the economy of Hong Kong from a manufacturing city to a financial centre in Asia also affects the availability of suitable jobs in new towns. Although manufacturing still employed a large percentage of the working population in 1981, its importance had declined. While the proportion of workers engaged in manufacturing diminished, the proportion of workers in wholesale, retail and office work increased, from 16 percent in 1961 to 28 percent in 1981. With the decentralization of population into new towns, the mismatching between the place of work and the place of residence was further aggravated and the pressure on the transportation network between new towns and main urban areas became more acute.

The development of new towns in Hong Kong is spectacular in terms of pace and scale. It is unquestionably a major achievement of urban planning. Despite that, too much emphasis has been given to public housing construction, but the provision of social facilities and transport has been overlooked. The emphasis on public housing is understandable in Hong Kong where it has long been a major social problem. More important, the Government has an overt public housing programme to improve the living conditions of its people. The development of public housing in new towns is rapid and always on schedule because the Housing Department has an annual production target to fulfil. Other departments, however, are not subject to this pressure. In fact, they are often inclined to give a low priority to the provision of facilities in new towns. Consequently, the provision of public facilities and internal/external transport in new towns often lags behind population growth. Many new town residents have to commute to main urban areas for employment on a transport system that lags behind the development of new towns (Yeh, 1985a, 1987).

E. Increasing Role of Urban Planning

Although Hong Kong advocates a laissez-faire policy, there is evidence that non-market forces play an important role in its economic growth. With the Government's involvement in the prices of rice, public utilities, transport, medical and health, education, and housing provision, Hong Kong is able to provide cheap labour for its economic development (Schiffer, 1985).

Urban planning in Hong Kong was largely a postwar activity. Although the Town Planning Ordinance was enacted in 1939, it was not until 1947 that a small Town Planning Unit was established in the Public Works Department and in 1953 that a Planning Branch was set up within the Crown Land and Survey Office of the Public Works Department (Town Planning Division, 1984). It was in the 1970s, when new towns were in process of planning and development, that the importance of planning was beginning to be recognized in Hong Kong. This was followed by a drastic increase in the number of town planners in the Government. The number of planners has increased from 5 in 1960 to 86 in 1980, and 171 in 1990. The population/planner ratio has increased from an astonishing low of one planner to 2.2 million people in 1950 to one planner to 34,513 people in 1990. However, the ratio is still much lower than that in the United Kingdom where there is one planner to 5,500 people. The recognition of the importance of planning of the community was manifested by the upgrading of the former Town Planning Office of the Buildings and Lands Department to a new Planning Department under the new Planning, Environment and Lands Branch on 1 January 1990.

The Town Planning Ordinance, the basis of urban planning in Hong Kong, is not as comprehensive as similar legislation found in other countries (Working Group on the Review of Town Planning Ordinance, 1988). It covers only existing and designated urban areas and has no direct power of development control and plan implementation. Development control has therefore to rely on other legislations such as the Building Ordinance and lease conditions of land sold or granted (Pun, 1983; Fung, 1988). The separation of planning from implementation reflects the low status of planning in Hong Kong. Urban planning so far has not been seen as a policy area by itself and is simply treated as a tool for carrying out the Government's policies (Bristow, 1984).

Planning in Hong Kong in the past was conceived as largely demand-oriented (Bristow, 1981). With the increasing recognition of the importance of planning, this is at present less true than in the past. A number of major forward looking plans were formulated to guide the development of Hong Kong into the 21st century. The role of planning in public housing and new towns development should also not be underestimated. Extensive planning input and co-ordination in land development are required in developing new towns, which on average accommodate 0.5 million people, and con-structing public housing estates that, in some cases, house a population larger than that in small British new towns. However, because of the late recognition of the importance of planning, development in the older dis-tricts has suffered from the lack of planning. The result is that open space and public facilities are generally under provided in these districts. With the benefit of planning, the new towns are better designed and have more open space than the main urban areas. Despite the constraints of the planning system in Hong Kong, urban planning has contributed significantly to improving the urban environment of Hong Kong and will play an important role in shaping the urban environment in the future.

Plans for Urban Development in the 21st Century

A. Territorial Development Strategy (TDS)

In view of the shortcomings of piecemeal planning and development, the Land Development Policy Committee in 1980 considered it necessary to for-mulate a comprehensive long term development strategy for Hong Kong in the 1990s and up to 2001. The Territorial Development Strategy (TDS) was not only concerned with meeting the population requirements for land, ser-vices and facilities, but also with sustaining the growth of key economic ac-tivities in Hong Kong (Hong Kong Government, 1985). The decision to formulate the Territorial Development Strategy was in part attributable to the recognition of the lack of coordination between urban development and transport provision, especially in the case of new towns where transport is still inadequately provided. The TDS took four years to prepare and was completed in 1984.

In the preparation of the Territorial Development Strategy, a special team was formed to conduct integrated land use and transport optimization studies with the help of computers (Eason, 1985). For the purpose of formulating the development strategy, Hong Kong was divided into five potential development subregions. They are: (i) the "metropolitan area"[1] of Hong Kong Island, Kowloon Peninsula, New Kowloon and Tsuen Wan; (ii) the North Eastern New Territories (NENT) comprising Sha Tin, Ma On Shan, Tai Po and Sheung Shui; (iii) the North Western New Territories (NWNT) including Tuen Mun, Yuen Long and Tin Shui Wai; (iv) the South Eastern New Territories (SENT) consisting of Junk Bay and Sai Kung; and (v) the South Western New Territories (SWNT) covering North Lantau, Peng Chau and Cheung Chau. Studies of the five subregions were undertaken by various government departments and secretariat branches in conjunction with consulting firms. The objective was to determine the long term development potential of each subregion and consequently recommend a preferred development strategy on a subregional basis. The five subregions were divided into forty-nine smaller zones in order to investigate the maximum urban land development potentials, the road and rail transport system of each subregion, and the incremental land development and infrastructure costs and benefits. The findings served as input to the Land Use-Transport Optimization (LUTO) model, which was employed to devise and evaluate various development options of the Territorial Development Strategy (Choi, 1985).

In the early stage of the TDS study, the future location of the international airport was recognized as a significant factor affecting the future development pattern of Hong Kong. While a number of development options concerning future airport location were considered, doubts were cast over the possible relocation of the existing airport in view of the uncertain political future of Hong Kong. As a result, two alternative long term growth patterns based on the existing airport location at Kai Tak were produced. Both options saw a need for major improvements and extensions of the existing planned highways and rail systems. Each represented an end-state plan for the year 2001; beyond then fundamental changes in basic assumptions might be necessary.

The common components of the two options suggested further development of the existing urban areas by reclamation at West Kowloon in Yau Ma Tei and at West Hong Kong near Green Island for public housing, and at Central; this development would be for expansion of business offices and Government cultural activities (Pryor, 1985). Another common component was the construction of the second cross harbour tunnel and passenger rail systems in order to link up: Sha Tin, North East New Territories with Tsuen Wan; West Kowloon with Tsuen Wan; and West Hong Kong with Green Island. The Preliminary Report of the Territorial Development Strategy was presented to the Executive Council in July 1984.

The formulation of the TDS was a breakthrough from the traditional piecemeal planning in Hong Kong and it provided an important tool to synchronize land use and transportation development. A new tier of subregional planning had been created between territorial and district planning by the TDS (Town Planning Division, 1984). The then Town Planning Office of the Buildings and Lands Department has undertaken to prepare structure plans for the five subregions of Hong Kong. Structure plans so prepared serve as subregional policy guidelines that translate territory-wide goals into subregional objectives and act as a link between the TDS and local/district plans. They are planned for fifteen years and relate closely to current implementation programmes. Also, they are more policy oriented than physical plans are and will act as a monitoring tool for the TDS at the subregional level. The first subregional plan prepared was for the North Eastern New Territories and subsequently most of the subregional plans were prepared. The subregional plan of the "metropolitan area," which is known as the "Metroplan," is at the final stage of formulation.

The TDS, through its subregional and sectoral studies, has given the best information available about land development potential and extensively examined development options for Hong Kong in the foreseeable future. It also provides guidance for investments in land and transportation developments in the 1990s and beyond.

B. Port and Airport Development Strategy (PADS)

The Port and Airport Development Strategy (PADS) Studies were initiated by the government in March 1988. The strategy is designed to meet the forecast port and air traffic growth of Hong Kong up to 2011, to ensure that all new port, airport, associated industrial and residential facilities, transport links and other infrastructure will be incrementally provided for according to an integrated and cohesive plan (Hong Kong Government, 1989b; Barnes, 1990; Morris, 1990). The selected development strategy, announced in October 1989, is to relocate the Kai Tak airport, built in 1925, to Chek Lap Kok, on the north coast of Lantau Island, with initial future port developments around the existing Kwai Chung container port and further port developments on the northeastern tip of the Lantau Island (Figure 4.2). The new airport will have two runways and will be on a site of about 1,000 ha. It will have the technical capability to handle up to 80 million passengers, 320,000 aircraft flights and over 4 million tonnes of air cargo annually. It will be capable of operating twenty-four hours a day. An airport support community of about 150,000 people will be built at Tung Chung next to the new airport. Industrial land will be provided in the area near to the new port and airport, and most of these lands will be on Lantau Island. The strategy requires a number of new transport infrastructures that will include the North Lantau Link, a dual three-lane road crossing from Tsing Yi, via Ma Wan, to Lantau Island; a dual three-lane expressways on North Lantau between the airport and the North Lantau Link; a new two land road bridge to serve port facilities in the Kwai Chung area at East Tsing Yi and at Stonecutters Island; a dual three-land road from the North Lantau Link to the new port peninsula that will later be extended, if necessary, via a tunnel to Hong Kong Island; a dual two-lane road around the Castle Peak coast. The strategy also includes a passenger rail line to connect the airport to Hong Kong Island via the North Lantau Link, Tsing Yi and the West Kowloon Reclamation. A fast service train will be provided for airport users from Kowloon and Central. A slower train will also be provided, stopping at a number of intermediate stations. The capital costs of the project are estimated to be HK$127 billion (US$16.3 billion) at 1989 prices. These costs do not include the costs of facilities that are part of the already committed, or planned, development programmes. Part of the costs of the PADS is hoped to involve private investment. It is hoped that PADS will provide Hong Kong with the infrastructure necessary to move forward into the 21st century.

The relocation of the airport will provide additional space for new developments in Kowloon, allow the present restrictions on the heights of

Figure 4.2: The Port and Airport Development Strategy (PADS)

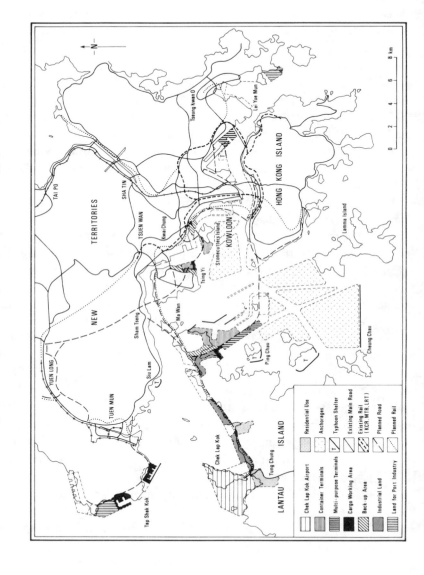

buildings in certain parts of Kowloon to be lifted, and reduce noise levels for the approximately 350,000 people suffering from high noise levels caused by aircraft landing and taking off. The new airport and port will help to boost and sustain economic activities of the city. The decision on the new port and airport locations have facilitated the formulation of the long term transport and land use plans for Hong Kong that were highly uncertain when the Territorial Development Strategy was formulated.

C. White Paper on Transport Policy in Hong Kong

The first Comprehensive Transport Study, completed in 1976, provided a broad framework for the development of the transport infrastructure up to 1991. It has formed the basis of transport policy in Hong Kong. The Second Comprehensive Transport Study was commissioned in 1986 to project the growth in transport demand up to 2001, and to appraise the transport infrastructure and policy proposals for dealing with the various transport needs in the future. It was completed in May 1989 and a Green Paper was published in June 1989 for public consultation. The White Paper "Moving into the 21st Century: The White Paper on Transport Policy in Hong Kong" was published in January 1990 (Transport Branch, 1990).

The major factors affecting a transport infrastructure development strategy include the relocation of the airport to Chek Lap Kok and substantial expansion of port facilities in Tsing Yi, Stonecutters Island, Tuen Mun and North Lantau; cross-border goods vehicle traffic that is forecasted to increase by more than three times between 1986 and 2001; a projected increase of over one million residents in the new towns and further development of commercial facilities on both sides of the harbour that will increase the number of long trips between the new towns and the urban centres as well as cross harbour journeys. The proposed network of road and railways will: provide the necessary links to support future airport and port facilities; provide efficient transport links to support the growth in goods and vehicle traffic between Hong Kong and China; extend the rail system to major population centres; relieve congestion in existing networks; and provide new roads and upgrade existing roads to relieve congestion and to improve road safety.

The White Paper has three main components. It covers transport infrastructure improvements, policies of expansion and improvement of public transport, and policies for managing road use. The proposed major road development programmes of the next decade include: North Lantau Expressway and Lantau Fixed Crossing to provide direct expressway link to the replacement airport at Chek Lap Kok; Route 3 to provide a third harbour crossing and major north-south road link connecting the border with the existing container port and the urban area; the Hung Hom bypass and the Kai Tak connector to provide new east-west road links in Kowloon; Route 16 to provide a new expressway connecting Sha Tin and West Kowloon, and Route 7 and Central-Wan Chai bypass to provide a continuous expressway along the northern and western shores of Hong Kong Island (Figure 4.3). The recommended railway projects are the Airport Railway, an extension of the Mass Transit Railway to Junk Bay, and a rail link connecting north-western New Territories and Tsuen Wan.

D. Metroplan[2]

The first consultation was carried out in April 1988 by the consultative booklet "Metroplan — The Aims" in April 1988. In December 1989, three initial options were prepared for public comment in the booklet "Metroplan — Initial Options." The main objective of the plan is "to bring about a better organized, more efficient and more desirable place in which to live and work" (Planning, Environment and Lands Branch, 1990). It aims to enhance Hong Kong's role as: an international port and airport; as an international business, finance and tourist centre; and as a centre for a diverse range of light manufacturing industry. A plan will be formulated to provide land to satisfy the future needs of the population and economic activities and to create a more acceptable urban environment. The Metroplan has not been finalized yet. Once finalized, it will change the urban landscape of Hong Kong significantly.

The Metroplan area covers Hong Kong Island, Kowloon, New Kowloon, Tsuen Wan, Kwai Chung and Tsing Yi. The time horizon for the Metroplan is 2011 and it provides a strategic framework to guide planning and development in the districts of the metroplan areas. It comprises a broad land use/transport plan showing major development proposals for target areas where there is a need for, and opportunity to, restructure the city. It will provide guidelines related to urban design, broad planning controls, urban landscape principles and the height and density of building development. A comprehensive landscape strategy, especially for the urban fringe and coastal areas will be provided. The metroplan area currently has a

Figure 4.3: Proposed Major Highways and Railways

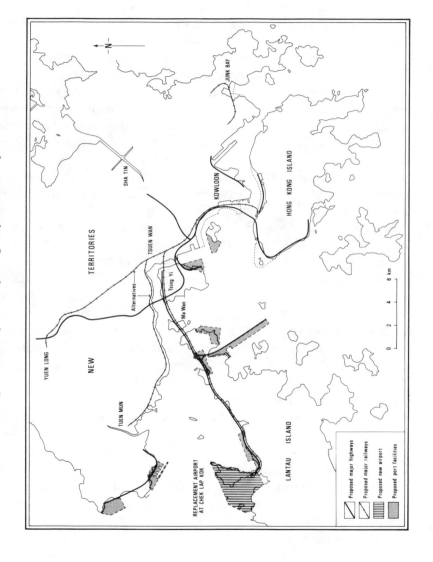

population of around 4.2 million out of the territorial total of 5.6 million people. The plan does not increase the existing population but improves the living environment. The majority of the forecasted increase of one million will be decentralized to non-Metroplan areas.

Six types of land are identified for future development (Figure 4.4). These include: (i) areas in needs of major changes, comprising areas where problems need to be redressed through more vigorous and comprehensive renewal; (ii) areas of selective change — basic land use structure is likely to stay, but where redevelopment to improved standards should be encouraged by making use of available opportunities; (iii) areas of limited change where there is a need for only minimal improvements, but where the existing enironmental conditions should be protected through careful development control and improved landscaping; (iv) areas of recent development where little improvement is needed; (v) potential new development area, that is, mainly comprised land from reclamation, including West Kowloon, Hung Hom Bay, Kowloon Bay, Tsuen Wan Bay, Green Island, Central-Wanchai, Aldrich Bay, and Siu Sai Wan and certain areas of hillside that can be formed into terraced sites; and (vi) urban fringe and coastline.

There is very little difference in the location of land reclamation and major transportation network of the proposed options. They were mainly taken from the Second Comprehensive Transport Study and PADS. The main differences among the three options are the distribution of principal commercial office centres and concentrations of industrial uses, the use of the Kai Tak site after the airport is relocated, and the different degree of removal of airport height controls. The options vary from the concentrated further expansion of the existing CBD to the development of more dispersed commercial office centres.

These plans have given Hong Kong a new opportunity to restructure the city. The relocation of the airport will make 230 ha of land available at the site of Kai Tak airport. It can be used to meet the future needs of land in the urban areas and for a relocation site for the renewal and decongestion of residential and industrial areas in the main urban area. The relocation of the airport may remove the airport height restrictions in some areas in the main urban areas to make it possible to permit redevelopment to a higher intensity where additional infrastructure and community services can be provided. The large land reclamation at West Kowloon and Central-Wan Chai will provide land for housing, commercial offices, hotels, industrial and

Figure 4.4: Areas in Need of, and Broad Opportunities for, Structural Land Use Change in Metropolitan Area

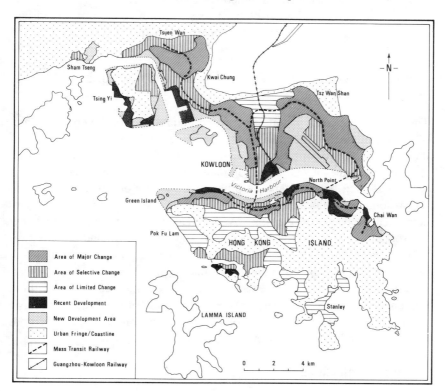

other community uses required for future development and redevelopment of the main urban areas, particularly Mong Kok and Wanchai. The relocation of the airport from Kai Tak will eliminate severe aircraft noise problems over large parts of north Kowloon. The risk of air disaster in the main urban areas should also be reduced. The developments of airport and port facilities at the Western Harbour and on North Lantau will attract industries and offices away from existing urban locations, leading to a more dispersed pattern of development within the "metropolitan area." The major road and rail transport links to the new airport and port facilities connected to the existing transport networks will provide a system for the movement of people and goods throughout the city. Many areas identified by the

Metroplan as areas in need of major changes will be redeveloped with the assistance of the Land Development Corporation, using a public-private partnership approach (Yeh, 1990b). This will improve the urban environment and change the landscape of the main urban areas.

Factors Affecting Urban Development in Hong Kong in the 21st Century

The Territorial Development Strategy has determined the general direction of Hong Kong's development into the 21st century. Upon the completion of the new towns development programme in the New Territories, emphasis will revert to the development of main urban areas. Land reclamation, which has long been a common practice in Hong Kong in expanding its land resources, will be actively carried out along the seashore of main urban areas. The subsequent Port and Airport Development Strategy and the Metroplan will determine more precisely the future form and direction of urban growth within the "metropolitan area." These plans were formulated on the assumption of continuous population and economic growth that would largely depend on the extent to which the Joint Declaration will be implemented between now and 1997, and the impact of the future economy, economic relations with China, population emigration, local politics, and information and communication technology.

A. Politics with China

The 8,000-word Joint Declaration specifies China's basic policies towards Hong Kong in the fifty years after regaining its sovereignty over Hong Kong in 1997. It also specifies how the "one country, two systems" would operate, in which Hong Kong's existing economic and trade systems will be maintained after Hong Kong is returned to the People's Republic of China. The main body of the agreement is made up of twelve basic policies of the Chinese Government towards Hong Kong, attached to which are three lengthy annexes dealing with specific issues.

China will designate Hong Kong as a Special Administrative Region (SAR) in 1997, as provided by Article 31 of the Chinese constitution. The third annex is devoted to the discussion of the land issue that was one of the main elements that triggered off the negotiations. It is only in this respect that China wants to assume a monitoring role in the activities of the Hong

Kong Government during the transitional period. This is understandable because land sales have always been a significant, though fluctuating, source of the Government's revenue. Each year they contribute, on average, around 10–20 percent of the total revenue. At the height of the property boom between 1980 and 1982, they generated as much as over 30 percent of the total revenue (Kwok, 1983). The basic land policy of the Hong Kong Government is to sell leases to the highest bidder at public auction. However, land for public rental and ownership housing, education, public utilities, welfare, religious and other charitable purposes is usually granted by private treaty. The premium charged for a private treaty grant varies from nothing for non-profit making uses to full market value for public utilities. Land was leased for terms of 75, 99 or 999 years in the early days. This has now been standardized in the urban areas of Hong Kong and Kowloon Peninsula to a term of seventy-five years, usually renewable for a further seventy-five years at a reassessed rent. Land leases in the New Territories and New Kowloon are normally sold for the residual period of ninety-nine years less three days from 1 July 1997.

Under the Joint Declaration, the existing leasehold system will continue and arrangements for the leasing of land will resemble the current practice in Hong Kong. Terms of the existing leases extending beyond 1997 will be honoured, and those that will expire before 1997 may be extended to 2047 without paying any additional premium. After 1997, holders of renewed leases or new leases granted after the Sino-British Joint Declaration will have to pay an annual rent of 3 percent of the rateable value of their properties. The present Hong Kong Government can issue new leases with terms lasting as late as 2047 through the existing land disposal system of public auction, tender or private treaty grant. However, in order to prevent the Hong Kong Government from selling off all the land, leaving Hong Kong's future Special Administrative Region (SAR) Government without a major source of revenue, it is stipulated that no more than 50 ha of land can be leased by the Hong Kong Government in a single year during the transitional period.

The Joint Declaration, especially the part concerned with the question of land, has removed a major uncertainty for landholders in the New Territories, where all leases were due to expire in 1997. The only difference between the current and the new systems is that the 3 percent rent now payable is fixed irrespective of any changes in future in the ratable value. Nonetheless, the Joint Declaration has eased some worries of local developers who once feared that China would charge a huge premium on renewed leases. However, there are still some uncertainties for the agreement has not specified, for instance, the legal status of leases that will extend beyond 2047, which perhaps is too far to be concerned with.

The promise that the sale of land in the New Territories can continue to 30 June 2047 should result in an increasing confidence in the property market. Purchasers of flats in the New Territories, who have been offered a lease of only about twelve years, are now given a term of sixty-two years. Indeed, land and property prices have increased drastically since the last property slump due to uncertainty in Hong Kong's political future.

China's influence in Hong Kong will inevitably increase in the 1990s. In order to achieve a smooth transition, there are many areas where cooperation among Britain, China and Hong Kong is required, such as the Joint Liaison Group for consultation on the implementation of the Joint Declaration and the Land Commission for monitoring land sales.

B. Future Economy

Uncertainty in Hong Kong's economy is one of the major problems facing urban development in the 21st century. The export-oriented open economy of Hong Kong is vulnerable to fluctuations in the world market and competition from neighbouring countries. Any change in its economic conditions can affect the funding and progress of the planned development projects. For example, the worldwide economic recession in the mid-1970s dealt a severe blow to the local economy, and consequently caused a delay in many planned public projects.

There is indication that Hong Kong is not doing very well compared to its neighbours recently. Its GDP growth has slowed down in recent years compared to its competitors in the region. Countries in Asia are growing rapidly (Ginsburg, 1988; Kraus and Lutkenhorst, 1986; Shinohara and Lo, 1989) and Hong Kong will be facing more severe competition in the 21st century. Future urban development will depend on its ability to sustain the present level of economic development.

C. Economic Relations with China

Even without the 1997 issue, Hong Kong's tie with China is expected to increase, given that the open door policy of China continues. Now the tie has definitely been strengthened after the signing of the Joint Declaration. China's adoption of an open door economic policy since 1978 has led to a rapid increase in economic links between Hong Kong and China. Since 1985, China has become Hong Kong's largest trading partner. Merchandise trade between Hong Kong and China has grown by 39 percent per annum in 1978 and 1988 (Hong Kong Government, 1990). China is now the largest market for Hong Kong's re-exports, and second largest market for Hong Kong's domestic exports. China is also the largest supplier of goods to Hong Kong. Hong Kong also overtook Japan in 1987 to become China's largest trading partner and accounted for 27 percent of China's overall external trade. China has, since 1979, been Hong Kong's largest re-export market as well as the largest source of goods re-exported through Hong Kong. In 1988 nearly 80 percent of Hong Kong's re-exports were related to China, either as a market or as a source of supply. Besides merchandise trade, various forms of invisible trade between Hong Kong and China also increased. These included tourism and travel services, transport services, financial services, and professional and other business services (Lau, 1986).

Hong Kong is the most important source of external investment in China. Many Hong Kong manufacturers have established compensation trade and outward processing arrangements with Chinese enterprises, mainly those in the Pearl River Delta region and Shenzhen Special Economic Zone. The growing economic relations between Hong Kong and China have added a new dimension to Hong Kong's economic growth.

The major form of foreign participation and investment in manufacturing in China is in the form of outward processing, which takes advantage of the cheap labour in China. Chinese partners provide the plant, labour, water, electricity and other basic facilities, while the foreign investor supplies machinery, materials, product design, and is responsible for marketing. The Pearl River Delta has significantly changed Hong Kong's traditional subcontracting relationship among small, medium and large factories. There is a new spatial division of labour between Hong Kong and the Delta (Sit, 1989).

Apart from providing transshipment services by the world's second largest and highly efficient container port in Kwai Chung, Hong Kong also has an efficient banking system to handle letters of credit for China. Such economic ties with China will have an increasing impact on urban development in Hong Kong, which is evident in the recent construction of the new

Hong Kong-China pier and headquarters of the Bank of China, and the expansion of the Kwai Chung container port. Chinese capital is playing an increasingly important part in property and infrastructure development in Hong Kong.

D. Emigration and Labour Shortage

The imminent change of Hong Kong to a Special Administrative Region of China has caused grave concern to some of the people in Hong Kong who are either refugees from China or their descendants. Since 1985, there has been an increasing trend of emigration to Canada, USA, and Australia, causing labour shortage in some sectors.

The changing economic structure of Hong Kong from manufacturing to financing needs people of higher levels of skill. According to a study by the Education and Manpower Branch of the Hong Kong Government, Hong Kong's first comprehensive manpower study that focussed mainly on the requirement for and the supply of manpower at different educational levels, there is an increasing demand for highly trained manpower (Education and Manpower Branch, 1990). Total employment is projected to increase by 119,572 persons or 4.4 percent between 1988 and 1996. The shift in employment is based on the structural change in employment in favour of trade and services industries that had taken place consistently during the 1980s. The restructuring of Hong Kong's economy will need more highly-educated and better trained workers. There is a shortage of workers who have a post-secondary education, particularly the upper secondary, sixth form, and university first degree.

People Hong Kong needs most in the next four years unfortunately are also those who are leaving Hong Kong most. There is a sharp increase in the number of emigrants since 1985 because of the 1997 issue. A recent study of emigration from Hong Kong by a special task force of the Legislative Council established in May 1988 showed that more than 90 percent of Hong Kong emigrants in 1988 have gone to Canada, USA, and Australia. The age profile of emigrants, as compared to the population, shows disproportionately more in the economic active age of twenty-five to forty-four and disproportionately fewer in other age groups. There is also a disproportionately large group of people with university degrees. Fifteen percent of the emigrants have degrees, although such people comprise only 3.5 percent of the total population. Twenty-five percent of the emigrants are professional, technical, administrative and managerial workers and they only constitute 5.5 percent of the total population.

The rapidly growing jobs in the professional, technical and managerial sectors unfortunately are those most severely hit by the brain drain. Many of these jobs can only be filled by people with degrees or higher qualifications. However, the survey shows that there will a shortfall of 36,734 persons with first degree qualifications in 1996. The government is actively trying to attract emigrants and students who are studying abroad to come back to Hong Kong to work.

Apart from the shortage of professional labour, there is also a shortage of unskilled and semi-skilled labour. The PADS and Metroplan projects will need many professionals and labourers. The supply of labour is not fast enough to cope with the growing economy. It was estimated that in 1988 there was at least a shortage of 128,000 workers (Joint Association Working Group, 1989). Labour shortage was felt in all economic sectors, with some sectors more severely hit than others. The highest vacancy rate was in construction, followed by manufacturing, wholesale, retailing and hotel. In May 1988, a special scheme allowing employers to import 3,000 skilled foreign labourers was introduced to meet the general shortage of skilled labour in Hong Kong. This foreign labour import scheme was further expanded in May 1990 to allow the import of 14,700 foreign skilled and semi-skilled labourers. Two thousand foreign workers in this scheme were reserved especially for the construction of the new airport and airport-related projects.

E. Local Politics

The introduction of district administration in 1981 and representative government in 1985 has opened up a channel for public participation in urban development. The district administration system in Hong Kong started in 1981 in response to the growing complexity of urban management associated with rapid economic and social changes that required a strengthening of the Government administration and an increase of citizen participation at the district level (Hong Kong Government, 1981). In order to improve district management and stimulate more public participation, a comprehensive district administration system with elected members was introduced on 1 June 1980, with the first election of 132 members held in 1982.

Under the district administration system, Hong Kong was originally divided into eighteen districts, with ten on Hong Kong Island and Kowloon and eight in the New Territories. The district number expanded to nineteen in 1985 with Kwai Chung/Tsing Yi separated from the former Tsuen Wan District. Although District Boards are free to discuss whatever they consider to affect the livelihood of local residents, their specific responsibilities are to advise the Government on the general well-being of the residents and workers in their districts, the provision and use of public services and facilities, the adequacy and priorities of government programmes, and the allocation of public funds for local public works and community activities. In an attempt to tackle the development issues encountered in districts, a number of committees such as Environment, Transport and Social Services are formed with co-opted members drawn from the local communities.

The environment, land use, and provision of transport and public facilities are problems that affect the daily life of residents in every district. Since each District Board has its own funds to spend on minor environmental improvement and public work projects, it is not surprising that these matters are most often discussed in District Board meetings. An environmental committee, whatever its name, is found in every District Board, while there are sixteen out of a total of nineteen District Boards that have traffic and transport related committees. Depending on the perceived needs, some districts even have a work projects committee to monitor public work programmes.

District administration has undoubtedly increased citizen participation in the previously restricted area of urban planning in Hong Kong. There are different objectives and levels of citizen participation in planning (Arnstein, 1969; Glass, 1979). District Boards in Hong Kong have been quite successful in building support for district issues and generating community input and information exchange between planners and District Board members, but somewhat limited in establishing direct communication with the general public, educating District Board members and the public on planning knowledge, and promoting decision making power (Mok Wong, 1983). Most of the items brought up for discussion are already at the detailed programming stage and it seems that District Boards have been used to generate support for plan implementation. The advice of District Board members is limited because they have to depend on government officials for information and technical expertise. In addition, their terms of reference restrict District Boards to advisory bodies without actual executive power (Fong, 1986).

Since their establishment in 1982, District Boards have made a significant impact on local environmental problems despite their limited powers and resources. They have given advice on matters that affect the daily living of the residents, and promoted local participation in recreational and cultural events. Their work ranges from organizing district celebrations for festivals, activities for the youth and the elderly to providing sitting areas, rain shelters, open space and recreational facilities. They have been successful in improving the environment by clearing obstructions and illegal structures in side streets and back lanes. Their efforts have also led to better bus and refuse collection services, more footbridges and car parks, and better provision of maxicab and ferry services.

F. Information and Communication Technology

Communication technology is often regarded as something that is space-extending and that allows individuals and firms to function within a geographically larger set of boundaries (Brotchie, 1984; Kellerman, 1984). New technology, particularly information and communication technology, allows people to exchange information and ideas without interpersonal contact. Communication is an important factor affecting office location (Goddard and Morris, 1975). Communication technology has helped to decentralize economic activities and population away from the city centre of the western cities. There is a rapid increase in the growth of telecommunications in Hong Kong, particularly in portable phones and fax machines. There are signs that Hong Kong is developing towards an intelligent city with a good information and communication network (Batty, 1990). The rapid development of communication technology in Hong Kong may have a great deal of impact on its future urban form, enabling Hong Kong to become a more decentralized city.

Conclusion

The urban development of Hong Kong in the 21st century requires speculation and crystal ball-gazing (Yeh, 1985b). The direction of urban development has been established by the Territorial Development Strategy, the Port and Airport Development Strategy and the Metroplan. The current dispersed pattern of urban development will continue, but major development and improvement will occur in the main urban areas through land reclamation and urban redevelopment. If the plans are successfully implemented, they will improve the urban environment of Hong Kong, particularly the older congested districts. Whether these plans will materialize depends greatly on the future political and economic development of Hong Kong. The 1990s will be a major turning point and test case in Hong Kong's history. The continual "stability and prosperity" of Hong Kong hinge upon the smooth transition of its existing system and government to the SAR government after 1997, which will operate on the "one country, two systems" principle. Although political uncertainty is not the sole determining factor in urban development, it does greatly influence the extent of foreign investment, which Hong Kong needs to maintain its position as a major financial and manufacturing centre in Asia. Future economic growth and urban development in the 1990s and beyond are dependent upon the good faith and close co-operation between Hong Kong and China.

With the district administration scheme and representative government paving the way, further democratization may materialize in the 1990s. Should it happen, urban planning and development policies would be more openly discussed and more citizen participation might also be allowed. The government is increasingly bringing important policy issues for discussion to district boards, a break-away from the long-established colonial administrative system of little consultation and public participation. Recent examples include the harbour reclamation studies, the Land Development Corporation for urban redevelopment, Electronic Road Pricing systems, the review of public housing allocation policies, the policy on housing subsidies to public housing tenants, and the Metroplan.

The demand for public participation in urban development matters is becoming more acute. Politics will become increasingly important in shaping future urban development in Hong Kong, especially with the introduction of direct election in the Legislative Council's election in 1991 that makes the Government more open to the public.

The Joint Declaration and Basic Law will not greatly affect the land administration and urban planning in Hong Kong as they have basically endorsed the continuation of the existing leasehold land tenure system until 2047. However, the 50 ha land sales restriction by the Joint Declaration will lead to a slower horizontal expansion of the city, a greater intensity of land use in the old urban areas, and higher land prices until this restriction is reviewed after 1997 (Li, 1990).

Urban development may be influenced not only by local politics but also by politics between Hong Kong and China. Recently, there are indications that China is stepping up its influence on urban development in Hong Kong. The Chinese government has cast doubts on the need for, and location of, future port and airport facilities as recommended by the Port and Airport Development Strategy announced by the Hong Kong Government in 1989. The project of building the new airport was halted and a series of talks carried out among the Hong Kong, British and Chinese governments on the scale and funding of the project. China also expressed concerns over the Town Planning Amendment Bill that extends development control to the New Territories for improving the rapidly deteriorating environment. Although the issue of building the new airport has been resolved by the signing of the Memorandum of Understanding Concerning the Construction of the New Airport in Hong Kong and Related Questions by the British Prime Minister, Mr. John Major, and the Chinese Premier, Mr. Li Peng, on 3 September 1991, it has caused grave anxiety among the people of Hong Kong over the degree of influence of the Chinese government on Hong Kong's affairs before and after 1997.

Urban development in very much related to prevailing social and political ideology. There has been speculation that because of the difference in the ideology of China with the existing system, there will be changes in the location, use, access to, and significance of urban space and structure in Hong Kong after 1997 (Cuthbert, 1987). However, whether this will happen depends very much on what type of interference that China would exert on Hong Kong and what type of changes that will occur in China.

NOTES

1. The "metropolitan area" is different from the common usage in other places in the world where it means the city and its surrounding commuting areas. In the TDS, it is referred to as the main urban areas of Hong Kong Island, Kowloon, and New Kowloon plus the Kwai Chung — Tsuen Wan New Town.
2. Metroplan is not a strategic plan for the metropolitan area of Hong Kong per se. It only covers Hong Kong Island, Kowloon, New Kowloon and Kwai Chung — Tsuen Wan which form the main urban areas of Hong Kong. "Metroplan" is one of the sub-regional plan of the five major sub-regions of the Territorial Development Strategy.

REFERENCES

Arnstein, Sherry (1969). "A Ladder of Citizen Participation." *Journal of American Institute of Planners*, Vol. 35, pp. 216–224.

Barnes, Graham (1990). "The Shape of Hong Kong after PADS." *Planning and Development*, Vol. 6, No. 1, pp. 2–6.

Batty, M. (1990). "Intelligent Cities: Using Information Networks to Gain Competitive Advantage." *Environment and Planning B: Planning and Design*, Vol. 17, pp. 247–256.

Bristow, M. R. (1981). "Planning by Demand: A Possible Hypothesis about Town Planning in Hong Kong." *Hong Kong Journal of Public Administration*, Vol. 3, No. 2, pp. 199–223.

——— (1984). *Land-Use Planning in Hong Kong: History, Policies and Procedures*. Hong Kong: Oxford University Press.

Brotchie, J. F. (1984). "Technological Change and Urban Form." *Environment and Planning A*, Vol. 16, pp. 583–596.

Chen, Edward K. Y. (1984). "The Economic Setting." In *The Business Environment in Hong Kong*, edited by David G. Lethbridge, 2nd edition. Hong Kong: Oxford University Press, pp. 1–51.

——— (1990). "The Hong Kong Economy in a Changing International Economic Environment." In *The Newly Industrializing Economies of Asia*, edited by M. Kulessa. Berlin: Springer-Verlag, pp. 91–110.

Choi, Y. L. (1985). "The LUTO Model and Its Applications in Hong Kong." *Planning and Development*, Vol. 1, No. 1, pp. 21–31.

Cuthbert, A. R. (1987). "Hong Kong 1997: The Transition to Socialism — Ideology, Discourse, and Urban Spatial Structure." *Environment and Planning D: Society and Space*, Vol. 5, pp. 123–150.

Eason, A. G. (1985). "Territorial Development Strategy Studies: A View of the Process." *Planning and Development*, Vol. 1, No. 1, pp. 4–7.

Education and Manpower Branch (1990). *A Statistical Projection on Manpower Requirements and Supply for Hong Kong*. Hong Kong: Hong Kong Government.

Fong, Peter K. W. (1986). "Citizen Participation and Administration Decentralization in Hong Kong." *Habitat International*, Vol. 10, No. 1/2, pp. 207–217.

Fong, Peter K. W. and Anthony G. O. Yeh (1984). "Public Housing Programme in Hong Kong: 1973–83." *EAROPH Journal*, Vol. 1, pp. 110.

——— (1987). "Hong Kong." In *Housing Policy and Practice in Asia*, edited by Seong-kyu Ha. London: Croom Helm, pp. 12–47.

Fung, Bosco C. K. (1988). "Enforcement of Planning Controls in Hong Kong." *Planning and Development*, Vol. 4, No. 1, pp. 21–26.

Ginsburg, Norton (1988). "Geography and the Pacific Century." *Asian Geographer*, Vol. 7, No. 1, pp. 1–11.

Glass, James (1979). "Citizen Participation in Planning: the Relationship between Objectives and Techniques." *Journal of the American Planning Association*, Vol. 45, pp. 180–189.

Goddard, J. B. and D. Morris (1975). *The Communications Factor in Office Decentralization*. Oxford: Pergamon Press.

Hong Kong Government (1981). *White Paper on District Administration in Hong Kong*. Hong Kong: Government Printer.

———— (1985). *Planning for Growth*. Hong Kong: Government Printer.

———— (1989a). *Hong Kong 1989: A Review of 1987*. Hong Kong: Government Printer.

———— (1989b). *Gateway to New Opportunities: Hong Kong's Port and Airport Development Strategy*. Hong Kong: Hong Kong Government.

———— (1990). *Hong Kong 1990: A Review of 1989*. Hong Kong: Government Printer.

Hong Kong Housing Authority (1974). *Annual Report 1973–74*. Hong Kong: Hong Kong Housing Authority.

———— (1981). *Annual Report 1980–1981*. Hong Kong: Hong Kong Housing Authority.

———— (1984). *A Review of Public Housing Allocation Policies: A Consultative Document*. Hong Kong: Hong Kong Housing Authority.

———— (1985a). *Green Paper: Housing Subsidy to Tenants of Public Housing*. Hong Kong: Hong Kong Housing Authority.

———— (1985b). *Report to Housing Authority on Public Consultation: Green Paper on Housing Subsidy to Tenants of Public Housing*. Hong Kong: Hong Kong Housing Authority.

———— (1986a). *Report of the Domestic Rent Policy Review Committee*. Hong Kong: Hong Kong Housing Authority.

———— (1986b). *Report of the Committee on Housing Subsidy to Tenants of Public Housing*. Hong Kong: Hong Kong Housing Authority.

Joint Associations Working Group (1989). *Report on Hong Kong's Labour Shortage*. Hong Kong: Joint Associations Working Group.

Kellarman, A. (1984). "Telecommunications and the Geography of Metropolitan Areas." *Progress in Human Geography*, Vol. 8, No. 2, pp. 222–246.

Kraus, W. and W. Lutkenhorst (1986). *The Economic Development of the Pacific Basin*. New York: St. Martin's Press.

Kwok, R. Y. (1983). "Land Price Escalation and Public Housing in Hong Kong." In *Land for Housing the Poor*, edited by S. Angel. Singapore: Select Books, pp. 328–345.

Lands and Works Branch (1984). *NTDD — A Decade of Progress*. Hong Kong: Lands and Works Branch, Hong Kong Government.

Lau Pui-king (1986). "Economic Relations Between Hong Kong and China." In

Hong Kong in Transition, edited by Joseph Y. S. Cheng. Hong Kong: Oxford University Press, pp. 235–267.

Leung, W. T. (1980). "Hong Kong's New Town Programme: A Social Perspective." In *Hong Kong: Dilemmas of Growth*, edited by C. K. Leung, J. W. Cushman and G. Wang. Hong Kong: Centre of Asian Studies, University of Hong Kong, pp. 375–395.

———— (1983). "The New Town Programme." In *A Geography of Hong Kong*, edited by T. N. Chiu and C. L. So. Hong Kong: Oxford University Press, pp. 210–227.

Li Si-ming (1990). "The Sino-British Joint Declaration, 1997 and the Land Market of Hong Kong." *Review of Urban and Regional Development Studies*, Vol. 2, No. 1, pp. 84–101.

Lin, T. B., V. Mok, and Y. P. Ho (1980). *Manufactured Exports and Employment in Hong Kong*. Hong Kong: The Chinese University Press.

Lo, C. P. (1975). "Changes in the Ecological Structure of Hong Kong 1961–1971: A Comparative Analysis." *Environment and Planning A*, Vol. 7, pp. 941–963.

———— (1986). "The Evolution of the Ecological Structure of Hong Kong: Implications for Planning and Future Development." *Urban Geography*, Vol. 7, No. 4, pp. 311–335.

Lui, Terry Ting (1983). "Undocumented Migration in Hong Kong." *International Migration*, Vol. 21, No. 2, pp. 260–276.

Mok Wong, Oi Yee-ann (1983). "Citizen Participation in Hong Kong: Its Application in Urban Planning." Unpublished M.Soc.Sc. dissertation, Centre of Urban Studies and Urban Planning, University of Hong Kong.

Morris, Kevin (1990). "PADS: An Overview." *Planning and Development*, Vol. 6, No. 1, pp. 7–13.

Planning, Environment and Lands Branch (1990). *Metroplan: The Foundation and Framework*. Hong Kong: Strategic Planning Unit, Planning, Environment and Lands Branch, Hong Kong Government.

Pryor, E. G. (1985). "An Overview of Territorial Development Strategy Studies in Hong Kong." *Planning and Development*, Vol. 1, No. 1, pp. 8–20.

Pun, K. S. (1983). "Urban Planning." In *Geography of Hong Kong*, edited by T. N. Chiu and C. L. So. Hong Kong: Oxford University Press, pp. 188–209.

Schiffer, J. R. (1985). "Anatomy of a Laissez-Faire Government: The Hong Kong Growth Model Reconsidered." In *State Policy, Urbanization and the Development Process*, edited by Peter Hills. Hong Kong: Centre of Urban Studies and Urban Planning, University of Hong Kong, pp. 1–29.

Shinohara, Miyohei and Lo Fu-chen (eds.) (1989). *Global Adjustment and the Future of Asian-Pacific Economy*. Tokyo: Institute of Developing Economies and Kuala Lumpur: Asian and Pacific Development Centre.

Sit, V.F.S. (1989). "Hong Kong's New Industrial Partnership with the Pearl River

Delta." *Asian Geographer*, Vol. 8, Nos. 1 and 2, pp. 103–115.

Skeldon, R. (1986). "Hong Kong and Its Hinterland: A Case of International Rural-to-Urban Migration." *Asian Geographer*, Vol. 5, No. 1, pp. 1–24.

Town Planning Division (1984). *Town Planning in Hong Kong*. Hong Kong: Town Planning Division, Lands Department.

Transport Branch, Hong Kong Government (1990). *Moving into the 21st Century: The White Paper on Transport Policy in Hong Kong*. Hong Kong: Transport Branch, Hong Kong Government.

Wang, L. H. and Anthony G. O. Yeh (1987). "Public Housing-Led New Town Development: Hong Kong and Singapore." *Third World Planning Review*, Vol. 9, No. 1, pp. 41–63.

Wigglesworth, J. M. (1971). "The Development of New Towns." In *Asian Urbanization: A Hong Kong Casebook*, edited by D. J. Dwyer. Hong Kong: Hong Kong University Press, pp. 48–69.

Working Group on the Review of the Town Planning Ordinance, Hong Kong Institute of Planners (1988). "Issues of Town Planning Legislation in Hong Kong." *Planning and Development*, Vol. 4, No. 1, pp. 2–7.

Yeh, Anthony G. O. (1985a). "Employment Location and New Town Development in Hong Kong." In *State Policy, Urbanization and the Development Process*, edited by Peter Hills. Hong Kong: Centre of Urban Studies and Urban Planning, pp. 60–85.

——— (1985b). "Planning for Uncertainty — Hong Kong's Urban Development in the 1990s." *Built Environment*, Vol. 11, No. 4, pp. 252–267.

——— (1987). "Spatial Impacts of New Town Development in Hong Kong." In *New Towns in East and Southeast Asia — Planning and Development*, edited by D. R. Phillips and Anthony G. O. Yeh. Hong Kong: Oxford University Press, pp. 59–81.

——— (1990a). "Unfair Housing Subsidy and Public Housing in Hong Kong." *Environment and Planning C: Government and Policy*, Vol. 8, No. 4, pp. 439–454.

——— (1990b). "Public and Private Partnership in Urban Redevelopment in Hong Kong." *Third World Planning Review*, Vol. 12, No. 4, pp. 361–383.

Yeh, Anthony G. O. and Peter K. W. Fong (1984). "Public Housing and Urban Development in Hong Kong." *Third World Planning Review*, Vol. 6, No. 1, pp. 79–94.

Yeung Yue-man (1990). "Cities that Work: Hong Kong and Singapore." In *Changing Cities of Pacific Asia: A Scholarly Interpretation*, edited by Yue-man Yeung. Hong Kong: The Chinese University Press, pp. 187–209.

Youngson, Alexander J. (1982). *Hong Kong: Economic Growth and Policy*. Hong Kong: Oxford University Press.

CHAPTER FIVE

Economic Reform and Regional Development in China in the 21st Century

Wing-shing Tang
Department of Geography, The Chinese University of Hong Kong,
Hong Kong
David K. Y. Chu
Senior Lecturer, Department of Geography, The Chinese University of
Hong Kong, Hong Kong
C. Cindy Fan
Assistant Professor, Department of Geography, University of California,
Los Angeles, USA

Introduction

Long before the events in Beijing in June 1989, researchers disputed over whether or not the policy and practice of regional development in China had changed over time. This debate was brought about by economic reforms beginning in 1978. Since then, food became more readily available with the introduction of the household responsibility system and adjustments in the procurement system in agriculture. Consumption goods became equally more available after structural changes in the industrial economy. External trade with the world economy increased by leaps and bounds, and investors outside China voted with their feet by pouring in investment. The debate, which began with these economic reforms, deals with the question of whether or not these reform measures have increased regional disparity. Or, put differently, is the East-West divide in China increasing or decreasing? Is the East-West divide still a relevant concept with which to understand regional disparity? (see Figure 5.1) While this debate was far from being settled, researchers were forced to start again from square one because of the events in 1989 as it is beyond any doubt that these events have caused policy changes: economic reform has been slowed down. Researchers must now start again to collect information on the possible effects of this "U-turn" on regional development in the 1990s and possibly the 21st century.

Figure 5.1: Province-level Administrative Divisions of China, the End of 1988

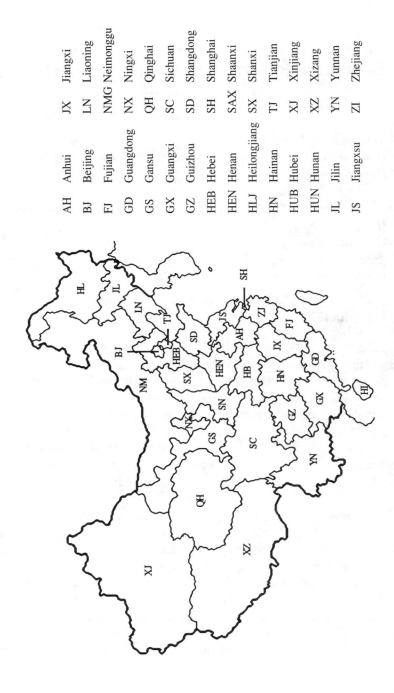

AH	Anhui	JX	Jiangxi
BJ	Beijing	LN	Liaoning
FJ	Fujian	NMG	Neimonggu
GD	Guangdong	NX	Ningxi
GS	Gansu	QH	Qinghai
GX	Guangxi	SC	Sichuan
GZ	Guizhou	SD	Shangdong
HEB	Hebei	SH	Shanghai
HEN	Henan	SAX	Shaanxi
HLJ	Heilongjiang	SX	Shanxi
HN	Hainan	TJ	Tianjian
HUB	Hubei	XJ	Xinjiang
HUN	Hunan	XZ	Xizang
JL	Jilin	YN	Yunnan
JS	Jiangxsu	ZI	Zhejiang

It is not our purpose to provide a full-fledged forecast of Chinese regional development. Nevertheless, this chapter attempts to make a modest contribution by providing some speculations based on a more in-depth understanding of the processes of regional development up to the 1980s. Our understanding emphasizes the geographical dimension. Recent literature in mainstream geography has emphatically argued that we must pay heed to the duality between economy and space (see Cooke, 1989; Duncan, 1989; Massey, 1984; Sayer, 1985). In our context, it means that we should not restrict ourselves to describing the spatial manifestations of economic development, including foreign trade. The way spatial organization in turn affects the development of the economy should also be investigated. That being so, it is beyond the scope of this chapter to provide a full elaboration on these issues. We only outline a simplified version of these arguments, as a more elaborate one can be found elsewhere (Tang, 1991).

The next section reviews the literature on regional development in China during the reform period and highlights how the literature addresses the dynamics behind regional development. Section 3 attempts to provide an informed account of the mechanisms at work. Regional development is understood in the context of a resource-constrained economy and a state-controlled society. Two mechanisms can be identified from this political economy: the geographic transfer of value and of revenue. These mechanisms have different effects depending on the contingent conditions of individual regions. In terms of time, the discussion will be divided into two parts: pre-reform and reform periods. A discussion of the former period is necessary, as it lays down the background for understanding the processes during the latter period. Section 4 will speculate on the future spatial development in the 21st century, while the final section summarizes the basic arguments of this chapter.

The Recent Literature

The literature has disproportionally focussed on the relationship between foreign trade — the cause, and regional development — the outcome at the expense of the role of other reform measures. Implicit in this emphasis is the undisputed role of the new development strategy since 1978 in initiating a redirection in the trade policy and its effects on regional development.

Since 1978, China's involvement in international trade has been significantly eased by the erosion of the so-called Maoist development strategy, which dominated the first three decades since 1949. The Maoist strategy was said to be based on the egalitarian principle and was implemented to redistribute resources to the interior to obtain spatially balanced development. The new leadership, since 1978, apparently has abandoned the formerly held notions of even development and self-sufficiency. Instead, current emphases include first, more interactions with the world through which advanced western technology will be imported, thereby facilitating modernization and second, an uneven development strategy based on regional comparative advantage and a broadly defined efficiency principle. The surge in foreign trade volume, from 10.2 percent of the gross national product in 1978 to 27.9 percent in 1987, is usually quoted as supporting evidence of the diminishing role of national self-reliance in determining state priorities (Lockett, 1989).

It has been observed that the new economic reform is based upon the recognition of the backwardness of the Chinese economy and the widely held conviction that foreign technology will provide a short-cut to technological modernization (Hsu, 1989). Hsu notes that China's recent foreign trade expansion has been largely led by economic growth, and suggests that in the long run, through obtaining needed investment, technology and equipment, foreign trade will serve as an engine of growth. Using employment data, Reynolds (1987) demonstrates that the job-creating effects of foreign trade vary with the composition of trading goods. Expanding labour-intensive sectors, such as agriculture and food processing, will maximize the job-creating benefits of foreign trade. He finds that in mid-1980s, foreign trade played a positive role in generating employment as import of agricultural goods declined and as import of machinery and transport equipment and other light industrial products increased.

Findings about technology transfer seem to be mostly negative, however. Chan et al. (1989) suggest that the goal of importing high-technology investment and skills has not materialized. This may be attributed to the conflicting objectives between China and her trading partners: China wishes to increase exports and absorb advanced technology, while most foreign investors are interested in the huge domestic market (Lockett, 1989). At the regional level, the urge to cash in so as to boost economic performance also means that, in practice, technology transfer is assigned a lower priority. In parts of the Special Economic Zones, for example, rapid developments in tourism, recreation and real estate contribute to profit-making rather than attracting advanced technology (Phillips and Yeh, 1989).

The effect of trade on regional restructuring in China, in terms of regional coordination and spatial inequality, constitutes another focus of discussion in recent literature. The lack of cooperation among provinces in the pre-reform years is well documented. Lyons (1987) observes that the principle of local self-sufficiency has led to slow output growth, fragmentation in the economy, excessive vertical integration and non-standardization of products. It is also well known that the lack of horizontal coordination between production units and between administrative units has contributed to economic inefficiency (Kirkby and Cannon, 1989; Lakshmanan and Hua, 1987). It is the intention of the central planners to ameliorate, if not totally resolve, all these problems induced by the spread effects of foreign trade by promoting cooperation among provinces. Towards this end, provinces are reclassified into regions by a modified schema of regionalization on the basis of their development levels. Under China's Sixth (1981–1985) and Seventh Five-Year Plans (1986–1990) broad regions are defined with unique development goals. In the Seventh Five-Year Plan, the interior is further divided into the central and western regions. The coastal region, which covers the narrow strip along the eastern coast, includes a large proportion of the nation's major industrial cities and all the Special Economic Zones.[1] Anticipated outcomes of the current strategy include increased commercial and commodity linkages between provinces and increased horizontal integration between production units. It is expected that the central region may supply the eastern region with energy desperately needed for its export-oriented industries, while foreign technology absorbed may trickle down in the other direction (Yang, 1990).

Nevertheless, these linkages remain abstract notions rather than realities. Rothenberg (1987) indicates that foreign investment results in enclaves of active trading areas such as the Special Economic Zones, which have little interrelationship with the rest of China. Phillips and Yeh (1989) find that most of the Special Economic Zones' linkages are among themselves or with neighbouring counties. It appears that most local authorities are less than enthusiastic about initiating cross-regional cooperation, when guidelines and coordination mechanisms are inadequate, when the risks involved seem to outweigh benefits, and when the legacy of regional competition and local protectionism is still strong (Lyons, 1987; Solinger, 1987).

The imperatives of achieving equality and spatial balance in development were stated in Mao Zedong's *On the Ten Great Relationships*. Nevertheless, the historical development gap between the east and the west, or between the coast and the interior, persisted during the pre-reform years (Cole, 1987; Fan, 1988; Lyons, 1987). Once again, the current emphasis on trade and foreign investment is considered to be an important factor in eradicating regional inequality. Accompanied with this wishful thinking is said to be a reversal in regional development policy. The new strategy takes into consideration differentials in regional endowment and encourages regional specialization followed by cooperation. Of late, the coast is targeted for rapid export-oriented industrial growth; the central region is encouraged to maintain its good agricultural and energy base to support the east and to provide import substitutes; and development in the west is to centre on animal products and mineral exploitation (Ji, 1989; Lockett, 1989). The coast may have benefited more from such a strategy than its counterpart, as noted by the distribution of state and foreign investments (Table 5.1). But, this increasing regional inequality need not worry the grumbling poor provinces as well as the central planners, since benefits accrued to the coast will trickle down to the interior in due course. In other words, regional inequality will finally disappear during the course of regional and international cooperation; this is an argument that resembles in nature those of Williamson (1965) and Keeble (1967).

Findings on the implications of this reversal in regional policy tend to be less conclusive. The creation of a political framework for growth, due to the open door policy and the decentralization of economic power from the centre to the local areas, has rendered the coastal region more attractive to foreign investment. Fan (forthcoming) finds that the economic returns to foreign trade involvement are greater in coastal and industrial provinces than in the rest of the country. Accordingly, the outcome of these changes in policy has been faster growth in the coastal region, while other regions slipped behind. Some evidence, based on statistical analyses of provincial economic data, tends to lead us to believe that the converse is the case. Drawing on recently published provincial data, both Lyons (1991) and Tsui (1991) argue that regional inequality in terms of coefficients of variation of per capita National Income Produced (*Guomin shouru*) and Gross Domestic Product (*Guonei shengchan zongzhi*) has narrowed during the reform period. The trend of these coefficients over time has been reproduced in

Table 5.1: Regional Distribution of Foreign Investment, 1979–1988

Provinces	Number of Contracts Signed	As a % of Nation	Actual Investment (US$'000)	As a % of Nation
National Total	98,931		19,429,101	
Beijing	538	0.54	1,416,690	7.29
Tianjin	313	0.32	847,720	4.36
Hebei	222	0.22	60,400	0.31
Shanxi	66	0.07	N.A.	
Neimenggu	N.A.		N.A.	
Liaoning	1,316	1.33	1,271,870	6.55
Jilin	227	0.23	123,301	0.63
Heilongjiang	255	0.26	236,100	1.22
Shanghai	959	0.97	2,523,620	12.99
Jiangsu	891	0.90	754,740	3.88
Zhejiang	541	0.55	462,670	2.38
Anhui	256	0.26	230,060	1.18
Fujian	2,086	2.11	947,490	4.88
Jiangxi	368	0.37	96,210	0.50
Shandong	563	0.57	440,020	2.26
Henan	218	0.22	164,390	0.85
Hubei	150	0.15	355,240	1.83
Hunan	171	0.17	106,500	0.55
Guangdong	88,975	89.94	8,133,340	41.86
Guangxi	309	0.31	399,870	2.06
Sichuan	208	0.21	422,640	2.18
Guizhou	56	0.06	34,010	0.18
Yunnan	48	0.05	27,430	0.14
Shaanxi	147	0.15	316,380	1.63
Xizang	N.A.		N.A.	
Gansu	N.A.		N.A.	
Qinghai	N.A.		N.A.	
Ningxia	N.A.		N.A.	
Xinjiang	48	0.05	58,410	0.30

Note: N.A. Data not available.
Source: Tang (1991)

Figure 5.2 to illustrate the point. Nevertheless, as argued in Tang (1991), one needs to interpret this kind of statistical evidence carefully on several counts. Since the statistical yardstick usually excludes "black market" activities, which have grown by leaps and bounds especially in the coastal region, we may not have captured the magnitude of regional inequality. That economic indicators have excluded non-economic indicators may also lend support to our reservation. In short, some analyses have cast doubt on the implicit assumption that foreign trade has the effect of improving regional inequality during the reform period.

Figure 5.2: NIP-based Regional Uneven Development Indices

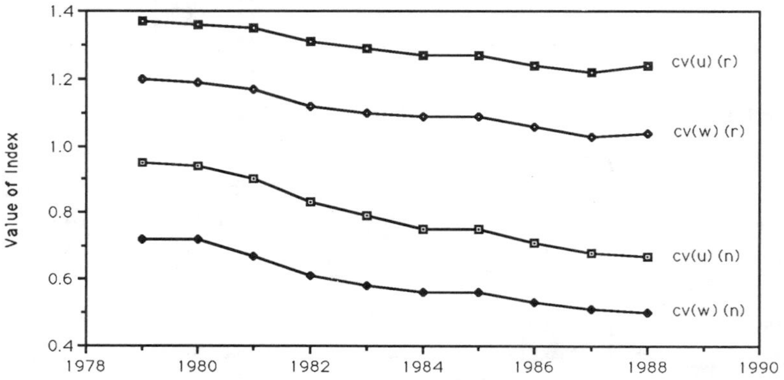

Notes: CV(U) = coefficient of variation (unweighted)
          CV(W) = coefficient of variation (weighted)
          r = real per capita National Income Produced
          n = nominal per capita National Income Produced
Source: Tang (1991).

The above summarizes the discussions in the literature regarding the changing relationship between foreign trade policy, urban reform and spatial development strategy. This literature is not without problems (Tang, 1991). First, it tends to take empirical facts and rhetoric at face value. For example, central planning is still dominant in the realm of goods circulation and the market mechanism is severely distorted; foreign trade, overseas investment and imported technology only accounted for a tiny proportion of the modernization effort. Uneven spatial development as a strategy is exaggerated, that is, greater attention to, and more capital investment in, the coastal region may or may not be the direct consequence. The skewed distribution of investment may be due to strategies with different purposes or intentions; it may be the unintended consequences of certain inherent structural mechanisms at work. One must make the distinction between regional policies with stated regional objectives and national policies with regional implications. It will be argued later that it is the latter that have contributed more to the regional development we observe.

Second, existing explanations also take rhetoric at face value. Partly because of the difficulty of collecting information and data, the literature tends to rely heavily on the official line explanation. Once a certain policy is adopted, it is often the case that information will be gathered to elaborate the policy and to highlight its positive consequences rather than to investigate and analyze the policy. Below, we will elaborate this argument with three examples: the notion of regional comparative advantage, the role of regional differentiation, and the triparite regionalization (coastal, central and western) as promulgated in the Seventh Five-Year Plan for the so called "export-led industrialization *cum* modernization."

Regional comparative advantage is a problematic concept. Many official policies claim to be designed with the promotion of regional comparative advantage in mind. In a politico-economic system that allows a greater mobility of resources across enterprises and regions, comparative advantage means that a region will specialize, using its endowments, and will trade with other regions or countries. In a system that attempts to control the distribution of resources, comparative advantage carries a connotation completely different from the efficiency principle as implied in the various versions of uneven development strategy. It is in fact a justification for the relaxation of control on particular regions or goods in circulation. It allows the developments of these regions to deviate from the central planners' original or proposed targets. It is regionalism, that is, what the regions think of as appropriate to them, rather than the consideration of regional endowment and specialization that shapes development paths. Thus the identical practices of producing particular goods for export, setting up Special Economic Zones, and favouring the coast carry different implications in different settings. It is then advisable not to follow the common practice found in the literature of taking uneven development strategy at its face value. Instead this should be subject to critical examination.

The existing explanations usually ignore the role of spatial development. While emphasizing regional comparative advantage, the literature tends to pay little attention to the role of regional differentiation in development. At most, one can recall only passing references to how the endowments of a particular region are employed in the production of certain goods and how certain zones are conducive to foreign and local investments. What exactly these regional endowments are is not fully understood. Our understanding seems to be restricted to a one-way analysis of the spatial implication of economic development policies. The extent to which regional variations in development help to shape economic reforms and development paths of provinces needs to be investigated before we can deepen our understanding of the interaction between space and policy.

When the country was divided into three regions according to the Seventh Five-Year Plan, it was done with political and administrative objectives. Control is easier if there are fewer actors around. But as we will show later, there are wide variations within each region. Guangdong is different from Liaoning, and Guangxi may have more similarities with Yunnan than with Jiangsu. Various provinces have also taken different paths of development. It is therefore important to employ the proper level of spatial disaggregation to reflect, rather than disguise, maximum diversity.

In sum, the existing explanations of recent changes in economic and regional development policies are inadequate. A more in-depth analysis of the mechanisms inherent in China's political economy is necessary for a better understanding of these changes and for any projection of future trends.

The Mechanisms at Work

Since the mechanisms currently at work are largely based upon those operating before 1978, we will discuss forces shaping Chinese policies in both periods. The mechanism of geographic transfer of value is found to be inherent to the resource-constrained nature of the economy, while the mechanism of geographic transfer of revenue is a by-product of the imperative to legitimation in a state-controlled society. Here we can summarize the arguments presented in Tang (1991).

A. Geographic Transfer of Value in a Resource-constrained Economy

Drawing on Kornai's (1980a) argument, China is a resource-constrained economy and this is an outcome of the adoption of central planning and the quest for rapid industrialization. The principal characteristic of this kind of economy is the continuous reproduction of shortages. While absolute scarcities associated with backward development may be an important cause of shortages, the latter do not necessarily depend on the former. Besides, shortages are not attributable to the irrationality of planners or policy makers; the problem is more systemic. Specifically, shortages are produced and reproduced by the interaction between the planning agents and subordinated individual agents such as enterprises and households. It is within this context that the shortages in energy, raw materials and industrial products persist during the preliminary stage.

One of the solutions to the shortage problem is to invest. Addition in new productive capacity is preferred to the expansion of existing facilities. The reasons behind this are systemic. First, increments of benefits associated with the former are tangible and can therefore be planned. This fits, and therefore reproduces, the ideology of planning, perhaps the author meant some specific "planned things," but as it stands, it is redundant. Second, unlike most increments of cost, most of the increments of benefit appear in the accounts of the governments. Thus, statistics can be complied to show how well the governments have performed. Third, increments of benefit can be disposed of by the governments while those associated with the expansion of existing facilities can only be decentralized. This point is especially important at a time when governments are losing control of the economy. Fourth, increments of benefit are visible immediately, while increments of cost, such as air and water pollution and those associated with massive migration of people, only appear later. For a regime that looks for immediate accomplishment, building new facilities seems to be ideal at least for propaganda purposes.

This investment hunger to ameliorate shortages interacts with the "comparative advantage" of some provinces to produce a spatial outcome. A cursory look at resource maps of China will show that provinces farther away from the coast possess the larger reserves of raw material and energy resources. As discussed in the preceding paragraph, increments of benefits associated with setting up production units for the extraction and primary processing of these resources in the interior provinces are superior to increments of cost. The costs of transporting these resources for further processing in the coastal provinces appear to be extended over a long period, while the benefits can be realized almost immediately. The outcome is that statistically, interior provinces have a larger proportion of their industrial productive capacity in resource extraction and the production of semi-finished commodities.

What is important to establish at this juncture is that the products of these industries are priced lower than their counterparts. Drawing on, once again, Kornai's (1980b:353–376) conceptualization of the price-fixing process in a shortage economy, it can be argued that the common scissors problem referred to in development literature also happens in China. (Development strategy of the day further reinforces this choice process.) Industrial products are priced higher than agricultural products and, within industry, light industrial products are priced higher than heavy industrial products which are in turn higher than mineral and resource products. In addition, the price structure and administrative system are so rigid that only little local variations exist.

Consequently, the coastal provinces can obtain low priced primary and semi-finished products from the interior provinces for further processing. On the other hand, other parts of the central planning system are so structured that the interior provinces are forced to use their limited revenues to buy higher priced products from the coast. Given that money has only a passive role to play in China, this unequal exchange is not so much detrimental to the purchasing power of the interior provinces, because they can, as will be argued below, live on subsidies. What is, however, more important is that this unequal exchange creeps into the calculation of various economic performance indicators (for example, Guo and Wang, 1988:66–67), which are sometimes used to rationalize investment preference. It is in this way that interior provinces are usually assessed as the last ones to invest in. Shortage breeds shortage. The interior provinces become increasingly underdeveloped, and, if unchecked, the disparity between the coast and the interior widens over time.

Translating these concepts into quantitative cartographic language, Figure 5.3 shows that the East-West divide was quite marked by the end of the pre-reform period. Transfer-out values (loss in values due to a larger proportion of extractive industries) and transfer-out values (gain in values due to a larger proportion of manufacturing industries) are calculated for provinces, and the status of "loser" or "beneficiary" is assigned. In 1980, it was still generally the case that the magnitude of transfer-out value decreased as one approached inland. With the possible exceptions

Figure 5.3: Geographical Transfer of Value, 1980

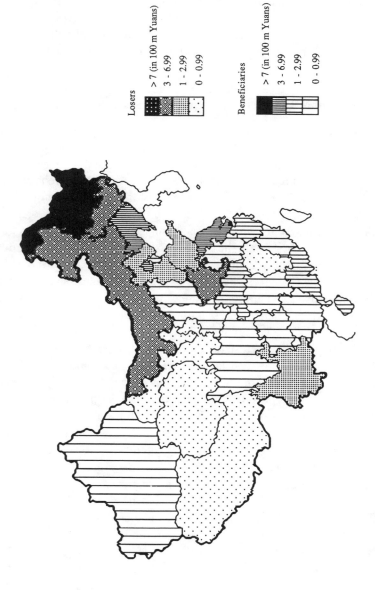

Losers

▓ > 7 (in 100 m Yuans)
▒ 3 - 6.99
▤ 1 - 2.99
░ 0 - 0.99

Beneficiaries

■ > 7 (in 100 m Yuans)
▤ 3 - 6.99
▦ 1 - 2.99
☐ 0 - 0.99

Source: Tang (1991).

of Xinjiang and Heilongjiang, the interior provinces were the "losers" in the geographic transfer of value. Shandong and Hebei were the two provinces along the coast that also belonged to this category. In contrast, other coastal provinces were the "beneficiaries" of this geographic transfer of value. In general, we can say that the calculations of values transferred have provided evidence to support the conceptual arguments outlined above.

B. Geographic Transfer of Revenues in a State-controlled Society

The politico-economic system that was discussed above also contributes to the geographical transfer of revenue. In China, the interests of the Chinese Communist Party, if not those of just a few people at the top echelon of the Party, are placed over the interests of society. As such, there is every need to legitimize the Party's existence by controlling every aspect of society for security reasons.

The control system, which the state implements, is always under attack. This is because, first of all, the control system is not always standardized or even legalized. Many control areas are not governed by well specified norms or rules (Whyte, 1989). One expects challenges based on different interpretations. Even in control areas where better specified norms are readily practised, challenge is still possible. Some individuals may begin to challenge socialist ideology when it confronts reality over time. With their constituents having interests at variance with those of the state, it is not difficult to conceive of resistance from local social units, including local governments. Furthermore, when tensions occur between inputs requested and allocated, the typical feature of a shortage economy, local governments usually challenge the central plans and hoard for inputs. In short, one of the structural dynamics of the Chinese state is that, while there is the imperative to control by the state, there is every attempt by local governments to counteract such control.

This structural dynamic takes on a concrete form depending on the mediation of local conditions. Some provinces possess conditions that either impel the state to control or foster the local governments' determination to counteract control. Ethnic tension, for example, may encourage the development of grievances among the non-Han national minorities. If these grievances have developed to such an extent that the minorities challenge the state rule, the state will not hesitate to take decisive action to restore security. Such actions may deprive the minorities of the opportunity to stimulate region-oriented development. Grievances will compound and call for more intensive local resistance. Then it becomes more imperative for the state to control for the sake of security, and the vicious cycle continues. If these provinces are also economically backward, as in the case of Xizang, Xinjiang, Neimenggu, Qinghai and Ningxia, there is the necessity of not only improving the living standard, but also ensuring the continual centralization of political power.

Mistrust of the non-Han nationalities discourages the state from granting too much autonomy to the minority provinces. Besides, for the sake of security, these provinces must be administered in such a way that the centre is always in full control. Moreover, the practice of central planning does not allow for too much deviation from the central planning system, if resources are still to be procured. Accordingly, the provincial institutional structure is bound to be the replica of that of the centre. Given the peculiar differentiation between urban and rural in the system of resource distribution, it is not surprising to find that state personnel retain their urban household status. Like production enterprises, administrative offices also have an inherent expansionary drive, resulting in a gradual increase in state personnel (Post and Wright, 1989:127–128). In other words, there is a continually expanding number of urban households from whom the state must try to seek their legitimation.

Besides, given that these provinces occupy strategic positions in national defense, security considerations have played an important role in shaping measures taken to improve the standard of living. It is not uncommon to adopt measures for security considerations rather than for local accumulation. In sum, in light of the necessity to maintain a strong control by the state and the impracticality of doing it through local accumulation, raising the standard of living by all sorts of subsidies seems to be the only option.

This form of stability promotion is implemented via the fiscal system. Although the trend since 1949 has been the expansion of the fiscal powers of the local governments, the system has basically remained one with unified control over revenues and expenditures (*tongshou tongzhi*). The state can, via the centre budget, redistribute funds and other resources from one province to another. Thus the control-countercontrol interaction appears via the fiscal system as inter-regional transfer of revenues. Specifically, the flow of revenue takes the form of urban subsidies. The latter make available to urban households commodities that are otherwise out of their reach. Subsidies may also be spent to support local production enterprises operating at a loss. Should these enterprises be left to go bankrupt, employment opportunities will be greatly reduced and stability jeopardized.

Figure 5.4 attempts to quantify the geographic transfer of revenues in 1978, the year-end of the pre-reform period. For each province, the amount of revenue transferred is obtained by dividing budgetary expenditures by budgetary revenues. One hundred percent refers to the situation where revenues balance out expenditures. Percentages above it mean that the local budgets are subsidized by transfers of revenue. The higher the percentage, the larger the amount of transfer-in revenues. Percentages below 100 mean that revenues are transferred out from the local budgets. The general message from Figure 5.4 is loud and clear: there is a discernible East-West divide in terms of transfer of revenue. With the possible exceptions of Ningxia and Heilongjiang, the amount of transfer-in revenue increases as one moves inland from the coast.

The interesting point to note is that these subsidies, however, have the negative effect of delaying structural change in the local economy. With subsidies pouring into these near-bankrupt production spheres, investment made in these problematic provinces are bound to be less "efficient" and with lower reproductive capacity. More importantly, since subsidy-induced productive and consumption commodities are manufactured in the more industrialized coastal provinces, the subsidies in fact represent a stimulus to their manufacturing industries.

The apparent outcome is that the larger the amount of subsidy the problematic provinces receive, the more underdeveloped they will be. This outcome has attracted the attention of some recent research — the most popular of all being Wang and Bai (1986) — but, as we have argued above, this is not the only mechanism affecting regional development. The mechanism of geographic transfer of value is also in operation. In addition, it is not, as argued by Wang and Bai, that underdevelopment is caused by too much state intervention. It has much more to do with the requirement of legitimation, the nature of the Chinese political economy.

In summary, the political economy underpinnings — the mechanisms of geographical transfer of values and of revenues — are found to have the tendency of perpetuating the underdevelopment of the problematic provinces, a large proportion of which is found in the interior.

Figure 5.4: Geographical Transfer of Revenues, 1978

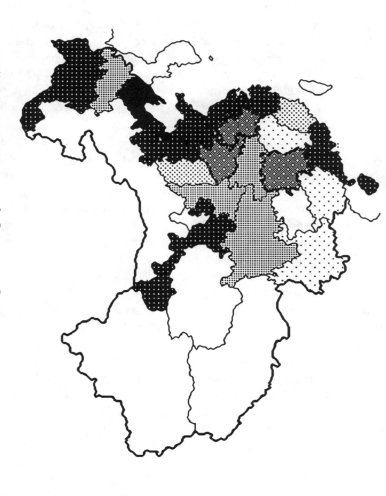

Expenses as a
% of revenues

> 170%

130 - 169.9%

110 - 129.9%

100 - 109.9%

90 - 99.9%

80 - 89.9%

40 - 79.9%

< 39.9%

Source: Tang (1991).

C. Relaxation of Control for Better Control Since 1978

Before examining the kinds of change economic reform has brought to the two mechanisms outlined above, a cautious note is needed on the nature of economic reform. Unless the nature of the state has changed substantially, and the events in Beijing in June 1989 have proved otherwise, the present economic reform in China is not systemic in nature. Reform measures are meant neither to solve all the problems inherent to a socialist system nor to up-root the current system and implant a new one (Guo *et al.*, 1988). Indeed, they basically consist of minimal decentralization designed to gain better control of society (see also Peter, 1987). Indeed, enclaves designed to take in foreign investment and technology are contained territorially as well as administratively. As a result, it is necessary to view these reform measures with a more realistic attitude. Specifically, one should not fall into the trap of exaggerating their impact without substantive evidence.

What this cautious note implies is that the structural forces underlying the two mechanisms of geographic transfer are still basically in operation. In spite of recent price reforms, the extent to which price structure is changed does little to obliterate the mechanism of geographic transfer of value. Price differentials between agricultural and industrial products, on the one hand, and between heavy and light industrial products, on the other, did narrow in the early 1980s. But they have started to widen again since the mid-1980s. The effect of change in price structure on the restructuring of spatial economy has not been forthcoming, at least not in the magnitude expected by reform advocates.

Conversely, some reform measures have actually contributed to the perpetuation of this mechanism. The intertwining influence of the decentralization of material allocation power to the local governments and fiscal reform is a case in point. Local governments nowadays are capable of allocating a larger number of resources than in the pre-reform period. Even among those categories that are considered of national importance, such as steel, iron ore, electricity and coal, the local governments are likely to have a say on the extra-plan portion after negotiation with the state. Fiscal decentralization (*fenzao chifan*), in fact, means that the local governments are responsible for growing expenditures with fewer revenues allocated from the state. To make both ends meet, local governments from the economically backward and resource-rich provinces, usually in the interior, must raise their revenues by investing in high profit-tax light industries. These local governments are indeed using their already low revenues, generated from resource extraction, to subsidize this light industrial production. Given their weak industrial base, light industrial investment is bound to be less "efficient." Besides, it would be difficult for the commodities produced to capture a decent market share in the industrially advanced provinces. In other words, although apparently these interior provinces have undergone sectoral change in their economies, they do not really benefit from such change. The other side of the story is that there is a continual value drain from industrially backward provinces to their industrially advanced counterparts. Undoubtedly, the former provinces can withhold resources desperately needed by the latter, as reported in the media as a regional blockade. Nevertheless, the resource-poor provinces are still able to alleviate their shortage problems, first, from the black market or the extra-plan portion and, second, through some kinds of regional "cooperation" or horizontal linkages. As noted, although these activities have not taken both the form and the magnitude perceived by the central planners, they do exist. In short, the geographic transfer of value is still very much in place, albeit in a slight different form.

With China's re-entry into the world economy, the substantial difference between local and world prices does have a role to play in perpetuating the existence of the mechanism. As argued by Woo and Tsang (1988), the Ricardian concept of comparative advantage would not operate in a socialist economy like China, which has absolute disadvantage in almost all lines of production. The only possible exception is light industrial products, which are either cheap, because of the availability of abundant cheap labour, or culturally distinctive, because of the availability of historically specific skilled labour. China is still able to under-sell her competitors in marketing these products, but at a cost. In order to maintain her competitiveness, China must make sure that production is kept at low cost. This means that wages, prices of producing goods and resources must be kept stable by various price and cost stabilization measures, including subsidizes. If these production activities were charged at world prices in producing goods, raw material and energy resources, they would lose their competitive edge immediately and disappear from the world market. Put differently, light industrial products for the world market are now subsidized by locally priced raw material and energy resources. The actual value transferred from resource-rich to resource-poor provinces is greater than in the pre-reform period.

Even worse, some of the revenues obtained from these light industrial producing provinces are not ploughed back into the state purse for second-round redistribution. When the import and export decision-making power is delegated to the Ministry of Foreign Trade and its local subordinates, as well as those enclaves with certain economic autonomy, they will choose to import and export goods that will bring them maximum benefits, disregarding the needs of the country. Consumer electronics and luxury cars are typical examples of goods that are least urgent imports for local accumulation. Although the imports help to enrich the coffers commanded by the importing units, they do so at the expense of depriving the interior provinces of funds for development. Values generated in the latter provinces, from resource extraction, are transferred overseas, to purchase imports, instead of being re-distributed via the state, as revenue transfers. The same logic applies to tax holidays and related land and infrastructure subsidies in coastal enclaves designed for foreign investment such as the three Special Economic Zones and fourteen open cities. This special treatment does not act as a catalyst for structural change in any provincial economies or between any two of them. Once again, the mechanism of geographic transfer of value is operating in a disguised form between the interior and the world economy.

Furthermore, reforms in industrial management have been directed to relax control on production enterprises. This relaxation has clearly stirred up another wave of expansion, demanding more resources and resulting in greater shortage (Wong, 1986). Production of raw material and energy resources must be raised, as exemplified in the investment allocation in the Seventh Five-Year Plan. This lays down the conditions for the perpetuation of the transfer mechanism.

Figure 5.5 shows the pattern of the transfer of value in 1985. Three points about the pattern are worth mentioning. First, the 1980 general pattern of having values transferred to the coast roughly persisted in 1985. Second, superimposed on this general East-West divide is the North-South divide. With Xinjiang shifting from a "beneficiary" to a "loser," and with Gansu perhaps deteriorating in its position as a "loser," northwest China has become a large region with transfer-out values. Similarly, north China has become worse off due to the "negative" developments of Shanxi (from

Figure 5.5: Geographical Transfer of Value, 1985

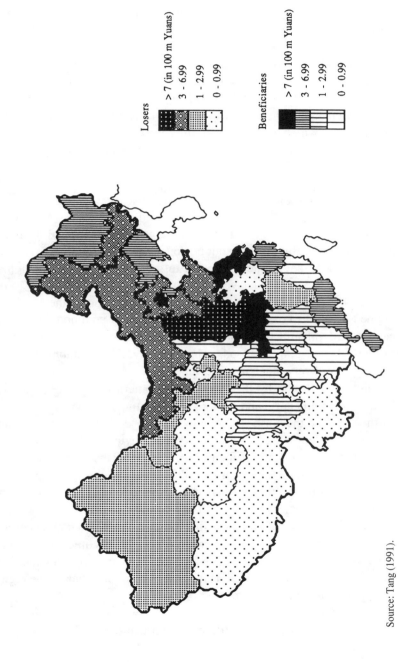

Losers

> 7 (in 100 m Yuans)

3 - 6.99

1 - 2.99

0 - 0.99

Beneficiaries

> 7 (in 100 m Yuans)

3 - 6.99

1 - 2.99

0 - 0.99

Source: Tang (1991).

a "beneficiary" to a "loser"), Hebei, Henan and Shandong (deteriorated in positions). With the exception of Anhui and Jiangxi (the two agricultural provinces), the rest — roughly the southern part of the country — has really benefited from economic reform. Third, development among provinces along the coast is increasingly uneven. Here, the North-South divide is even more apparent, since Hebei and Shandong — the two provinces with transfer-out values — have slipped even further behind Jiangsu, Zhejiang and Guangdong, which have instead improved their positions as "beneficiaries." These differential developments have demonstrated the variations in response from provinces with contrasting local conditions.

Regarding geographic transfer of value, this does not mean that such a mechanism is no longer in operation when fiscal reform has reduced the amount of funds available to the state for redistribution. As noted earlier, local governments of interior provinces are forced to expand their feeble industrial bases. But this may not be done with local funding. To make up the difference, they request the state to grant them greater autonomy as offered to the coastal enclaves. This has, once again, taken the form of subsidies. Also, as in the pre-reform period, a portion of the subsidies is drained off to the coastal provinces in the form of commodities that they cannot still manufacture, including traditional consumer durables and fashionable consumption goods. That is to say, the geographic transfer of revenue is still very much in place, albeit in a slightly different form.

This is confirmed by the 1988 spatial pattern of revenue transfers in Figure 5.6. With Gansu and Heilongjiang shifting their positions drastically, the west and the northeast are now clearly "deficit" regions, relying on revenue transfers. Conversely, the coastal provinces of Beijing, Tianjin, Jiangsu, Shanghai and Zhejiang have remained the core that transfers revenues to the state budget. It is in this sense that the spatial pattern has changed very little after ten years of economic reform. However, another pattern certainly emerges as a result of reform. In response to fiscal reform, a significant number of provinces that formerly contributed revenues to the state now either reduce their contribution or become dependent on redistribution from the state. The coastal provinces together mentioned above are the only exceptions. This has the effect of reducing the regional variations in revenue transfers.

To summarize, the compound effects of economic reform have resulted in a regional pattern slightly different from that of the pre-reform period.

Figure 5.6: Geographical Transfer of Revenues, 1988

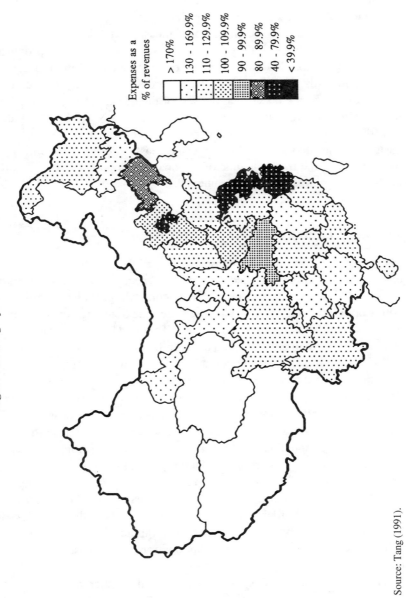

Expenses as a
% of revenues

> 170%

130 - 169.9%

110 - 129.9%

100 - 109.9%

90 - 99.9%

80 - 89.9%

40 - 79.9%

< 39.9%

Source: Tang (1991).

Reform measures have not significantly altered the conditions of the two mechanisms of transfer. The resulting regional pattern has vividly indicated the continual operation of these mechanisms. But, some provinces are capable of capitalizing on the reform measures to develop their local economies. This has certainly been the case of some coastal provinces, which possess more favourable spatial organizations and more pragmatic attitudes towards growth. These coastal provinces, mostly in the south, have grown at a rate faster than the rest of the coast, thereby generating a new dimension of regional uneven development — a North-South divide. It is a divide that reflects the influence of decontrol measures in a still basically controlled society. Insofar as the coast in general is pulling ahead of the interior, the final outcome of regional development in China during the reform period is increasingly uneven.

The 21st Century

The crackdown on student demonstrations in 1989 reflects the need to recontrol the over decontrolled economy and society. The action itself did not solve the problems associated with decontrolling. Rather it limited the policy options available to the Chinese state. The tiptoeing between control and decontrol becomes more and more difficult. The immediate need for stability results in the introduction of centralization and austerity measures. Freezing liquidity and devaluation of *Renminbi* have the effect of lowering inflation, but at the cost of restricting the embryonic market mechanism. Price reform, which was designed to normalize the relationship between different commodities, manufactured products and services was brought to a halt. On the one hand, the inflation rate was reduced, but on the other, transfer of value and transfer of revenue continue and subsidies of one form or other persist. By centralizing the import and export system again, problems associated with paternalism and ministerial/territorial rivalry are also alleviated momentarily. Through these measures, the state is capable of keeping its house in order, at least for the time being. But the conditions for the existence of the two mechanisms of geographic transfer of revenue and value have been kept intact. Also, options for the future are accordingly restricted.

The Chinese state plans to open up inland frontier towns along the Sino-Russia and Sino-Mongolia borders and river ports along the Yangzi in

the Eighth Five-Year Plan (1991–1995), partly to soothe the disquiet poorer provinces and partly to become less dependent on the over decontrolled regional economies of the south-east. However, given the shortages in raw materials and energy resources, such a spatial development strategy will leave the existing distortions of value, revenue and uneven state controls largly unchanged, if not worsened. In other words, provinces with rich deposits of energy and mineral resources will be kept under strict state control while the mechanism of subsidizing manufacturing and exports in some cities to obtain foreign hard cash will persist. The open cities and areas will receive less state capital investment and subsidies and will have to find their own way of financing. Accordingly, foreign investment and trade will be very important to these areas, and economic restructuring will become inevitable. These open up opportunities for foreign capital participation and in the short run China may import more capital goods and needed technologies. In short, to reinforce its control, the Chinese state has designed a development strategy that tends to perpetuate the division of the country, activated by the earlier economic reform, into a dual-space system: areas dominated by stricter control or close space, and those by looser control or open space. This dual-space system is very much in line with the dual-track system found in the economic sphere, where the extra-plan component stands side by side with the plan component.

As the 21st century approaches, it is fairly safe to predict that the existing political economy will last for some time. So will the dual-space system. Minute changes will be introduced into the closed space, but will not reverse its logic. The resultant relationship among trade, economic reform and regional development will therefore heavily depend on the operational effectiveness of the dual-space system, and needless to say, the political developments during these years. Given China's size, there will be enormous regional differentiations. A likely outcome, at the risk of over-generalization, is that some, but not all, of the coastal provinces will pull ahead further by reaping the benefits of operating with open space, while the other coastal provinces remain stagnant, since open space is no panacea to all coastal provinces. Most inland provinces will likely suffer the negative effects of close space. But there are some exceptions. Through continuous transfer of revenues and possibly transfer of value, the physically well endowed inland provinces will witness steady growth (its steadiness will be quite remarkable because its non-openness will save it from global economic fluctuations). The Sino-Russian and Sino-Mongolian frontier cities and towns and the river ports along the Yangzi will be able to reap some benefits from the more relaxed system of state control and from more local initiatives. But the chaos of transition from one system to another are inevitable.

It will be extremely difficult to predict what will happen beyond the short term scenario, because the stability brought by the acceptance of the dual-space system will be short-lived and costly and is hardly a long term solution due to the inherent incompatibility of the two components. It is certain, however, that a capitalist spatial pattern of development, as found in many developing countries, will not emerge unless the nature of the Chinese state changes drastically and there is a comprehensive and coordinated programme of economic reform measures. As long as these conditions do not materialize, regionalism co-operation in the dual-space system will continue to produce an autarkic, as well as uneven, regional development.

Summary and Conclusion

This chapter has speculated on the regional development of China in the 21st century. We have done so, first, by reviewing the literature. This was found wanting due to its inability to understand the processes behind regional uneven development. To make up the difference, a preliminary understandiing has been provided by referring to the political economy as a starting point of enquiry. It is found that such a system encourages the workings of two mechanisms. The geographic transfer of value is derived from the interaction among the expansionary drive, the shortage in energy and raw material, the administered price differentials, the spatial endowment differentials and industrial planning, all in a resource-constrained economy. The geographic transfer of revenue is an outcome of the interaction among the centralized fiscal system, the control-countercontrol conflict between the state and its subordinates and the spatial endowment differentials, all within a state-controlled society. During the pre-reform period, there was a clear East-West divide in terms of regional development. Many provinces in the interior, which are forced to concentrate on low-priced resource extraction, have to rely on state redistribution to cover their expenses on high-priced manufacturing products from the coast. The differential

between east and west widens as the economy develops. During the reform period, these two mechanisms are very much in place, although the spatial outcome has been less clear-cut. The East-West divide is confused by the emergence of a dual-space system, where a close space (under strict state control) stands side by side with an open space (with loose control). The dual-space system will likely persist in the 21st century, at least in the beginning. Unless there is a genuine systemic change leading to comprehensive and coordinated reform, this spatial pattern will remain intact for some time.

This chapter has shown that regional development in China has been under-researched. We are still not in a position to predict boldly on the basis of our understanding of the processes at work. The understanding provided above relies heavily on a conceptualization of the systemic features. Deep in its spirit is the assumption that systemic features take precedence over policies and ideologies in explaining regional development. Future research must be devoted to examining how the interaction of these three dimensions shapes regional policy and practice.

NOTES

1. The tripartite regionalization used in the Seventh Five-Year Plan is as follow:

    Coastal: Liaoning, Beijing, Tianjin, Hebei, Shandong, Jiangsu, Shanghai, Zhejiang, Fujian, Guangdong, Hainan and Guangxi;

    Central: Neimenggu, Shanxi, Jilin, Heilongjiang, Henan, Anhui, Hubei, Hunan and Jiangxi; and

    Western: Gansu, Shaanxi, Ningxia, Sichuan, Guizhou, Yunnan, Xizang, Qinghai and Xinjiang.

    The province-level administrative division of China at the end of 1988 has been included in Appendix 1.

REFERENCES

Chan, J.C.M., N. Y. Li and D. Sculli (1989). "Labour Relations and the Foreign Investor in the Shenzhen Special Economic Zone of China." *Journal of General Management*, 14, pp. 53–61.

Cole, J. P. (1987). "Regional Inequalities in the People's Republic of China." *Tijdschrift voor Economische en Sociale Geografie*, 78, pp. 201–213.

Cooke, P. (1989). "Locality, Economic Restructuring and World Development." In

Localities, edited by P. Cooke. London: Unwin Hyman, pp. 1–44.

Duncan, S. S. (1989). "Uneven Development and the Difference that Space Makes." *Geoforum*, 20, pp. 131–139.

Fan, C. C. (1988). "The Temporal and Spatial Dynamics of City-size Distributions in China." *Population Research and Policy Review*, 7, pp. 123–157.

——— (forthcoming). "Foreign Trade and Regional Development in China." *Geographical Analysis*.

Guo Fansheng and Wang Wei (1988). *Pinkun yu Fazhan (Impoverishment and Development)*. Hangzhou: Zhejiang Remin Chubanshe.

Guo Shiping, Yi Changtai and Gong Wenmi (eds.) (1988). *Huigu, Pinggu, Zhanwang (Review, Assessment and Prospect)*. Changsha: Hunan Kexue Jishu Chubanshe.

Hsu, J. C. (1989). *China's Foreign Trade Reforms*. Cambridge: Cambridge University Press.

Ji Chongwei (1989). "China's Foreign Trade Strategy." *Beijing Review*, 31 July–6 August, pp. 29–32.

Keeble, D. E. (1967). "Models of Economic Development." In *Social-Economic Models in Geography*, edited by R. J. Chorley and P. Häggett. London: Methuen, pp. 241–302.

Kirkby, R. and T. Cannon (1989). "Introduction." In *China's Regional Development*, edited by D.S.G. Goodman. London: Routledge, pp. 1–19.

Kornai, J. (1980a). *Economics of Shortage A*. Amsterdam: North-Holland.

——— (1980b). *Economics of Shortage B*. Amsterdam: North-Holland.

Lakshmanan, T. R. and C-I. Hua (1987). "Regional Disparities in China." *International Regional Science Review*, 11, pp. 97–104.

Lockett, M. (1989). "Foreign Trade." In *China's Regional Development*, edited by D.S.G. Goodman. London: Routledge, pp. 57–76.

Lyons, T. P. (1987). "Interprovincial Trade and Development in China: 1957–1979." *Economic Development and Cultural Change*, 35, pp. 223–256.

——— (1991). "Interprovincial Disparities in China: Output and Consumption, 1952–1987." *Economic Development and Cultural Change*, 39, pp. 471–506.

Massey, D. (1984). *Spatial Division of Labour: Social Structures and Geography of Production*. London: Macmillan.

Peter, S. (1987). "Reform and Paternalism in China: Some Theoretical Concerns." *International Regional Science Review*, 11, pp. 59–73.

Phillips, D. R. and A.G.O. Yeh (1989). "Special Economic Zones." In *China's Regional Development*, edited by D.S.G. Goodman. London: Routledge, pp. 112–134.

Post, K. and P. Wright (1989). *Socialism and Underdevelopment*. London: Routledge.

Reynolds, B. L. (1987). "Trade, Employment, and Inequality in Postreform China."

Journal of Comparative Economics, 11, pp. 479–489.

Rothenberg, J. (1987). "Space, Interregional Economic Relations, and Structural Reform in China." *International Regional Science Review*, 11, pp. 5–22.

Sayer, A. (1985). "The Difference that Space Makes." In *Social Relations and Spatial Structures*, edited by D. Gregory and J. Urry. London: Macmillan, pp. 49–66.

Solinger, D. J. (1987). "Uncertain Paternalism: Tensions in Recent Regional Restructuring in China." *International Regional Science Review*, 11, pp. 23–42.

Tang, W. S. (1991). "Regional Uneven Development in China, with Special Reference to the Period Between 1978 and 1988." *Occasional Paper,* No. 110. Hong Kong: Department of Geography, The Chinese University of Hong Kong.

Tsui, K. Y. (1991). "China's Regional Inequality, 1952–1985." *Journal of Comparative Economics*, 15, pp. 1–21.

Wang Xiaoqiang and Bai Nanfeng (1986). *Furao de Pinkun* (The Impoverishment of Abundance). Chengdu: Sichuan Chubanshe.

Whyte, M. K. (1989). "Who Hates Bureaucracy? A Chinese Puzzle." In *Remaking the Economic Institutions of Socialism: China and Eastern Europe*, edited by V. Nee and D. Stark. Palo Alto: Stanford University, pp. 233–354.

Williamson, J. G. (1965). "Regional Inequality and the Process of National Development: a Description of the Pattern." *Economic Development and Cultural Change*, 3, pp. 3–45.

Wong, C.P.W. (1986). "The Economics of Shortage and Problems of Reforms in Chinese Industry." *Journal of Comparative Economics*, 10, pp. 363–384.

Woo Tunoy and Tsang Shuki (1988). "Comparative Advantage and Trade Liberalization in China." *Economy and Society*, 17, pp. 21–51.

Yang Dali (1990). "Patterns of China's Regional Development Strategy." *The China Quarterly*, 122, pp. 230–257.

PART III

Environmental Pressures

River System and Water Resources Management in Pacific Asia for the 21st Century

Ian Douglas
Professor of Geography, University of Manchester, Manchester, United Kingdom

The continental lands of Pacific Asia contain some of the most densely populated alluvial lowlands of the world, yet those lowlands are also among the most hazardous, being subject to flooding in some seasons and to differing degrees of drought and water deficiencies in others. Exploitation of these lowlands has relied on effective water management and river engineering, yet on virtually all these rivers, developments in the catchment areas upstream are altering flow regimes, water quality and sediment loads. Questions are being constantly raised about the ability of existing water management practices to meet the rising demands for water in newly industrializing and urbanizing countries and about their ability to deal with the impact of water-related activities stemming from rapid socio-economic and technological changes (Hufschmidt and Kindler, 1991).

Ensuring that the needed quantities of water are available in the right place at the right time with right quality is one of the major challenges of resource and environmental management for Pacific Asia in the 21st century. Management problems differ from river to river, some being plagued with seasonal drought or flood, others by high sediment loads and still others by the consequences of people's actions in the catchment areas. In insular Pacific Asia, river basins are much smaller and the problems of land use change and forest exploitation loom largest in water resource use and development.

In terms of relief and fluvial geomorphology, the eastern margin of the Tibetan plateau is one of the most fascinating regions of the world. The major rivers of southeastern Asia almost all arise here, converging in the region of Yunnan, then dispersing in different directions (Figure 6.1). The westernmost river, the Brahmaputra, rises in Tibet to the north of west Nepal, flows eastward for 1,500 km north of the Himalaya before turning abruptly south at about 95°E and entering Assam and, eventually, the Bay of Bengal. The Irrawaddy and the Salween rise near the centre of Tibet and flow southeastwards to Yunnan, where they turn south to flow 1,500 km to the Andaman Sea. The Mekong also rises in the centre of the Tibetan plateau but after passing through Yunnan flows southeastwards to the southern part of the South China Sea. North of the Mekong, the Red River of Vietnam and the Pearl (Zhu Jiang) of southern China, rise in Yunnan and flow southeastwards and eastwards respectively to the South China Sea. The Yangtze (Chang Jiang) rises on the Tibetan plateau and flows southeastwards to Yunnan, before turning north and then east to enter the East China Sea. Further north, the Yellow River (Huang He) rises on the eastern margin of the Qinghai plateau, north east of Tibet, and flows through a series of angular reaches before discharging into the Gulf of Chihli.

The high plateau origins of the largest rivers means that the runoff of their upper courses is largely controlled by seasonal snowmelt, while the whole region is dominated by seasonal rainfall regimes, especially the southwest monsoon from May to August. Tropical cyclones, or typhoons, exert an important influence to more than 7° north of the equator, especially in Vietnam and southern China.

The Huang He (Yellow River)

With a mean suspended sediment concentration of 37,600 mg/l and a sediment yield of 2,100 tonnes/km^2/yr, the Huang He is rightly considered the world's muddiest river. Of this sediment load, 90 percent comes from the loess plateau region in the middle course of the river. Up to 25 percent of the sediment delivered to the head of the alluvial fan at Xiaolangdi is subsequently deposited between the dikes restraining the river along its course across the North China Plain. Deposition is rapid enough to raise the channel bed 10 cm/yr and consequently the channel flow is now generally

Figure 6.1: The Main River Systems in Pacific Asia

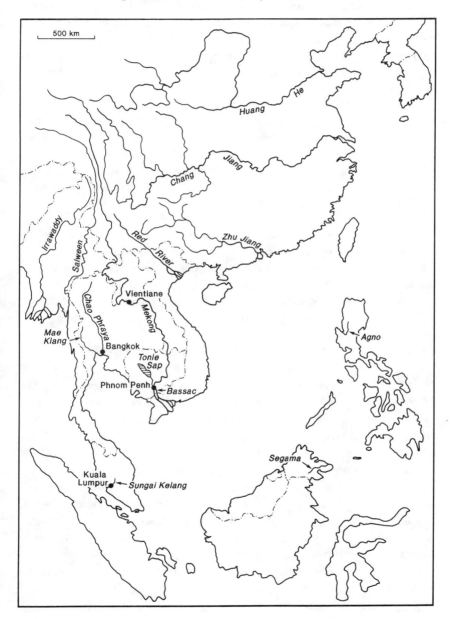

between 3 m and 5 m, and in places 10 m, above the plain outside the dikes (Douglas, 1989). The basin sediment system of the Huang He is at a critical stage where constant effort to evacuate peak water and sediment flows through the endiked channel across the alluvial fan depositional tract may be disrupted by any major natural or people-caused events upstream affecting peak discharges or sediment loads. Huang (1988) has described the problem succinctly:

> Simply stated, embankment strengthening alone is doomed to failure in the race against channel siltation. Should the river break at its most dangerous locality, the resulting flood would directly affect an area with more than 150 million inhabitants. The only dependable remedy for this problem is soil conservation on the loess highlands, for if the lower Yellow River is not so heavily silt-laden, our engineers can easily grapple with the problem of river control.

The key to silt reduction in the loess highlands is to protect the surface against raindrop impact and detachment. Active gully enlargement is almost ubiquitous on the loess plateau where sediment concentrations in runoff reach 100,000 mg/l. Erosion rates of 18,600 tonnes/km^2/yr are recorded in parts of Shaanxi (Derbyshire, 1990). Raindrop splash, rilling, gullying, slurry flow and sliding of loess blocks combine to produce persistently high sediment yield, that of the Dali River in Shaanxi averaging 19,600 tonnes/km^2/yr from 1959 to 1969. However, much of the actual soil loss occurs from within the gully systems, in the Wuding river system, 30–62 percent of the erosion occurs on the interfluves between gullies, but 38–70 percent within the gullies (Jiang et al., 1981). Determinations of caesium 137 levels in soils indicate similar proportions, 7–20 percent of the eroded material coming from interfluves and 74–93 percent from the gullies (Zhang et al., 1989). Although revegetation of actively eroding gullies is difficult, maintenance of a good plant cover on the interfluves not only reduces erosion there, but encourages infiltration and so lowers the runoff to gullies and thus the potential for erosion with gullies (Huang, 1988). Much of the eroded sediment is trapped behind dams or erosion control works with the catchment, but nevertheless flood flows with extremely high sediment concentrations are carried into the endiked plains section of the river, where the coarse particles of more than 0.05 mm diameter account for more than half the accretion within the dikes (Zeng and Zhou, 1989).

Despite the importance of watershed management and soil conservation,

North China often is short of water and multi-purpose reservoir construction has long been part of the strategy for managing the Huang He. The main stem of the river is regulated by a chain of eight reservoirs from the Longyang Gorge Dam upstream in Qinghai province to the Sanmenexia Dam, with a ninth at Lijia Gorge in Gansu under construction and a tenth, the Xiaolangdi Dam, on the lower river, now under construction. The Yihe and Louhe tributaries in Henan, which at times contribute up to 50 percent of the flow of the Huang He across the plain, are dammed; the Guxian Reservoir on the Lohe being due for completion in 1992 (Yuan, 1991). The variability of the sediment load in the endiked plains course of the Huang He is increased by the operation of regulating valves on the reservoir dams. In dry years the valves are closed and sediment is deposited in reservoirs, while in wet years, especially during floods flows with high sediment concentrations, gates are opened and sediment is scoured out of reservoirs adding to the load carried across the plains (Zuo and Zhang, 1990).

The Chang Jiang (Yangtze River)

The hydrologic behaviour of the Chang Jiang has long been a major concern of the Chinese people. The earliest flood-mark of the Three Gorges section of the river dates from 1135 A.D. (Cheng, 1989). The earliest hydrological station on the river dates from 1865 and the greatest flood in the historical record of the Three Gorges section was a flow of 110,000 m^3/s in 1987, with the mean annual runoff at the mouth estimated at 29,300 m^3/s (Wei and Zhao, 1983) and the sediment yield as 280 tonnes/km^2/yr (Gu and Douglas, 1989). The main stem of the river, the Jingsha Jiang, rises in the dry eastern plateau of Tibet and has the lowest mean runoff per unit area of all the upper tributaries of 0.00915 m^3/km^2/s, compared to a mean flow of 0.021 m^3/km^2/s in the Mian Jiang in western Sichuan. In a normal year, the flooding of the various tributaries and the main Chang Jiang do not coincide. However, in an abnormal year, if storms affect the southern tributaries later than usual, the flood peaks of the southern tributaries and that of the mainstream may combine to form an exceptional flood, such as the historic flood of 1931. If the flood on the mainstream comes earlier than usual it may combine with the peak wet season discharges of the southern tributaries to create a catastrophic event, such as the flood of 1935 (Cheng, 1989).

Land degradation in the middle and upper portion of the Chang Jiang basin has led to a doubling of the river's sediment load since 1958 (Li and Cheng, 1987). The 533 million tonnes total annual sediment transport at Yichang is about one-third that of the Huang He. Two areas and problems dominate the sediment supply, the severe debris flows, yielding up to 33,000 tonnes/km^2/yr of sediment, in the steep, rugged area along the Yunnan-Sichuan border, and severe agricultural soil erosion in eastern Sichuan, especially in the catchment of the Jialin River. Although the Jialin accounts for only 15.5 percent of the catchment area and 15.9 percent of the runoff above Yichang, it contributes 30.4 percent of the total sediment discharge.

Debris flows are found in steep folded and faulted terrain with slopes of over 30°. They are triggered by heavy intense rainstorms of over 40 mm in an hour, which are particularly likely to occur in the western part of the Sichuan basin. The frequency and magnitude of such mass movements have been accelerated by steepland clearance for grazing and the exploitation of forests for fuelwood. The southern part of the upper Chang Jiang catchment, north of Kunming, also contributes a large amount of sediment through debris flows (Gu and Douglas, 1989).

Unstable slopes are a particular problem in the Three Gorges section between Chongqing and Yichang. Near Wanxian, for example, four landslides in a 16 km reach of river have a combined debris volume of over 50 million m^3 (Li and Wan, 1989). The whole section has some 177 landslides, several exceeding 10 million m^3 each. Much of this mass movement is due to the steeply dipping friable weak mudstone beds in the Triassic and Jurassic sedimentary sequences (SSTC, 1988). Failure along bedding planes may be accelerated by changes in the water balance caused by loss of vegetation, but even without people's actions, this area would suffer severe mass movement.

These landslides and the erosion of cultivated land and the many debris flows further upstream combine to produce serious river sediment problems for the Three Gorges multipurpose hydroelectric and water resource project which, on 2 August 1991, the Chinese government finally decided to build. The controversy over this huge project has had world wide attention, but it illustrates a classic dilemma of water resources management, that of the big project as opposed to hundreds of small scale works. In many ways, the big project has some advantages when multipurpose water use is required. The potential saving of 40 million tons of coal by generating electricity represents a huge sum of money for supporting ancillary navigation and flood control benefits. Larger vessels will be able to proceed upstream to Chongqing and the reservoir will reduce flooding downstream of the gorges. However, the benefits will fall unevenly regionally, helping those in the downstream lowlands, but with severe costs to some 750,000 to 1 million people who will have to be resettled and probably causing difficulties in and around Chongqing where the reservoir waters will eventually be at the present summer high water levels virtually all the year. The balance nationally, environmentally, socially and regionally between positive benefits and negative costs in this case is extremely delicate.

The Zhu Jiang (Pearl River)

The Zhu Jiang drains the hills of southern China that receive high rainfalls from the south-west monsoon in the summer months. The mean annual depth of runoff is 820 mm, compared with 531 in the Chang Jiang and only 86.5 in the Huang He (Chen, 1985). Exceptional rains, particularly when associated with typhoons can produce major flooding. In 1915 a flood on the Beijiang and Xijiang tributaries inundated 4.5 million ha of farmland and affected 3 million people. Large parts of Guangzhou city were flooded (Pan et al., 1983).

Much of the terrain is deeply weathered with red oxisols that erode relatively easily when vegetation is removed. Although the average sediment yield for the whole basin is 260 tonnes/km^2/yr, parts the upper Xijiang basin suffer severe gullying and have yields five to six times higher. Even the establishment of orchards, which provide a permanent tree cover, has been seen as damaging to the soil, as rills and gullies develop between the trees. Severe gullying of some of the deep soils is widespread in parts of the catchment area.

The catchment requires careful land management. Both a series of earth dams in major gullies (Xi, 1990) and a careful scheme of soil conservation planting (Zhu, 1990) have been advocated to reduce erosion. The zoning proposed involves a forest cover near hill summits, giving way to tea gardens below. Downslope from the tea would be another forest belt, giving way to orchards, with grazing or forage near the slope foot and paddy rice cultivation on valley floors and flood plains. Such integrated management of the landscape maximizes both rural output and soil and water conservation. Doubt remains, however, as to the ability of such schemes to reduce erosion in the gullies that already exist and to reduce further forest exploitation in the search for fuelwood.

The Red River (Songkoi)

Above the delta, the Songkoi, whose rectilinear alignment is one of the most striking features of the river patterns of continental Pacific Asia, is deeply entrenched and crosses from China into Vietnam at only 85 m above sea level. The steepness of the terrain in the catchment area means that response to rainfall is rapid and flooding is extremely variable. Wet season high flows can occur at almost any time from June to October and may exceed dry weather flow by almost forty times. While runoff from the shales and schist terrain is rapid, there is also some slower flow through limestone groundwater systems that both tends to prolong high flows, but may also cause renewed rises in water level downstream. The delicate drainage system of the delta requires careful maintenance if agricultural productivity is to be preserved and flooding avoided.

The main channels of the Songkoi and its tributaries flow on natural levees across the delta and do not function as local drains. Another set of channels drains areas between the levees. Saline water intrusion along the coast remains a problem, but through a system of casiers, basins enclosed by dikes and equipped with gates to regulate the inflow and outflow of water, the needs of irrigation, drainage and prevention of saline incursions can be met. The almost complete system of embankments, whose foundations were laid 2,000 years ago, is unique in southeast Asia, and results both from the long Annamite civilization in the area and the absolute necessity to protect the delta lowlands against the extraordinarily flashy floods of a river the size of the Songkoi (Volker, 1983). Without such protection, nothing, not even rice, could be grown.

The Mekong River

Vientiane marks the emergence of the Mekong from its mountain tract on to the lowlands. The catchment area of the Mekong above Vientiane is 299,000 km^2, while above Kratie (Table 6.1) it is 646,000 km^2. The mean

Table 6.1: Characteristics of the Major Rivers of Pacific Asia

Rivers	Catchment Average Maximum Average Maximum Mean					
	Area km^2	Pptn mm	Flood Flow m^3 s^{-1}	Annual Flow m^3 s^{-1}	Silt Conc mg l^{-1}	Annual Sediment Load t km^{-2} y^{-1}
Huang He	751,871			1,480	37,600	1,080
Chang Jiang	1,827,000			32,190	12,100	280
Zhu Jiang	442,100			7,800		
Red	120,000	1,500	35,000	3,900	7,000	
Mekong	795,000	1,380	76,000	14,800	597	435
Chao Phrya						
Kelang	1,260	2,250				806

annual flow at Vientiane is 0.161 m^3/km^2/s, while downstream at Kratie it is 0.233 m^3/km^2/s, the higher discharge at the lower station reflects the relative aridity of the Tibetan plateau and the significance of the monsoon rains in the lower catchment. Below Kratie, seasonal overbank flow into the deltaic area begins. At Phnom Penh, the Mekong divides into two branches, the eastern, still called the Mekong, carrying 80 percent of the flow, with the other 20 percent going down the Bassac to the west. Some of the Mekong water also spills westward into the Tonle Sap, with a corresponding outflow after the Mekong flood peak has passed. The Tonle Sap regulating system has long been thought capable of augmentation and control, improving flood protection and land reclamation, as well as providing for power generation and release of water to combat saline intrusion into the delta (Aki and Berthelot, 1974; Sewell, 1966; White, 1964). In 1957 the United Nations Economic Commission for Asia and the Far East (ECAFE) published a report, Development of Water Resources in the Lower Mekong, which proposed damming the Mekong and some of its tributaries for hydro-electricity generation, extended irrigation, flood control and improvement of navigation. Control of the Mekong would bring many benefits: drowning of rapids impeding navigation; prevention of abnormally high floods in the delta; raising the water level of the Tonle Sap in the dry season to improve fishing; greater dry season flow into the delta would reduce incursions of saline water; improvement of crop yields through better water supply, especially in dry areas of north-east Thailand

(Fryer, 1970). The far-sighted plans for the Mekong would have changed many environments, but did lead to a recommendation that about 7 percent of the area of the basin, mainly upland forests should be left as protected areas in their natural state. The forests around the proposed dams would slow down soil erosion and reservoir siltation as well as provide for wildlife conservation in a system of national parks (McNeely and Wachtel, 1988). The political upheavals and warfare that have beset Laos, Kampuchea and Vietnam since the 1960s have prevented many of these ideals from being achieved.

The 170,000 km^2 of northeast Thailand have 18 million people on one-third of the Thai territory, but erratic rainfall and generally poor soil conditions make agricultural productivity low and economic growth slower than in the rest of Thailand. With the long dry season, irrigation is necessary in this part of Thailand, but in 1990, only 0.9 million ha, out of 9.73 being cultivated, had access to some forms of public or private irrigation. Even if supplies were to be improved, estimates suggest that only about 20 percent of the agricultural land in this part of the Mekong basin is potentially cultivable (Sethaputra et al., 1990).

Seasonal water levels in the Bassac River at Long Xuyen show considerable variation from year to year, peak levels (maximum annual stage) ranging from 2.24 to 2.95 m a.s.l. (Hatien datum) in the thirty years from 1937 to 1966 (Thomson, 1968). Characteristically, river stage is lowest in May and rises from June to October when the peak stages are reached (see p.139 Figure 6.1). The delta area itself is affected by rains from the northeast monsoon from November to January, the two heaviest one day rains at Can Tho from 1920 to 1966, of 198 and 159 mm, both occurred in November.

The Chao Phraya River

The Chao Phraya Basin is usually divided into three zones, the Upper, Middle and Lower (Takaya, 1987). In the headwater areas of the mountains and valleys of the upper basin, deforestation has been a major problem, the percentage of northern Thailand covered with forest declining from 67 percent in 1973 to 47.4 percent in 1988 (Witthawatchutikul and Tangtham, 1990). The valley floors are normally used for wet-rice cultivation, with water control by weirs and irrigation channels. However, increasing population has meant the enforcement of strict rules on land and water distribution. Competition for water for agriculture, energy, industrial, domestic, tourist and aquaculture uses, as well as the extension of upland agriculture through poppy-substitution programmes, have increased the water problems of the upper basin (Sethaputra *et al.*, 1990).

In the Mae Klang sub-basin, a tributary of the Ping, for example, more than twenty communal irrigation systems divert water for rice irrigation. However, the 2.5–4.5 percent annual growth of the hill peoples on the mountain slopes has greatly affected water resources through land use changes, especially deforestation. As a result of these new hill villages and the introduction of such crop practices as cabbage cultivation to reduce the poppy-growing areas, farmers in the lowland and upland areas are coming into competition for water resources during the dry season. Development schemes have pushed two communities into direct confrontations, the one being encouraged to grow three crops of rice a year, the other to continuously cultivate cabbages. Since 1973, the total annual discharges of the Mae Klang have declined from around 225 to 150 thousand m^3 (Sethaputra *et al.*, 1990).

Events such as those in the Mae Klang affect many of the upper basins of the Chao Phraya system and thus the flows of water into the middle and lower reaches of the river. Two major dams, the Bhumipol and Sirikit, regulate the lower river and the Bangkok surface water supply, their huge storage capacities making reliable dry season supplies available (Takaya, 1987). Flows into the Bhumipol Dam have declined since 1975, primarily as a result of reductions in the flow of the Ping River by the construction of other reservoirs upstream (Peetanonchai, 1990). In addition to the rapid expansion of municipal and industrial water use in the Ping Basin, the irrigated area of the basin has doubled since 1975, indicating a trend to further depletion of inflows to the Bhumipol Dam.

Upstream conflicts are paralleled in the delta area, where the growth of Bangkok causes concern that the Chao Phraya may not be able to deliver sufficient flow to meet all the requirements of abstraction by the Metropolitan Waterworks Authority (MWA), irrigation, combatting seawater intrusion, and conveying wastewater being directly dumped into the river. The MWA pumps the majority of its raw water supply from the Chao Phraya near Bang Pa-in and obtains a small amount from deep wells that are being phased out in an attempt to overcome the land subsidence problem caused by excessive groundwater withdrawal. Between 1978 and 1981, the average land subsidence in the eastern part of the Bangkok Metropolitan Region (BMR) was over 10 cm/yr, and part of the area was already below sea-level and thus subject to frequent flooding. Excessive use by many more private than MWA wells required action to develop piped surface water supplies and to end MWA pumping in critical areas by 1987. However, according to the Department of Mineral Resources (DMR), although up to 1987 groundwater use expanded at only 2.3 percent per year, after 1988 it increased at 5 percent per year, and the MWA continued to use groundwater to meet short term shortages of surface water. For industrialists in a period of economic expansion, groundwater use has proved cost effective. As industry expands in the outer areas with poorer infrastructure, the demand for groundwater may grow further (Sethaputra *et al.*, 1990). Users of groundwater pay far less than the social cost of groundwater pumping and, because of lax enforcement, often nothing at all. Failure to price groundwater at a level that takes account of the costs caused by subsidence and flooding is in effect subsidising their overuse and the consequent environmental and social impact (Mekvichai *et al.*, 1990).

While the delta landscape has been transformed to one where roads are usually always passable and rice is cultivated all year, the water balance of the delta is still delicate. Bangkok has changed from a city of canals to a city of overcrowded highways with continual risks of flooding. The large dikes that protect Bangkok will have to be strengthened, for the city is now a people-made waterproofed island, reliant on dikes and the efficiency of the pumps that evacuate water from its deep drainage system. The reliability of agricultural water supplies depends on both the regulations of land cover changes in the headwaters and the use of price mechanisms to achieve more efficient water use in the delta.

The Sungai Kelang, Malaysia

The Sungai Kelang is typical of the streams draining the western flank of the Main Range of peninsular Malaysia, but, as the most developed river basin in the country, it illustrates how increasing urbanization and growing affluence transform water resource problems and lead to severe degradation of rivers and riverine amenities. About 25 percent of the basin is covered with forest and swamp, 41 percent by agricultural uses, mainly rubber and oil palm plantations, 5 percent by active and abandoned tin mining land and

29 percent by urban land uses. The Kelang Gates dam, where the main river passes through the prominent resistant quartz dike of the Kelang Gates Ridge, provided the original water supply of the city, but it has now been supplemented by the Batu Dam on a tributary and by inter-basin transfers from the Selangor, Langat and Semenyih rivers. So great is the urban consumption of water that no compensation water is released from the two dams upstream. During dry periods in the urban area, low river flows are unable to dilute and flush out incoming liquid and solid wastes (Low and Balamurugam, 1991). In 1983, more than 1 percent of the Kuala Lumpur population had latrines directly over the river where faecal coliform accounts greatly exceeded WHO standards. Such a situation is unlikely to change while a large squatter population remains. Wastes from industry add to severe heavy metal contamination, mercury contents of the water and sediment on the Kelang estuary being 1.69 g/l and 0.2 mg/kg respectively (Law and Singh, 1987).

The overriding contaminant of water in the Kelang system is, however, sediment. Urban development on the deeply weathered granites and partially metamorphosed sediments of the Kuala Lumpur area exposes clayey and sandy regolith material to the erosive action of raindrops. Bare soil sites are easily rilled and gullied and steep cut slopes are subject to slumping and soil slippage. The private housing market suffers rises and falls, as in other major urban areas, with land developers clearing land in the hope that they will be able to sell houses in a rising market and often leaving construction bare and inactive when land prices drop. These bare sites are major sediment sources. Some gullies are now visible; they are up to 10 m deep and have developed in the last two or three years (Leigh, 1982). As the urban area has expanded, construction has moved on to steeper and steeper sites away from the city centre. Platforms for house construction are made by cut and fill operations leaving unconsolidated material which, if left unprotected, erodes readily and adds to the silt loads of streams. As headwaters become encumbered with sediment, material is carried into the major tributaries and the Kelang itself, raising the stream bed and inducing more frequent flash flooding.

The typical evolution of a construction-affected tributary is for it to alter from a narrow, deep winding stream to a wide shallow braided stream to cope with higher peak discharges and peak sediment concentrations (Douglas, 1978, 1985). Such changes produce severe channel modifications downstream, causing scour around bridges that are too small to cope with increased flows and a great deal of bank erosion, often threatening riverine structure and frequently causing distress in squatter communities that have settled on flood plains because they have nowhere else to live.

Major widespread flooding in 1926 led to river regulation and channel widening in the 1930s and another flood in 1971 saw renewed channel enlargement during the 1980s. Each of these operations served to ensure the rapid passage of storm turnoff through the city centre, but further downstream, the high levels of water in the embanked and regulated main river caused swollen tributaries to back-up and flood adjacent premises and roads. The modern concrete-lined channel in the city centre has to be kept clear of sediment. Although built-up areas yield relatively little sediment, newly urbanizing tributaries still have yields of 1,750 to 2,283 tonnes/km^2/yr (Balamurugan, 1991). Such yields are over ten times those in the partially disturbed forest headwaters of the Kelang and indicate the off-site, downstream costs of rapid urbanization without sufficient concern for urban soil conservation.

The Sungai Segama, Borneo

The islands of Pacific Asia have suffered profound modification by the people's exploitation of tropical forests: by 1987 the island of Borneo alone accounted for almost 60 percent of the world's export trade in tropical hardwood timbers (Brookfield et al., 1990). The rapid selective commercial logging in the Malaysian states of Sabah and Sarawak and the combination of logging and land clearance in Kalimantan are having profound effects on rivers, at whose mouths large muddy plumes project forth into the waters of the surrounding seas. The impact of land disturbance is superimposed on relatively high natural erosion rates due to the low resistance to erosion offered by the Tertiary mudstones that occupy a large part of the sedimentary rock sequences that dominate Borneo's geologic structure. The muddiness of most Borneo rivers is not entirely a consequence of people's actions.

The Sungai Segama drains areas of undisturbed natural lowland dipterocarp forest and areas that have been selectively logged in the last twenty years. Detailed observations of small tributary streams have identified the intensity of natural erosion and the changes in sediment yield caused by logging (Douglas et al., 1990, 1992; Spencer et al., 1990).

Three stages of commercial logging in a 0.54 km^2 catchment in the upper Segama basin caused great changes in the sediment yield, with marked increases after initial logging road construction, a further increase after trees were removed for 37 m on either side of the road and an even bigger increase when selective logging of the remainder of the catchment was carried out. Immediately after logging, major storms evacuated 20 tonnes/km^2 in two hours, sediment concentrations remaining well over 1,000 mg/l for 120 to 180 minutes. After logging ceased, ground cover creepers quickly spread over most of the bare areas and vigorous regrowth of ground vegetation occurred. However, roadside erosion continued along the main logging truck routes while several abandoned log-dragging tracks became gullied, thereby increasing the drainage density and the speed with which storm runoff reached the river channels. Under natural forest less then 5 percent of the rainfall reaching the ground runs off as overland flow, while on abandoned logging tracks about 55 percent of rainfall runs off the surface. Such gullies continue to act as sediment sources long after logging has ceased. Storm flows also scour out some of the sediment that had built up on the channel bed and floodplain during logging activity and thus sediment yields from the logged catchment were still two to five times greater than those from a nearby natural catchment eighteen months after logging had ceased. With an estimated sediment yield of 1,650 tonnes/km^2/yr over the logging period, erosion rates in the affected parts of the Segama catchment approach those of some of the Chinese rivers affected by intense agricultural activity.

The net result of all the logging activity is that drainage networks are extended and new, long-lasting sediment sources are created. Forest roads and log-loading areas are frequently not blocked off by simple earth mounds to prevent rapid runoff, rill development and gully formation. Downstream, channels become aggraded and fine silt and sand cover many gravel and boulder bars. Channel widening and shallowing may occur, tending towards the type of metamorphosis seen in the urban channels in Kuala Lumpur. Eye-witness accounts tell of so much sediment being deposited by floods on lowland paddy fields that the land has built up almost to the level of the distributary channels of irrigation systems, reducing the ability of water to flow under gravity to all parts of the rice-growing area. A high off-site cost of logging is being paid by people and communities that in no way benefit from the logging activity. The problem, like those of the loess plateau of the Huang He or the urban subdivisions of Kuala Lumpur, can be greatly reduced by preventing the sediment from leaving the logging site by simple, low-cost earthworks. If commercial forestry is to be sustainable and environmentally acceptable, such conservation measures, already the norm in the tropical forests of Queensland, will have to be adopted and enforced in all timber concessions.

The Agno River, Luzon, Philippines

The Agno River drains 13,900 km^2 of mountain ranges and alluvial plain inhabited by 3.1 million people in the western part of central Luzon. The mean annual rainfall is 2,208 mm and the depth of runoff is 1,959 mm. Floodplains covering 1,810 km^2 of the northeastern part of the basin are often inundated, affecting up to 1.5 million people. Much of the flooding is through breaches in a dike system that has become increasingly vulnerable to erosive floodwaters. Unregulated development on the floodplain has reduced channel capacities while erosion on the surrounding hillslopes has added to the sediment load. Urban development is competing with irrigation in demand for additional water (Briones, 1991).

The Agno Basin catchments are suffering from severe land degradation, with particular problems caused by tailings from copper and gold mines that have been silting up channels and floodplains. Erosion control measures have not been as successful as planned, despite many executive orders and presidential decrees concerning the management of the upland zones of the Agno Basin. Indeed, the combination of a plethora of orders and ineffectual government supervision and administration are seen as major factors in the continuing land degradation (Briones, 1991). The lack of overall basin planning, and the conflicting attitudes of the various authorities concerned with water has now been recognized by the Philippine National Water Resources Council and a new policy encouraging conservation, development and optimal utilization of water is being put into action.

Conclusions

Population growth and increasing industrial activity to meet the needs of a growing international trade and local middle class have placed increasing demands on water and land resources. Achieving a balanced multi-purpose use of water in Pacific Asia requires more and more comprehensive river basin planning with greater attention to the role of local communities and also requires individual enterprises and groups to take increasing responsibility for their actions. No longer can any land user consider the land a free good to be exploited at will without regard for the consequences. Responsibility for good husbandry of the land in the widest sense must be shared through all levels of society, from individual land holder or land user right through to governments. As the countries of Pacific Asia become increasingly industrialized and urbanized, freedom from environmental hazards, such as flooding and landsliding will become taken for granted as will the availability of good quality, safe drinking water and adequate disposal of used polluted waste water.

Water and land just cannot be taken for granted. These aspects of the living environment have to be at the forefront of all planning and development exercises. The tremendous effort needed in the small, but excessively crowded, territory of Hong Kong to cope with geotechnical mass movement problems in a densely urbanized area and the detailed Japanese planning to cope with earthquakes and related hazards indicate the scale of investigation and research that is needed for safe urban development and sustainable rural production in Pacific Asia. Only by adequate environmental understanding and geographical awareness by the educated public will there be sufficient popular pressure for attention to these matters by national authorities. Pacific Asia thus faces a major challenge for safeguarding its rivers and water resources. The techniques are available, all that is needed is the will to diffuse and adopt them.

REFERENCES

Aki, A. and R. Berthelot (1974). "Hydrology of Humid Tropical Asia." In *Natural Resources of Humid Tropical Asia.* edited by UNESCO. Paris: UNESCO, pp. 145–158.

Balamurugan, G. (1991). "Some Characteristics of Sediment Transport in the Sungai Kelang Basin, Malaysia." *Journal of the Institution of Engineers, Malaysia*, 48, pp. 31–52.

Briones, N. D. (1991). "Agno River Basins, Luzon, Philippines." In *Approaches to Integrated Water Resources Management in Humid Tropical and Semiarid Developing Countries*, edited by M. M. Hufschmidt and J. Kindler. Paris: UNESCO, pp. 129–161.

Brookfield, H., F. J. Lian, K. S. Low and L. Potter (1990). "Borneo and the Malay Peninsula." In *The Earth as Transformed by Human Action*, edited by B. L. Turner II, W. C. Clark, R. W. Kates, J. F. Richards, J. T. Mathews and W. B. Meyer. Cambridge: Cambridge University Press, pp. 495–512.

Chen Zhizai (1985). "China's Water Resources and Its Utilization." *Geojournal*, 10, pp. 167–171.

Cheng Xuemin (1989). "Design Criteria for Flood Discharge at China's Hydro Schemes." *International Water Power and Dam Construction*, 41 (4), pp. 14–17.

Derbyshire, E. (1990). "Loess and the Loess Plateau of North China." In *The Geography of Contemporary China: The Impact of Deng Xiaoping's Decade*, edited by T. Cannon and A. Jenkins. London: Routledge, pp. 100–101.

Douglas, I. (1978). "The Impact of Urbanisation on Fluvial Geomorphology in the Humid Tropics." *Geo-Eco-Trop*, 2, pp. 229–242.

——— (1985). "Urban Sedimentology." *Progress in Physical Geography*, 9, pp. 255–280.

——— (1989). "Land Degradation, Soil Conservation and the Sediment Load of the Yellow River, China: Review and Assessment." *Land Degradation and Rehabilitation*, 1, pp. 141–151.

Douglas, I., A. T. Greer, T. Spencer, W. Sinun and Wong Wai-meng (1990). "The Impact of Commercial Logging on a Small Rain Forest Catchment in Ulu Segama, Sabah, Malaysia." *International Association of Hydrological Sciences Publication*, 192, pp. 165–173.

Douglas, I., T. Greer, Wong Wai-meng, Kawi Bidin, Waidi Sinun and T. Spencer (1992). "Controls of Sediment Discharge in Undisturbed and Logged Tropical Rain Forest Streams." Proceedings of the Fifth International Symposium on River Sedimentation (in the press).

Fryer, D. W. (1970). *Emerging South-East Asia*. London: Philip.

Gu Hengyue and I. Douglas (1989). "Spatial and Temporal Dynamics of Land Degradation and Fluvial Erosion in the Middle and Upper Yangtze Basin, China." *Land Degradation & Rehabilitation*, 1, pp. 217–235.

Huang Bingwei (1988). "River Conservancy and Agricultural Development of the North China Plains and Loess Highlands: Strategies and Research." *Great Plains Quarterly*, 6, pp. 218–224.

Hufscmidt, M. M. and J. Kindler (1991). *Approaches to Integrated Water Resources Management in Humid Tropical and Arid and Semi Arid Zones in Developing Countries*. Paris: UNESCO.

Jiang Deqi, Qi Leidi and Tan Jiesheng (1981). "Soil Erosion and Conservation in the Wuding River Valley, China." In *Soil Conservation: Problems and Prospects*, edited by P. C. Morgan. Chichester: Wiley, pp. 461–479.

Law, A. T. and A. Singh (1987). "Distribution of Mercury in the Kelang Estuary." *Pertanika*, 10, pp. 175–181.

Leigh, C. H. (1982). "Urban Development and Soil Erosion in Kuala Lumpur, Malaysia." *Journal of Environmental Management*, 15, pp. 35–45.

Li, J. and K. Cheng (1987). "The Erosion Process in the Middle and Upper Reaches of the Yangzi River." *International Association of Hydrological Science Publication*, 165, pp. 483–487.

Li Tianchi and Wan Shumin (1989). "Landslide Hazards Regions in the Middle River Valley of the Chang Jiang." *Mountain Research*, 6, pp. 8–10.

Low Kwai-sim and G. Balamurugam (1991). "Urbanization and Urban Water Problems in Southeast Asia: A Case of Unsustainable Development." *Journal of Environmental Management*, 32, pp. 195–209.

McNeeely, J. A. and P. S. Wachtel (1988). *Soul of the Tiger: Searching for Nature's Answers in Exotic Southeast Asia*. New York: Doubleday.

Mekvichai, B., D. Foster, S. Chomchan and P. Kritiporn (1990). *Urbanization and Environment: Managing the Conflict*. Research Report No. 6. Bangkok: Development Research Institute Foundation.

Pan Qingshen, Zeng Jingxian, Yu Wenchen, Li Chunan, Wang Zhikun and Zhou Kaiping (1983). "Experiences in Flood Prevention and Control in China." *United Nations Department of Technical Cooperation in Development Natural Resources/Water Series*, 11, pp. 35–105.

Peetanonchai, B. (1990). "The Impact of Water Resources Development in the Upper Basin on the Inflow of the Downstream Reservoir." Paper presented at the UNESCO Regional Workshop on Watershed Management and Development, Kuala Lumpur, 19–23 February, 21 pp.

Sethaputra, S., T. Panayotou and V. Wangwacharakul (1990). *Water Shortages: Managing Demand to Expand Supply*. Research Report No. 3. Bangkok: Development Research Institute Foundation.

Sewell, W.R.D. (1966). "Mekong River Plan: A Challenge in International Cooperation." *Water Power*, 18, pp. 179–184 and 239–247.

Spencer, T., I. Douglas, T. Greer and W. Sinun (1990). "Vegetation and Fluvial Geomorphic Processes in South-east Asian Tropical Rain Forests." In *Vegetation and Erosion*, edited by J. B. Thornes. Chichester: Wiley, pp. 451–469.

State Commission of Science and Technology (SSTC). Ministry of Geology and Mineral Resources, PRC (1988). *Landslides and Rockfalls of the Yangtze Gorges*. Beijing: Geological Publishing House.

Takaya, Y. (1987). *Agricultural Development of a Tropical Delta: A Study of the Chao Phraya Delta*. Monographs of the Center for Southeast Asian Studies, Kyoto University, 17. Honolulu: University of Hawaii Press.

Thomson, R. L. (Chief) (1968). *Land Reform Vietnam. Pilot Drainage and Irrigation Project Tranh Quoi, An Giang Province Feasibility Study*. Washington, D.C.: Department of the Army, Engineer Agency for Resources Inventories, Appendix A.

Volker, A. (1983). "Rivers of Southeast Asia: Their Regime, Utilization and Regulation." *International Association of Hydrological Sciences Publication*, 140,   pp. 127–138.

Wei Zhongyi and Zhao Chunian (1983). "Natural Conditions in the Proposed Water Transfer Region." In *Long Distance Water Transfer: A Chinese Case Study and International Experiences*, edited by A. K. Biswas, Dakang Zuo, D. E. Nickum and Changming Liu. Dublin: Tycooly, pp. 97–125.

White, G. F. (1964). "Vietnam: the Fourth Course." *Bulletin of the Atomic Scientists*, 20 (10), pp. 6–10.

Witthawatchutikul, P. and N. Tangtham (1990). "Rural Community Watershed: Another Approach in Watershed Management for Thailand." Paper presented at the UNESCO Regional Workshop on Watershed Management and Development, Kuala Lumpur, 19–23 February, 10 pp.

Xi Chengfan (1990). "Better Land Use and Reclamation of the Red Soil Hilly Region of Southern China." *Geojournal*, 20, pp. 365–368.

Yuan Jiang. "Taming Floods." *World Water and Environmental Engineer*, November, p. 45.

Zeng Qinghua and Zhou Wenhao (1989). "Soil Erosion in the Yellow River Basin and Its Impacts on Reservoir Sedimentation and the Lower Yellow River." *International Association of Hydrological Sciences Publication*, 184, pp. 123–130.

Zhang Xinbao, Li Shaolong, Wang Chenghua, Tan Wanpei, Zhao Qingchang, Zhang Yiyun, Yan Mei Qiong, Liu Yalun, Jiang Jingjang, Xiao Jule and Zhou Jie (1989). "Use of Caesium 137 Measurements to Investigate Erosion of Sediment Sources within a Small Drainage Basin in the Loess Plateau of China." *Hydrological Processes*, 3, pp. 317–323.

Zhu Hejian (1990). "The Present Sate and Development Orientation of Land Utilization in Mountainous Red Earth Regions of China — Take Fujian Province." *Geojournal*, 20, pp. 375–379.

Zuo Dakang and Zhang Peiyuan (1990). "The Huang-Huai-Hai Plain." In *The Earth as Transformed by Human Action*, edited by B. L. Turner II, W. C. Clark, R. W. Kates, J. F. Richards, J. T. Mathews and W. B. Meyer. Cambridge: Cambridge University Press, pp. 473–477.

CHAPTER SEVEN

Urbanization and Water Resources Management in ASEAN Countries towards the Year 2000

Kwai-sim Low
Professor, Department of Geography, University of Malaya, Kualu Lumpur, Malaysia

Introduction

The Association of South East Asian Nations (ASEAN), lying within the humid tropics, consists of a group of rapidly developing countries, namely Brunei Darussalam, Indonesia, Malaysia, the Philippines, Singapore and Thailand. Recent years of double-digit economic growth have produced very rapid environmental transformation in these countries. The major feature of this transformation was the conversion of forests to agricultural and urban lands on a scale that was described as a new "great age of clearance" (Brookfield, 1988). The forces behind such transformation have been a rapid growth of population in these countries and a need to develop resources for urbanization and industrialization.

ASEAN countries today are densely populated and population growth is rapid and accelerating. In 1985 these countries registered an estimated population of 395 million and this is expected to reach 525 million by the year 2000. Population growth rates vary with the countries and range from 1.09 percent in Singapore to 2.25 percent in the Philippines (Table 7.1) compared to an average global growth rate of 1.8 percent between 1980 and 1990 (United Nations, 1978) and 0.6–0.7 percent in developed countries (Maione, 1988).

Urban population growth rates are very much higher, averaging 4.0 percent (excluding Singapore and Brunei), and reflect a massive rural-urban

Table 7.1: Population Statistics of Southeast Asia

	Indonesia	Malaysia	Philippines	Thailand	Singapore	Global
Population 1985	166.4	15.6	54.5	51.4	2.6	4836.7
(Millions) 2000	222.4	20.5	74.1	65.5	3.0	6161.8
Population Density Persons/sq km	87.0	47.0	182.0	100.0	4404.0	36.0
Percent urban pop. growth rate	25.3	38.2	39.6	19.8	100	41.0
Total	1.74	2.12	2.25	1.61	1.09	1.63
Urban	4.3	4.2	3.6	4.3	1.09	2.4
Rural	0.8	0.8	1.3	0.9	—	1.1
Median age	20.2	20.7	19.4	21	27.2	23.5
Life expectancy	56.0	68.6	63.5	64.2	72.8	61.1
Infant mortality (per 1000)	74	26	45	39	9	71
Age 15–64 (%)	57.7	58.4	56.1	60.1	70.4	60.7
GNP (US$)	530	2,000	580	800	7,420	—

migration brought about by a prolonged economic boom since the early 1960s. Thus, while in 1950, there were only two cities, Jakarta and Manila, that had populations of more than 1 million, by 1980 there were more than six such cities (Table 7.2). It is also estimated that by the year 2000 there will be at least ten cities of over 1 million people. Three of the largest cities, Bangkok, Jakarta and Manila, are expected to grow into megacities, each projected to have over 10 million people with Jakarta expected to have about 17 million comparable to the total population of Malaysia today.

The primacy of these cities is well documented (McGee, 1967; Pryor, 1979) and together with other national capitals such as Kuala Lumpur, they hold the keys to economic development. All have important economic functions, whether commercial, financial or industrial. Hence they are also large consumers. For example, Bangkok, built on the alluvial deposits of the Chao Phraya River, with a population of nearly 5 million people is at least fifty times larger than the next largest city, Chiangmai, and possesses almost 80 percent of all the telephones, 50 percent of the motor vehicles and consumes over 80 percent of the electricity and potable water supply in Thailand (Phantumvanit and Liengcharensit, 1989). Metropolitan Manila

**Table 7.2: Southeast Asian Cities with Population of over 1 Million People
(adopted from Brunn & Williams, 1983)**

Cities	Population (in thousands)		
	1950	1980	2000
Manila	1,532	5,593	12,683
Singapore	484	2,260	3,029
Bangkok	964	4,258	11,030
Kuala Lumpur	241	978	1,766
Jakarta	1,565	7,191	16,933
Surabaya	679	2,273	5,038
Bandung	511	1,836	4,126
Semarang	371	893	1,858
Medan	245	989	2,270
Palembang	277	859	1,876

has 8 million people or 30 percent of the total urban population in the Philippines settled within an area of 636 km^2. The urban population congestion has caused serious shortages in amenities such as water and electricity (Jimenez and Velasquez, 1989). Similarly, Kuala Lumpur, although not as definite an example of primacy as Bangkok, Jakarta or Manila, contains the bulk of the commercial and institutional establishments in Malaysia. These problems are further compounded by intense competition for the already limited natural resources by the industry, agriculture, housing and tourism sectors. Phantumvanit stressed in a 1990 report that:

The sustainability of growth could be undermined if resources degradation, poverty and resource conflicts persist for long. Sustainability calls for the maintenance of the productive base and for the enhancement of both society's and nature's resilience. Yet advancing deforestation, a growing income gap and proliferating natural resource conflicts serve to undermine this....

Across this commonality of population pressure and resources degradation, the management of water resources is the most significant. The aim of this paper is to examine some of the underlying issues of water resources management in the ASEAN countries and what strategies these countries adopt to overcome them.

Identification of Problems and Issues in Water Resources Development

In ASEAN countries, the management of water resources can be discussed within the context of the development of available water resources and pollution of these resources caused basically by activities aimed at higher economic development. While priority has been accorded to the development of the water resources sector to meet the requirements for domestic, industrial and agricultural demands as well as for hydropower development, the threat of pollution of water sources is increasing due to population growth, the rapid rate of urbanization and industrialization as well as the inadequate provision of sanitary facilities in these countries.

A. Water Resources Development

Development of surface water as the major source of raw water supply continues to be the main focus of national water agencies since surface runoff constitutes a high percentage of the total annual rainfall. In Malaysia, surface runoff constitutes about 56 percent of the annual total rainfall, estimated to be 990 billion cubic metres (bcm), while groundwater accounts for only 6 percent. Due to the uneven distribution of surface water and the need to increase the availability of water, dams are constructed to store surplus water during wet periods. Hence, the development of multi-purpose dams, especially in water-stress regions, and the implementation of inter-basin and inter-state water transfers from water surplus to water-deficit areas are given due priority. Now in Malaysia, there are 54 dams in operations with a total live capacity of 12 bcm that is available to meet the demand of the various users (Sixth Malaysia Plan, 1991–1995). Of these, eleven were developed for hydropower while the remaining dams were for water supply, irrigation and flood mitigation. In addition, nine dams are at various stages of construction and seven still under feasibility study. The locations of these dams are shown in Figures 7.1 and 7.2.

While the water resources management situation is highly complex, water resources development in these countries is further hampered by certain inherent geographical characteristics such as climatic variability and the size of the river basins, both of which underpin water resources development efforts.

Figure 7.1: Location of Dams in Peninsular Malaysia

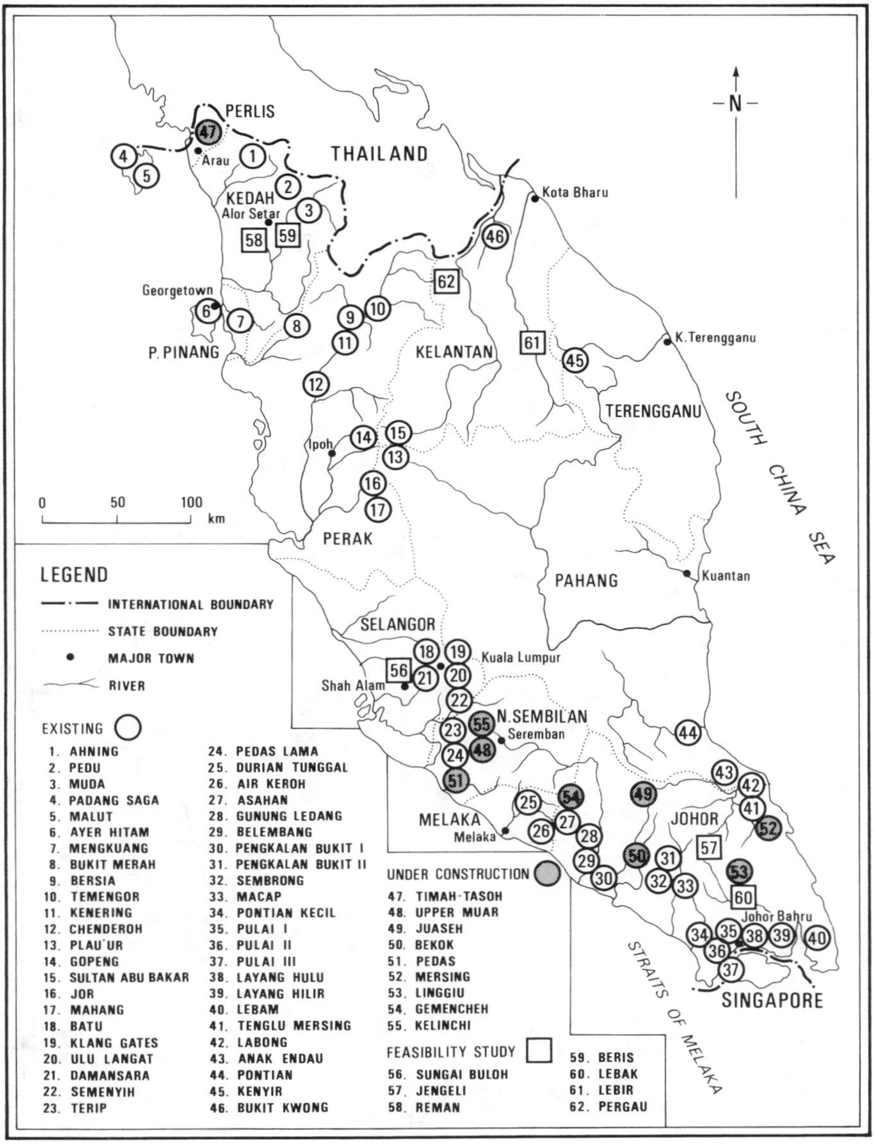
N
PERLIS
Arau
THAILAND
KEDAH
Alor Setar
Kota Bharu
Georgetown
P. PINANG
KELANTAN
K.Terengganu
TERENGGANU
SOUTH CHINA SEA
Ipoh
0 50 100 km
PERAK
PAHANG
Kuantan
SELANGOR
Kuala Lumpur
Shah Alam
N.SEMBILAN
Seremban
MELAKA
Melaka
JOHOR
Johor Bahru
SINGAPORE
STRAITS OF MELAKA
LEGEND
INTERNATIONAL BOUNDARY
STATE BOUNDARY
MAJOR TOWN
RIVER
EXISTING
1. AHNING
2. PEDU
3. MUDA
4. PADANG SAGA
5. MALUT
6. AYER HITAM
7. MENGKUANG
8. BUKIT MERAH
9. BERSIA
10. TEMENGOR
11. KENERING
12. CHENDEROH
13. PLAU'UR
14. GOPENG
15. SULTAN ABU BAKAR
16. JOR
17. MAHANG
18. BATU
19. KLANG GATES
20. ULU LANGAT
21. DAMANSARA
22. SEMENYIH
23. TERIP
24. PEDAS LAMA
25. DURIAN TUNGGAL
26. AIR KEROH
27. ASAHAN
28. GUNUNG LEDANG
29. BELEMBANG
30. PENGKALAN BUKIT I
31. PENGKALAN BUKIT II
32. SEMBRONG
33. MACAP
34. PONTIAN KECIL
35. PULAI I
36. PULAI II
37. PULAI III
38. LAYANG HULU
39. LAYANG HILIR
40. LEBAM
41. TENGLU MERSING
42. LABONG
43. ANAK ENDAU
44. PONTIAN
45. KENYIR
46. BUKIT KWONG
UNDER CONSTRUCTION
47. TIMAH-TASOH
48. UPPER MUAR
49. JUASEH
50. BEKOK
51. PEDAS
52. MERSING
53. LINGGIU
54. GEMENCHEH
55. KELINCHI
FEASIBILITY STUDY
56. SUNGAI BULOH
57. JENGELI
58. REMAN
59. BERIS
60. LEBAK
61. LEBIR
62. PERGAU

Figure 7.2: Location of Dams in Sabah and Sarawak

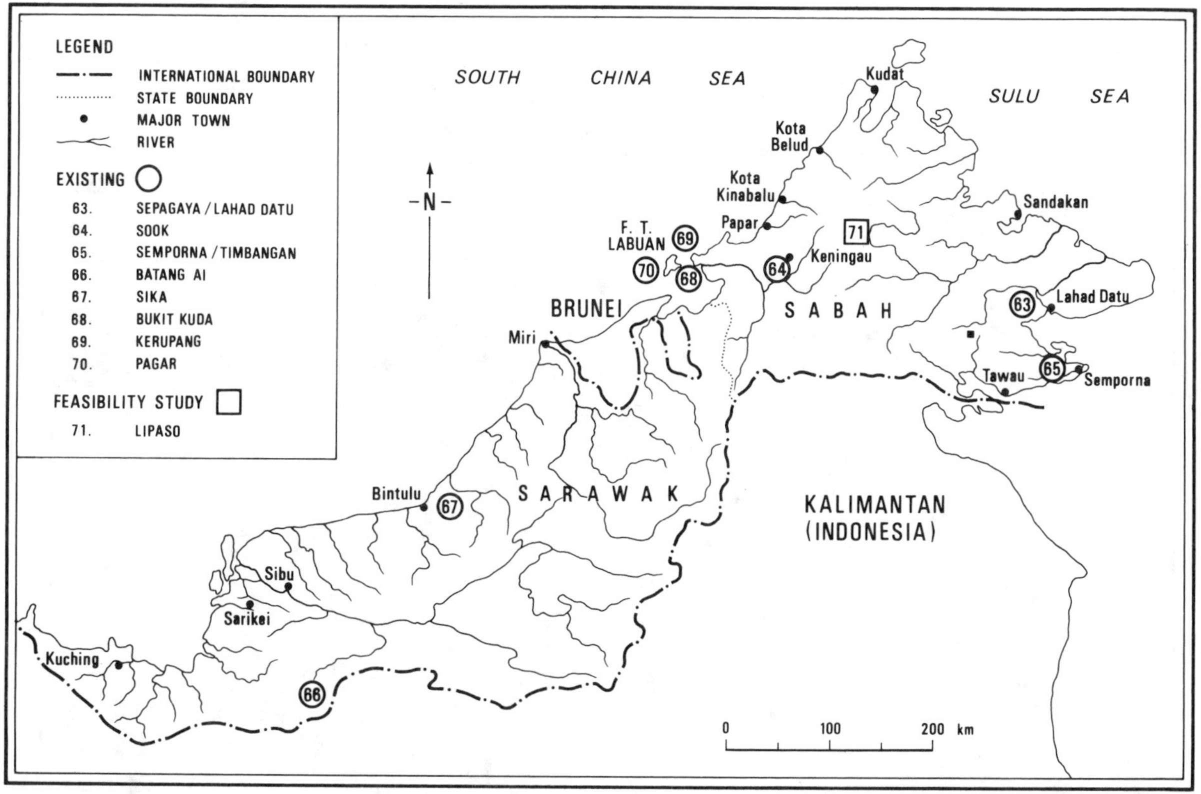

LEGEND

— · — · INTERNATIONAL BOUNDARY
· · · · · STATE BOUNDARY
● MAJOR TOWN
⋏ RIVER

EXISTING ◯

63. SEPAGAYA / LAHAD DATU
64. SOOK
65. SEMPORNA / TIMBANGAN
66. BATANG AI
67. SIKA
68. BUKIT KUDA
69. KERUPANG
70. PAGAR

FEASIBILITY STUDY ☐

71. LIPASO

B. Climatic Variability

All the major urban cities in ASEAN lie entirely within 10° north and south of the equator and, accepting the definition of Chang & Lau (1983), are within the humid tropics which will have a minimum of 4 1/2 wet months in a year. However, some of the urban centres obtain their water from dams and reservoirs located in the upper parts of the watersheds and even sometimes outside the humid tropics, such as the headwaters of the Chao Phraya in Thailand. Any climatic variabilities in these areas will therefore have severe implications on supplies downstream. Climatic variabilities are known frequently to occur in the ASEAN region. The average annual rainfalls range from 1,000 mm to as high as 4,000 mm with marked seasonal concentrations (ACST, 1982). Areas in the higher latitudes such as northern Thailand that can be classified as sub-equatorial (though still within the humid tropics) experience more seasonality with 50 percent of the annual rainfall occurring in two to three months and water stress during the remainder of the year.

Furthermore, the region is affected by the Northeast and Southwest monsoons, the former occurring between late October and early January, the latter between May to September. Depending on the locations of the countries, heavy rainfalls occur with intervening relatively dry months. For example, during the Northeast monsoons, the equatorial trough lies just north of the equator between longitudes 60°E and 160°E. Cyclonic vortices often develop in this trough over the South China Sea because of the interactions of air-sea mixing causing conditional instability. These disturbances migrate south westwards picking up additional moisture during their long trip across the South China Sea and deposit heavy rain to the east coasts of Peninsular Malaysia, Sabah and Sarawak and the eastern regions of Thailand and Kalimantan. The Southwest monsoon on the other hand, occurring between May to September, brings heavy rains to the west coasts of Sumatra, Java and west Peninsular Malaysia. The strong influence of these two monsoons causes two hydrological phenomena: floods and droughts. Floods, due to the concentration of rain in a short period of time are more common than droughts. Prolonged droughts, however, have been known to occur regularly, especially when intensified by the reversal of the Walker circulation in the periodic El-Nino/Southern Oscillation (ENSO). Taking the average evapotranspiration rates as constant, about 4–5 mm/day or 120–150 mm/month, many parts of the region receive rainfall less than this amount for four to five months in a year. In Kuala Lumpur, for example, 40–50 percent of its monthly rainfalls are below 150 mm. In Thailand, water deficits are even higher in the eastern and northern regions during the inter-monsoonal months. Witthawatchutikul (1988) showed the persistence of water deficits between December and April and how they affect the yields of root crops (cassava) in the Rayong Watershed in eastern Thailand.

On the other hand, flood-causing rainstorms with maximum twenty-four hour rainfall exceeding 600 mm have been recorded in all major cities in ASEAN. Similarly, maximum monthly rainfall totals of 2,000 mm have also been recorded in all these cities except Singapore. Thus, climatic variability is a major underlying causative factor of water problems in the humid tropical cities.

C. Sizes of River Basins and Location of Urban Centres

Another major difficulty in developing water resources in ASEAN is the size of their river basins. A large proportion of the highly populated land is either on small or medium sized islands scattered throughout the region, with the exception of Thailand. This type of islandic landmass does not give rise to large river basins. The largest river basin is the Chao Phraya Basin with an area of about 120,000 km^2. The largest basins in Peninsular Malaysia, Indonesia (excluding Kalimantan) and the Philippines are in the range of 20,000–50,000 km^2 but there are only six of these. Paradoxically most urban centres are located within very small river basins, whose sizes do not exceed 2,000 km^2. The sizes of these basins pose several problems. First, urban activities often impose pollutants and sediment loads into the river systems which, because of their small sizes, do not have the capacity to assimilate and dilute. Second, the volume of water available is relatively small (because of the small catchment area with minimal natural storage) and hence, when the water is polluted, it effectively reduces the net amount available for use. Furthermore, the relief-length ratios exhibited in the river basins are usually high and under the humid tropical conditions with highly weathered soils, the delivery of sediments into the river network is very efficient thus constantly polluting the water sources.

Kuala Lumpur is a good example. The city is located in the heart of the Kelang River Basin with a catchment area of about 1,200 km^2. Due to heavy demands for potable water, water in the two dams upstream is never released to compensate downstream flow. This has in many ways magnified the water pollution situation. Only a few kilometers downstream of the dams, extremely low flows in the river, especially during the dry seasons in February and July, are unable to dilute and flush the incoming effluents generated by the urban population and their activities, and the river has been transformed into an open sewer. In addition, housing development and road construction in the foothills bordering the river valley have brought an average of 500 tonnes/km^2/yr of sediment downstream of the city of Kuala Lumpur. A large proportion of the potable water has therefore to be brought into the city by inter-basin transfers from the nearby Semenyih River, which again will have to be augmented by the year 2000 by other river basins further away to meet the rapidly growing water demands of the urban population. About 75−85 percent of the clean water consumed is returned to the rivers in a polluted state.

Such management of water resources for urban areas is not unique in the large cities of ASEAN due to the relatively small river basins. In areas where there is an excess of water as in the island of Borneo, the demand is minimal due to the low population density. The distribution of population in Sarawak or Kalimantan, for example, is hardly more than 5 persons/km^2, and hence does not justify the cost of developing large water resources projects unless hydro-electricity is also tapped. In fact, it is hydro-electricity rather than water supply that overrides most considerations to develop the water resources in the upper reaches of such river basins in this area. This certainly is the case in the Batang Ai Dam in Sarawak where hydro-electricity is fed onto the national electricity grid to supply the city of Kuching, the capital of Sarawak, while potable water supply for the city is obtained from a number of tributaries through direct river abstraction and not from the dam.

Thailand is an exception. The river basins in Thailand are large, but receive the lowest annual rainfalls compared to the other countries in the region. The largest river, Chao Phraya, has abundant water, but the major usage is for agriculture. The withdrawal of water for irrigation has increased the fluctuations on the supply side of the water balance and the released water is often contaminated with fertilizers and pesticides. In both cases, the problem is not simply to deduct consumptive use from runoff. It is much more complex because it is related to the land use pattern in the river basins where generally urban enclaves bear the brunt of the problems because of their locations downstream. Thus, Bangkok relies more on groundwater than most other cities in the region, and although this has often been cited as contributing to land subsidence in the city, it is the only solution. In the last decade, Bangkok has resorted to inter-basin transfers of water, especially from the hilly Kanchanaburi Province southwest of Bangkok. Here again, hydro-electricity takes priority over water supply, although the objective of augmenting potable water to Bangkok has been met to a certain extent. There have also been suggestions made that water could be transferred from the Mekong into the Chao Phraya as it has been estimated that the former has an excess of about 950 MGD of water (Phantumvanit & Liengcharensit, 1989). This again reflects the complexity of water management in the years to come because inter-basin transfers, especially across political boundaries, are often delicate issues.

Pollution of Water Resources

In ASEAN, water resource management now, and towards the year 2000, has to take into consideration a series of options to abate a multitude of water problems that include water pollution, sewage disposal, effluent discharges into water courses, sedimentation and floods. The section below will enumerate some of these major problems and how they affect the water courses and the efficiency of the mitigating measures.

A. Water Pollution

Water pollution forms part of the first category of problems caused by activities aimed at economic development. Water pollution can be defined as "anything causing or inducing objectionable conditions in any water course and affecting adversely any use, or uses, to which the water may be put" (Klein, 1957). The word "uses" in this definition is particularly meaningful with respect to water pollution in the ASEAN urban centres where uses of rivers are diverse. The waters in the urban rivers are a source of drinking water, a conveyance for sewage disposal, a mode of transportation, a recreational spot, a source of food and more often than not, a rubbish dump. With ever progressive urban development and population pressure, many of these rivers are increasingly being polluted; they become turbid, septic and emit unbearable odours. Several rivers have even been classified as "biologically dead" where the dissolved oxygen content in the water is zero. Thailand's Chao Phraya River is nearly dead south of Bangkok and many types of fish and prawn life have disappeared from the lower stretch of the river. Coliform bacteria, originating in human waste, surpass acceptable limits even in the mid-sections of the river north of Bangkok. The major sources of water pollution are sewage effluent and untreated faecal matter from riverine residents, industrial effluent and untreated industrial wastes, domestic and industrial garbage, and sediment.

B. Sewage Disposal and Water Pollution

Water pollution by sewage is a universal problem and not confined to rivers running through large cities in the region. Sewage, if adequately treated and disposed of, poses very minimal pollution or health problems. However, sewage treatment and disposal require heavy capital outlay that cities like Bangkok, Jakarta, Manila and, to a certain extent, Kuala Lumpur, would rather spend on something yielding more immediate benefits. Thus, for example, in Bangkok in the early 1980s, only 60.8 percent of the sewage was treated, while the rest was discharged raw into vacant lands or into rivers and canals (Xoomsai, 1988). It is estimated that outside Bangkok, at least 40 percent of the untreated sewage ends up in rivers and canals (Table 7.3). In urban areas in Malaysia, more than 9 percent of the population have no sanitation facilities at all with most of them either using pit privies or latrines directly over rivers. Even in Kuala Lumpur, the largest and best kept city in Malaysia, more than 1 percent of its population in 1988 still used rivers, mainly the heavily polluted Kelang River, as a mode of sewage

Table 7.3: Methods of Waste Water Disposal in Bangkok
(adopted from Xoomsai, 1988)

Methods	Percentage of Population		
	Bangkok Metropolis	City Core	Outer Districts
Dumping into public sewers	60.8	75.1	13.8
Drainage into vacant land	5.0	3.2	4.1
Septic tank	1.0	0.7	3.8
Cesspool latrine or left on ground	13.1	7.2	31.9
Disposal into rivers or canals	18.2	12.5	44.5
Other means	1.9	1.3	1.9

disposal. In 1980 that faecal coliform counts in the Kelang River ranged from 113,000–160,000 per 100 ml (Law, 1980), which were extremely high compared to the WHO standard of 100 per 100 ml for bathing waters. In 1989, the coliform counts were still the same. The situation is similar in Jakarta where less than 75 percent of the population are served by some form of sanitation while the rest resort to habitual means of pit privies or water courses (Douglas, 1983).

The population of these cities cannot be blamed for pollution of the rivers because they have no choice. Neither can the sanitary engineers nor public work authorities be expected to take the blame because they usually work under tight budgetary and technical constraints. The development and management of sanitation facilities, or for that matter, any public facilities are directly related to the availability of funds. In nearly all cases, big cities are governed by local authorities with limited financial allocations. Hence, as long as funds are not forthcoming, the problem of water pollution will remain a major issue in the 21st century.

C. Industrial Growth and Water Pollution

The recent rapid growth of the manufacturing and processing industries has brought with it major problems in terms of water pollution. Although the economic impact of these industries is only of recent origin, the pollution caused by them has reached unacceptable proportions in many cities. During the early years of industrialization in Malaysia and Thailand in the 1960s and early 1970s, the environment was sidestepped in pursuit of economic growth. This has proved to be a costly decision. Many industries in Kuala Lumpur and Bangkok are now actually polluting the very rivers from which they abstract waters for their own use. Even though legislation has required industries to treat their wastes before discharging into rivers, the regulations were never complied with in the early 1970s when industrialization gathered momentum. It was only in the early 1980s when the governments came down hard with stringent standards and severe penalties that factories started treating their wastes.

The average BOD of water samples taken upstream and downstream of the industrial Shah Alam area in Malaysia, for example, showed a 30-fold increase after construction of the factories. The ecology of the river downstream of the area was dominated by pollution-resistant flora and fauna and there was little evidence of clear water species. In 1988, after a lapse of fifteen years, at which time the industrial estate had grown larger, the same place was sampled again and the BOD was found to be just as high (DOE, 1988). The pollution problem due to industrialization was reflected in the Philippines through the number of litigations pending since 1973 (Marlay, 1977).

D. Deforestation, Soil Erosion and Sedimentation

Sediments are the most serious pollutants in most of the rivers in ASEAN. Rapid urbanization in the past two decades has resulted in clearance of large areas of forests, particularly in the urban fringes. Increasing population, demands for employment, housing and food have resulted in development in environmentally sensitive areas in and around large cities such as Kuala Lumpur, Bangkok, Manila and Jakarta.

During the 1980s Thailand's forest were being destroyed at a rate only surpassed in Asia by Nepal. Ecologists say the country now only has about 18 percent forest cover, including degraded areas in official forests. Forest destruction has caused a fall in water supplies around deforested water-sheds and, while a ban on logging slowed forest encroachment, some 8 million people live illegally in reserve forests (FEER, 1991).

Suspended sediment loads of rivers flowing through these cities are very high. Intensively cultivated river basins in Java and the Philippines con-tribute large volumes of sediments in the rivers. The Tjatjaban and Tjeloetoeng rivers in Java were reported to carry suspended loads of 2,500 and 1,350 $m^3/km^2/year$ (Douglas, 1978). The tributaries of the Kelang River in Kuala Lumpur carry an estimated suspended sediment loads of 250–550 $m^3/km^2/year$. The sediments are often deposited on flat flood plains near the city, resulting in raised river beds and frequent floods. Hyper-concentrations of sediment have been reported in the Kelang River following land clearance. Douglas (1978) recorded a maximum concentra-tion of 81,230 mg/l following a 75 mm rain that fell in forty-five minutes in Air Batu River where land was being cleared for housing construction. Suspended sediment concentrations above 10,000 mg/l following periods of heavy rainfall are common in many urban rivers in Malaysia. This situation is similar in Manila and Jakarta. Clearing of urban fringes has caused excessive sediment delivery into the rivers and canals. The canals in Jakarta that were meant to carry sewage and flood waters are now almost useless for flood protection. It is also not uncommon for urban rivers in the

Philippines and Indonesia to carry suspended sediment concentrations of above 5,000 mg/l during high flows.

Water Resources Management

There have been strong lobbies for "sustainable development" in recent years to ensure that the water resource is available in the quantity and quality that is required. Although this has been strongly advocated as a form of management policy option in the ASEAN countries, the techniques used have not been perfected. One of the major setbacks has been financial, rather than technical constraints. For example, it is only in 1989 that a central sewage system has been completed in Kuala Lumpur, and even then it serves only half the city.

Although it has not yet come to the stage where the shortage of water could impose limits on population growth and economic expansion as in central Africa, nevertheless the signs are ominous. Two major developments will be very important in the future: water equity and water pricing. These two developments will form the fundamental issues in the 21st century and will be elaborated below.

Water equity is related to the availability of water on a per capita basis. At present, population growth is accelerating and its growth rates are not declining. In fact, various development policies in ASEAN have implications that will increase rather than decrease growth rates. This means that there will be a less equitable share of water per capita if there are no further long term development plans to increase water supply. Notwithstanding, there is already a shortage of water to meet agricultural and industrial demands. ASEAN countries being located in the fastest growing areas of Pacific Asia will also require more water per capita unit of goods produced when economic expansion is implemented. Growth in irrigation-intensive farming, soaring water consumption by industry, households and the tourism industry and the growing need of water for power generation, have led to tension over water resources. Large enterprises are at present finding it extremely difficult to locate their industries in designated industrial locations because of the shortage of water, and have resorted to ground-water supplies to augment their requirements. In Bangkok, the extraction of groundwater has caused sea water to seep into wells 20 km from the coast. Equitable distribution of water will therefore become very important in future. Changing patterns of population consumption, affluence and agricultural patterns of production will also mean a higher demand for water. Existing water resource development has not kept pace with the demands and the gap keeps widening every day. The future scenario will be one of an acute shortage of water based on population growth, climatic variability and the size of the river basins. Water resource development plans have therefore to be instituted now to narrow the gap and the projected demands. The future economic growth in each country will be highly dependent on a good supply of water.

Related to the above, water pricing will become a more important policy and management issue in the future. Water development for potable, agricultural and industrial uses requires large capital expenditures that will put a dent in a large part of the total national budgets. The internal rate of return on these costs is often low because water is seen partly as a social cost. Therefore, water pricing is kept artificially low for the consumers, with the government bearing the heavy burden of subsidizing the cost. There are already signs that many governments are not able to subsidize water to the consumers even with soft loans from World Bank or other financial instruments. Under such circumstances, there will definitely be an increase in water cost to consumers. In Malaysia there are plans to privatize more water supply projects and these will involve the implementation of commercial accounting systems and increasing efficiency in revenue collection. In addition, studies will be undertaken on these projects to ensure that the affordability for consumers and competitiveness of industrial users will be safeguarded. The question is the amount that the government is prepared to subsidize and the consumers are prepared to pay.

Questions of equitable distribution and water pricing will be more prevalent in countries that share common political and watershed boundaries. For example, Singapore, which will have a water shortage problem, is willing to develop and buy water from Peninsular Malaysia on a permanent basis. Their joint effort with the Johore Government to develop the Linggiu Dam is one of the ways to increase and ensure a steady supply of water to the country. Thailand, Cambodia, Laos and Vietnam will also have common grounds for discussion in future over the development of the Mekong river basin. Such efforts will not only be related to water distribution rights and pricing but also the issues relating to using of the waterways for fishing and transportation, control of effluent discharge and pollution.

The latter is very important since it will reduce the amount of water for potable use and increase the cost of development. Other countries which do not share common boundaries or watersheds will also see a reduction in freshwater supply due to pollution unless stringent standards and enforcement are effected to control effluent discharges into the watercourses. Gazettement for preservation of the upland areas for water catchments is very successful in Malaysia but not in the Philippines where such areas are used for farming and settlements. In the final analysis, less supply can only mean higher cost to the consumers and a less equitable share to those unable to pay since many countries are also thinking of privatizing the development and distribution of water to reduce the financial burden of the government.

A water management scenario will not be complete without mentioning the efforts of governments to control water pollution through river rehabilitation programmes. Such river rehabilitation programmes are designed essentially to control water pollution through landuse planning by resiting polluting factories and squatters away from river banks, deepening and realigning channels and relocating sewage effluent outfalls, all of which are intended to reverse pollution. The cost is often very high, as seen in the cleaning of the Kallang River in Singapore (or even the River Thames in England). Given the limited financial resources in the region, such efforts may be thwarted and the problem of pollution will persist in future. Moreover, environmental problems are difficult to control because of low levels of literacy and the general lack of media coverage, political will, and community participation. Given this scenario and the rapid pace of industrial and economic development in these countries, the urban water problem can only escalate in the future unless serious water resources planning and management are given their due attention.

Conclusion

The experiences of ASEAN cities point to the universal problems associated with the provision of an adequate supply of quality municipal water to a rapidly growing population. In the past many municipal water agencies have operated on marginal financial and manpower resources, and, because of the massive investments involved in water supply infrastructure development, population growth has outstripped water resources development. Projected demands of municipal water in these countries are expected to increase at a rate higher than urban population growth by the year 2000. This demand will undermine the capacity of the national water authorities to provide sustainable water supplies of the quantity and quality required, but the challenge will have to be met. Planning will play a major role in ensuring an adequate water supply for the cities. Unfortunately, existing administrative systems have not set up institutions within the broader framework covering their relationships with the overall processes involved in an integrated urban and water resources management systems. In this respect, regional and national planning must supersede local planning as cities are increasingly being forced to expand their sources of water supply. Moreover, water resources planning of the future will have to adopt a more imaginative approach than has been the case in the past where crisis management seems to be the order of the day. A more realistic financial and accounting system for cost recovery of investments expended will have to be established to help enhancing the overall performance of the sector. It is therefore expected that pricing and equity will play a more important role in the future. The outlook for water for the cities should be viewed with cautious optimism. Though rapid economic, social and political changes are taking place in these countries that will strain existing water supply systems, the water demands can be met through a coordinated water resources planning approach that involves consideration of viable alternatives.

REFERENCES

ACST (1982). *The ASEAN Compendium of Climatic Statistics*. Jakarta: ASEAN Committee on Science and Technology.

Brookfield, H. C. (1988). "The New Great Age of Clearance and Beyond: What Sustainable Development is Possible?" In *People of the Tropical Rainforest*, edited by J. Denslow & C. Padoch. Berkeley and Los Angeles: University of California Press.

Chang, J. H. and L. S. Lau (1983). "Definition of the Humid Tropics." Paper presented to the IAHS Hamburg Meeting, Paris, France.

DOE (1988). *Environmental Quality Report of the Department of Environment, Malaysia*.

Douglas, I. (1978). "The Impact of Urbanization on Fluvial Geomorphology in the Tropics." *Geo-Eco-Trop*, Vol. 2, pp. 229–242.

————— (1983). *The Urban Environment*. London: Edward Arnold Publication.

FEER (1991). "Victims of Success." *Far Eastern Economic Review*, 19 September, p. 44.

Jimenez, R. D. and A. Velasquez (1989). "Metropolitan Manila : A Framework for Its Sustained Development." *Environment and Urbanization*, Vol. 1(1), pp. 51–58.

Klein, L. (1957). *Aspects of River Pollution*. New York: Academic Press.

Law, A. T. (1980). "Sewage Pollution in Kelang River and Its Estuary." *Pertanika*, 3(1), pp. 13–19.

Maione, U. (1988). "Present and Future Perspectives on Water Resources in Developed Countries." *Journal of Hydrological Science*, Vol. 33, pp. 87–102.

Marlay, R. (1977). "Pollution and Politics in the Philippines." Paper in International Studies, Southeast Asia Series, No. 43, Ohio University.

McGee, T. G. (1967). *The Southeast Asian City: A Social Geography of the Primate Cities of Southeast Asia*. London: G. Bells and Sons.

Phantumvanit, D. and W. Liengcharensit (1989). "Coming to Terms with Bangkok's Environmental Problems." *Environment and Urbanization*, Vol. 1(1), pp. 31–39.

Pryor, R. J. (1979). *Migration and Developments in Southeast Asia : A Demographic Perspective*. Kuala Lumpur: Oxford University Press.

United Nations (1978). Department of International Economics and Social Affairs Population Studies, No. 72. New York: United Nations, pp. 1–39.

Witthawatchutikul, P. (1988). "Watershed Research at Rayong, Thailand." Proceedings of Seminar on Watershed Research and Management Practices. ASEAN-US Watershed Project. Universiti Pertanian, Malaysia.

Xoomsai, T. N. (1988). "Bangkok : Environmental Quality in a Primate City." In *Environmental Quality Issues in Asian Cities*, edited by P. Hills and J. Whitney. Project Ecoville Working Paper 43. Hong Kong: University of Hong Kong, pp. 1–23.

CHAPTER EIGHT

Improving Upland Utilization in Southern China and Neighbouring Areas

R. D. Hill

Reader, Department of Geography and Geology, University of
Hong Kong, Hong Kong

Background on Hill-country Problems

Since 1949 the population of China and its neighbours has doubled and despite current anti-natal policies in China, especially, the population will continue to grow steadily for some decades. This will be so even if those policies change in response to changing perceptions of such demographic consequences as a rapid decline in birth-rates and burdensome family dependency rates. Since around 1910, the area of arable land per person in China has fallen from around 0.22 ha to about 0.11 ha in 1990 and is projected to fall to 0.06 by the year 2050 (Cai, 1990:339). From 1957 urban and industrial construction, together with desertification and soil erosion, have resulted in a loss of cropland by about 40.7 million hectares although this has been partly compensated by the reclamation of some 25.1 million hectares of "wasteland" to give a 1990 total under crops of 126.7 million hectares (Cai, 1990:337).

Fortunately, the increase in agricultural production has so far been able more than to keep pace with population growth; though since 1984 this has become less and less true. However, there are excellent grounds for believing that production increases in the lowlands of southern China, Vietnam and Thailand cannot continue to grow rapidly beyond levels that are already high or, as in northeastern Thailand and central Vietnam, appear to be limited by such intractable environmental problems as highly-peaked hydrological regimes and water shortage. While the technology may exist for such increases in the short term, it is doubtful that their implementation through such measures as even greater fertilizer and pesticide application will be economically feasible or, in the longer term, environmentally desirable. Increasingly, the law of diminishing returns will apply and opportunity costs will rise. Since it is Chinese government policy to foster development *in situ*, in part because of the enormous cost of rapid urban growth, the question of increasing production from hill areas will become even more crucial. At the social and political levels, too, this issue will be important for there is a danger in allowing upland/lowland differences in living standards to become excessive even in authoritarian states.

In the environmentally-similar regions of Vietnam, similar problems, compounded by severe climatic difficulties in the centre and north of the country, also exist. In contrast, the Thai problems relate partly to the economic and social integration of minority peoples though, there too, the fact that the lowland rice frontier has effectively closed has put upland areas under severe pressure from lowlanders lacking sufficient land for wet rice cultivation. There seems little doubt, for instance, that plough cultivation on even gently-sloping land for such dry crops as Kenaf (*Hibiscus* spp.) induces large sediment yields, at least locally.

So far as forests are concerned, the picture is distinctly unpromising. Between 1949 and 1981 about 67 million hectares of forest are estimated to have been destroyed, reducing the total to 121.4 million hectares which represents only 0.11 ha per person compared with a global average of 1.07 ha. The current rate of cutting is thought to be about 50 percent higher than the rate of regrowth (Cai, 1990:340).

In southern China and in neighbouring areas, interested individuals, forestry and agricultural research and extension agencies are, of course, very much aware of such issues. Effective action, however, has been limited by several factors, including lack of funds, narrowly-based programmes of research, difficulties in extension to the local areas as well as by a lack of linkage with relevant research outside the immediate region in which it is accomplished. The current focus upon hill forestry, for instance, is excellent as far as it goes, but forestry suffers from long lead-time to harvest, virtual economic "sterilization" of the land until then, a need for rather large areas to be viable for some forms of production (e.g. pulp and paper), a limited range of products, food-supply problems and a basic inability to support more than quite low population densities. In addition there are serious problems of control and questions of land owner-ship. Alternative strategies are clearly needed.

Current Utilization

At this point upland utilization strategies can be little more than enumerated. Shifting cultivation, especially its short term variant, bush-fallowing, is widespread, particularly among minority groups in most parts of the region, with the consequence that commercially-usable "natural" forest scarcely exists. Environmental scientists have long held that this form of exploitation causes serious damage by increasing runoff and consequently accelerating both erosion and sedimentation. However, in the absence of long term, con-trolled catchment experiments throughout most of the region, it is difficult clearly to distinguish such accelerated processes from "normal" ones, par-ticularly when there appears to be increasing evidence that exceptional events bring about very rapid erosion and sedimentation (During a recent typhoon in coastal Guangdong, for example, half a metre of sediment was deposited in the lower courses of the worst-affected catchments within only three days). Questions remain. Just how far and how fast do sediments travel in the hill country? Is the obvious aggradation of the upper courses of streams, such as along the Thai-Burmese border, really a cause for concern? At what rates do sediment yields decline as slopes revegetate? At what speed do they revegetate and which factors control this? Are trees really a satisfac-tory form of erosion control or would deep-rooting perennial shrubs or grasses such as *Vetiver* offer superior control of surface wash and rill erosion? Can a combination of trees and grass not only offer superior control but also give direct economic returns at reasonable levels? The answers, as yet, are very partial and for large areas scarcely exist.

In addition to shifting cultivation or bush fallowing, the fundamental purpose of which is food-getting, there are many other utilization strategies which, however, generally exclude any significant form of livestock-raising. A major use of phytomass is for fuel. In China's rural areas, just under half of the fuel consumed (in coal equivalents) is thought to be in the form of phytomass, wood, twigs, grass, even roots grubbed from the soil. In eastern Hunan, for example, Li (1983) has estimated an annual firewood consumption of 1.5 cubic metres per person, representing the annual dry matter increment of between six and thirteen are of woodland. In the southwestern province of Yunnan, Liu (1983) has estimated an annual fuelwood consumption of 17.4 million cubic metres, accounting for 70 percent of total fuel consumption in the early 1980s.

Not all the phytomass harvested from the hills is for domestic fuel purposes. In western Guangdong, for example, there is a local trade in phytomass, much of it for industrial purposes such as brick-making, lime-burning and sugar-refining. An allied, and thermally more efficient use of upland phytomass, is for the generation of biogas (The thermal efficiency of traditional fire-places is said to be around 10 percent compared with up to 45 percent for biogas. See Chen Rongjun, 1988). Digested materials comprise hillside grasses, crop residues, animal and human wastes.

Dried grass, ground into a meal, is also becoming of some significance as feedstuff for stall-fed animals and pond fish. However, natural grasslands in the region are thought to suffer a number of disabilities. Since a three to four month dry season is the rule, production falls dramatically at that time while early wet season production has a high moisture content. At the same time native grasses tend to be low in protein, high in silica (especially in the dry season) and rate relatively poor in terms of palatibility and digestibility. The investigation of deep-rooting shrub browse is little advanced.

A further agricultural and sylvicultural use of upland phytomass is as compost, though its use for this purpose, like that for fodder is very labour-intensive. Such use is limited to highly nutrient-demanding crops such as sugarcane and cassava rather than for rice, wheat or groundnuts for which chemical fertilizers are preferred.

A basic issue in respect to the utilization to upland phytomass that needs to be addressed is an economic one. As development in the regional economies takes place, it might be expected that the relative costs of labour and transportation will rise making some forms of phytomass use un-economic and ultimately reversing their apparently adverse environmental impacts.

However, such a time seems rather far off, especially in China where limited opportunities for migration continue to result in a "piling up" of people in rural areas. There is little doubt that, in southern China, at least, both the quantity and quality of upland phytomass is declining. In Fujian province, for example, the annual increment of wood is estimated at around 9 million cubic metres against a utilization of 13 million cubic metres. In

Hainan province the living stock of wood fell by half between the early 1950s and 1980 (Li, 1983). At the same time grasslands have degenerated. In Dengfang *hsien*, Hainan, grasslands of fair quality including such species as *Phaseolus ninimmus* and *Evovulus alsinoides* have been replaced by grasslands dominated by low-quality species such as *Miscanthus floridus*, *Arundinella hirta*, the fern *Dicranopteris*, together with other poor species such as *Imperata cylindrica*, *Miscanthus sinensis*, *Digitaria longifera* and *Eragrostis cylindrica* (Hou, 1984; Chen Chaohui, 1985). Significantly, such changes have thus far made only a limited impact upon the international scientific community.

A further basic problem is the control of burning. It must be admitted that legal sanctions against uncontrolled burning are totally ineffective. So are fire-control techniques. Only in wealthy places such as Hong Kong can fires, once started, be controlled to some degree, but even there costs are so high that in open country fires are generally left to burn themselves out. Though the question has yet to be studied scientifically, it is claimed that burning the uplands results in an increase of nuturients in the runoff that may be diverted to agricultural use by irrigation.

Research on Hill Country

Generally, current research investigations in southern China tend not to be reported internationally (Thailand is a similar area where it is so reported). There are thus, right at the outset, problems of communication in which international scholarship and organizations could be expected to become involved. Obviously, this is not where the basic efforts should be, though initial resolution of such problems is important.

Rather the research effort should concentrate in two major areas, the environment and land utilization systems. Suggested subject areas may be set out schematically. To enumerate these is not to suggest that nothing has been done, rather, given that hill country covers several million hectares remarkably little is known especially internationally.

A. Basic Environmental Investigations

1. Vegetation   — phytomass standing crop, productivity
               — fire ecology and regeneration
               — current off-takes and uses

2. Soils — nutrient status and cycling
        — stability, erosion and mass movement, sediment trans-
          portation and deposition
        — water-balance and soil microclimate
These topics would be approached initially from the standpoint of
different types of vegetation covers and current utilization.

3. Hydrology — rainfall partitioning, especially overland flow
        — runoff, quantitative and qualitative aspects
        — stream regimes and relationships with land use
          and vegetation

4. Zoology — identification of actual and potential pests, ecology
          and dynamics

5. Agrometeorology & agroclimatology
        — identification and forecasting of paths of cyclonic
          storms, economic analysis of their effects
        — identification and forecasting of dry spells and cool
          spells, their physiological and economic effects and
          their spatial dimensions
        — analysis of the mutual relations of crop type and plant-
          ing patterns upon local climates
        — investigation of techniques and economics of trapping
          occult precipitation for tree-crop and forest estab-
          lishment

B. Agriculture and Agro-forestry

An essential preliminary step here is to establish details of current uses at a
level beyond that obtainable from existing remote-sensing and geographic
information systems. For example, it is scarcely known how productive (in
terms of phytormass) existing scrub- and grasslands are nor how harvested
biomass is partitioned. Fire is extremely common, yet not much is known
of fire-ecology and, especially, the reasons why fires are set.

The prime problem is to devise, test and extend technically and economically viable alternative hill-country land utilization systems. Some are
already known to be technically feasible, at least in part, for example,
dairying based partly upon *Pennisetum* fodder, afforestation with *Acacia*,
Cunninghamia, *Eucalyptus* or *Pinus massoniana*. In principle single-
species, even-aged stands, have serious shortcomings unless they are of

very small extent. The vulnerability of *Leucaena* and *Pinus massoniana* to insect attack is now well-established and is exacerbated in single-species stands. *Eucalyptus* is said to reduce runoff in some circumstances, though some species withstand or regenerate well from fire. Large, even-aged stands are clearly advantageous in large-scale industrial lumber production systems but where planted areas may comprise only a few tens or hundreds of hectares controlled by a local community, if all or most of the trees are even-aged, production may be excessively peaked, especially in the general absence, at that level, of sylvicultural knowledge.

A further consideration related to afforestation is the question of the effects of using species known to produce rather acid litter upon the soil and consequently upon second and subsequent cycles of production. So far as is known, this has not yet been investigated in the region, though in New Zealand later cycles of production with *Pinus radiata* are reported to show depressed yields on some soils, especially rather free-draining ones.

It must be said that many approaches to forestry have resulted in "adversarial" relationships with rural people struggling to feed themselves from forests and scrublands that they consider to be their property rather than that of a distant and less than benign government among whose representatives the forester ranks. Consequently, except perhaps in Thailand, little is known of the social and economic bases of people — forest interactions (see, for example, The Northeast Thailand Upland Social Forestry Project, 1987). Some subject-areas for particular attention may be enumerated:

1. Agronomy   — tree-crops
              — hill-grown fodders, especially shrubs
   (because deep-rooting and less susceptible to winter drought)
   Though regarded as a crop for semi-arid region the legume *Cajanus cajan* (pigeonpea) may be useful. It is to be oversown experimentally into rough grassland in Hong Kong.
2. Sylviculture — multi-purpose: fuel-wood, timber, fodder
              — construction and general timbers
              — problems of monoculture, especially pests
              — effects of commonly-used planted species upon soil and long term prospects for successive crops
              — "non-wood" products such as fungi

C. Erosion Control

Substantial areas of hill-country, several million hectares, are to a greater or lesser degree experiencing accelerated erosion, though in the absence of a significant number of base-line studies and comprehensive surveys it is difficult to be precise as to how widespread and how intense such erosion may be, how far, how fast and in what quantity sediments travel and are deposited. Accelerated erosion falls into two basic classes: that which can be controlled biologically (by planting trees, shrubs or grasses) and that which cannot and thus requires structures for control, for example, gullying or geologically-weak substrates.

Key areas for investigation include:

— ground covers for control, especially if they can be used for rough grazing. Vetiver grass (*Vetiveria zinzanoides*) is promising and has been used in the Himalayan region, southern India and Fiji. It is about to be planted on an experimental basis in Hong Kong
— tree and shrub covers
— development of appropriate methods for aerial oversowing and their economics compared with hand methods

The Case of Guizhou Province

Guizhou is one of several provinces in South China in which hill-country problems bulk largely. Of an area of some 170,000 sq km, about two-fifths is reckoned by the Chinese authorities to be eroded. Relatively high rates of loss are reported, even where the vegetative cover is good, since slopes are often very steep and rainfall intensities are high. On the limestone (which covers 70 percent of the province) soils are thin with, usually, a very sharp transition to bedrock. Soil loss from areas of weak rocks such as weathered basalt and Permian shales is thought to be especially high.

Population densities are high, with a crude density of about 175 persons per square kilometer and an "agricultural" density of 480 persons per square kilometer (urban population included). The annual population growth rate averages 1.5 percent but rises to 3.5 percent among some minority groups of which there are 46 in the province. Over half of the counties are below the official poverty line of 300 *yuan* per family annual income. The cropped area is about 1.9 million hectares with, on average, sixteen people dependent on each hectare. To this may be added about 4.3 million hectares of grazing land, virtually none of it improved, on each hectare of which seven people depend. To put the figures another way, each person "has" 0.063 ha of cropland, a further 0.14 ha of rough pasture, together with 0.56 ha of forest, most of which is degraded.

Against this background, little more can be done than to identify possible areas for further study and improvement. The first is cut-and-carry fodder utilization systems.

A. Cut-and-Carry Fodder and Erosion Control

Cut-and-carry cattle and buffalo-rearing is quite widespread in the province though there appears to be no published study on it. Characteristically, farmers own one to three cattle or buffaloes that are kept in stalls and fed on phytomass cut daily from public hill lands and carried back to the farm in pannier baskets or, where accessible, by road or path, by pony-cart. Animals are kept for milk and buffaloes, especially, for ploughing on flat lands or ploughable slopes.

Unlike neighbouring Guangdong, where significant areas of public hill lands are cut intensively for wood and grass fuel, in Guizhou the availability of coal for domestic as well as industrial use tends somewhat to reduce the intensity of cutting on the hill-slopes. There is, nevertheless, some cutting for fuel in the province.

A number of important practical and scientific questions concerning the ecology and economics of this form of production have been identified.

— Since the upland being public land, receives no fertilizer, not even from animals (since they generally do not graze it directly), what sustainable level of nutrient transfer can be expected?

— What is the frequency of dry-season burning and what are the reasons for this (e.g. maintenance of legume/grass cover, improvement in nutrient-content of irrigation water)?

— How do rates of sediment yield relate to cutting frequency and intensity?

— What are the prospects for improving the productivity of such public-access hill lands, e.g. by oversowing?

— What are the prospects for the introduction of better management of such lands given that they are of public access?

— Assessment of the need for, and social and political acceptability of, "privatization," subdivision and enclosure of hill lands or the development of user groups that might more effectively manage the use of such lands.

— What are the prospects for improving the transportation of phytomass, e.g. by bicycle, bearing in mind that improved access, especially when coupled with loans for stock now available, might increase pressure on hill phytomass?

— What are the non-fodder uses of upland phytomass, e.g. fuel, biogas digestion?

— Would plantings of tropical/sub-tropical shrub/tree legumes be feasible bearing in mind that many are deeper-rooting than grasses and are better able to withstand dryness? Is there sufficient depth of soil on "cone-karst" slopes (which are widespread) for this to be feasible?

— Would road-side and terrace-edge plantings of fodder shrubs/trees be feasible, bearing in mind that many species would compete with adjacent crops for nutrients, light or both thus depressing crop yields?

— What are actual and potentially-feasible annual fodder production curves and are they sustainable in the medium and long term?

The investigation of these and related questions will require the cooperation of individual scientists, their employers, university students and, especially, farmers. Though its use in China is not at all widespread, the use of key farmers as low-level, paid researchers has been successful elsewhere, of course with appropriate supervision. At the same time, such key farmers, if successful in identifying (with scientific workers) appropriate, sustainable, upland utilization strategies, would be expected to act as informal extension agents (This assumes, of course that farmers willingly share information — something which requires proof).

There are as yet no data on rates of soil loss from hill-slopes, but prompt consideration will need to be given to the role of tree-planting both for erosion control, for farm timber (and fuel where needed) as well as for ultimate sale. The slopes that are particularly steep and too distant from homesteads to be attractive to farmers as regular sources of cut-and-carried biomass are obvious candidates for afforestation.

There seems little doubt that trees can be grown successfully both on slopes with a continuous soil mantle and on those where it is patchy, though care must be taken to protect them from cutting and livestock (if there are such, grazing freely) during the establishment phase.

In order to obtain a good strike rate, especially on limestone "pocket" soils where soil-covered surfaces may range from 40–70 percent and may be very thin, simple hand-seeding is unlikely to be successful and aerial oversowing, as has been attempted in Guangdong, is even less so. Seedlings in bags with pelletized fertilizer are likely to have much greater success and it is more likely that farmers will care for them if they plant them themselves rather than for direct-seeded seedlings grown *in situ*.

A particular problem will be to avoid losses in the first dry season. In many areas hand-watering is not a feasible option given that domestic water may have to be hauled from distant wells. The steep and broken slopes of cone karst especially, the difficulty of simply walking over the surface, let alone carrying water, is considerable. Mobile pumps and hoses may be technically feasible but the cost is likely to be beyond contemplation.

While it is generally assumed that trees are suitable for erosion control, so far as is known, there has been no systematic investigation of the relative efficiency of various species in this respect. Obviously, in a given environment and location there is likely to be an optimal combination of species, balancing net benefit as timber, fuel and fodder against efficiency for erosion control purposes.

For higher, more temperate areas, pampas grass may offer possibilities and for lower more tropical areas *Vetiver* may be suitable for erosion control. Neither is good-quality fodder. This is important since good-quality fodders are likely to be environmentally-sensitive, or require significant input (which no farmer can afford and would not use anyway on public-access lands). More importantly, vigorous low-quality fodder is likely to suffer less cutting or grazing pressure and thus continue to be effective in erosion control, especially if planted, as recommended, in a double-row hedge along the contour.

While large areas have obviously been deforested and may be suffering from soil erosion, there is little doubt that trees will grow satisfactorily but they will be grown only where they will not unduly compete economically with essential food crops or rough fodder.

Species of trees possibly worth further trials and extension include:

(a) *Albizzia* spp.: Especially *A. lebbek* that casts light shade, fronds may add nitrogen and organic matter to soil. Shallow-rooting, good timber. Lower elevations only.

(b) *Leucaena* spp.: Despite problems with pests, good fodder, firewood. Lower elevations only.

(c) *Salix* and *Populus* spp.: Known to grow well in cooler upland areas. Valuable as timber, fuel and probably also as fodder though the latter is very inadequately tested.

(d) *Cupressus* spp.: Has already planted in some areas and appears to do well but may depress crop yields on adjoining fields.

(e) *Pinus massoniana* and *Cunninghamia lanceolata*: Have already planted in some areas and does quite well at lower elevations but likely to depress crop yields if grown close to them.

(f) *Melaleuca leucodendron*: Grows well at lower elevations but is known to produce very acid litter. Much the same is true of most *Acacia* and *Eucalyptus* spp. These cast quite dense shade, eventually forming single species stands with an open floor if planted into scrub. Consequently of limited use for erosion control except insofar as they reduce raindrop impact. *Acacias* generally are of limited or no value as fodder and some *Eucalypts* may be positively toxic in the event that stock can be persuaded to eat their leaves.

A particular problem is that the numbers of large livestock appear to be building up in response to the relative ease with which loans may be obtained for their purchase and to a substantial government subsidy (at least at Huaxi) on purchased feedstuffs (On a scheme at Huaxi farmers in 1990 paid 38 *fen*/kg for bagged feed against an open market price of 78 *fen*/kg. Loans averaged 8,000 *yuan* each, enough to buy three animals). But neither purchased feed (even if subsidized), nor farmers' own improved pasture, vegetable wastes (mainly rice and wheat straw and maize stalks), nor road-side grazing or cutting necessarily suffice to support the animals. On a 0.6 ha family farm at Huaxi with seven milk cows the minimum daily cut was reported to be 50 kg of hillslope phytomass rising to 140 kg or more at times in winter. Such pressures, if representative, are considerable.

The improvement of the yield of grass fodder from public-access hill lands is likely a matter of considerable importance. Casual observation and experience in a number of tropical areas with erect non-spreading grass species such as vetiver (*Vetiveria zinzanoides*) suggests that these, where planted on the contour as double-row hedges, may trap surface wash more effectively than trees. As mentioned earlier it is ironical, yet important, that such species provide relatively low-quality fodder, since if their quality is high they may well be cut or grazed close to extinction. Suggestions for further trials and/or extension include:

Pampas grass — for cooler areas
Paspalum — for warmer areas
Vetiver — for warmer areas

Medicago has already been used for over-sowing but with what success I do not know.

B. High Plateau Open Range Improvement

The Wei Ning area, a limestone plateau region at an elevation of 2,200–2,500 m, is one in which livestock are grazed in enclosed fields or on the open range. Farmers are used to handling stock. Private small farmers graze mixed flocks of ten to twenty sheep, cattle and sometimes pigs on spontaneous pastures that have long replaced the subtropical montane forest of the region. However, the basic food supply comes from *Solanum* potatoes as a sole crop or an intercrop with maize, grown in ridges both on flat and sloping land. The slopes are roughly terraced but because the slopes are remarkably uneven the terraces are small, sometimes only a row or two of crops in width. Moreover the orientation of the cultivation ridges with respect to the slope seems quite haphazard and is not infrequently normal to the slope instead of parallel to it as good practice requires. The terraces may slope considerably, up to about 5°–7° and consequently do not fully control surface wash.

The two basic agricultural activities clearly induce two forms of soil erosion. Much of the pasture is closely-grazed (and this close to the presumed peak production associated with the June/July rainfall peak). Significant bare areas occur. Characteristically these bare patches appear to cover areas from about 50 sq m up to several hectares. They appear to have been initiated by accelerated sheet wash following eating out and trampling of the soil cover. On the upslope side of such patches there is usually a scarplet 30–40 cm high and this presumably migrates upslope. Some of the larger bare patches show signs of rill formation and a few more extensive ones have begun to gully. The practice of grazing pigs may assist the initial opening up of the sward by rooting. Though conditions in June are favourable to plant growth, virtually no plant colonization on bare patches was observed (It may be that native grasses are autumn-seeding and that by the time seeds are naturally-distributed the surface of the bare patches is too dry to obtain a strike).

The control of erosion on public-access lands is unlikely to be easy not least because stock numbers appear to be rising. This is in response to relatively easy access to loan moneys. The Committee for the Eradication of Poverty in Wei Ning county for example has, since 1986, given small, low-interest loans (averaging about 300 *yuan* at 0.06 percent/yr) to 90,000 families, many of whom have subsequently purchased livestock. The World Bank has also allocated 1.5 million *yuan* for sheep projects in the county.

So far as was observed no erosion control measures are being taken on public-access grazing lands. However the Soil Conservation Bureau, part of the provincial Department of Agriculture, has recently begun work in a project area of about 2,000 sq km is the Upper Yangtze catchment. While no information on the policy for the selection of areas for erosion-control treatment was forthcoming in the field, it will be important that areas selected will have a good prospect of recovery in the short and medium term. Badly-damaged areas in which recovery is likely to be slow and expensive may have to be left aside at this point.

On public-access grazing land an obvious approach is pasture improvement, though any such improvement would necessarily be by way of a direct subsidy in that, apparently, no mechanism currently exists for the recovery from users any of the costs of such improvement. Limited local experiments show that the burning of "natural" pasture and scrubland, followed by crushing using animals followed by the sowing of cocksfoot and white clover results in the establishment of a satisfactory pasture. This combination, without added fertilizer, has been tried only on a limited scale and there must be some doubt as to its long term persistence especially if grazing is uncontrolled (The trial was made on a state farm). The same consideration applies with even greater force to the ryegrass/white clover/*Vicia* combination that has also been tried with somewhat less success than cocksfoot and white clover.

On enclosed lands, where grazing can be controlled, pasture development has taken a different course. Here the Da Shan experiment station, now partly funded by New Zealand, has been active since 1980. Initially the focus was on ryegrass and clover, a combination known to require substantial fertilizer input, particularly at this site where the soil, paradoxically since the country rock is limestock, is rather acid, possibly as a result of having been derived partly from blanket peat that may be presumed to have existed when the region was covered in subtropical montane forest. The highest-yielding combinations are (in order of productivity):

> red & white clover + ryegrass & fescue
> red & white clover + cocksfoot & fescue $\Big\}$ all for *in situ* grazing
> red & white clover + ryegrass
> red clover + cocksfoot – for cutting

Fertilizer applications are quite heavy, in the first year 60 kg phosphate/ha followed, after emergence, by 75 kg N (as urea), 60 kg P and 75 kg K. Such levels are almost certainly quite beyond the reach of ordinary farmers.

For improved pasture-based systems to be attractive to small farmers grazing their own land it is fundamental that a truly low-input system be devised since the high cost of artificial fertilizer is likely to be beyond their financial reach. Larger farms, including state farms, may be able to bear the capital cost of investing in high-quality pastures but even so doubts remain as to both technical and, especially, economic feasibility. At Da Shan ryegrass and white clover were sown (on plough) in 1985 yet had to be resown in 1987. Soils are obviously highly variable over very short distances, even a few metres. Patches have been invaded by weeds and poorer pasture species including introduced Yorkshire fog and *Lotus major* as well as herbs like *Artimisia* some species of which are known to be poisonous to livestock.

No data were forthcoming on annual pasture production curves either for improved or unimproved pastures. Given the substantial variation in monthly rainfall and below zero winter temperatures it may be expected that there are problems in maintaining production during the winter. Except at the highest levels on the plateau (around 2,500 m above sea level) there appears to be virtually no ploughable land available for such temperate fodders as turnips or *chou moullier*. Presumably animals are carried through the winter using stored crop residues and whatever else is available. This must be a matter of concern since December lambing is usual.

While the main thrust of research and development has been towards grass pasture, an area for further investigation, in addition to the no-fertilizer or low-fertilizer approach, is shrub or tree browze. This approach, of course, is one that temperate pastoralism has, for the most part, not taken (It should be remembered that the climate of high plateaux is not truly temperate but subtropical montane). In the Andes, for example, lupin (*Lupinus* spp.) is of some value locally. Sage-brush, though generally considered to be a plant of semi-arid regions, does tolerate cold and may be worth a trial for growth without fertilizer. Shrub/tree browse has, in principle, several advantages over most grasses. Species tend to be relatively deep-rooting. Thus they not only survive drought better but also draw upon soil nutrients from deeper, less-leached horizons. Once mature, free-grazing animals cannot extirpate them entirely unless the herdsman cuts them excessively. Trees will also provide timber and firewood. Some consideration should be given to making long term trials employing this approach.

The case of Guizhou illustrates the considerable complexities of devising workable alternatives to the existing upland use strategies. One more basic issue for China as a whole is the question of the degree to which the uplands represent an "input bank" upon which lowland systems continually draw. One writer has suggested that as much as 80 percent of the "natural" input (i.e. those other than fossil energy and, of course, sunlight) derived from the uplands. While most improvement strategies for the uplands are unlikely to harm a basic input such as irrigation water, at least insofar as quantity is concerned, there are many imponderables. What is certain is that improvement cannot wait until full, scientific studies are made. Rather science and praxis must go hand in hand.

ACKNOWLEDGEMENTS

I am grateful to my doctoral candidate, Mr. Chen Rongjun, for drawing my attention to a number of Chinese-language sources and summarizing their major findings. The University of Hong Kong supported travel to Guizhou and the Department of Geography, Guizhou Normal University provided travel in the province as well as making all arrangements for my visit.

REFERENCES

Cai Yunlong (1990). "Land Use and Management in PR China, Problems and Strategies." *Land Use Policy*, 7(4), pp. 337–350.

Chen Chaohui (1985). *Hainan Dao Cao de Liyong yu Niuyang Muye Fazhan Fangxiang. Hai Nan Dao Redai Nongye Ziran Ziyuan yu Quhua* (The use of pasture and the direction of developments in animal husbandry on Hainan Island. Agricultural and natural resources in the Tropics and their zonation on Hainan Island.)

Chen Rongjun (1988). "Energy and Nutrient Flow through Detritus Food Chains." In *Agricultural Ecology and Environment*, edited by M. G. Paoletti, B. R. Stinner and G. G. Lorenzoni. Amsterdam: Elsevier Science Publisher B. V.

Hou Xueyu (1984). *Fazhan Hainan Dao Da Nongye Yingcai Qu de Fangzhen he Tujing. Shengtaixue yu Da Nongye Fazhan* (Principal policies and approaches to the development of Hainan's agriculture). Anhui: Keji Publishing, pp. 201–222.

———— (1984). *Cong Shengtaixue de Guandian Tan Wo Guo Nanfang Shandi Qiuling de Liyong Fangxiang he Ruhe Fazhan Xumuye* (On the use of mountains and hills and the development of animal husbandry in southern China from the viewpoint of ecology). Shengtaixue yu Da Nongye Fazhan. Anhui: Keji Publishing, pp. 96–101.

Li Changhua (1983). *Nanfang Shandi Shengtai Pingheng Pohuai de Zhuyao Yuanyin de Chu Bu Fenxi* (Preliminary analysis of the main causes for the destruction of ecological balance in mountain areas of southern China). Lun Shengtai Pingheng: China Social Sciences Publishing, pp. 143–153.

Liu Cheng (1983). *Luelun Yunnan Zi Yuanli Yong he Baohu Shengtai Pingheng Wenti* (On ecological balance between utilization and conservation of resources in Yunnan). Lun Shengtai Pingheng: China Social Sciences Publishing, pp. 154–162.

Northeast Thailand Social Forestry Project (1987). *Case Studies of Human-forest Interactions in Northeast Thailand*. Khon Kaen: Ford Foundation.

PART IV

Transport and Communication Innovations

Transport and Communications in the Pacific Economic Zone during the Early 21st Century

Peter J. Rimmer

Senior Fellow, Department of Human Geography, Research School of Pacific Studies, Australian National University, Canberra, Australia

> The causes, character and significance of urban development can be best understood by analyzing cities in terms of their transnational linkages... (Smith and Feagin, 1987:5).

Since the early 1980s, the attention of scholars has been captured by rapid urbanization and economic restructuring of the Pacific Economic Zone — an area encompassing Australasia, East and Southeast Asia and the west coast of North America but excluding Central and South America, and the Pacific Islands (Nagatsuka, 1987). Interest has centred on the emergence of "world cities" within the Zone that act as pivots in global finance, international trade, knowledge-based industries, communications-related services and a transnational matrix of corporate decision-making and control (Friedmann, 1986; King, 1990). Examples include Hong Kong, Los Angeles, San Francisco, Seattle, Seoul, Singapore, Sydney, Taipei and Tokyo. Another focus has been the work on the ecological consequences of hyper-urbanization and industrialization in mega-cities of low-income countries (Douglass, 1989). Bangkok, Beijing, Jakarta, Manila, Shanghai, Tianjin and Wuhan, with populations expected to be in excess of five million by the year 2000, are such cities. Consideration has also been given to the different conditions under which the internal structures of mega-urban regions have emerged in Japan, Korea, Thailand (the Bangkok–Central Plains region), Malaysia (the Klang Valley), Indonesia (the Greater Metropolitan Region of Jakarta), Taiwan (the Taipei–Kaohsiung belt) and China (the Hong Kong–Macau belt) (McGee, 1990).

Surprisingly, little heed has been paid to changes in the capacity and structure of the essential external infrastructures that weld cities and megaregions within the Pacific Economic Zone together. Yet they underlie the regional production and distribution of goods and services and movements of capital, labour and information. In a bid to rectify this neglect, key issues are raised here about transport and communication networks and movements of commodities, people and information in the Zone during the early years of the 21st century. Which will be the key urban concentrations and how will they be connected? More specifically, what will be the respective roles of container shipping, air freight, air passenger and telecommunication services? Finally, how are changes in these networks related to likely trends in research and development?

Forecasting trade volumes and growth trends in the Pacific Economic Zone is a notoriously difficult enterprise. Not only are they affected by cyclical changes in the world economy, but by the varying pace of structural adjustment in different countries. While allowing for the progressive switchover from oil to gas in the long term, the study assumes the persistence of existing vehicles (and their derivatives), ports, trading patterns and procedures for the next fifty years (Allen, 1989). The role of transport and communications technology in shaping major Development Corridors is highlighted. Then interest centres on commodity movements by examining: (i) the emergence of regional hub ports and their container shipping connections; and (ii) the development of air freight. This leads to a study of air passengers and terminals in the short term and the emergence of superhubs in the longer term. Finally, telecommunications are discussed. Recognizing that Japan will play a pivotal role in reshaping the Pacific Economic Zone into the early years of the 21st century, a recurrent sub-theme is to highlight its specific connections with the rest of the world by examining freight, passenger and communications networks.

The Pacific Economic Zone

Urbanization has been a keynote of the Pacific Economic Zone's formation that has also been marked by the emergence of Japan as a major centre of capital surplus, the rise of the Newly Industrializing Economies and the reorientation of the United States and Australasian economies towards

Pacific Asia. Forecasts suggest that urban population will increase from 800 million in 1990 to 1 billion in the year 2000 — 45 percent of the Zone's total (Douglass, 1989). Regardless of the level of national urbanization, the dominant trend is the rise of the Zone's large metropolitan cities with populations in excess of five million. As shown in Figure 9.1, mega-cities in the year 2000 will include Los Angeles, Tokyo, Osaka, Seoul, Beijing, Shanghai, Hong Kong, Manila, Bangkok and Jakarta (the projections exclude Tianjin and Wuhan). The populations, however, understate their degree of control within national economies measured in terms of manufacturing employment, banking and number of motor vehicles. While it is tempting to focus attention on conventional cities or mega-regions, such a strategy would provide a misleading guide to the future of the Zone's transport-communications and land use system. Consideration has to be given to non-metropolitan space.

Cities, Mega-regions and Development Corridors

The existing metropolitan centres are artefacts reflecting cumulative connections between infrastructure, production and the built-environment prior to the 1970s. These are summarized in Table 9.1. Since the early 19th century they have arisen from the Zone's progressive integration into the world economy as part of the periodic superimposition of imported, modern transport and communications technologies over pre-existing, trading links connecting city-states. Many of the cities grew as mercantile communities between 1870 and 1910 following the introduction of steam-powered ships, railways and trams and the electric telegraph that provided the means for collecting and exporting a range of local commodities to Europe and North America. Much of their existing mega-regional structure, however, stems from the restructuring between 1920 and 1970 that was triggered by the spread of motor vehicles, aircraft and telephones. They not only cut travel times and transport costs but widened the market for emerging multinational corporations with branches in metropolitan port-cities and capitals. Thus, the introduction of technological innovations is associated with the addition of new infrastructure leading to existing networks being refashioned, downgraded or abandoned.

Since the early 1970s, a fresh bout of restructuring has occurred within the Pacific Economic Zone accompanying the changeover from an industrial to an information society emphasizing knowledge-intensive

Figure 9.1: Major Urban Centres with Populations in Excess of Two Million in the Year 2000

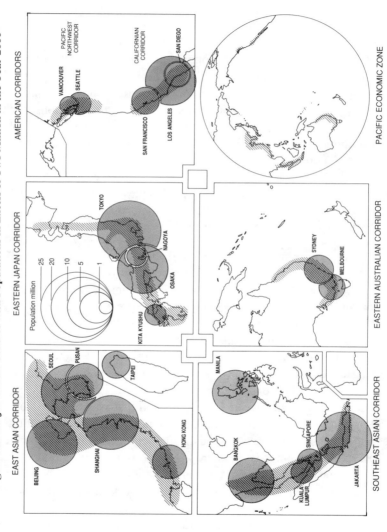

Source: United Nations, 1987.

Table 9.1: Key Features in the Development of the World Economy and the Pacific Economic Zone Since 1780

Time Scale	Infrastructure Networks		Production	Urban Form
	Transport	Communications		
Pre-capitalist/transition 1780–1850	Man, animal, sail, river canal	Mail	Individual proprietorship engaged in worker and outworker system (i.e. primitive accumulation)	Port city states
Industrial (competitive) production, 1860–1910	Steamship, Tramway, Elevator (1870 rail 85%; canal <10%, road <10%)	Telegraph (information sparse and skewed distribution)	Small-to-medium regional/national firms (confined to one branch of an industry such as textiles and steel) with homogeneous workforce and large reserve of surplus labour	Major port-cities
Corporate (monopoly) production, 1920–1970	Motor vehicle, Aircraft (1960: road 85% rail <10%)	Telephone, Radio	Large-scale national/multinational business organizations producing homogeneous commodities across a range of industries (oil, motor car, appliances and petrochemical) with segmented labour force, dependent small firm sector and state assistance	Metropolitan ports (point of tangency between the intra-continental and inter-continental transport systems)
Global production 1980–	Jumbo aircraft container ships bulk carriers (2000: road 75%, air 20%, rail 5%; 2050: air 65%, road, 35%)	Computerized telecommunications	Large global network corporations controlling smaller production units exploiting local resources (including universities) — a reflection of the growth of an international financial market, new international divisions of labour and greater number of locations with good potential	Development Corridors providing a new innovative milieu with major nodes benefiting from being financial centres, headquarters of network corporations and communications hubs

Note: Percentages for different modes in column two are based on total network length in the United States (see Andersson, 1990).
Source: Derived from Gibson and Horvath, 1983; Soja, 1989: 157–189; Andersson, 1990.

goods and services. Simultaneously, a new infrastructural arena in which a fresh set of economic and political activities can occur is being created by advances in transport and communications such as container shipping, jumbo jets and the extensive application of information technology to road traffic. This new, denser infrastructure, based on multi-layered links, has intensified the network character of the world economy and speeded the flow of knowledge about innovations by facilitating point-to-point contacts between dispersed coastal and continental locations (Batten, 1990).

Also, the new infrastructure has allowed export-oriented, global network corporations, responsible for information processing, to use smaller production and distribution units to develop both local resources and links with universities as part of their intensive research and development activities. In the process, attention has shifted from central place hierarchies of conventional cities and mega-regions to network hubs within Development Corridors where infrastructure endowment is closely correlated with high levels of knowledge, culture and accessibility (Batten, 1990). These, in turn, are synonymous with prosperity. They are akin to Andersson's (1990) macro-economic Corridor (C-region) in Europe that stretches from the southeast of England to the north of Italy encompassing the Cambridge-London-Oxford-Reading, Munich and Stuttgart regions.[1]

Six Development Corridors are recognized in the Pacific Economic Zone (cf. Rimmer, 1989):

(a) the *Pacific North West Corridor* stretching from Vancouver to Eugene;

(b) the *Californian Corridor* from San Diego to Sacramento;

(c) the *Eastern Japan Corridor* from Sapporo to Kagoshima;

(d) the *East Asian Corridor* from Nakhodka in the Soviet Union to Hong Kong with a possible extension to Hanoi;

(e) the *Southeast Asian Corridor* from Chiang Mai to Bali; and

(f) the *Eastern Australian Corridor* from Cairns to Adelaide.

No node, however, dominates any of the six Corridors.

Indeed, the Corridors are the ongoing battleground for commercial and financial hegemony between rival contestants (e.g. Los Angeles–San Francisco, Portland–Seattle, Osaka–Tokyo, Beijing–Shanghai, Bangkok–Singapore and Sydney–Melbourne). Also, the Corridors are prime targets for high-speed trains (e.g. Los Angeles–San Diego, Vancouver–Portland,

Seoul–Pusan, Beijing–Shanghai, Sydney–Canberra–Melbourne) and a mag-lev super train (Tokyo–Osaka). Before suggesting how infrastructure endowment and research and development in these Corridors are related, advances in freight and passenger transport, and computerized telecommunications systems need to be detailed. Initially, interest is centred on container shipping and airfreight distribution hubs because, as Batten (1990:85) highlights, most investment is concentrated on nodes rather than link structures.

Container Ports

The fortunes of container ports reflect the structure of trade and transport interdependence within the Pacific Economic Zone. Key trade facts, therefore, have to be highlighted before discussing likely future developments. Between 1977 and 1987, the Zone's share of world exports increased from 33 percent to 38 percent; the equivalent figures for imports were almost 34 percent and 40 percent respectively (Table 9.2).

Table 9.2: Pacific Economic Zone's Share in World Gross Domestic Product, Imports and Exports (in percentage)

Zones	World GDP		World Imports		World Exports	
	1977	1987	1977	1987	1977	1987
Japan	10.7	15.8	7.0	6.4	8.2	10.3
NIES	1.1	1.8	3.0	5.1	2.8	5.6
China	2.6	2.0	0.6	1.5	0.7	1.9
ASEAN	1.7	1.4	3.0	3.2	3.4	3.7
ANZ	1.7	1.2	1.5	1.5	1.6	1.4
Pacific-Asia	*17.8*	*22.2*	*15.1*	*17.7*	*16.7*	*22.9*
North America	33.7	32.7	18.6	22.2	16.2	15.1
Pacific Economic Zone	*51.5*	*54.9*	*33.7*	*39.9*	*32.9*	*38.0*
Western Europe	32.9	32.9	39.4	49.3	47.1	50.4
Rest of World	15.6	12.2	26.9	10.8	20.0	11.6
World	*100.0*	*100.0*	*100.0*	*100.0*	*100.0*	*100.0*

Note: Acronyms: GDP = Gross Domestic Product (New Zealand is included in Rest of World); NIES = New Industrializing Economies (Hong Kong, South Korea and Taiwan); ASEAN = Association of Southeast Asian Nation, including Singapore); ANZ = Australia and New Zealand.

Source: Garnaut, 1989:39, 51.

The heightened economic integration of the Pacific Economic Zone is confirmed by trade intensity indices in Table 9.3. It shows that the growth and redirection of the Zone's trade is attributable both to: (i) its greater importance in the world economy stemming from trade between the Far East and North America and, to a lesser extent, with Western Europe;[2] and (ii) the increase in Intra-Zonal flows, particularly among countries in Pacific Asia. The latter have stemmed from active investment and

Table 9.3: Trade Intensity Indices Involving the Pacific Economic Zone, 1978 and 1988

1978							
	Pacific Economic Zone					Other	
	Japan	NIEs	ASEAN	ANZ	North America	Western Europe	Rest of World
Japan	—	4.1	3.0	2.1	1.5	0.3	1.3
NIEs	2.1	1.5	2.6	1.7	1.9	0.4	0.7
ASEAN	4.1	2.1	5.3	1.5	1.1	0.3	0.6
ANZ	4.2	1.9	2.5	4.2	0.7	0.4	0.8
North America	1.3	1.2	0.9	1.2	1.7	0.5	1.3
Western Europe	0.2	0.3	0.4	0.6	0.4	1.3	1.4
Rest of World	1.1	0.7	0.6	0.3	1.0	1.0	1.2
1988							
	Pacific Economic Zone					Other	
	Japan	NIEs	ASEAN	ANZ	North America	Western Europe	Rest of World
Japan	—	2.4	2.2	1.9	1.8	0.5	0.9
NIEs	2.0	1.7	1.6	1.3	1.7	0.4	0.4
ASEAN	2.8	2.0	4.6	1.5	1.0	0.3	0.7
ANZ	3.7	2.2	2.0	4.9	0.6	0.4	1.9
North America	1.5	1.8	0.9	1.3	1.7	0.5	1.0
Western Europe	0.3	0.3	0.3	0.6	0.4	1.5	1.1
Rest of World	1.1	0.5	0.5	0.4	0.7	1.0	1.6

Note: The trade intensity index measures the relative significance of a particular trade flow independent of the scale of either partner's trade, and is defined from country's i's exports to country j as the share of i's exports going to j (x_{ij}/x_i) relative to j's imports (m_j) in world imports (T) less i's imports. $I_{ij} = (x_{ij}/x_i) / (m_j / T - m_i)$.
Source: International Economic Data Bank, Australian National University.

technological transfer in East and Southeast Asia by global network corporations based in Japan, particularly after the revaluation of the yen following the Plaza Accord of 1985 (Yoshida, 1987). Subsequently, both South Korea and Taiwan have followed Japan's lead into Southeast Asia.

Translated into cargo volume, the Pacific Economic Zone is expected to feature as the world's largest distribution centre by generating 200 million tonnes of freight and growing at the conservative rate of 2–3 percent per year until 2000 (Miyazaki, 1989). Another 100 million tonnes of cargo is likely to be moved between Japan and East and Southeast Asia due to the horizontal division of labour and the resultant interchange of industrial products. Assessments based on quantity, however, are misleading because rising incomes and higher value intermediate and capital goods from a more sophisticated economy will require better quality services by both sea and air. As reflected in the shift in the building of new containerships, and slot ownership, these quantity and quality projections have been outstripped by a marked growth in the Far East's merchant fleet (Table 9.4).

This growth has arisen from "newbuildings" being available at exceptionally low prices and the entry of independent newcomers less impeded by traditional protectionist barriers. Notable newcomers are Hong Kong's Orient Overseas Container Line, Singapore's Neptune Orient Line, and, above all, Taiwan's Evergreen Group that has one of the world's largest container fleets. Fierce competition and a so-called overtonnaging problem,

Table 9.4: Handling of Eastbound Cargoes from Japan and the Far East to the United States by National Shipping Groups, 1986 and 1987

Shipping Groups	1986				1987			
	Japan	Far East	Total		Japan	Far East	Total	
	thous TEU	thous TEU	thous TEU	%	thous TEU	thous TEU	thous TEU	%
Japanese	268	239	507	20.6	246	352	598	22.8
American	182	513	695	28.2	153	390	543	20.7
Far East	184	674	858	34.8	203	857	1,060	40.4
European	115	217	332	13.5	102	245	347	13.2
Other	21	50	71	2.9	15	57	72	2.7
Total	770	1,693	2,463	100.0	719	1,901	2,620	100.0

Note: Rounding errors occur in columns.
Source: Kaiji Sangyo Kenkyujo, 1989.

however, has resulted which has been characterized by: rates being halved on Trans-Pacific routes; the start of fixed-day of-the-week services; freight conferences; losing market shares leading to the formation of consortia, operating agreements and amalgamation of carriers; and the deregulation of agreements among carriers and the offering of service contracts (Yamada, 1988).[3] No recovery from this temporary and exaggerated problem of overcapacity is anticipated before 2000.

A. Load Centres

An examination of the pattern of container ports in Pacific Asia during 1988 highlights the demise of the exclusive hinterland concept and concentration of cargo at a limited number of highly competitive major ports. The inland rail connections, however, are not shown (Figure 9.2). Load centring in the American Corridors was focussed on the key terminals of Los Angeles, Long Beach, Oakland, Seattle and Vancouver. They offered landbridge services by double-stack trains and tractor and trailer combinations to other parts of North America. These services have diverted cargo from United States east coast ports. With the advantage of being the closest Asian ports to North America, pivotal load centres in Japan were centred on Tokyo Bay (Tokyo–Yokohama) and Osaka Bay (Kobe–Osaka). In the East Asian Corridor the dominant hubs were Hong Kong, Kaohsiung, Keelung and Pusan. Singapore, the world's busiest container port, services the Southeast Asian Corridor. As the basic infrastructure (e.g. container freight stations and inland container depots) and landbridge services by rail were relatively undeveloped in Asia all of these load centres, with the exception of Pusan, depended upon complementary feeder ports and short-distance shipping services, a task well-suited to national carriers (Yamada, 1989). No port in the Eastern Australian Corridor, however, handled 1 million TEU per year. This situation of a very few ports attracting all cargo from a region was brought about by bigger ships and the scale and geographical scope of large carriers and consortia rather than from the abandonment of the traditional multiport approach and changes in the structure of mainline itineraries (Gilman, 1988).

Load centring, like containerization, will continue into the 21st century with greater use being made of high cube and specialized containers, feeder networks and inland depots as carriers concentrate on fewer routes and seek to obtain economies of scale from newer vessels (Marti, 1988). Already fourth generation container ships with capacities of 4,500 TEU — the

Figure 9.2: Container Ports and Major Container Shipping Routes in the Pacific Economic Zone, 1988

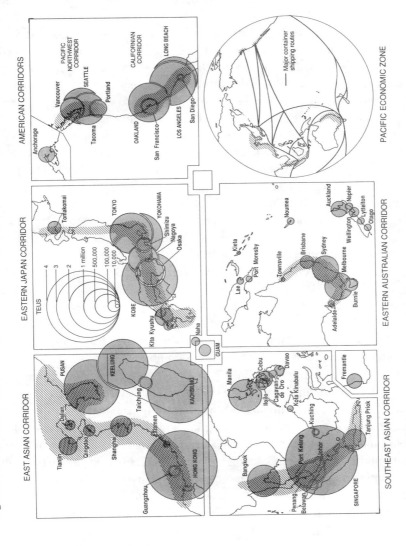

Note: Ports with more than one million TEU are in capital letters.
Source: CI, 1989.

"jumbo conships" — have exceeded the dimensions of the Panama Canal (post-Panamax). They require extended depths (14–15 metres), super-gantry cranes with an outreach of over 40 metres and an increased length of wharf. The trend towards larger container ships is, however, unabated and accelerating with fifth-generation vessels (ultra-Panamax) being mooted with 6,000–7,000 TEU capacity and a speed of 22–25 knots. These developments will involve major load centres in purchasing the most advanced infrastructure and technology to match increases in vessel size so that they can stay ahead of competitors. In addition, shipowners will need to be large enough to control a significant share of the market to warrant the purchase of larger ships and the chassis required to move containers into the interior of the United States. There is, however, no sign that the number of ports is being reduced or competition diminished. Ultimately, the outcome is likely to be a range of first, second and third division ports rather than a few superports and feeders (Gilman, 1988).

Port planners in the United States suggest that there will be two rail-fed ports on the West Coast of North America focussed on San Pedro Bay (Los Angeles–Long Beach) and Puget Sound (Seattle–Tacoma), though Oakland should not be discounted — it is the headquarters of the American President Line and an export outlet from the Mid-West via the Southern Pacific Rail-road (Fleming, 1989). Within Asia, container throughput will treble by the year 2000 and, with further increases in vessel size, hub and feeder development, will be pronounced. Tokyo Bay and Osaka Bay ports are unlikely to maintain their past prominence. These ports will switch from concentrating on cargo handling to a range of functions combining distribution, industry and residence as part of the Ministry of Transport's plan for decentralizing activities to thirteen ports during the early 21st century. Spurred by the privatization of port terminals, Kaohsiung, Hong Kong and Singapore are seen as vying for the supreme hub position with, for example, Kobe–Osaka, Pusan and Tokyo–Yokohama being cast as major regional ports and Port Klang and Tanjung Priok (Jakarta) ranking third. These changes are likely to be accompanied by fewer, but more sophisticated, shipping companies on the mainstream east-west route between East and Southeast Asia and the United States that is dominated in varying degrees by Japan, Korea and Taiwan (Table 9.5). In turn, these carriers are being transformed into multi-modal transport operators to take advantage of the increased productivity of container shipping, port operations and inland movements.

**Table 9.5: Movement of Full Containers between East and
Southeast Asia and the United States, 1986 and 1987**

Countries	Eastbound				Westbound			
	1986		1987		1986		1987	
	thous TEU	%	thous TEU	%	thous TEU	%	thous TEU	%
Japan	771	31.3	719	27.5	653	42.0	772	42.1
China	99	4.0	143	5.5	60	3.9	81	4.4
Hong Kong	222	9.0	246	9.4	133	8.6	156	8.5
Taiwan	827	33.6	887	33.8	288	18.5	342	18.6
Korea	311	12.6	368	14.0	229	14.8	266	14.5
East Asia	1,459	59.2	1,644	62.7	710	45.8	845	46.1
Indonesia	42	1.7	42	1.6	42	2.7	41	2.2
Malaysia	25	1.0	31	1.2	20	1.3	23	1.3
Philippines	46	1.9	50	1.9	50	3.2	68	3.7
Singapore	61	2.5	64	2.4	49	3.2	52	2.8
Thailand	60	2.4	72	2.7	29	1.9	34	1.8
Southeast Asia	234	9.5	259	9.8	190	12.3	218	11.9
Total	2,463	100.0	2,622	100.0	1,553	100.0	1,835	100.0

Note: Rounding errors occur in columns.
Source: Kaiji Sangyo Kenkyujo, 1989.

B. Multimodal Transport Operators

The transformation of major shipping companies into integrated transport
operators should proceed apace by the early 21st century. However, mid-
dle-market competitors offering round-the-world services (notably
Taiwan's Evergreen Group) and minimum cost port-to-port services (such
as those provided by Korea's Hanjin Container Line) are likely to persist
along with others on secondary routes. In the process, the wholesale port-
to-port operation should have been largely superseded by a customized,
shipper-oriented, door-to-door service satisfying specific packaging and
routing requirements. This will be effected by the former shipping companies, typified by American President Line and Sea-Land of the United
States, Maersk of Denmark, and K-line (Kawasaki Kisen Kaisha), Mitsui
OSK Line and Nihon Yusen Kaisha (NYK) of Japan, because they have the
necessary financial capability, expertise for trade and transport regulations,

procedures and practices, and an international network of offices linked by modern communications.

These multimodal transport operators (MTO) will undertake responsibility and liability for moving the container from a source in one country to a destination in another using a variety of modes — sea, truck and double-stack train — under a single transport document transmitted by a completely paperless electronic data interchange (EDI) system (Kuroda, 1987).[4] By undertaking cargo consolidation and fixed-day of the week services, underpinned by expert electronic systems indicating the position and status of the container, multimodal transport operators will offer value-added services (e.g. computerized information, and efficient terminal operations) (Yamada, 1987). Through being able to comprehend, manage, and possibly control, the economics of the move, they will extend their streamlined logistics management activity to cover production scheduling, warehousing and delivery to industrial firms. This will enable the latter to adopt the "just-in-time" practices already used by Japanese car companies based in the United States (Honda, Nissan Motor, Toyota Motor, Toyo Kogyo and Mitsubishi) and American department stores, both of which operate with near-zero inventories (i.e. with a little buffer stock to cover for non-delivery or unpunctuality). As carriers are supplying inventory control the door-to-door service is fast becoming a work-station-to-work-station exercise. Most multimodal transfers of cargo will be a continuous operation during the first decade of the 21st century with the prospect of automated cargo handling systems being commonplace (Frankel, 1990).

C. Sea-Air

Multimodal transport operators will also interlink their ocean and coastal shipping-rail-road activities with air freight services to cater for high valued, small quantity and diversified types of freight, thus becoming truly full transport enterprises (Akiyama, 1984). For instance, the Zone's largest container shipping company, the Evergreen Group, has plans to purchase aircraft, possibly to by-pass investment in multimodal operations (Chinnery, 1989). While international sea-borne cargo has slowed, air freight in world trade has grown to challenge the role of ports as the chief conduit for the movement of high-priced goods requiring speedy service (e.g. semiconductors, fashion clothing and perishables).

By 2000, 10 percent of high value cargo in international trade will move by air (Frankel, 1990). Although high-speed superconductor seacraft (1,000 TEU capacity with a speed of 50 knots) are likely to trim the speed advantage of air cargo there is much emphasis in Japan on multimodal transport operators connecting both seaports and airports and designing combined bimodal sea-air routes, such as: (i) Tokyo to Vancouver by sea and by air from there to Europe and Africa; and (ii) Tokyo to Singapore or Dubai by sea and by air from there to Europe. Discussion in considering air freight movements, therefore, is concentrated on Japan.

Airfreight

Since the recession of the early 1980s, the freight industry in Japan has grown from being subordinate to passenger transport into a business in its own right. This has been brought about by the shift from heavy industry to assembly and processing and a preference for light, thin, short and small commodities (*kei-haku-tan-sho*), such as lighter car engines and small computers (Walker, 1989a, b). The resultant need for careful handling, speed and reliability has been fulfilled by air transport.

Freight growth has been marked by: (i) the advent of wide-bodied aircraft (Boeing B747, Lockheed L1011 Tristar and MacDonnell Douglas DC10) possessing large underfloor cargo compartments (capacity 40 tonnes); (ii) dedicated freight terminals; and (iii) cargo reservation and tracking systems. Attention here, however, is focussed on three organizational changes: (i) the establishment by airlines of their worldwide cargo activities as in-house systems; (ii) the creation by air freight agents and forwarders of their own national systems for eventual worldwide coverage; and (iii) the expansion of the international activities by integrated multimodal carriers (e.g. Federal Express and United Parcel Service) from bases in the United States (Kobayashi, 1989). Before discussing these changes in order to understand developments in the 21st century, airfreight origins within Japan and destinations of consolidated freight forwarders' cargoes to other parts of the world are considered.

A. Origins and Destinations

An examination of the origins of airfreight in Figure 9.3 shows that the New Tokyo International Airport at Narita is pre-eminent within Japan and is reputed to be the world's largest cargo airport. The prime destinations for

Figure 9.3: Airfreight from Japanese Airports to Overseas Locations, January–May 1989

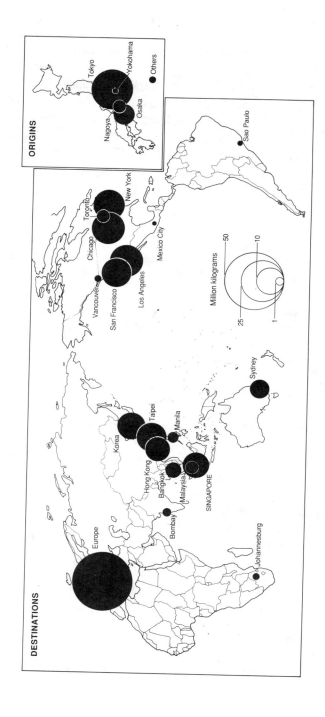

Note: Origins refers to airfreight and destinations to consolidated export cargo handled by forwarders.
Source: *Space*, 1989.

consolidated freight forwarders' goods highlight the dominance of the three major economic blocs — the United States, Europe and Inner Asia. Their importance has been heightened by the division of labour between domestic bases in Japan and diversified overseas production centres. Comprising electronics and non-electrical goods from high-tech industries, the consolidated cargo volumes for the highly-competitive United States market shows that New York, Los Angeles and Chicago are more or less on a par whereas San Francisco is smaller. Figures for the prosperous European market are not broken down but shipments from Japan to Western Pacific Rim destinations underline the importance of trade within Inner Asia following the establishment of off-shore bases, especially in high-value economic parts. In particular, growth has been marked in Hong Kong, Seoul, Singapore, and Bangkok (which is seen as possibly the biggest hub in Southeast Asia). All offer attractive sites for agents consolidating cargoes from Development Corridors on behalf of overseas buyers. Saudi Arabia is the only prominent airfreight destination outside the major zones. Carriers have sought to consolidate their networks by reinforcing central delivery points in the United States and road services in North America and Europe (hubbing on Frankfurt and Amsterdam).

There is, however, no comparable information on the origin of imports dominated by fresh foodstuffs, including meat and vegetables from Australia, seafood from India and fruit and flowers from Southeast Asia; express parcels and component parts; and the counter-flow of high-tech and high-value goods from the United States, Europe and the Newly Industrializing Economies. Consequently, it is difficult to trace the effects of the appreciation of the yen and creation of a domestic demand-oriented economy since 1985. The main outcome, however, has been to reduce the directional imbalance that is highly correlated with the Pacific Rim exchange rate index and trends in the world economy, notably the transformation of the United States service economy, just-in-time developments and industrialization of Asian-Pacific economies.

Constraints on supply may limit the two-digit percentage growth in airfreight demand in Japan, however, as both Narita (Tokyo) and Osaka airports are used to their capacity. Surprisingly, no effort has been made to establish a dedicated all-freight airport. Until the completion of the second phase of Narita's construction and the off-shore New Kansai Airport, any increase in freight capacity will have to rely on a few additional trips, use of "combi flights" (half passenger, half freight) and the deployment of larger planes, such as Singapore Airlines B747-300 freighter with a capacity of 109 tons (equivalent to thirty-eight pallets, thirty standard international containers or any combination thereof). Other than excluding transit cargoes, few changes can be made in routing and service frequency in response to variations in demand. Consequently, organizational changes are examined.

B. Organizational Changes

Traditionally, the air cargo business in Japan has been the preserve of local firms. Freight forwarders picked up and delivered and the airlines provided the line haul service. This situation was revolutionized by a memorandum of understanding between Japan and the United States in 1985. Three years later, this has led to the entry of Federal Express into the Japanese market. An immediate reduction in rate levels for light-weight commodities following its entry has been coupled with an improvement in information services. The latter have involved Federal Express in introducing its Cosmos system. It indicates the location of the consignment and other management information as part of its door-to-door package and has had a marked impact on both local freight forwarders and competing airlines. Its impact was compounded by Federal Express's takeover of the world's largest cargo airline, the Flying Tigers, as part of its plans to create a global network for intercontinental express freight in competition with DHL International, Australia's TNT and its United States rival, United Parcel Service (which entered the Japanese market in 1990).

Federal Express' scheduled flights for its high-priority, logistics service were tailored to the needs of high-technology industries, and are, therefore, different from both traditional airfreight business. Nevertheless, the emergence of this global mega-competitor, combining both forwarding and line haul functions, is likely to cause a realignment and reorganization of the industry. Already Federal Express is occupying fourth place among the top ten scheduled international airfreight carriers (Table 9.6). The response of the other carriers has led to a multinational alliance between the world's three largest operators — Japan Airlines, Lufthansa and Air France — and joint route agreements made, for example, between British Airlines and Singapore International Airlines (London–Singapore), British Airlines and Japan Airlines (London–Tokyo) and Cathay Pacific and Lufthansa (Hong

Table 9.6: Top Ten Scheduled International Freights Carriers, 1988–1989

International Freight Carriers	1988		1989	
	Freight mill. tonne-km	Increase percent	Freight mill. tonne-km	Increase percent
Lufthansa	3,450	7.4	3,810	10.5
Japan Airlines	3,230	7.9	3,400	5.2
Air France	2,990	7.9	3,120	4.6
Federal Express	2,750	23.1	2,960	7.4
Korean Air	1,880	18.0	2,360	25.7
British Airways	2,020	43.5	2,170	7.6
KLM	1,870	8.9	1,990	6.5
Singapore Airlines	1,450	12.7	1,680	15.9
Cathay Pacific	1,170	19.0	1,270	8.5
Alitalia	1,000	13.1	1,090	8.6

Note: The Federal Express takeover of the Flying Tigers in 1988 is reflected in the following years data. Singapore Airlines figures are for the year to 31 March.
Source: Westlake, 1990b:59.

Kong–Frankfurt). These developments suggest that regional consortia will be developed and oligopolisation is imminent.

Airlines with headquarters within Pacific Asia, such as Nippon Cargo Airlines, Cathay Pacific, Japan Airlines, Korean Air and Singapore International Airlines, have responded to this competition and the region's high growth prospects with an expansion programme. As prime passenger and cargo route sectors do not necessarily coincide, their programme is based on pure freight aircraft rather than "combi" versions. Whereas All-Nippon Airways has created a separate cargo airline, Japan Airlines has a freight department within the main airline to maximize its options. Korean Air has followed a similar strategy by introducing five B747-400 freighters and converting two B747-200 from passenger to freight use to develop Seoul as a cargo hub for the United States and European markets — a global strategy that permits it to act as a consolidator for its own intercontinental services (KMI, 1990). Conversion costs an estimated US$20 million (including hush kits on some models to meet noise regulations) compared with US$120–140 million for a new freighter. The latter has the advantage of greater range, low maintenance, fuel and crew costs. Nevertheless, as the saving of one hour of transit time from the introduction of a new freighter does not generate extra income, the retrofit conversion of available aircraft during the early 1990s will lead to increased competition. Much will depend on recognition of the cyclical nature of airfreight demand and the continued utility of in-house computerized reservation systems for the airfreight business and industry in general.

(a) Demand: There is no consensus on the likely worldwide rate of growth over the next decade. Assuming global stability, estimates based on a strong correlation with Gross National Product (GNP) range from between 6.5 and 10 percent with above average rates of growth being predicted for the Asia-Pacific market, notably the Intra-Asia, Far East-Europe and trans-Pacific routes. At the centre of world growth, airlines based in Pacific Asia are likely to boost their overall share from 24 percent in 1988 to 28 percent in 2000 to be on a par with Europe and challenging the United States at 32 percent. Continuing efforts, therefore, will have to be made to improve the functions of in-house cargo reservation and tracking systems.

(b) Cargo Reservation Systems: As in-house cargo reservation systems do not create demand or encompass all parties involved in the door-to-door transit of goods they are likely to be questioned in future (Aiwa, 1989). The pressing need is to link separate information systems and to share point-of-sale data on both trade and transport as part of a broad spectrum of economic activities, especially with the development of computerized Customs-clearance systems in many countries. This requirement should see the closed corporate or industry in-house system transformed into an open one responsible for the movement of commodities. In this new arrangement air transport will be regarded as a link in the commodity chain between different economic activities so that just-in-time deliveries can be realized with the sharing of standardized electronically processed and stored data in all directions (including destinations and inter-mediate points). Attempts to standardize international trade data are well advanced in America and Europe, but there have been delays within Pacific Asia.

Air Passengers

Between 1970 and 1986, the average annual growth of the Pacific Economic Zone's passenger traffic was more than 10 percent compared with 6 percent for the world as a whole. Again, there is no concensus on predictions. McDonnell Douglas, the aircraft manufacturer, anticipates world growth to the year 2010 to be 7.7 percent compared with 11 percent for the North and Mid-Pacific, 10 percent for Intra Asia and 8 percent for Far East-Europe. The International Air Transport Association (IATA) forecasts that Asian traffic will grow between 10 and 14 percent until 1995 and will double its share of all scheduled traffic to 40 percent by the year 2000. Before considering short term developments in the early 21st century and long term prognostications for 2040 an idea of the magnitude of likely changes can be derived from examining variations in linkages between 1979 and 1989.

A. Past patterns

Interest in examining air passenger networks is centred initially on non-stop services that exceeded more than twenty flights per month in August 1979 and 1989 respectively. During the earlier period, flight activity was concentrated on linking the East Asian and Southeast Asian Corridors though China was isolated (Figure 9.4). A distinct "main street" existed between Jakarta and Taipei; Bangkok, Hong Kong and Singapore were major pivots with both Manila and Seoul figuring prominently. Tokyo served as the major interchange between these airports and the American Corridors — a reflection of a liberal bilateral agreement between Japan and the United States. Clearly, Anchorage and Honolulu performed key roles as only San Francisco in the American Corridors reached the minimum threshold of twenty flights. The number of flights, however, may not have been a true reflection of the relative importance of airports at this time. Among the dispersed set of airports in the American Corridors the number of flights had been suppressed by the advent of wide-body jets since the early 1970s (i.e. the 350 seat 747s which doubled the capacity of the DC 8s and 707s). This phenomenon may also explain the limited number of direct connections with the Eastern Australian Corridor. Only Bangkok, Hong Kong and Tokyo had major external connections with airports outside the Pacific Economic Zone.

By August 1989, the pattern had changed with the intensification of connections between the three Asian Corridors — Eastern Japan, East Asian and Southeast Asian — and increased links between them and the American and Australian Corridors (Figure 9.5). The "main street" between Jakarta and Taipei persisted. Specifically, Hong Kong's pivotal role was

Figure 9.4: Twenty or More Non-stop Air Passenger Flights in the Pacific Economic Zone, August 1979

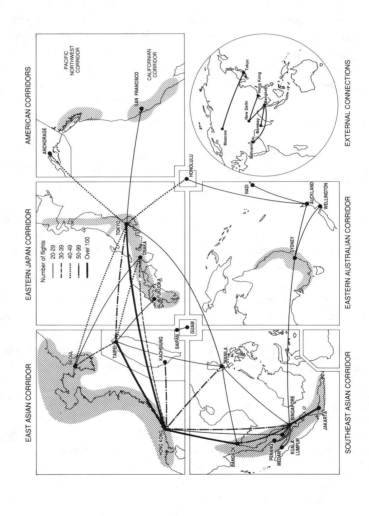

Note: Inset shows external non-stop connections.

Source: ABC, 1979.

Figure 9.5: Twenty or More Non-stop Air Passanger Flights in the Pacific Economic Zone, August 1989

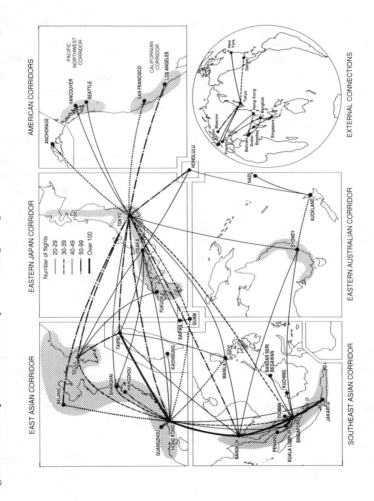

Note: Inset shows external non-stop connections.

Source: ABC, 1989a, b.

enhanced by connections with China and Bangkok by its function as a fuelling base on the one-stop Australia-Europe flights. The marked change was confirmation of Tokyo as the dominant gateway to Pacific Asia. This stemmed from Tokyo's strong local market within the Eastern Japan Corridor and its being a fuel stop on trans-Pacific flights. Tokyo's non-stop connections with major gateways in the American Corridors has been enhanced at the relative expense of Anchorage and Honolulu. Two factors have been responsible for Los Angeles overshadowing San Francisco in California and Seattle and Vancouver battling for dominance in the Pacific Northwest. These are: (i) rapid service expansion, associated with increased hub and spoke developments on the domestic network (created after the *Airline Deregulation Act*, 1978); and (ii) the subsequent consolidation of international passengers.

The minimum threshold of twenty flights, however, masked an increase in the number of trans-Pacific flights to non-Japanese destinations resulting from: (i) the noted capacity constraints at the New Tokyo International Airport at Narita; (ii) the growth in East Asian and Southeast Asian passenger markets; and (iii) unsuccessful United States pressure on Japanese authorities to ease its economic regulation of international aviation. Other key features were the closer integration of the Eastern Australian Corridor with the Asian Corridors and the marked increase in non-stop ultra long-distance flights. For instance, Tokyo has frequent flights to New York, Dallas, Frankfurt and London.

B. Short Term Developments

Given the likely continuation of double-digit growth into the 1990s to accommodate passengers and tourists, changes in the pattern of flights by the beginning of the 21st century are expected to occur through: (i) technological developments in aircraft; (ii) the spate of airport developments planned for Pacific Asia; and (iii) changes in organizational structure arising from the extension of passenger reservation systems.

(a) Technological developments: Recent developments in passenger aircraft have concentrated on the marketing benefits of ultra-long-range, non-stop operations. Boeing has developed the B747–400, McDonell Douglas the MD11, and Airbus the A340. As a result of improvements in materials technology, fuel efficiency and additional fuel capacity all of these aircraft have an extended range of operation. This will benefit those routes on which aircraft have periodically to reduce payloads because of adverse weather conditions. Investigations are also being made into increasing the seat capacity of aircraft and folding wing spans to overcome constraints of cost, land availability and environmental considerations associated with expanding or building new airports to meet the expected rise in jet fleet numbers (Westlake, 1990a).

(b) New airports: New hubs are planned in Hong Kong (1997), Osaka (1993) and Seoul (n.d.) which, together with existing airports in Bangkok, Manila, Shanghai, Singapore and Taipei, are expected to accommodate the rapid growth in demand and the inevitable spillover of connecting traffic from Narita. As congestion is most pronounced in Japan, developments there are highlighted. Although designed for 7.5 million, the volume of passengers at the New Tokyo International Airport at Narita had almost tripled from 6.4 million in 1978 to 18 million in 1988 (Damrot, 1990). As capacity is limited by the single runway, night curfews and the restrictive practices of air controllers, existing services have to be rescheduled and the introduction of new ones postponed (Hansen and Kanafani, 1990). The short term resolution of this problem is: (i) to expand the existing international airports at Osaka, Haneda (Tokyo International) and Narita by additional runways and new passenger terminals (though land acquisition at Narita has been slowed by political opposition and environmental concerns); and (ii) to build the New Kansai International Airport. The latter US$7 billion, one-runway project is being constructed on reclaimed land in Osaka Bay and will be connected to the mainland by a two-lane bridge. It will incorporate a tri-level terminal building to integrate international and domestic flights and operate twenty-four hours a day to accommodate additional passenger, charter and cargo flights. Like the other new hubs in Hong Kong and Seoul, Kansai's success will depend on "connecting traffic" at Narita being diverted. This move would involve passing on Narita's higher terminal costs to passengers and removing some of the fifth freedom landing rights enjoyed by United States airlines that permits them access to the Japanese market en route to other Asian destinations (Hansen and Kanafani, 1990).

(c) Passenger reservation systems: Both single-user, computerized reservation systems and multi-user, global distribution systems have been developed to accommodate the massive passenger upsurge following the introduction of the B747s. Unlike airfreight, the reservation system creates value by meeting a passenger's specific requirements in concluding a transport contract and supplying unidirectional and unilateral information between the airline as producer and the traveller as consumer. Competition between airlines to extend their respective passenger booking systems has led to a handful of companies in North America taking control. As this oligolopolistic development is nearing completion, contestants are seeking predominant positions on a global scale. These airlines are merging into larger groups geographically based in Continental Europe and Asia. The air passenger network, however, is still an immature system. Indeed, the development of the domestic hub and spoke system developed in the United States described by Hansen and Kanafani (1988) is unlikely to find global expression before the middle of the 21st century.

(c) Superhubs

Air passengers are likely to triple by the year 2040. At that time, six predictable issues are anticipated to dominate airport construction: the growth of both passengers and cargoes; changes in airport technology; more runways and better terminals; integration of security and terminal designs; an increase in the importance of environmental concerns; and better integration between ground and air networks (Stoner, 1990). As moving airports from congested inner-city areas to peripheral locations within 50 km and 80 km of existing areas has not provided a lasting solution, a new air transport system is being planned. It is based on a set of superhubs for handling new classes of aircraft (e.g. supersonic and hyper-sonic). These vast airports will be located between 160 km and 800 km from existing population centres as shown in Figure 9.6. This study, how-ever, does not take into account the possibility of off-shore airports (and cities).

Domestic links will be provided by: (i) supertrains and high-speed ground transport; and (ii) tilt-wing or tilt-rotor aircraft that are able to land and take-off vertically and carry between fifty and seventy-five passengers to and from inner city terminals sited on small parcels of land. At the airport automated people movers, capable of carrying between 1,000 and 16,000 passengers per hour, will make the necessary transfers at the central ter-minal between domestic feeder systems and long-haul aircraft stationed at remote piers (or satellites). Parallel automated and programmed rail sys-tems able to operate at 55 kph will handle baggage between landside and

Figure 9.6: A Future Superhub Air Network

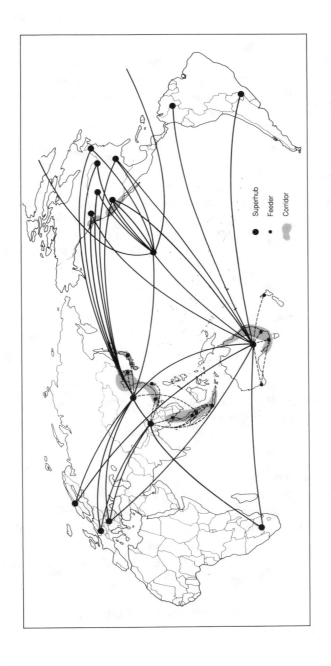

Source: Based on Stoner, 1990:13.

airside areas. Although it is feasible to send baggage twenty-four hours ahead of a flight, passenger security necessitates the two being identified together. Past experiences with both domestic services in the United States and international services suggest hubs are not stable as carriers divert to secondary airports once they are congested. Will this happen with super-hubs after 2040, or is this the ultimate hub and spoke system? Before this issue can be resolved telecommunications have to be discussed (see Rimmer, 1989).

Telecommunications[5]

International markets for computerized telecommunications are increasing at 9 percent per year with growth rates in the Pacific Economic Zone outstripping this figure. Already, the creation of satellite circuits has been the focus of much discussion because of their facility in transmitting to all points simultaneously, ease of repair, and their use by the banking and financial brokerage industry. Hence, interest here is concentrated on the development of submarine fibre-optic cable networks that link the Zone's major cities. They promise to overcome the slight, but significant, delay inherent in satellite transmission and facilitate the use of high-speed code transmission (MPT, 1988; Lee, 1989). Following the explosion in the Zone's demand for international telephone calls, the new network is designed to overcome a feared gridlock in satellite communication and microwaves (the Pacific Intelstat satellite is almost fully used and addition-al relief will not be available until 1993).

A. Fibre-Optic Networks

As shown in Figure 9.7 the entire network will interconnect Development Corridors within the Pacific Economic Zone by the mid-1990s. The twin American Corridors will be linked with the Eastern Japan Corridor which, in turn, will be connected to the East Asian and Southeast Asian Corridors through two different routes. Connections will also be made with the Eastern Australia Corridor and New Zealand and linked back to the California Corridor through Hawaii.

Fibre-optic cables carry information using the transmission of laser-generated impulses of light through glass fibres. They can accommodate more telephone calls at a lower cost than the traditional "analogue"

Figure 9.7: Network of Fibre-optic Cables in the Pacific Economic Zone, Showing Dates of Completion

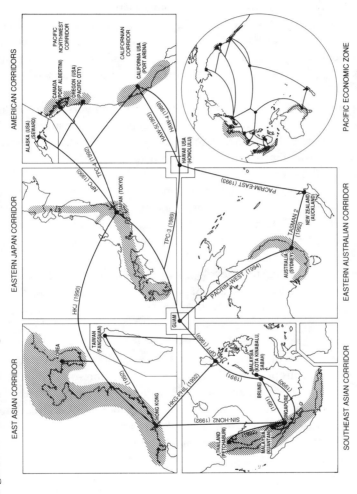

Note: An additional development due for completion in 1995 is linked between Ullang Do (South Korea) and Hamada (Japan) and Nakhodka (Siberia) which, in turn, will be connected to Moscow and other European cities.

Source: Based on Clowes, 1989.

submarine copper cables that carry information electronically. They guarantee crystal-clear quality for both voice and data transmission that eliminates the static and cross-talk of the copper cable and the echoes experienced when using satellites floating 36,000 km above the Pacific. Unlike satellite transmission, fibre-optic cables offer security for the transmission of sensitive data from banks and other institutions as they cannot be tapped. Also, they will be used for a variety of business services including the next genera- tion of FAX (Group IV), high-definition television, international video-conferencing and enhanced, value-added services for global network corporations engaged in financial transactions and the use of computer-aided design.

Key corporate players are vying to provide these networks. For example, the major United States carrier, AT&T and its twenty-two partners, linked Port Arena in the Californian Corridor through Hawaii Cable 4 and Trans-Pacific Cable 3 to Japan and Guam with a further link to Infanta in the Philippines and Taiwan. A rival venture, comprising Pacific Telecom Cable of the United States, Japan's International Digital Communications and Britain's Cable & Wireless, has provided the North Pacific Cable that supplies: (i) a direct link between Pacific City in the Pacific Northwest Corridor of the United States and Miura in Japan; (ii) a spur to Alaska; and (iii) an extension to Hong Kong and Korea. AT&T and its partners are endeavouring to match this development with an alternative fibre-optic cable, Trans-Pacific Cable 4, that will provide a direct link between the twin American Corridors, notably California's Port Arena and Canada's Port Albertini, and the Eastern Japan Corridor. When completed this "global digital highway" will connect Corridors in the Pacific Economic Zone with cities in the United States (interconnected by 40,000 km of cables) and through them to Europe through the Trans Atlantic fibre-optic link. Given the technical advancement in fibre-optic technology, coupled with internationalization of markets and customers and the liberalization of regulatory structures, decreasing unit costs are anticipated together with a fall in industry profits — a pattern already evident in international telephone calls in Japan.

B. International Direct Dialing from Japan

As telegrams and telexes are both declining and mail more or less constant in Japan attention is focussed on the rapid escalation in international telephone calls (including facsimile communications). The origins of international direct dialing, shown in Figure 9.8, are concentrated in the Eastern Japan Corridor with a large number of calls focussed on Greater Tokyo (including Kawasaki and Yokohama), a smaller concentration in the Kansai area (Osaka, Kobe and Kyoto), and outliers at Nagoya and Hiroshima. Although the United States and Australia are undifferentiated, the destinations underline the importance of Development Corridors in Western Europe, East Asia and Southeast Asia. Apart from Saudi Arabia, links were weak with Africa, Central and South America and the Middle East. This pattern reflects the close relationship between telephone use and regional location of Japanese overseas corporations.

Besides the telephone, the transmission of information also involves: (i) computerized telecommunications (telematics), which include E-mail, facsimile, teletex, video-conferencing and videotex; and (ii) teleports that provide these services to a building complex or geographical area so that dispersed logistics functions can operate as a single enterprise. Without detailed information on these activities in Japan, international direct dialing calls are used to illustrate that Development Corridors depend upon the export of information. Extrapolating from European experience, these Corridors possess an intrinsic network character that may be contrasted with those large urban hubs that also generate creative activities (Batten, 1990). Apart from the scope for synergistic economic development between research and development and teleport, airport, seaport and road capacities, the Corridors offer greater potential for knowledge expansion within and between polycentric settlements.

This synergism has been recognized by global network corporations in Japan as they have used modern transport and communications technology, including their own leased circuits, to target all five Development Corridors for research and development activities and scientific collaboration. The structure of the circuit arrangement reflects the nature of their prime activities. For instance, the international leased networks of city banks and securities firms are centred on a triangular network with the three world financial capitals — London, Tokyo and New York — at the vertices (MPT, 1988). Those of general trading companies radiate from Eastern Japan with the North American, European and East Asian Corridors at the end of the rays. The Southeast Asian and Australian Corridors are seen as prime sites for technopolises.

Figure 9.8: Calls by International Subscriber Dialing from Major Japanese Cities to Overseas Countries, 1983

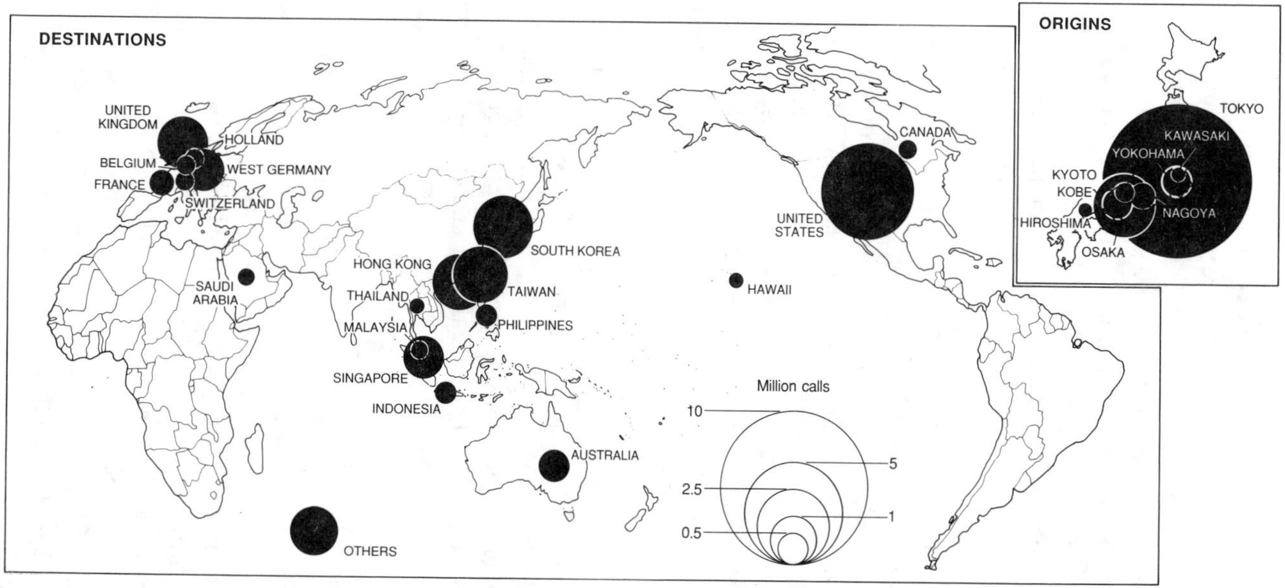

Source: Pers. comm.

Conclusion

This study is an initial contribution to the task of forecasting developments in the Pacific Economic Zone. Of necessity, it has involved keeping up with technologies, assessing the effects of multimodal arrangements, understanding problems in trade facilitation and developing an appreciation of protectionist arrangements (Peters, 1989). Specifically, it has focussed on the ramifications of variations in the nodality of the command centres, and density of transport and communication networks linking the Development Corridors that have emerged in the Zone since the 1970s. For the most part it has concentrated on freight and passenger networks and pinpointed the hub and spoke networks that have arisen in sea and air transport following deregulation in the United States and the rise of the multimodal transport operator.

If the relationship between the Corridors and Research and Development is to be understood, more effort will have to be devoted to comprehending the significance of the import and export of information based on basic research and applied science (e.g. inventions, patents and publications). The importance of understanding the relationship between telecommunications and community creativity within the East Japan Corridor is already appreciated. It will have to be extended to other parts of the Zone before the potential economic synergies of the other Development Corridors can be tapped (Batten, 1990).

As Australia is battling immediate economic problems, the likely Corridor changes involve overcoming legal and institutional barriers to trade. They require the development of a community of Electronic Data Interchange and deregulation rather than any infrastructural modification (though a land bridge and double stack trains have been investigated). Major adjustments are likely to occur within the East Asian and Southeast Asian Corridors. Rapprochement involving China, Japan, the Koreas and the Soviet Union will have important repercussions on market diversification and prospects for additional feeder cargo and information for handling by recognized seaport, airport and teleport hubs, notably Osaka Bay, Tokyo Bay and Seoul-Pusan, and other, as yet, unheralded nodes (Rimmer, 1990).

Similarly, Taiwan, and Kaohsiung in particular, stand to benefit from any reorientation of sea and air trade and traffic with China, presumably at the expense of Hong Kong. Also, the Taiwanese are endeavouring to benefit from the progressive switch of industry to Southeast Asia by locating their off-shore activities to take advantage of Singapore's superior sea-air connections. Although much emphasis in this study has been given to Japan's influence on the Pacific Economic Zone's market place these developments suggest that its importance during the early part of the 21st century is likely to wane with the overseas Chinese and China as the pacemakers. Before these possibilities are put into context, connections between Development Corridors in the Pacific Economic Zone and their counterparts in the Europe Community and other parts of North America would need to be investigated.

ACKNOWLEDGEMENTS

I am indebted to both Barbara Banks and Christine Tabart for research assistance and to Kay Dancey, Cartographic Section, Research School of Pacific Studies, The Australian National University, Canberra for drawing the accompanying figures.

NOTES

1. Outside the macro-economic corridors in Europe and the United States (undefined) Andersson (1990) recognized that small corridor regions were being created by channelling investment into transport and communication infrastructure and cultural activities.

2. The main goods moving from East Asia to the United States include manufactured commodities including electrical appliances (video and office equipment) and high-tech electronic machinery and apparatus (computers and semiconductors), knocked-down motor vehicles and textiles and intermediate manufactured goods and components).

3. Service contracts followed deregulation in the United States. The *Shipping Act, 1984* allows carriers to enter into agreements with shippers which offered discounts for meeting an agreed volume over a specified period.

4. Electronic data interchange (EDI) is the standard means of document exchange among computers for international trade.

5. The transmission, emission and reception of signals, writing, images, sounds or information of any nature through wires, fibre optics, satellite links, broadcast or electromagnetic systems between locations.

REFERENCES

ABC (1979). *ABC World Airways Guide, August 1979*, 2 vols. Dunstable: ABC Travel Guide Ltd.

——— (1989a). *ABC World Airways Guide: Blue Book, August 1989*. Dunstable: ABC International.

——— (1989b). *ABC World Airways Guide: Red Book, August 1989*. Dunstable: ABC International.

Aiwa, Motoo (1989). "International Airfreight Information Systems: Their Present Status, Future Task." *Airfreighting Guide, 1989–1990, Supplement*. Tokyo: Shipping and Trade News, pp. 18–19.

Akiyama, Tomomasa (1984). *Comparative Study of Transportation Costs by Air and Containership*. JAMRI Report, No. 4. Tokyo: Japan Maritime Research Institute.

Allen, J. E. (1989). "Visions for World Transport in the Next 50 Years." *Proceedings ICHCA 19th Biennial Conference May 29th–June 2nd 1989*. Stockholm: International Cargo Handling Carriers Association.

Andersson, A. E. (1990). "The Emerging Global Network of C-regions." *Cosmo Creative '90: International Forum on Logistical Development and Its Regional Consequences in Osaka — Towards a Cosmo Creative City, 17–18 July 1990*. Osaka: Osaka Prefectural Government (and others), pp. 57–64.

Batten, D. F. (1990). "Network Cities Versus Central Place Cities: Building a Cosmo-creative Constellation." *Cosmo Creative '90: International Forum on Logistical Development and Its Regional Consequences in Osaka — Towards a Cosmo Creative City, 17–18 July 1990*. Osaka: Osaka Prefectural Government (and others), pp. 83–85.

CI (1989). *Containerisation International*. London: National Magazine Co.

Chinnery, K. (1989). "Air Raid Alert." *Intermodal Asia*, Winter, pp. 21–23 & 37.

Clowes, C. W (1989). "Round the Pacific by Light Beam." *Asia Technology*, 1(4), pp. 27–28.

Damrot, S. (1990). "The Japanese Airport Squeeze." *Asia Technology*, 2(3), pp. 15–16.

Douglass, M. (1989). "The Future of Cities on the Pacific Rim." In *Pacific Rim Cities in the World Economy: Comparative Urban and Community Research*, Vol. 2, edited by M. P. Smith. New Brunswick: Transaction Publications, pp. 9–66.

Fleming, D. K. (1989). "On the Beaten Track: A View of US West-Coast Container Port Competition." *Maritime Policy and Management*, 16(2), pp. 93–107.

Frankel, E. (1990). "Future Technological and Operations Developments in Intermodal Transport." Unpublished paper presented at the 2nd KMI International

Symposium on The Public Sector's Role in Logistics for the 21st Century, hosted by the Korean Maritime Institute (KMI), 2–7 July, p. 24.

Friedmann, J. (1986). "The World City Hypothesis." *Development and Change*, 17, pp. 69–83.

Garnaut, R. (1989). *Australia and Northeast Asian Ascendancy: Report to the Prime Minister and Minister for Foreign Affairs and Trade*. Canberra: Australian Government Publishing Service.

Gibson, K. and R. Horvath (1983). "Aspects of a Theory of Transition within the Capitalist Mode of Production." *Environment and Planning D: Space and Society*, 1, pp. 121–138.

Gilman, S. (1988). "Prospects for Development of Multimodal Transport Systems." In *Changes in the World Shipping Environments and Counter-Strategies toward the Year 2000*, International Maritime Seminar, 25–26 July. Seoul: Korean Maritime Institute, pp. 237–266.

Hansen, M. and A. Kanafani (1988). "International Airline Hubbing in a Competitive Environment." *Transportation Planning and Technology*, 13, pp. 3–18.

——— (1990). "Airline Hubbing and Airport Economics in the Pacific Market." *Transportation Research A*, 24A(3), pp. 217–230.

KMI (1990). *2000 Nyeondae ul Hyang Han Urynara Hanggong Sanup Yeu Jung Jang gi Bal Jeon Bang Hyang Yeongu* (Research report on mid- and long term directions in the development of the Korean air industry for the 21st century). Seoul: Korean Maritime Institute.

Kaiji Sangyo Kenkyujo (1989). *Sekai no Shuyo Chiiki Kan Tekisen Niuyoki Ryo Chosa* (Survey report of the volume of liner shipping on the major world routes). Tokyo: Kaiji Sangyo Kenkyujo (Japan Maritime Research Institute).

King, A. D. (1990). *Global Cities: Post Imperialism and the Internationalization of London*. London and New York: Routledge.

Kobayashi Masato (1989). "Airfreight Transport: Current Situation and Future Outlook." *Airfreighting Guide, 1989–1990, Supplement*. Tokyo: Shipping and Trade News, pp. 10–14.

Kuroda Hideo (1987). "Kokusai Fukugo Unso no Genjo to Mondai" (Problems and activities of international multimodal transport). *Kaigai Sangyo Kenkujo*, 250, pp. 9–27.

Lee, B. (1989). "Teleports and Global Networks: Australian Opportunities." *International Telecommunication and the Global Economy: Policies and Opportunities, Proceedings of a Circit Conference*. Melbourne: Centre for International Research on Communication and Information Technologies, pp. 44–47.

MPT (1988). *White Paper 1988: Communications in Japan*. Tokyo: Ministry of Posts and Telegraph.

McGee, T. G. (1990). "The State and Urbanization in Asia: The Emergence of Desakota Regions." Unpublished paper presented at the Conference on States and Development in the East Asian Pacific Rim, held at the University of California, Santa Barbara, 22–25 March.

Marti, B. (1988). "The Evolution of Pacific Basin Load Centres." *Maritime Policy and Management*, 15(1), pp. 57–66.

Miyazaki, Tatsuo (1989). "Japanese Ports and Overview on Trade and Transportation." Unpublished paper presented at the 16th General Conference of the International Association of Ports and Harbors, held in Miami, Florida, April, 19pp.

Nagatsuka Seiji (1987). *The Pacific Rim Era and the Shipping — Effects of the Economic Developments of Asian Nics on Seaborne Trade and the Shipping.* JAMRI Report, No. 19. Tokyo: Japan Maritime Research Institute.

Peters, H. J. (1989). *Seatrade, Logistics and Transport.* Policy and Research Series, No. 6. Washington, D.C.: The World Bank.

Rimmer, P. J. (1989). "Japanese Communications Developments and the Australian-transport Land Use System: The Missing Link." *Transactions of Multi-Disciplinary Engineering*, GE 13(2), pp. 57–72.

——— (1990). "Ports, Inland Transport Linkages and Inland Development: A Western Pacific Rim Conspectus." Unpublished paper presented at the 2nd KMI International Symposium on The Public Sector's Role in Logistics for the 21st Century, hosted by the Korean Maritime Institute (KMI), 2–7 July, 55 pp.

Smith, M. P. and J. R. Feagin (1987). "Cities and the New International Division of Labor: An Overview." In *The Capitalist City: Global Restructuring and Community Politics*, edited by M. P. Smith and J. R. Feagin. Oxford and New York: Basil Blackwell, pp. 2–34.

Soja, E. (1989). *Postmodern Geographies: The Reassertion of Space in Critical Social Theory.* London and New York: Verso.

Space (1989). "Consolidated Export Cargo Classified by Destination and Forwarders." *Space*, July, pp. 84–85.

Stoner, I. (1990). "Airports for the Twenty-first Century." *Asia Technology*, 2(3), pp. 12–14.

United Nations (1987). *The Prospects of World Urbanisation Revised as of 1984–85.* New York: United Nations.

Walker, S (1989a). "Air Growth Hinges on Asia." *Intermodal Asia*, Spring, pp. 14–19.

——— (1989b). "The Rise and Rise of Express Freight." *Intermodal Asia*, Winter, pp. 18–23.

Westlake, M. (1990a). "Altitude Sickness." *Far Eastern Economic Review*, 15 March, pp. 42–44.

——— (1990b). "Airfreight: A Shift of Emphasis." *Far Eastern Economic Review*, 4 October, pp. 58–59.

Yamada Hideo (1987). *Where Conference and Non-Conference Carriers Meet:*

What Fixed Day-of-the-Week Service Aims At. JAMRI Report, No. 23. Tokyo: Japan Maritime Research Institute.

——— (1988). *Container Shipping — Unmasking of Overtonnaging.* JAMRI Report, No. 29. Tokyo: Japan Maritime Research Institute.

——— (1989). "Perspective on the Short-sea Liner Trades in Asia." Unpublished paper presented at Marintec China 1989 Conference, Shanghai, 30 November.

Yoshida Shigeru (1987). *Changes in Japan's Foreign Trade Structure Induced by the Tremendous Strengthening of the Yen, and Merchant Shipping.* JAMRI Report, No. 24. Tokyo: Japan Maritime Research Institute.

CHAPTER TEN

Planning Rural Transport for the 21st Century: Some Pointers for Indonesia

D. C. Johnston

Senior Lecturer, Department of Geography, University of Canterbury, Christchurch, New Zealand

Two main forces will shape the pattern of rural transport in Pacific Asia as the region moves into the 21st century: changing levels of demand for movement; and the degree to which demand can be met by the supply of transport facilities. It is clear that demand for transport will increase steadily as subsistence activities are incorporated into market economies, as rural dwellers increasingly seek off-farm employment, as disposable incomes grow, and as amenities such as clinics and schools become more accessible. There is much less certainty that the provision of rural transport facilities can keep pace with the demand for transport. Each country faces its own set of economic pressures and, with continual growth in the range of competing claims on national budgets, "piecemeal" additions to the rural transport network have difficulty in matching the economic and political returns available from other expenditure options.

In fact, the central issue is even more basic than the availability of funds. There is a gross lack of information on the transport situation in rural areas. Thus it is virtually impossible to define the real magnitude of the "rural transport problem" or to critically evaluate the accepted wisdom of contemporary approaches of rural transport improvement. Most attempts to evaluate rural transport problems simply assume the over-riding desirability of all-weather roads and motor vehicles without any careful evaluation of the "appropriateness" of this model in the context it is meant to serve. Part of the problem undoubtedly lies in an unbounded faith in the flexibility of the motor vehicle as the solution to all transport problems. Even more important is the lack of information on the rural transport situation to show what the patterns really are and what the needs might be.

This chapter draws mainly on data from Indonesia in a first systematic attempt to describe the aggregate dimensions of rural transport in a Southeast Asian country and to evaluate the appropriateness of the available information base for decisions that allocate public funds to rural transport improvement. It is shown that standard sources of planning information fail to address the real issues of rural transport. Given the continuing use of such sources of information, we might expect that rural transport improvements will continue to focus on the "road and motor vehicle fix" and thus perpetuate the neglect of the reality of the rural transport scene. The 60–70 percent of national populations who live in rural areas have the right to demand a more sensitive approach to their transport problems.

Project and Area Based Planning

Planning for investment in transport infrastructure could proceed from two main bases: project or areal. Project based planning focuses on specific problems in existing infrastructure: a section of road needing resealing, a bridge that should be widened, or the enlarging of a public transport depot. Area-based planning, on the other hand, involves comparing the situations of a set of areas or regions — normally ones with administrative significance (e.g., districts or provinces) — to identify those areas that are deficient in some ways relative to others. These two approaches are fundamentally different in their philosophies and in the likely nature and pattern of the improvements that they generate.

Project based planning focuses on specific problems in existing facilities — projects are therefore easily identifiable, finite, and defined by some visible shortcomings in the physical infrastructure or in the operation of the transport system. They are, for these same reasons, eminently suited to orthodox economic evaluation by methods such as cost-benefit analysis. Indeed, one wonders at times whether suitability for economic analysis is the main reason why some transport improvements are proposed.

Yet such methods have been criticized for a number of reasons, perhaps the most significant being the bias towards situations with high traffic volumes and therefore against areas with relatively low levels of movement. Economic evaluation also depends upon the valuing of all elements of cost and benefit in monetary terms; items with no ready valuation such as noise pollution, environmental damage or improved access, may be noted, but do not enter the calculus. Furthermore, considerable importance is attached to forecasts (both "with-" and "without-" project) of future traffic levels, of future savings in vehicle operating costs, of future savings in travel time, and of future savings in accident costs. All such forecasts present difficulties over the short term, let alone over the twenty to thirty years life of a transport project.

It should also be noted, certainly in the context of rural transport, that the solutions adopted are inevitably defined by the problem identified: the deteriorated pavement is resurfaced; the washed-out bridge is repaired and the gap in the road network is filled by a new road. There appears to be a fixed mind-set that sees the narrow technical options of all-weather road and motor vehicle as the only feasible ways of improving transport in rural areas.

Even more serious, the projects that actually emerge from this mind-set overwhelmingly concentrate on the physical infrastructure alone. The planners' assumption must be that vehicles and transport services will materialize as if by magic. That may well happen but one should also ask: who provides the services and how appropriate are the services for the target population?

The first point is not clearly resolved in the literature, though it is believed that transport operators are often urban-based traders who not only provide transport services but also function as purchasers of farm produce and, possibly, suppliers of rural credit, too. Such a situation could very easily work against the interests of the farmer.

The second point, however, is abundantly clear to anyone who visits the rural Third World. Roads and vehicles may well be readily available in rural areas, but the visitor also sees ample evidence of modern physical infrastructure being used in traditional ways. Farm produce is carried in head or shoulder loads, by hand carts, by bicycle or by animal transport. The only conclusion possible is that the motor vehicles available are not responsive to the needs of the rural population.

The project-based approach therefore appears to be inappropriate in situations where inequalities are present in the provision, or in the ability to use, infrastructure. It would seem to be most useful in situations where the socio-economic makeup is relatively homogeneous and where the network of physical infrastructure is essentially complete. Orthodox economic analysis might then be used to evaluate maintenance or improvement proposals without having any untoward effect in compounding disadvantages faced by those peripheral to the network.

Area-based planning, in contrast, seems the logical way of approaching situations with large disparities in the provision of physical network and/or in the ability to use services. By definition, the technique focuses on relative deficiency and therefore should minimize the tendency for investment to concentrate in areas already well served. Furthermore, an area-based approach allows the consideration of situations where the solution to a transport difficulty is not predefined — thus there is potential for creative thinking that may generate transport improvements more appropriate to the needs of rural people.

Area-based planning does not lead to proposals that are readily amenable to economic analysis simply because it deals with areal aggregates rather than specific problem sites. Rather than worrying about estimating costs and benefits for the area concerned (which could be done, though at considerable administrative cost), it is more productive to focus on the advantages of the area-based approach.

First, the absence of a single scale of evaluation relevant to all the issues involved in rural transport forces the analyst to recognize that a number of dimensions could be used to define transport deficiency. This means that explicit and clear objectives for rural transport improvement must be established. Then, and only then, can the planner choose the measures needed to assess transport deficiency. Insisting on measures that relate to stated objectives provides scope for evaluating the "performance" of the improvements that are implemented and thus invaluable feedback for the planning process.

Second, the area-based approach is singularly appropriate for a decentralized planning system where investment funds are granted to an areal unit for expenditure according to the needs defined by its own people. Few observers would argue that central government bodies have a clearer appreciation of local needs and resources than local units. While it could be argued that local government does not have the technical expertise and experience to implement some kinds of projects, it is also a truism that one cannot develop experience without being allowed to try.

An area-based approach to transport planning that allowed flexibility in both problem definition (type and extent of transport deficiency) and in the nature of the proposed improvements, could be a significant advance over project-based methods. This especially is true where transport infrastructure was not complete and where development planning was driven by a concern for equity rather than simplistic notions of economic efficiency.

This chapter will therefore concentrate on illustrating an area-based approach to rural transport planning. The aim of the exercise is to explore various ways of identifying areas that are deficient in transport facilities relative to other areas within the overall territory being examined.

In reality, of course, it would be expected that this kind of analysis would lead to investment in those areas defined as deficient in order to reduce disparities. Such an expectation, furthermore, involves an assumption that investment in transport facilities will be beneficial to the population concerned. It is vital that this assumption be recognized as an assumption and to understand that benefits will not automatically flow from each and every investment in transport improvement. Consequently, transport improvements must be designed to be appropriate for the needs of the target population and thus maximize the chances of actually realizing the anticipated benefits.

The question that arises therefore is, how can one identify areas deficient in transport conditions? What measures could be used and to what effect? These questions will be explored by using provincial level data from Indonesia which is one of the few countries with data collection systems that allow innovative approaches to an examination of rural transport patterns. Similar analyses could be carried out for any country with an appropriate data-base or at any level of territorial authority. In Indonesia, for example, the same principles could be applied to districts (*kabupaten*) within provinces or sub-districts (*kecamatan*) within districts. At any level the analysis would help identify those areal units most deserving of developmental funds to help improve its transport conditions.

Here the provinces are ranked on each measure and, for display, classified into three equal groups (terciles). The provinces in the top group are therefore identified as the least deficient while those in the bottom one third are the most deficient. There is nothing sacrosanct in this procedure.

Quintiles or some system of "threshold" values could equally be used to separate less deficient from more deficient.

Measures of Transport Deficiency: Orthodox

The most obvious measures of transport deficiency are those that involve the physical availability of the transport system: the density of roads and the availability of vehicles. Raw data required for these measures (road lengths and vehicle numbers) are usually readily available through government authorities responsible for road construction and maintenance and for vehicle registration. When converted to density or per capita forms they can be ranked, grouped and mapped (Figure 10.1).[1] Both measures demonstrate wide disparities in transport conditions within Indonesia and quite different spatial patterns. Java and Bali reveal the densest network of roads (noting, however, that information on road length was not available for Jakarta). Vehicle availablity (not mapped here) has significant high points in Sumatra and Kalimantan as well as Jakarta, Yogyakarta and Bali. However, both of these measures present problems for the assessment of deficiencies in rural transport conditions.

The value of vehicle availability as a measure of transport deficiency is reduced by an awareness that vehicles are largely concentrated in urban areas and therefore much less readily available to the rural population than might appear to be the case. Data to examine this assertion could not be obtained for Indonesia. However, information drawn from the 1970 Census of Population and Housing of Thailand shows that automobiles were ten times more available in municipal areas than in villages (Table 10.1). The figures are not directly transferable to Indonesia but it is reasonable to expect a similar result there also.[2] Rural people, then, do not gain the

Table 10.1: Vehicles in Households — Thailand 1970

Vehicle Type	Percent of Households with Vehicle		
	Municipal Areas	Sanitary Districts	Villages
Bicycle	28.6	41.3	29.6
Motorcycle	14.8	11.5	5.4
Automobile	13.3	5.8	1.3

Source: National Statistical Office, 1973, *Population and Housing Census 1970: Whole Kingdom*. Bangkok: National Statistical Office, p. 153.

Figure 10.1: Road Density: 1983

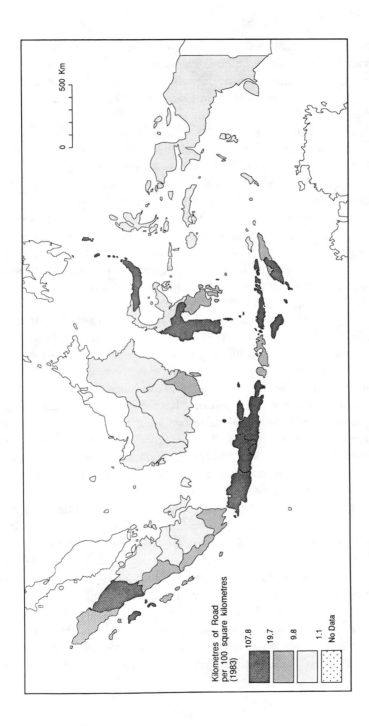

Kilometres of Road
per 100 square kilometres
(1983)

107.8

19.7

9.8

1.1

No Data

500 Km

benefits of vehicle ownership that are so often assumed in Western-oriented views of transport problems. The bicycle, however, seems to be a much more meaningful index of transport ownership in Indonesia and is documented for rural households in 1985 (CBS, 1987a). Ownership levels reach a high of nearly 62 percent of households in Yogyakarta and range down to 0.8 percent in Irian Jaya.[3]

Road density, like vehicle availability, is only superficially useful as an index of rural transport deficiencies. Road density values are distorted by the inclusion of areas of non-agricultural land (mountains, water bodies and urban areas) and also by counting lengths of road that serve primarily non-rural purposes (inter-city highways and urban streets).

Some of these difficulties can be resolved by employing more appropriate measures of "area" and "road" in order to meet the objective of assessing the availability of infrastructure in rural areas. Information on the area of cultivated land in each province is available for 1983 and 1986 (CBS, 1985b, 1987a, 1987b). Furthermore, Indonesian road statistics at the provincial level are broken down according to administrative responsibility. It is therefore possible to separate national, provincial and municipal roads from district roads. Taking district roads as an index of roads serving rural purposes is not a perfect solution as the figures include streets in those urban areas that do not qualify as municipalities (*Kotamadya*). It is felt, however, that the exclusion of national, provincial and municipal roads provides a better approximation to the infrastructure available in rural areas. As data were available for all but two provinces in 1983, that year was selected for the calculation of road density in terms of cultivated area. Kalimantan, in particular, stands out as an area of transport deficiency according to this measure.

It could be argued that different types of agriculture require different levels of access to roads and possibly the deficiency measure could be modified accordingly. There are, however, more basic problems with this kind of measure. The first is that any assessment of transport deficiency in terms of road density (however defined) has a very strong tendency to predispose planners to the view that the deficiency should be overcome simply by investing in more roads.

Secondly, defining transport deficiency as a relative shortfall in the density of roads ignores the function(s) that roads are supposed to perform. Some planners might argue that rural roads are designed primarily to serve the needs of agriculture. This, however, is a rather short-sighted view. A little reflection soon reveals that the fundamental function of a road (or transport in general) is to serve the needs of the population. Agriculture has no existence independent of the cultivators and cultivators have transport requirements that go beyond the marketing of crops. The main question raised by road density as a measure of transport deficiency is illustrated in Figure 10.2. Two provinces have the same land (and cultivated) area, the same population and the same length of road. According to a density measure they have the same level of transport deficiency. If, however, roads are intended to connect people (or settlements) to the national space economy then province B is much better served than province A.

Figure 10.2: Road Density: A Measure of Transport Deficiency?

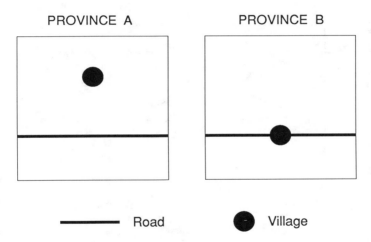

Measures of Transport Deficiency: Innovative

Assessing the transport system in terms of the degree to which it provides connections to people or settlements would therefore seem a much more appropriate measure of transport deficiency than road density. Indonesia, in fact, is one of the few countries that has conducted surveys that provide this kind of information.[4] Figure 10.3 displays the transport situation in terms of the proportions of villages which have all year vehicle access. Java and Bali are relatively well served according to this measure. It is also interesting to

Figure 10.3: Rural Villages with All-year Vehicle Access (1976/1977)

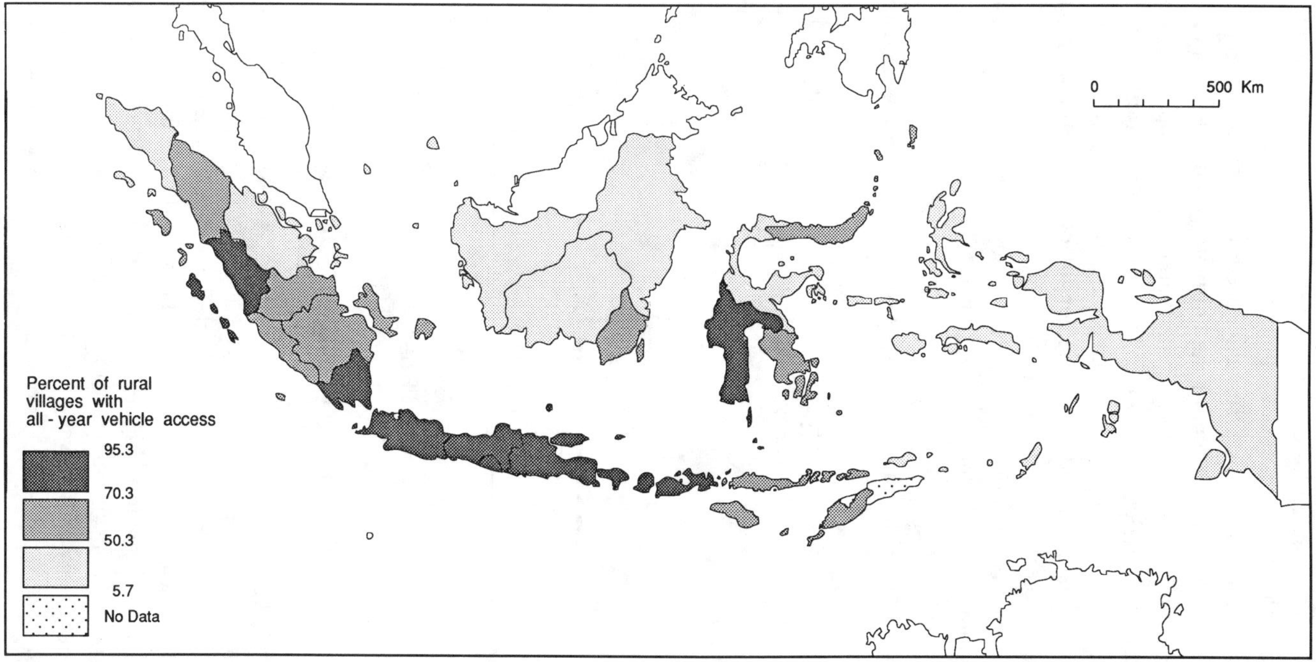

Percent of rural
villages with
all - year vehicle access

95.3

70.3

50.3

5.7

No Data

500 Km

0

note that Lampung, rated as "deficient" in terms of road density on cultivated land, is now in the top bracket! On the other hand, Irian Jaya, the Moluccas and three provinces in Kalimantan seem to be singularly disadvantaged. It is instructive to explore why this might be so.

The 1976/1977 Survey of Social Facilities in Villages recorded the main means of access to each village. Most rural villages were served by roads but, for the country as a whole, 11.1 percent operated primarily through water transport. At province level the proportion rises as high as 81.5 percent in the case of Central Kalimantan. A road-based view of transport deficiency would regard Central Kalimantan as a major problem area: only 5.7 percent of villages had all year vehicle access. Such a viewpoint would also face major difficulties if a road-based solution to the problem was implemented as wide rivers and extensive swamps render road construction extremely expensive. The settlement pattern, not surprisingly, is adapted to transport primarily by river. It is instructive, therefore, to review the question of whether water access should be regarded as a transport problem that, ideally, would be solved by building roads.

Roads and waterways both provide ready access to a channel for the movement of people and freight and neither, in principle, require the construction of a purpose built terminal to gain access to the transport vehicle: vehicles stop on the side of the road; boats moor against or nose into the river bank. Roads do have an advantage in that they can be used without a separate vehicle — walking is a significant way of moving people and goods in rural Indonesia. Waterways, on the other hand, require some kind of boat as swimming is rarely used as a mode of transport except in emergency or recreation. That said, however, it is probably easier for a rural household to obtain or purchase a boat of some kind than it is to get an equivalent vehicle to operate on roads.

Paddle power is, of course, less effective when going upstream but, then again, it is hard to cycle uphill. The most important advance that can be made in transport is to move from human power to mechanical power (or to sails in the case of water transport). Outboard motors cost no more than motorcycles and offer greater carrying capacity (and comfort) if a somewhat slower speed. In the absence of vehicles owned or borrowed, rural people depend on transport services provided by others and in principle there would seem to be little difference between providing a public transport service on a road or on a waterway. Finally one can note that waterways require relatively little expenditure on construction or maintenance.

On balance, therefore, it is argued that there is little significance in the difference between road and water access in the sense of providing either basic or improved (motorized) transport conditions. The two forms of transport could therefore be taken together to represent the base situation of access to rural villages (Figure 10.4).[5] On this combined measure West Kalimantan is the only Borneo province to be rated as "deficient" though it comes only just ahead of bottom ranked Irian Jaya. Aceh is now the third most "deficient" province.

Although household ownership of vehicles does provide the passport to improved transport conditions that is most familiar to Western eyes, it is also clear from the limited amount of data available that relatively few rural households in developing countries own motor-powered vehicles. Those without access to vehicles are therefore dependent on public transport services or must resort to using physical infrastructure in traditional ways. The potential importance of public transport must not be underestimated, especially in terms of the long distance linkages that it can open up: to new marketing opportunities, to government services, to high level education and medical care or to distant social contacts. For Indonesian provinces in 1976/1977, the proportions of villages that enjoyed public transport services run from a high of 90.5 to a low of 20.5. The "deficient" provinces on this measure range all across Indonesia from Riau to Irian Jaya. Perhaps surprisingly, given the high density of population and excellent trunk road infrastructure, Central Java's proportion falls below that of the best served group of provinces.

The real significance of public transport services varies with the degree to which villagers need to leave the village itself to gain access to important amenities. Indonesia can pride itself on a remarkable effort to make primary schools available in villages. Yet there were, in 1976/1977, several provinces where fewer than 75 percent of villages had schools. Similar tabulations from the Survey of Social Facilities in Villages data indicate that, at the provincial level, the proportion of villages with some kind of medical facility ranges from 88.6 percent to 12.5 percent.[6]

The full meaning that such data hold for the rural population does not emerge until the analysis explores the links between facility availability and public transport. Villages that have a facility are not an issue (depending,

Figure 10.4: Rural Villages with Water or All-year Vehicle Access (1976/1977)

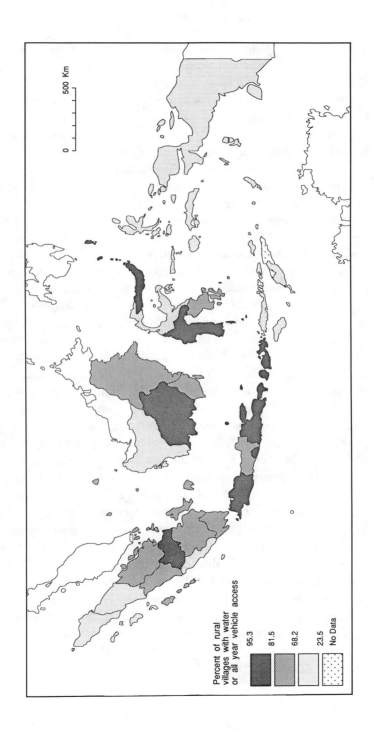

perhaps, on the quality of the facility); villages with no facility but with public transport links to facilities available elsewhere, are not quite so favoured. The real need for attention, however, are those villages that have neither the facility nor public transport (Figure 10.5). But the analysis must be tempered by recognizing that a village might be too small to warrant the presence of a facility. However, the planning process should not stop here. It must go on to find ways whereby the required kind of service can be made available: whether by formal or informal facilities within the village; by a mobile facility shared with other villages; or by providing a public transport service to a location possessing the facility.

One other point, that deprivation in terms of access to facilities is more apparent than real because of proximity to a neighbouring village possessing a facility, should readily be testable. Given adequate data, the mean distance to the nearest medical facility can be calculated for those villages that possessed neither facility nor public transport: for seven provinces in 1976/1977 this mean distance exceeded 20 km. At this level the analysis can give an unfair impression of conditions. In some cases, the number of villages (and the population) concerned is only a very small proportion of provincial totals, though this is no consolation to the villagers affected.

However, given the objective of exploring alternative approaches to the allocation of funds for the improvement of rural transport conditions, it is necessary to go beyond this point. How can one translate transport deficiency measures into statements about desirable or necessary levels of funding? It should be clear that the problems are not going to be solved within one year or even a few years. The issue is therefore one of allocating an annual budget among territorial units according to "need."

The problem could be handled by way of explicit national statements on the role expected of rural transport, the selection of appropriate measure(s) and the identification of "deficient" regions. The budget could then be allocated in proportion to the number of villages or people in those regions. However, there is a danger here that regions are regarded as either "deficient" or "non-deficient" when, in fact, the issue is one of degree. This can be counteracted by using the deficiency measure (or some explicit combination of measures) as an index of rural transport "need." Funding can then be allocated to each region in proportion to that index. The point is illustrated in Figure 10.6. Assuming that rural transport "need" is defined in terms of access to medical facilities, the index used is based on the population of villages

Figure 10.5: Rural Villages with neither Medical Facility nor Public Transport (1976/1977)

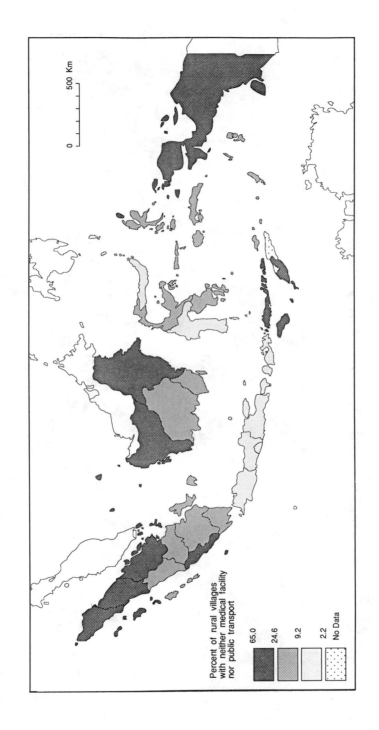

Percent of rural villages
with neither medical facility
nor public transport

65.0

24.6

9.2

2.2

No Data

500 Km

Figure 10.6: Possible Allocation of Rural Transport Funds (Provinces)

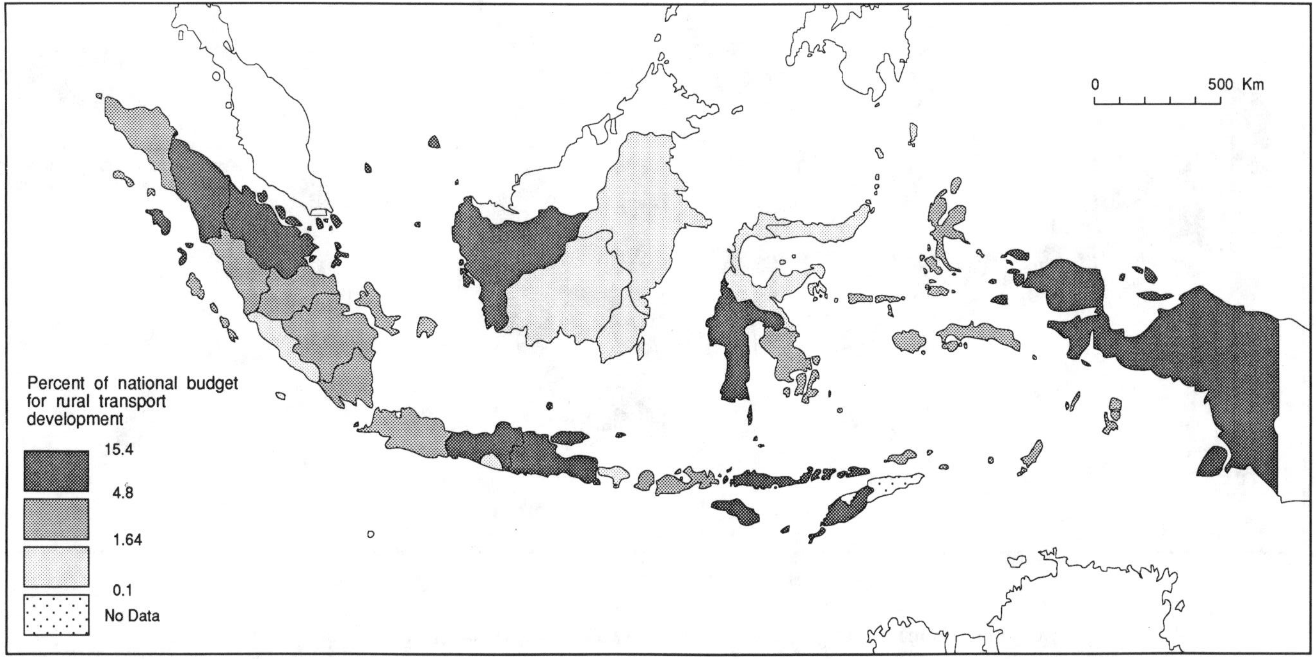

500 Km

Percent of national budget
for rural transport
development

15.4

4.8

1.64

0.1

No Data

that have neither medical facilities nor public transport. This population figure is then weighted by the distance, in each case, to the nearest medical facility on the grounds that larger funds will be required to overcome the problems of more isolated villages. The resulting pattern shows an intriguing combination of provinces with large affected populations, but small distances (Central and East Java) and those with small populations in very isolated villages (Irian Jaya and West Kalimantan).

The same point is explored at a larger scale in Figure 10.7 which maps the index for regencies (*kabupaten*) to show the spatial distribution of "need for funds for rural transport" within the provinces of Java. Similar analyses could be performed for sub-districts within regencies or even for villages within sub-districts.

One further major issue must be noted with regard to rural transport conditions. So far the analysis has focussed on the external links available to villages. These are undoubtedly important as they help conditioning the role that the village has in the wider nation state — economically, socially, politically and from a welfare point of view. However, as mentioned earlier, the Indonesian village is a territorial and administrative, rather than a settlement, unit. Individual villages may cover a considerable area, consist of several distinct hamlets and involve a range of transport conditions (Table 10.2).

This point leads to the whole question of intra-village transport needs. These include travel to and from farm land (with or without the movement of inputs or produce), the collection of firewood and household water

Table 10.2: Intra-Village Transport Conditions: Kabupaten Garut

Number of villages visited (Desa)	35
Number of Hamlets (Kampung)	596
Average distance from village office to the most distant hamlet (kms)	3.4
Percent of hamlets accessible by:	
Bicycle	39.1
Motorcycle	37.2
Jeep	27.7
Truck	26.7
Motor Car	23.7
Percent of hamlets with a school	22.0

Source: Field survey (1988).

Figure 10.7: Possible Allocation of Rural Transport Funds (Regencies in Java)

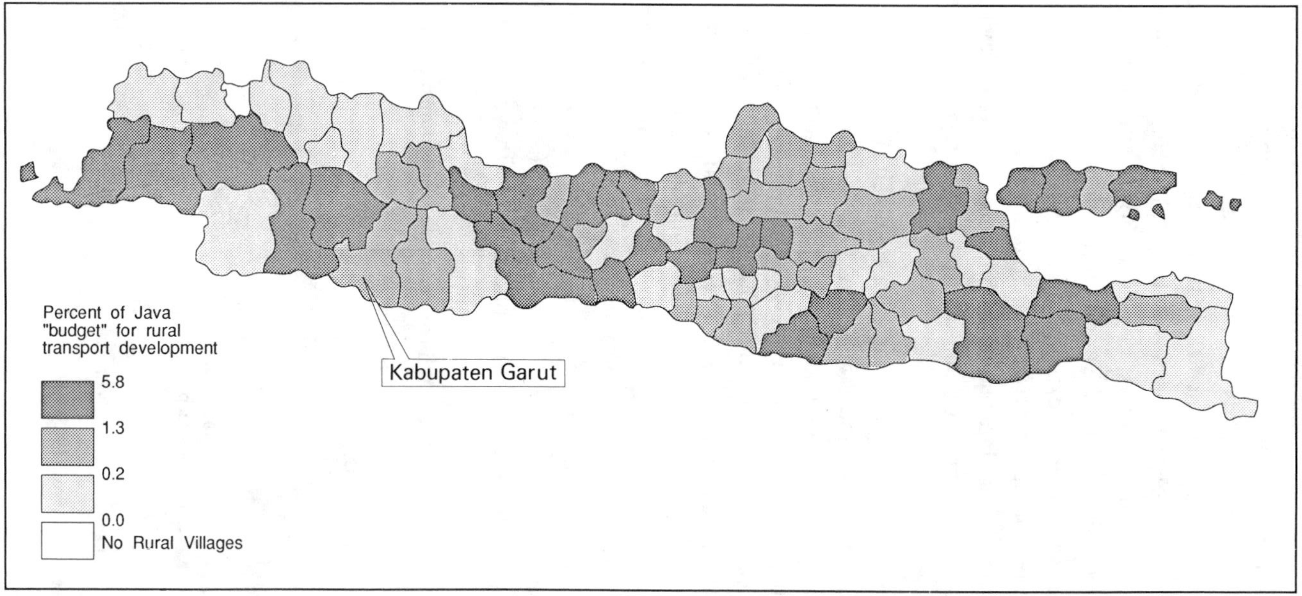

Percent of Java
"budget" for rural
transport development

5.8
1.3
0.2
0.0
No Rural Villages

Kabupaten Garut

supplies, as well as travel to school, to market, to clinics or to social and religious occasions. Only rarely have these transport needs been documented, but it is clear that very considerable burdens may be involved (Barwell and Malmberg, 1986).

The author's survey of villages in Kabupaten Garut (in West Java as shown in Figure 10.7) investigated this very point by recording every trip made by household members that exceeded 100 m.[7] Two survey periods covering both wet and dry seasons and totalling six weeks were covered. It is clear from the results so far available (wet season survey only) that village transport needs are very largely met by walking (Table 10.3).

Table 10.3: Summary Mobility Data: Kabupaten Garut

Hamlet	Method of Access	Trips by Mode of Transport: Walking					
		Mean Distance (kms)	Mean Load (kgs)	Walk Trips as a Percentage of All Trips			
				Trips	Load	Ton/Kms	Time
Cilimus	A	1.8	8.5	81.4	10.3	3.9	75.3
Sadangayah	A	2.4	22.0	93.6	41.0	26.6	90.7
Cocayur	A	1.6	8.4	61.8	26.1	8.2	63.5
Tegalparung	F	0.9	3.7	66.1	62.1	9.8	46.5
Pangkokan	A	1.8	10.2	78.2	23.1	4.2	42.4
Jaringao	S	3.8	6.6	90.9	79.7	42.1	61.8
Sukatani	S	1.3	28.5	76.8	82.1	34.4	59.6
Kiararungkad	S	1.2	27.4	84.5	67.8	33.9	67.3
Panyingkiran	S	0.9	30.7	86.1	8.4	1.0	46.8
Ciroyom	S	1.5	22.6	89.1	63.0	29.5	80.5
Cintakarya	A	1.4	6.3	85.8	4.9	2.1	72.5
Cipeundeuy	F	3.1	39.7	93.4	82.9	64.2	76.1
Jamilega	F	1.0	23.2	91.1	96.7	74.4	93.3
Bungbulang	F	1.9	16.9	90.7	79.3	50.2	83.8
Bojong	F	0.6	11.3	94.4	73.0	19.1	75.9
Jangkar	F	1.8	22.5	98.8	97.9	73.4	94.2
Sukawangi	S	1.4	12.9	94.4	58.7	24.9	79.5
Ciingga	F	1.6	9.0	89.8	87.8	38.0	72.6
Warungloa	A	2.3	17.4	85.6	41.5	14.9	64.5
Citapen	F	2.1	26.3	98.9	99.5	80.3	95.4

Method of Access: F = Foot access only
             A = All year access by motor vehicle
             S = Seasonal access by motor vehicle

Source: Field survey (1988).

Average distances are not great and are obviously affected by the relative proximity of the most frequently used destinations such as schools, mosques and village shops. The notable point, however, is the size of the mean load carried, especially in view of the numerous cases of small loads such as school books, digging hoes or harvesting knives that were enumerated. Clearly a major burden is shouldered even in those villages where motorized modes are available.[8]

This importance of human powered transport needs to receive considerable emphasis: transport and human costs are relatively high; the travel time involved could be invested in other activities; and human powered transport is totally ignored in any study that focuses on extra-village links. Furthermore, there is a danger that the employment implications of a knee-jerk "let them use motor vehicles" approach to rural transport improvement can be overlooked. Planners must be sensitive to the realities of transport conditions affecting rural areas and work towards meaningful ways of reducing the burdens that villagers face.

Although it provides no ready-made solutions to rural transport problems, the area-based approach offers a way forward. But it does require a commitment to a decentralized development planning system and it does depend on the availability of appropriate information so that development funds can be directed to where the needs are greatest. It is worth drawing attention, therefore, to the Indonesian system that generated much of the data in this chapter.

Each village (the lowest unit in the official hierarchy of territorial units) receives a formal questionnaire and the village head (a government official) is responsible for having it completed. The original survey of this kind was carried out by the Central Bureau of Statistics and concentrated on the presence/absence of social facilities. More recently, the surveys have been organized by the Rural Development Office and seek much more information and much greater detail. There is reason to believe, on the basis of completed questionnaires viewed by the author, that recent surveys have demanded too much of village officials and the quality of the response has suffered.

Nevertheless it is worth suggesting that surveys including questions along the lines of those in Table 10.4 be conducted to establish the data required for an area-based approach to rural transport planning. In addition to the details identified in Table 10.4, the survey would need to record

Table 10.4: Village Level Survey for Area-based Planning

Does this village have land access?	Yes/No

If yes: For how many weeks in the year is that access disrupted? ...

Does this village have water access?	Yes/No

If yes: For how many weeks in the year is that access disrupted? ...

Which method of access is most important?

Land ...	Water ...	Both Equal ...

If land access is available:

What type of road surface?	Concrete/Tar ...
	Gravel/Metal ...
	Earth ...

Can the village be reached by motor vehicles?

Never ...

Only very rarely ...

Usually, but road is sometimes disrupted ...

In all weather ...

If water access is available:

What are the main modes of propulsion?

	Major	Minor	Rare	Absent
Human Power				
Sail				
Outboard Motor				
Inboard Motor				

Do public transport services reach this village?	Yes/No

If yes: Which modes of public transport are available?

Animal ...	Bicycle ...	Motorcycle ...
Motor vehicle ...	Train ...	Paddle Boat ...
Sail Boat ...	Motor Boat ...	

If no: How far to the nearest public transport? ... Km

How do people travel to public transport? ...

What modes of transport are used to travel/carry produce to and from farms?

	Major	Minor	Rare	Absent
Walking/Porterage				
Animal Power				
Bicycle				
Motorcycle				
Boat				
Motor vehicle				

information on the population of each village; on the facilities within the village; and on the distance (and/or travel time) to get access to facilities not present. Village level data of this kind can easily be aggregated to each successive level in the hierarchy of territorial units. Simple calculations of the kind used in the paper can then identify those units which are "transport deficient" in some clearly specified sense. Allocations of development funds can then be directed to the transport deficient areas.

Conclusion

The conclusions of this chapter are both speculative and concrete. They are concrete in that a specific approach to the planning of rural transport improvements has been suggested. Furthermore, some specific ideas have been put forward on the collection of the data necessary to implement that approach. The speculations that are made operate at two different levels.

First, there is the argument that rural transport conditions will demonstrate little real improvement as long as the planning process is essentially project-based. This follows from the belief that standard methods of economic analysis are largely volume driven: funds for infrastructure maintenance or improvement will therefore go to those locations that have relatively high traffic volumes. Localities with low levels of traffic or without existing infrastructure will be neglected. Ultimately the process leads to a concentration of funds in and around the core (at each level of spatial resolution) and disinvestment in the periphery. In the end the issue is speculative because there are virtually no data by which it can be tested. Rural transport conditions are not adequately reflected in standard data collection systems.

A second speculation builds on an element of the first. Even if appropriate data did become available to allow an area-based planning process, there is no certainty that the claimed advantages of the system would eventuate. Would clear objectives be established for rural transport improvement? Would these be used to define appropriate measures for data collection? Would the data be used to derive measures of transport deficiency at different levels in the territorial hierarchy? Would development funding be allocated according to the relative levels of deficiency? Would the areas receiving funding be able to develop innovative ways of dealing with their transport problems? It does not take a determinedly pessimistic view of official structures to conclude that the geographies of rural transport in the 21st century are not likely to be very different from those of the 20th unless there are significant changes in the process of planning and implementing rural transport improvements.

NOTES

1. All the maps are drawn on the basis of dividing the ranked provinces into three equal groups (in the manner of quartiles): high, medium, and low. The low third is taken as an indication of the provinces that are "transport deficient."

2. A survey conducted by the author in Kabupaten Garut, West Java during 1988 revealed that, of the 639 rural households recorded, only 0.6 percent possessed a motor vehicle and 4.1 percent owned a motorcycle. National figures (urban plus rural), based on 1985 data for the total numbers of vehicles are: 5.1 cars/trucks and 13.3 motorcycles for every 100 households (Central Bureau of Statistics, 1987a, 1989).

3. The author's survey in Kabupaten Garut indicated that 2.2 percent of households owned bicycles. The big difference between this figure and that for West Java rural households overall in 1985, 21.4 percent, is probably due to the very hilly nature of the study area.

4. The Survey of Social Facilities in Villages (1976/1977) recorded the presence/absence of a wide range of facilities (including transport) in Indonesia's 60,000 villages (Central Bureau of Statistics, 1977, 1979 and 1980). Similar information can be obtained from surveys carried out in 1980; 1983 and 1986. The most detailed information available to the author comes from the 1976/1977 survey and so that is reported here. It should be noted that the 1976/1977 survey did not cover Timor Timur and that none of the villages in the province of Jakarta were classified as rural.

5. It is possible that villages depending on water access might not enjoy all year access because of storms or floods. No information is available on the proportions of villages affected in this way.

6. Medical facility, in this context, includes: hospital, clinic, infirmary public health centre, maternity hospital, general practitioner, midwife or para-medical personnel.

7. Field assistants were instructed to record only those trips that went outside the hamlet of residence. Unfortunately, this condition was not fully observed and so tabulations have been prepared on the basis of a distance restriction. Undoubtedly, the exclusion of trips under 100 m serves mainly to reduce the importance of walking as as a mode of a mode of transport.

8. No record was made in the study area of any examples of animal-power transport. However, water buffalo were used in the area to plough paddy fields while horse and "buggy" combinations provided taxi services in Garut City.

REFERENCES

Barwell, I. J. and C. Malmberg (1986). *Makete Integrated Rural Transport Project: Preliminary Findings from Village Survey*. Geneva: International Labour Office.

Central Bureau of Statistics (CBS) (1977). *Social Facilities in the Villages of Sumatera, Jawa, Bali, NTB, Sulawesi Selatan I*. Jakarta: Central Bureau of Statistics.

——— (1979). *Social Facilities in the Villages of Sumatera, Jawa, Bali, NTB, Sulawesi Selatan II*. Jakarta: Central Bureau of Statistics.

——— (1980). *Social Facilities in the Villages of Nusa Tenggara Timur, Kalimantan, Sulawesi kecuali Sulawesi Selatan, Maluku dan Irian Jaya*. Jakarta: Central Bureau of Statistics.

——— (1985a). *Statistical Yearbook of Indonesia 1984*. Jakarta: Central Bureau of Statistics.

——— (1985b). *Agricultural Census 1983: Land Utilization by Province and District*. Jakarta: Central Bureau of Statistics.

——— (1987a). *Population of Indonesia: Results of the 1985 Intercensal Population Survey*. Series SUPAS, No 5. Jakarta: Central Bureau of Statistics.

——— (1987b). *Agricultural Survey: Land Area by Utilization in Java*. Jakarta: Central Bureau of Statistics.

——— (1987c). *Agricultural Survey: Land Area by Utilization in Outer Java*. Jakarta: Central Bureau of Statistics.

——— (1989). *Statistical Yearbook of Indonesia 1988*. Jakarta: Central Bureau of Statistics.

National Statistical Office (1973). *Population and Housing Census 1970: Whole Kingdom*. Bangkok: National Statistical Office.

PART V

Demographic and
Labour Force Trends

The Dynamics of Population Ageing into the 21st Century: ASEAN and Selected Countries of Pacific Asia[1]

Warwick Neville
Associate Professor and Chair, Department of Geography,
University of Auckland, Auckland, New Zealand

In the second half of the 20th century East Asia has been notable for its relatively modest rates of population growth compared with other major regions in the less developed world. Over the last twenty years the differential has increased as fertility has fallen, reducing average annual growth rates to little more than half their level at the beginning of the period. However, the scale of reduction was extremely uneven among the countries of ASEAN and the other more industrialized countries of Pacific Asia (Japan, Hong Kong, South Korea and Taiwan): on the basis of population growth rates Japan is a case apart, more analogous to the countries of Europe; Brunei, Malaysia and the Philippines have maintained high rates of growth still well above 2 percent per annum; and the other countries have all recorded significant declines that, except for Indonesia, have been quite substantial (Table 11.1).

The consequences of the overall decline in the rates of population growth are wide ranging but particularly pertinent in the economic, social and political contexts as indicated by the extensive existing literature. This chapter, however, focuses primarily on the demographic consequences of the decline in rates of growth and particularly of fertility: as population growth rates fall, increasing attention must be paid to the composition of the existing population. In this instance the age structural shifts will be analyzed and note taken of the immediate implications of ageing over the

Table 11.1: Average Annual Growth Rates for Selected Regions and Countries, 1955–1960 to 1985–1990

Geographical Unit	Percent			
	1955–1960	1965–1970	1975–1980	1985–1990
World	1.86	2.06	1.74	1.73
Africa	2.35	2.63	2.95	3.00
Europe	0.80	0.67	0.45	0.22
Latin America	2.76	2.60	2.28	2.09
Asia	1.95	2.44	1.86	1.85
East Asia	1.53	2.42	1.41	1.31
Selected countries				
Brunei	4.99	4.40	3.41	3.40
Hong Kong	4.22	1.31	2.73	1.36
Indonesia	2.11	2.33	2.14	1.62
Japan	0.93	1.07	0.93	0.44
Malaysia	3.02	2.66	2.32	2.31
Philippines	2.84	3.17	2.53	2.48
Singapore	4.48	1.97	1.30	1.09
South Korea	3.09	2.25	1.55	1.19
Taiwan	3.46	3.19	1.98	1.13
Thailand	2.96	3.08	2.44	1.53

Sources: United Nations (1989a); Republic of China (1990).

fifty-year period 1970 to 2020. Other compositional changes can also be expected as a result of internal differentials in fertility rates between ethnic groups in some of the countries listed, but will not be discussed here. Because of demographic factors other than the decline in national increase (notably the role of international labour migration and the adoption of pronatalist policies in countries such as Malaysia and Singapore) differences between countries are likely to be further accentuated (Neville, 1990a) and these will be variously exacerbated or reduced by non-demographic influences.

The Setting

There is a very wide range in population numbers between Indonesia (fifth largest national population in the world with over 180 million in 1990) and

Japan on the one hand and Brunei (267 thousand) and Singapore on the other (Table 11.2).[2] Such differences in size make valid comparisons difficult and also influence the scale of the resultant impact. In every instance, despite stabilization or decline in growth rates, population numbers are expected to continue to increase — even in Japan for which fifty-year growth (1970–2020) would amount to only 25 percent and thirty-year growth (1990–2020) to only 5 percent. Apart from Brunei's very small population, the Philippines and Malaysia are expected to grow most rapidly. Such an outcome would result in the Philippines moving from a population size comparable to that of South Korea and Thailand in 1970, to double that of South Korea in 2020 and about the same as Japan had been in 1970, a state of affairs that could prove extremely disadvantageous.

Table 11.2: Population Numbers and Growth, 1970–2020

Countries	Total Population thousands			Change 1970–2020	
	1970	1990	2020	thousands	percent
Brunei	136	267	442	306	225
Hong Kong	3,942	5,841	6,913	2,971	75
Indonesia	118,368	180,514	253,560	135,192	114
Japan	104,331	123,457	129,916	25,585	25
Malaysia	10,439	17,339	26,556	16,117	154
Philippines	36,677	62,409	105,289	68,612	187
Singapore	2,074	2,702	3,220	1,145	55
South Korea	31,923	43,582	53,888	21,965	69
Taiwan	14,680	20,752	27,469	12,789	87
Thailand	34,354	55,702	78,118	43,764	127

Sources: Country censuses; United Nations (1989a); Zachariah and Vu (1988); Republic of China (1990).

Whatever the level of population growth, under the medium variant projections all countries will experience a significantly increased degree of ageing. Some writers and many readers of such assertions interpret these statements as predictors of an immediate, overwhelming component of elderly people in the population, but there are a number of preliminary stages and, for most countries, several decades before that eventuality is likely to emerge. The preoccupation with the elderly as a substantial segment of the population (for example, ESCAP, 1987; Heisel, 1984; Martin, 1988) is a recognition that, while the *numbers* of aged have gradually been increasing as a function of improved health, standards of living and consequently lowered mortality and raised life expectancy, the decline in fertility is producing changes of a quite different order in the *relative* size of the elderly component of populations.

Many countries in Western Europe are at a more advanced stage of the current experience of this ageing process, with others (notably other countries of European settlement) somewhere between Western Europe and most of the examples of countries in this study. Those societies have already confronted many of the consequences of a sustained age structural shift by developing appropriate economic and social mechanisms to deal with this phenomenon. Of equal importance has been the recognition that, while the demographic process is similar, the coping mechanisms appropriate to these Asian societies are likely to be different (Jones, 1988), given contrasting cultural values, economic resources and social expectations.

The purpose of this chapter is to assess the interim features of these ageing populations which, well before the emergence of the large proportions of aged people in most of these countries, will be contending with issues and benefiting from age adjustments affecting the rest of the population. In such a context, population ageing is a process in which the enlarged elderly component might be regarded as the culmination of a demographic cycle, but there are many intervening changes in age distributions that may be considered deleterious or beneficial depending on the perspective with which they are viewed.

The age structural changes are primarily a function of the movement from past high fertility rates, but have also been contributed to by declining mortality and the consequential rise in life expectancy. For most of these countries in the 1950s, public health programmes, medical therapies and improved standards of living had made limited inroads into overall mortality levels as reflected by expectation of life at birth.

In the late 1950s, Japan, Hong Kong, Singapore and Taiwan were recording life expectancies in the early sixties for males and females combined, but the other countries had levels of life expectancy in the early fifties or less and the lowest (that of Indonesian males) was under forty years. Steady progress resulted in considerable improvements by the late 1970s: Indonesia averaged only fifty years for both sexes, but all others exceeded sixty; Japan, Hong Kong and Singapore (and probably Brunei) had life expectancies over seventy years. In the late 1980s, expectation of life at birth in Indonesia was still only fifty-six years, but the Philippines, South Korea and Thailand were in the mid to upper sixties, and all other countries were seventy years or above. The projections anticipate that by 2020 all countries will have life expectancies of seventy years or more, and Hong Kong and Japan are likely to exceed eighty years for both sexes combined.

Although survival to older ages on average clearly influences the numbers of people at older ages, the proportional distribution by age-group is much more strongly influenced by fertility. In the 1950s, Total Fertility Rates (TFRs, expressed as children per woman of reproductive age) in all of these countries except Japan (2.1) were well over 4.0, and in all but Hong Kong and Taiwan were 6.0 or higher. By the late 1980s, only Brunei and the Philippines had TFRs in excess of 4.0 and Hong Kong, Japan, Singapore, South Korea and Taiwan had TFRs of 2.1 or less, with the lowest of 1.7 or 1.8 in Hong Kong, Japan and Singapore.

The assumptions of the future projections adopted in this chapter anticipate that Hong Kong, Japan and Singapore will remain at or about their current sub-replacement levels through to 2020, that South Korea may join them at that level, and that the other six countries will converge on a TFR of 2.1 by 2020 at the latest (Taiwan is already at that level, Thailand will reach it a little earlier than 2020). Given the high fertility record of the Philippines in particular, the often uncertain and uneven responses within and between countries to the regulation of fertility, and the announced reversals in adopting pronatalist population policies in Malaysia and Singapore (and perhaps, less directly, in Japan) the assumptions used may prove inappropriate and the projections progressively less adequate. For the purposes of this chapter, the possibility that the projections adopted may provide inaccurate forecasts is not a serious deficiency:[3] accepting the projected population structures and totals as broadly indicative makes possible the identification of the fundamental age structural shifts and their implications.

The age and sex-specific projections adopted here are those of the United Nations (1989a) global estimates and, in the case of Brunei and Taiwan (for which the United Nations does not publish data) the World Bank projections published slightly earlier (Zachariah and Vu, 1988). Complementary information, based on the same set of United Nations projections, has also been drawn from the assessment of world population prospects (United Nations, 1989b). In all instances the medium variant has been chosen: this adopts the medium assumptions for all three components of growth (mortality, fertility and migration), details of which are spelled out in the source volume (United Nations, 1989b: 13–26).

In the analysis that follows, 1970 is adopted as the base year and an assessment is made of the recent past (1970–1990) and of future developments (1990–2020) providing an evaluation of major shifts over the fifty-year period (1970–2020). The basic elements of population size at each of the three main dates and of the implied numerical and overall percentage change from 1970 to 2020 have already been noted in Table 11.2. The conclusion should not be inferred from this data that changes are simply linear; the discussion demonstrates that this is not so, but these data indicate the net result of the more detailed analyses that follow.

Age Structure

Youthful populations predominated in these countries in 1970, reflecting the high birth rates of the 1950s and 1960s. The impact of predominantly adult immigrants slightly modified this element in Hong Kong, but only Japan clearly failed to conform to this widespread pattern of child dominance in the age structure. With the exceptions of Hong Kong, Japan, Singapore and Taiwan, where the decline in fertility was already evident in reducing the size of the childhood age groups, the youthfulness of these populations was reaching its peak and the annual increments of births through the 1970s levelled off and in some instances began to decline.

A. Shift in Age Distribution

The rise in median ages in all cases usefully summarizes the process of shift in age distribution (Table 11.3). So large were the child components in 1970 that only Hong Kong and Japan had median ages of twenty or more and several countries had medians of little more than seventeen years of age. In the following twenty years to 1990 the median ages of most countries reflected the marked shift to older populations consequent upon fertility decline. The main exception was the Philippines that maintained a median below twenty years of age; Malaysia and Indonesia recorded modest increases, also reflecting the limits of their fertility decline; Thailand aged a little more. Except for Brunei, all other countries had median ages over twenty-six, and Japan's was already over thirty-seven years of age. In the twenty years 1970 to 1990, the median ages had shifted upwards by up to ten years, largely reflecting the changes in numbers of births. In addition, the effects of the large numbers of young adults involved in non-permanent international labour migration, especially in the case of the Philippines and to a lesser degree for Thailand, accentuate the youthfulness of these populations. In Brunei, immigrants, mainly from the nearby states of Malaysia, tend to have the reverse effect (Neville, 1990b), and Hong Kong also has been influenced by the selective movement of some sectors of the adult population (Skeldon, 1990: 161). Japan is by far the most distinctive case, recording a median age of over thirty-seven years in 1990, which is older than the median ages for most West European countries.

Table 11.3: Median Population Age, 1970–2020

Countries	Years					
	1970	1980	1990	2000	2010	2020
Brunei	17.8	20.4	24.3	25.9	28.6	32.2
Hong Kong	21.2	26.0	31.1	35.8	39.6	42.6
Indonesia	18.2	19.4	21.8	25.3	29.2	32.7
Japan	29.0	32.6	37.2	39.5	41.6	44.5
Malaysia	17.4	19.5	21.7	24.5	28.1	31.9
Philippines	18.5	18.7	19.8	21.7	24.6	28.1
Singapore	19.7	24.5	29.9	34.9	38.8	41.4
South Korea	19.0	21.8	26.6	30.9	35.3	38.6
Taiwan	18.9	23.0	26.9	30.5	33.1	36.1
Thailand	17.3	19.9	22.9	27.1	30.8	34.3

Sources: Country censuses; United Nations (1989a); Zachariah and Vu (1988); Republic of China (1990).

The continuing redistribution by age over the next three decades is mainly dependent on the level of fertility decline maintained in these population. If the TFRs follow the medium variant as predicted by the United Nations projections and decline from the 1970 levels of around five children per woman (substantially lower in Hong Kong, Japan and Singapore) to about 2.1 or less in 2020, then the median age will be over thirty in all of these countries except the Philippines, and over forty in Hong Kong, Japan and Singapore.

A more comprehensive assessment of the shift in age structure over the fifty-year period is provided by the five functional age groups depicting children (0–14 years), young adults (15–24 years), young-mature adults (25–44 years), old-mature adults (45–64 years) and the elderly (65 years and over) (Table 11.4). As recently as 1970, children comprised 40 percent or more of these populations in all countries except in Hong Kong, Japan and Singapore; in Japan, children already comprised less than a quarter of the total population and were greatly outnumbered by the young-mature adults born between 1925 and 1945. For most of these countries, the proportion of children will decline over the fifty-year period to 2020 to virtually half, or even less, of the 1970 percentages, if the projection assumptions are fulfilled. Even in the twenty years to 1990, all countries were estimated to have reduced the child component of their populations by between 8.7 and 16.0 percentage points except for much smaller reductions in the Philippines (which remains high) and Japan (which was already very low).

During the following thirty years to 2020, countries that have not already experienced major reductions in the child share of the total population are expected to undergo such changes, whereas those where children already comprised less than 30 percent in 1990 can anticipate less severe contraction. By 2020, only in the Philippines are children likely to comprise over a quarter of the population, and in Hong Kong, Japan, Singapore and South Korea, they can be expected to constitute as little as 15–18 percent of the total. In Hong Kong, Japan, Singapore and South Korea, the shift away from youthful populations had already, by 1990, resulted in an absolute and substantial reduction in the *numbers* of children. By 2020, actual numbers of children are expected to be fewer than in 1990 in these same countries and also in Indonesia, Malaysia, Taiwan and Thailand. In Brunei and the Philippines, despite the age shift, the numbers of children in 2020 will still be larger than at the two earlier dates. For eight out of the ten countries this shift from youthful to mature populations is therefore a very radical change with important long term implications for each of these societies in such areas as manpower, reproductive capacity and human welfare.

The proportional decline in the young-adult population (15–24 years) has been less pervasive than that of children (Table 11.4). Several countries, notably Indonesia, South Korea and Thailand are in the later stages (1970– 1990) of an upsurge in numbers and proportions of young adults, and

Table 11.4: Percentage Distribution of Population by Functional Age Groups, 1970, 1990 and 2020

Countries	Age Group (percent)					
	0–14	15–24	25–44	45–64	65 & over	Total
Brunie						
1970	43.5	21.2	22.6	10.0	2.7	100
1990	34.8	16.5	31.1	13.5	4.1	100
2020	22.8	15.6	30.1	22.2	9.3	100
Hong Kong						
1970	37.0	19.7	23.1	16.3	3.9	100
1990	22.0	15.8	36.2	17.2	8.8	100
2020	16.3	11.5	25.3	30.1	16.8	100
Indonesia						
1970	44.0	16.4	26.1	11.0	2.5	100
1990	35.0	21.3	26.3	13.5	3.9	100
2020	22.5	15.4	31.3	23.0	7.8	100
Japan						
1970	24.0	19.0	31.8	18.1	7.1	100
1990	18.5	15.4	28.8	25.6	11.7	100
2020	15.4	12.1	23.2	25.8	23.5	100
Malaysia						
1970	44.9	19.2	21.5	11.3	3.1	100
1990	36.2	20.1	27.9	12.0	3.8	100
2020	23.1	15.3	31.6	22.2	7.8	100
Philippines						
1970	43.0	19.3	23.2	11.0	3.5	100
1990	40.1	19.8	25.8	10.9	3.4	100
2020	26.6	18.0	31.3	18.2	5.9	100
Singapore						
1970	38.8	21.7	23.3	12.9	3.3	100
1990	22.8	16.9	38.4	16.3	5.6	100
2020	16.8	12.0	25.6	30.4	15.2	100
South Korea						
1970	42.1	17.8	24.7	12.1	3.3	100
1990	26.5	20.4	32.1	16.3	4.7	100
2020	18.1	13.3	27.8	29.6	11.2	100
Taiwan						
1970	40.5	20.2	23.7	12.8	2.8	100
1990	28.7	17.7	32.1	15.5	6.0	100
2020	21.1	13.7	28.1	25.5	11.6	100
Thailand						
1970	45.2	18.6	22.7	10.4	3.1	100
1990	32.6	21.8	28.8	12.9	3.9	100
2020	22.1	14.9	29.4	25.2	8.4	100

Sources: Country censuses; United Nations (1989a); Zachariah and Vu (1988); Republic of China (1990).

Malaysia and the Philippines have experienced a similar but smaller change. However, beyond 1990, these countries will emulate the 1970–1990 experience of the other five in showing the effects of sustained fertility decline as young adults too, decline in relative importance within their populations as a whole. In Indonesia, South Korea and Thailand the percentage point reduction is particularly substantial (5.9, 7.1 and 6.9 respectively), with Malaysia and Singapore not far behind recording reductions in the young adult share of the total population of just under 5.0 percentage points. In numerical terms, however, later reductions in the TFRs of previous decades continue to produce expanding *numbers* of young adults through 2020 in Brunei, Malaysia, the Philippines and (at a slower rate) in Indonesia and Taiwan; but Hong Kong, South Korea and Thailand can expect to record smaller numbers in this group in 2020 than in 1990, while Japan and Singapore are likely to have young adult numbers in 2020 which are 21 percent and 14 percent respectively lower than their *1970* young-adult totals.

The shift in age structure has resulted in increases in the proportion of the population aged 25–44, 1970 to 1990, in all of these countries except Japan (Table 11.4). Although relatively small in Indonesia and the Philippines, the impact is substantial in all the other countries (apart from Japan). Because of their postwar fertility experience and the timing of the upsurge and sharp decline in their TFRs, Hong Kong and Singapore both have their largest baby-boom cohorts concentrated at these ages, resulting in more than 36 percent of the population in each case in this functional age group. The only other countries in which this was the largest age group in 1990 were Japan (28.8 percent), South Korea and Taiwan (32.1 percent). Because of the timing of the progression of the largest cohorts through the adult ages by 2020 this 25–44 age group will be the largest in six of the countries and will be exceeded by the next older group only in Hong Kong, Japan, Singapore and South Korea.

By 1990, the impact of the shift in the age structure had become sufficiently far reaching for all but the Philippines to record an increase in the proportions concentrated in the older mature-adult group aged 45–64 (Table 11.4), although the shift at these ages was relatively small, 1970 to 1990, in all countries but Japan. Even in the Philippines, however, as in the other nine countries, improvements in morbidity and the rising expectation of life assured large increases in actual numbers of people in the 45–64 age

group. By 2020, both absolute numbers and the proportions of each population at these ages will have increased to such a degree that those countries
in the vanguard of the ageing process (namely Hong Kong, Japan, Singapore and South Korea) will have their largest numbers and therefore
largest proportions in this functional age group.

By far the smallest numbers are still to be found in the elderly age group,
65 and over (Table 11.4). Consequently, as a share of the total population,
proportions in each of the populations in 1970 and 1990 seldom reach
double figures — again with the exception of Japan with 11.7 percent
elderly people in 1990. Nevertheless, the aged comprise a growing segment
in all these populations and only the Philippines recorded a situation in
which the elderly declined as a proportion of the total 1970 to 1990 (i.e., did
not expand as rapidly as the population overall). With the lapse of time, the
impact of the shift of the larger cohorts to these older ages is beginning to
become apparent by 2020, particularly for Hong Kong, Japan (where the
elderly will be approaching a quarter of the total population), Singapore,
South Korea and Taiwan.

The net demographic impact of these changes over the fifty-year period
1970 to 2020 can be demonstrated by relating age-group growth to total
growth (see p. 272 Table 11.5). On assumptions made to construct the
projections, the medium variant would result in low levels of growth in the
larger, younger cohorts, and above average growth in the smaller, older
cohorts so that there is a general convergence in the size of quinquennial
age groups in all of these countries (Figure 11.1), resulting eventually in the
classic age structure of mature populations. As Table 11.5 shows, this
results in the more mature populations actually recording substantially less
growth in younger age groups than in their populations as a whole (all of
which are predicted to grow, see p. 261 Table 11.2), whereas the elderly are
expected to increase twice as fast (in the Philippines) and up to more than
twelve times as rapidly as the whole population in Japan.

Some care is required in interpreting these and other calculations since
the functional age group classes are of unequal size; while they relate
usefully to childhood, labour force entry and the like, the varying age spans
can be misleading. Furthermore, as previously noted, the change from 1970
to 2020 is not a simple linear one and other demographic factors (notably
migration) also intervene to disrupt the smooth graduation of cohorts (already uneven as a result of fluctuating fertility) from one age group to the

**Figure 11.1: Age Pyramids for Populations of the Selected Countries
of Pacific Asia, 1970, 1990 and 2020**

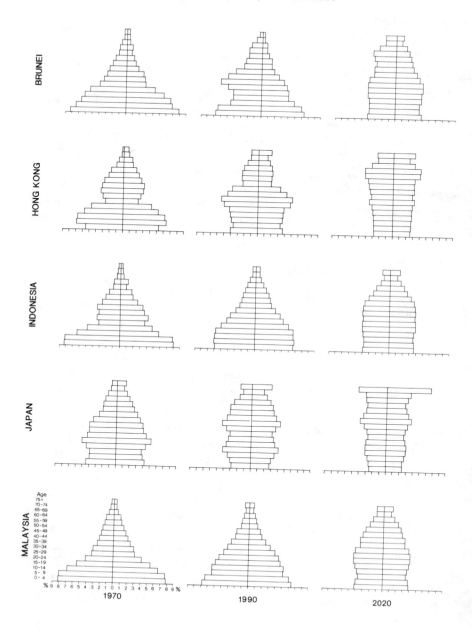

**Figure 11.1: Age Pyramids for Populations of the Selected Countries
of Pacific Asia, 1970, 1990 and 2020** (cont'd)

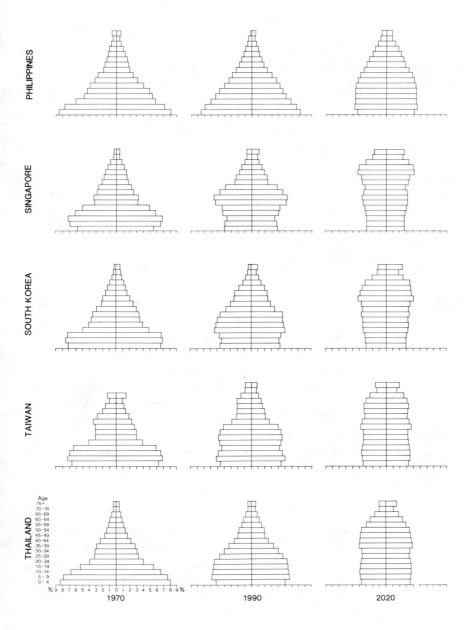

Table 11.5: Index of Growth in Functional Age Group Numbers Relative to Total Population Growth, 1970–2020

Countries	Age Group Index*				
	0–14	15–24	25–44	45–64	65 and over
Brunei	31	62	148	275	455
Hong Kong	−30	3	123	298	863
Indonesia	8	89	137	303	492
Japan	−82	−83	−36	310	1,259
Malaysia	20	67	177	258	355
Philippines	41	90	153	202	206
Singapore	−60	−26	128	483	1,099
South Korea	−40	37	131	452	688
Taiwan	−3	31	141	313	779
Thailand	9	64	152	354	408

* The index equals percentage growth of age groups 1970–2020 ÷ percentage growth of total population 1970–2020 × 100; a score of 100 indicates the same relative growth as in the total population. Total population growth rates 1970–2020 used for this calculation are listed in the final column of Table 11.2.

Sources: Country censuses; United Nations (1989a); Zachariah and Vu (1988).

next, so that significant real fluctuations may be discounted by this simplified evaluation. Also selection of different time periods gives different impressions of impact: a fifty-year period continues to age the entire population present in 1970 at least as far as the old-mature adult ages (45–64 years), and it is in the older age groups that survival of larger numbers than ever makes the greatest impact in redistribution of the population by age. However, while these are the people already present in 1970 and their numbers can be predicted according to established probabilities, the numbers that follow in the 1990s and 21st century become progressively less certain and their influence on the relative age distribution more unpredictable.

B. Demographic Implications

The major shift in distribution towards older age groups that has been described here in some detail, has important implications for the relationships between age groups. Demographic age dependency ratios measure the relative balance of broad age groups in terms of their numerical size between those deemed, on the basis purely of their age, to be potential "dependents" (0–14 years plus 65 years and over) and those who might be regarded as potential "supporters" (15–64 years). Although this dependent relationship is only notional and in some respects even less suited to Asian countries than it is to Western societies, the broad change over time is indicative of the shifting emphasis from youth to maturity and beyond. Despite these reservations, the appropriateness of these arbitrarily specified age groups is increasing because of the greater educational opportunities and expanded proportions participating in the formal economy in all of these countries, and is arguably a better general indicator than an assessment of the support segment of these societies in terms only of the formally defined "economically active" group.

Age dependency ratios were extremely high for all of these countries (except Japan) in 1970, ranging from just under 700 in Hong Kong to 931 per thousand in Thailand indicating, in the latter case, more than nine dependents for every ten adults under 65 (Table 11.6). Many of the ratios were still very high in 1980, but by 1990 all had declined to some degree and some very substantially, a function of the reductions in the TFRs and consequently the reduced child component and the concomitant expansion of adult age groups as the large earlier cohorts move through the adult ranks. The smallest reductions are attributable either to the delayed fall of the birth rate that maintained child dependency at very high levels 1970 to

Table 11.6: Age Dependency Ratios, 1970–2020

Countries	per thousand*					
	1970	1980	1990	2000	2010	2020
Brunei	858	708	638	578	470	473
Hong Kong	693	471	445	444	407	495
Indonesia	868	791	637	527	461	434
Japan	451	484	433	497	584	636
Malaysia	921	767	667	571	450	448
Philippines	870	831	769	662	550	481
Singapore	728	466	396	394	379	470
South Korea	830	608	454	416	404	414
Taiwan	764	567	531	469	448	485
Thailand	931	720	576	460	445	439

* Population aged 0–14 and 65 years and over per thousand population aged 15–64 years.
Sources: Country censuses; United Nations (1989a); Zachariah and Vu (1988); Republic of China (1990).

1990 (as in the Philippines) or to the declining impact of birth rates that fell much earlier and already had resulted in very low dependency rates (as in Japan where the ratio actually rose slightly through 1980 before falling even lower by 1990). As expected from the earlier analyses, the same four countries seen to be in the vanguard of the age structural shift were those with 1990 dependency ratios below 500: Hong Kong, Japan, Singapore and South Korea.

After 1990 the dependency ratios for all the countries other than Japan will tend to converge within a narrow range between 414 and 495 per thousand, a consequence of the increasingly similar projection assumptions being made for all of these countries particularly in relation to fertility. However, even apart from Japan, there is a marked difference between those countries that recorded early fertility decline and those that followed much later: the former had achieved even lower dependency ratios which, by 2020 will be rising again, whereas the countries in the latter group have ratios that are still moving down. This phenomenon is directly attributable to the timing of the impact of the two major components of the age dependency ratio: children and the aged.

For most countries the recent past has been a period of heavy child dependency whereas the elderly, particularly if defined as those 65 (rather than 60) years of age and over, have generally comprised a negligible component. In 1970, the elderly in Japan numbered nearly 300 for every thousand children in the population, but at that stage, the elderly in all other countries were a minor element of the dependency burden — less than 10 percent that of child dependents (Table 11.7). By 1990 the situation had changed significantly in Hong Kong, Japan, Singapore and Taiwan with the aged comprising a group at least one-fifth the size of the child dependent group and about two-fifths in Hong Kong and more than three-fifths in Japan. Elsewhere, the elderly remained a minor element in the overall dependency burden.

By 2020, elderly dependents in Japan will number 50 percent more than child dependents, and Hong Kong and Singapore will have age dependents split roughly equally between children and the aged (Table 11.7). In most other countries listed, however, the aged will still comprise a much smaller dependent element than children — especially in Indonesia, Malaysia, the Philippines and Thailand — but even in South Korea and Taiwan the elderly population will only be a little over half that of the child population.

Table 11.7: Aged-Child Ratios, 1970–2020

Countries	per thousand*					
	1970	1980	1990	2000	2010	2020
Brunei	62	74	118	167	245	406
Hong Kong	106	253	398	542	655	1,026
Indonesia	57	79	110	169	249	344
Japan	294	384	633	909	1,124	1,533
Malaysia	69	91	106	138	223	339
Philippines	81	81	85	102	142	221
Singapore	86	174	243	336	514	907
South Korea	78	112	179	272	414	620
Taiwan	69	126	208	323	377	549
Thailand	68	93	120	188	251	378

* Population aged 65 years and over per thousand population aged 0–14 years.
Sources: Country censuses; United Nations (1989a); Zachariah and Vu (1988); Republic of China
(1990).

C. Societal Implications

A major shortcoming of most studies of the process of population ageing is the tendency to dichotomize the outcome: to regard the balance between children and the elderly as depicted by the aged-child ratio, and the economic and social realities that reflects, as the only issue. Certainly the emergence of a large elderly population (both in numbers and proportions) is the ultimate and arguably the most significant outcome of this demographic cycle if only because it is likely to produce a less transient phase than earlier stages of the transition from the predominance of child dependency to the predominance of aged dependency. But populations have, in this sense, been "aged" before — even though in rather different global circumstances — and substantial fluctuations in birth rates can reasonably be expected to recur further into the future.

More central to this chapter, however, is not what may occur after the emergence of these large aged populations but what occurs in the transitional process leading up to them: the implications of the ageing process between the poles of predominantly youthful and predominantly old populations. These implications are more concerned with the *absolute* numbers involved than in the *relative* (i.e. the proportional) distribution of the population by age: whatever the demographic significance of the

proportional balance between age groups, the demand for work and services, for example, is a function of actual numbers (*inter alia*) which may
well be expanding even though proportions may be contracting.

The massive shift taking place from youthful to predominantly mature
adult populations should not be allowed to obscure the fact that in several
of these countries the child population did not peak until 1990 or later, and
that even then the numbers themselves remain fairly stable at a high level
(though not necessarily higher than 1990, as previously noted) in those
countries that have been later in moving through this ageing process
(Brunei, Indonesia, Malaysia, the Philippines and Thailand). Consequently,
if the needs of children are to be adequately met, particularly in education
but also in other areas such as antenatal and child health care, this does not
imply a freeing up of resources but a continued and possibly even increased
commitment if improvements are to be achieved. Even towards the end of
the period under discussion (2020) and beyond, when the elderly population emerges as larger and more significant than ever, there is likely to be
little scope for any trade-off from the resources previously allocated to the
needs of children. In all the larger populations other than Japan's, children
will still outnumber the elderly by two or three times and in any case, given
the established practices for care of the aged in those societies, diversion of
resources to any major forms of institutionalized care for the aged is still
unlikely to be the issue it is becoming in Japan — and in the smaller
populations of the countries further through that transition.

Trends in the numbers in the young adult group, 15–24 years, provide a
useful indication of the size of the entrant cohorts to the labour force and
advanced education as greater resources are deployed at all levels of education and as labour forces become more formally structured and demand
more entrants with training and education. In the majority of these countries
the rapid and large expansion of this functional age group between 1970
and 1990 accentuated the difficulties of creating (mainly urban-based)
employment opportunities that would productively absorb the expanding
numbers involved and consequently perpetuated the major bottleneck that
has long resulted in substantial unemployment, underemployment, informal activity and a considerable element of discouraged and economically
inactive young adults.[4]

These difficulties are likely to persist in Brunei, Malaysia, and the
Philippines as expansion in numbers at these ages (15–24 years) continues

well into the 21st century. In Indonesia and Thailand, numbers peak around the turn of the century and decline thereafter as the flow-through effect of the reduced fertility of earlier decades is felt. The remaining countries all experienced peak numbers in this functional age group rather earlier (around 1980 or 1990, even earlier in Japan) with three countries, Japan, Singapore and Taiwan, displaying a bimodal distribution over time for these ages. The real significance of this demographic phenomenon will be determined by the nature and scale of economic development and the consequent demand for labour (an issue that might force even the Japanese government to consider countenancing the introduction of legal foreign guest workers; Ogawa and Tsuya, 1988: 58). Already in the 1980s, the two smallest states in population terms (Brunei and Singapore) needed significant numbers of working-age migrants to supplement the local labour force (Neville, 1990b; Pang, 1988) and in the case of Singapore, despite attempts to substitute advanced technologies for labour, there were of the order of 150,000 foreign workers (excluding expatriate technical, managerial and professional personnel) employed at the end of the 1980s.

The conventional functional age-group categories do not readily accommodate one major subset of the total population: reproductive females, who are conventionally regarded as those aged 15–49 years. The current and projected growth of this group results in unprecedented numbers of potential childbearers in these populations. Although the argument tends to become somewhat circular given that the fertility rates adopted for the medium variant projections cannot be independent of the women experiencing them, the large numbers do imply widespread fertility regulation if the child population is to be of the order projected by this variant. It is this assumption that was queried in the introductory discussion of fertility in the light of the reversal to positively pronatalist policies now being pursued by countries such as Malaysia and Singapore (and in a much less explicit way in Japan). Suffice to note that females of reproductive age (15–49 years) around 1970, at a stage when birth rates in these countries were all at least beginning to show a significant decline (and some were already recording substantial reductions), comprised between 21 and just over 24 percent of their total populations except in Japan and Singapore where they exceeded 28 and 27 percent respectively.

In the four countries furthest into the ageing process (Hong Kong, Japan, Singapore and South Korea), the concentration of females in these reproductive ages is believed already to have peaked by 1990 (and much earlier in Japan) at between 27 and 30 percent of total population. This female population is expected to peak in the other countries at between 27 and 29 percent about the turn of the century (Taiwan and Thailand), or one decade (Indonesia, Malaysia) or two into the 21st century (probably the Philippines; Brunei, with only 25 percent in this group by 2020, may still not have reached its peak by then). The significance of these large proportions is that they occur concurrently not only with declining birth rates but with stabilizing and in some instances even reducing numbers of children in their populations. In the case of Indonesia, for example, by far the largest country population in this group, this requires that in 2020, 68 million women between them should have only 10 percent more children under the age of 15 than 29 million women had in 1970.

The bulk of the labour force is concentrated in the two mature adult groups aged 25–44 years and 45–64 years, although definitional problems regarding the nature of work and of labour force participation make accurate evaluation somewhat problematical in most of these countries (for example, Neville, 1985, 1986, 1988). However, the concern of this chapter is mainly with the potential impact of these expanding functional age-group populations on production and consumption. In Brunei, Indonesia, Malaysia, the Philippines, South Korea, Taiwan and Thailand these combined age groups, which represent the bulk of the labour force, are expected to expand substantially right through the period to 2020. Of these countries, only South Korea and Thailand will have surpassed their peak in the young mature age group (25–44 years) so that further expansion beyond this date (if not of the 25–44 year old ages, certainly in the 45–64 year age group) can be expected in most of these populations. For the remaining countries, numerical contraction in these combined age groups will have begun before 2020: the upward surge in numbers can be expected to have occurred by the turn of the century in Japan and by 2010 in Hong Kong and Singapore. The young-mature adult group (25–44 years) peaked in 1980 in Japan, in 1990 in Singapore and will do so in 2000 in Hong Kong. The momentum of this shift carrying forward to the old-mature adult group (45–64 years) determines the later apex for the overall 25–64 years group in these three societies.

The significance of these shifts in age distribution for all of these countries is that these are the age groups in which productive skills and experience are concentrated, and, because of current trends in economic development (with the possible exception of the Philippines), it is these groups that are primarily benefiting from rising living standards. The expanding entrepreneurial and salaried or waged sectors in particular, represent a substantial element with significant discretionary spending to constitute greatly expanded markets for consumer goods and services that until quite recently were the preserve of a small elite.

The consummation of the population ageing process is evident in the expanding elderly population that reaches its largest numbers in all of these countries in 2020 and will continue to expand beyond that time as the large groups in the mature adult ages graduate to these more advanced ages. Whereas high levels of fertility and youthful populations ensured that those aged 65 and over remained only a small segment of the total population, declining death rates and rising life expectancy (not only at birth) have assured substantial expansion of *numbers* of elderly. The problem of numbers, and the huge disparities between countries, while significant for all ages, becomes particularly acute in addressing the needs of the elderly. For example, in 2020, although the elderly in Indonesia will comprise a mere 7.8 percent or so of the population, they will number nearly 20 million — about the total population of Taiwan in 1990; and Japan, with 23.5 percent of its population in the elderly category will have over 30 million aged people in 2020 — more than the total populations projected at that date for either Malaysia or Taiwan.

The shift in proportions of elderly to levels now current in Western societies is therefore not imminent in most of these countries (apart from Japan and to a lesser degree, Hong Kong, Singapore and Taiwan) since the aged (65 years and over), in 1990, still comprised only a minor part of these populations: about 4 percent or less in most, a little more in South Korea (see p. 267 Table 11.4). However, despite the anticipation of the greatest upsurge in the elderly component occurring after 2020, the size of the increases in the intervening period commands attention. The numbers to be catered for, privately or publicly, in providing work or care or medical facilities, are of a different order from 1970 or even 1990. One ameliorating factor arising from the relative rapidity in the expansion of the aged component of the population will be the relatively large proportions of young elderly and small proportions of old elderly people (Jones, 1988:4) which can be expected temporarily to dampen the demand for facilities and care for the frail, the disabled and the sick who are most likely to be in the old elderly group. Overall, the importance of the eventual outcome of this demographic cycle of the ageing process has been widely recognized and is beginning to be addressed in most of these countries (Chen and Jones, 1989)[5] with Japan, already confronting many of the acute issues still only incipient elsewhere, providing relevant experience and advice (Kuroda and Hauser, 1981; Ogawa, 1982, 1987).

Conclusion

Modification of the youthful age structure and its shift towards greater maturity is well under way in all ten countries. Already at the country level for most of these societies there have been investigations of the issues needing to be addressed to ensure adequacy of support systems for the aged who will emerge as a major component of the total populations twenty or more years into the next century (or a little earlier if, as some studies have done, the threshold of old age is defined as 60 years of age instead of 65 as here).

There are a number of significant changes to be anticipated in the interim, however, and despite the limited lead time they too are worthy of more detailed attention. Major issues to be considered include both the positive and negative impacts of stable or declining child and young adult components and the concomitants of an expanded reproductive segment in these populations. The implications also need to be assessed for both the production and consumption aspects of the bulk of the population for whom work opportunities and purchasing power are significantly different from preceding generations, and the linkages between these elements that manifest themselves in institutional, familial and other societal adaptations.

From the more narrowly demographic point of view, conceptual and theoretical issues are being advanced by the understanding of the ageing process being experienced in Asia, notably in the case of Japan. The received wisdom, somewhat counter intuitive when first argued by writers such as Coale (1964), recognizes the predominance of past fertility as a determinant of age structure. As noted by Kono (1989), mortality improvements occur particularly among children and youth in the early stages of the demographic transition and there is less scope for a reduction in mortality in the mature to aged population. Consequently the reduced mortality effect is subsumed within the much more substantial influence of fertility with the increased life expectancy from the base of the age pyramid reinforcing the "juvenation" (Kono's term, 1989: 111) of the population. Progress through the demographic transition, the supersession of infectious and parasitic by degenerative diseases, the reduction of infant, child and young adult mortality levels, and improvements in diet and life style as concomitants of economic and social development provide opportunity for mortality improvements among the mature to elderly age groups. Therefore, even before the really major changes in proportional representation cause percentages of children to decline and of elderly to increase, numbers of aged are expanding, and with the overall decrease in the growth rate of the total population their growth rate comes to exceed that of the rest of the population. In general, when mortality decline for the aged exceeds that for children and young adults who already have low probabilities of dying, the continuing enhancement of life expectancies at older ages further promotes population ageing. Eventually the effect of mortality may become greater than that of fertility under certain conditions in explaining changes in age structure in low mortality, aged populations (Kono, 1989: 114, 122; Martin, 1988).

From a practical point of view, the demographic analysis is a reminder that the cohorts that will reach 65 years by 2020 are already adults in these populations, and given the well established (and improving) probabilities of survival to this age and beyond, and the small size of any net gains or losses of permanent migrants, broad numbers can readily be assessed and will be of the order of the populations projected here. Equally important is that, in the ageing process of the whole population in each of these countries, discordant cohort flows (reflecting earlier fluctuations in fertility) will result in surges of supply and demand in the human components of production and consumption, and efficient monitoring and adjustment of resources will therefore be essential. There are great benefits to be gained from appropriate deployment of human capital both before and during the onset of an aged population.

NOTES

1. The focus is on the insular and peninsular states that tend to comprise the more industrialized countries of the region. Although still a colony, Hong Kong is discussed on the same basis as the other nine countries. Abbreviations adopted throughout this paper include: Brunei, for Brunei Darussalam; South Korea, for the Republic of Korea; and Taiwan, for the Republic of China. Some of the

ideas developed here were first presented in a paper on the countries of ASEAN at a Commonwealth Geographical Bureau Workshop at The Chinese University of Hong Kong in December 1990 (Neville, 1990a). The present article first appeared in the *ASEAN Economic Bulletin*, 9, 1 July 1992, published by the Institute of Southeast Asian Studies, and is reproduced with the kind permission of the publisher.

2. The difficulty of projecting population numbers, particularly for small states, is well demonstrated in this case: actual census counts indicated that Brunei's 1990 population exceeded 300 thousand and Singapore's was over 3 million. In order to maintain the overall integrity of the statistics, updating of individual cases has not been attempted.

3. Others have provided evaluations of various projections of the United Nations (for example, Pflaumer, 1988).

4. The author recognizes the inappropriateness of applying some of these terms to these countries. The comments are intended to be indicative of the supply implications of the demographic dimension rather than evaluative of the economic system and the nature of labour participation.

5. This volume provides a summary for the countries of ASEAN (excluding Brunei) of country studies carried out during 1987 to 1988; for documentation of these individual studies refer to Neville (1990a).

REFERENCES

Chen, Aiju and G. Jones (1989). *Ageing in ASEAN: Its Socio-Economic Consequences*. Singapore: Institute of Southeast Asian Studies.

Coale, A. J. (1964). "How a Population Ages or Grows Younger." In *Population: The Vital Revolution*, edited by R. Freedman. New York: Doubleday-Anchor, pp. 47–58.

ESCAP (1987). "Population Aging: Review of Emerging Issues." *Asian Population Studies Series*, 80. Bangkok: United Nations.

Heisel, M. A. (1984). "Aging in the Context of Population Policies in Developing Countries." *Population Bulletin of the United Nations*, 17, pp. 49–63.

Jones, G. W. (1988). *Consequences of Rapid Fertility Decline for Old Age Security*. Seminar on Fertility Transition in Asia: Diversity and Change, Bangkok (unpublished).

Kono, S. (1989). "Population Structure." *Population Bulletin of the United Nations*, 27, pp. 108–124.

Kuroda, T. and P. M. Hauser (1981). "Aging of the Population of Japan and Its Policy Implications." *NUPRI Research Paper Series*, No. 1.

Martin, L. G. (1988). "The Aging of Asia." *Journal of Gerontology*, 43(4), pp. S99–113.

Neville, W. (1985). "Economy and employment in Brunei." *Geographical Review*, 75(4), pp. 451–461.

———— (1986). "Economic Development and the Labour Force in Thailand." *Contemporary Southeast Asia*, 8(2), pp. 131–150.

———— (1988). "Dimensions of the Labour Force in the Philippines." *Malaysian Journal of Tropical Geography*, 18, pp. 29–41.

———— (1990a). "Prospective Population Growth and Age Structural Shift in the Countries of ASEAN." Paper presented at the Commonwealth Geographical Bureau Workshop, The Chinese University of Hong Kong (unpublished).

———— (1990b). "The Population Composition of Brunei." *Singapore Journal of Tropical Geography*, 11(1), pp. 27–42.

Ogawa, N. (1982). "Economic Implications of Japan's Ageing Population." *International Labour Review*, 121(1), pp. 1–17.

———— (1987). "Implications of the Aging of Population for Socio-economic Development and National Plans and Policies — Lessons from the Japanese Experience." *Asian Population Studies Series*, 80, pp. 59–74.

Neville, W. and N. O. Tsuya (1988). "Demographic Change and Human Resources Development in Asia and the Pacific." *NUPRI Research Paper Series*, No. 40.

Pang Eng-fong (1988). "Development Strategies and Labour Market Changes in Singapore." In *Labour Market Developments and Structural Change: The Experience of ASEAN and Australia*, edited by Eng-fong Pang. Singapore: Singapore University Press, pp. 195–242.

Pflaumer, P. (1988). "The Accuracy of U.N. Population Projections." *American Statistical Association: Proceedings of the Social Statistics Section*, pp. 299–304.

Republic of China (1990). *Statistical Yearbook of the Republic of China, 1990*. Taipei.

Skeldon, R. (1990). *Population Mobility in Developing Countries*. London: Belhaven Press.

United Nations (1989a). *Global Estimates and Projections of Population by Sex and Age*. New York.

———— (1989b). *World Population Prospects, 1988*. New York.

Zachariah, K. C. and M. T. Vu (1988). *World Population Projections, 1987–88 Edition*. Baltimore: World Bank.

CHAPTER TWELVE

The Malaysian Labour Force: Into the 21st Century

Leslie O'Brien
Asia Research Centre, Murdoch University, Perth, Western Australia

Introduction

In 1957, when Malaya[1] gained formal political independence from Britain, it was a typical colonial society. The economy was essentially an extractive one, based upon the mining of tin and the plantation production of rubber. The corporate economy, which mainly comprised these mines and plantations, as well as large trading houses, banks and insurance companies, was characterized by a high degree of foreign ownership and control. The lion's share of local ownership was held by Chinese interests. Manufacturing made an insignificant contribution to gross domestic product (10.4 percent in 1965) and employed but a small proportion (6.3 percent) of the labour force (Malaysia, 1971, Table 2–5:31; Malaysia, 1977, Table 7.13:440). At that time "manufacturing" largely consisted of the production of consumer non-durables, in very small-scale enterprises. Most investment and consumption goods were imported from abroad, which, in an environment of increasing demand, meant that the country faced the potential of ever increasing balance of payments difficulties (Kay, 1975; Amin, 1976; Taylor, 1979).

In 1957, the population of the Malay peninsula was 6.28 million. Malays and other indigenous people comprised 50 percent of the population, Chinese 37 percent and Indians 11 percent (1957 Population Census data, cited in Malaya, 1970:51–54). At that time the country was marked not only by this racial heterogeneity but also by an association of race/ethnicity and economic function. The majority of the indigenous Malay population were tied to the land and involved in semi-subsistence production, small-holder agriculture, forestry and fishing activities. Town-dwelling Malays performed the majority of the administrative functions of government, or worked in a variety of low-skilled roles elsewhere in the public sector. Although poverty knows no ethnic boundaries, and there were, and are, wealthy and powerful Malays, this group had the lowest levels of household income. The towns, generally, were centres of trade and commerce. They were populated largely by ethnic/immigrant Chinese workers and entrepreneurs. Chinese, who were spread throughout the class system and the division of labour, also provided the bulk of the labour in the mines. Chinese, and most especially Indians, comprised the plantation agriculture workforce. Indians not engaged as plantation labour filled jobs as railway workers, medical orderlies and the like (Malaya, 1949; Malaya, 1960; Malaysia, 1971; Malaysia, 1977). Table 12.1 details the employed labour force by industry and ethnicity in 1957. Table 12.2 details the employed labour force by occupation and ethnicity at that time.

Table 12.1: Percentage Distribution of the Employed Labour Force by Industry and Ethnicity, Peninsular Malaya, 1957

Industrial Sector	Malays	Chinese	Indians
Total Agriculture	60	25	14
• Agriculture, Forestry, Hunting and Fishing	80	18	1
• Agriculture Products Requiring Substantial Processing	43	31	25
Mining and Quarrying	18	68	12
Manufacturing	20	72	8
Construction	32	48	18
Utilities	33	26	36
Commerce	16	65	17
Transport etc.	36	39	22
Services	40	34	15
Other	36	46	16
Total	47	36	15

Notes: 1. Derived from Malaysia, 1977, Table 7.13(a):441.
2. The columns do not total 100 percent because the category "Others" has been omitted.

Table 12.2: Percentage Distribution of the Employed Labour Force by Occupation and Ethnicity, Peninsular Malaya, 1957

Occupational Category	Malays	Chinese	Indians
Professional, Technical and Related	41	38	11
Administrative, Executive and Managerial	17	62	12
Clerical	27	46	20
Sales and Related	16	66	17
Agricultural Occupations	62	24	13
Miners, Quarrymen and Related	7	86	5
Transport and Communication Occupations	42	40	16
Craftsmen, Production Process Workers and Labourers	24	56	20
Service, Sport and Entertainment Occupations	40	33	13
Total Economically Active Population	47	36	14

Notes: 1. Derived from Malaya, 1960, Table 14:128–136.
   2. The columns do not total 100 percent because the category "Others," who comprised 3 percent of the economically active population, has been omitted.

In marked contrast to the situation at Independence, Malaysia today is increasingly an urban and industrialized society. The production of primary products is still of great importance within the economy, but the agricultural sector has been modernized, mechanized and diversified away from rubber. Malaysia today is one of the world's foremost producers of palm oil. Major inputs into gross domestic product (GDP) are also obtained from oil and natural gas. Trade and commerce, which were significant in the pre-colonial period and during the era of direct colonial rule, have expanded. One of the most marked socio-economic changes in the post-Independence period has been the development of manufacturing. By 1990, this sector contributed 27 percent to GDP and 60 percent to exports (Malaysia, 1991, Table 1–2:20, Table 1–3:22). Although the importation of investment goods places a strain on the country's resources, the volume of manufactured exports is such as to ameliorate these costs. In the period 1957 to 1990, Malaysia has thus changed from a society that was politically and economically tied to an imperial homeland, to one that is now fully incorporated into the capitalist world economy, yet rapidly developing within that set of interlocking constraints. What factors have caused these changes? What is the likely future direction of Malaysia's development?

Internal Factors

A. Early Development Strategies

The social and economic transformation that has taken place in Malaysia is the outcome of both internal developmental policies and practices, as well as external events at the level of the global economy. Insofar as internal policies and practices are concerned, the decision by the first post-colonial government to upgrade and extend the country's infrastructure, to diversify agriculture away from rubber, and to give impetus to the development of import-substitution manufacturing laid a solid foundation for later development efforts (Malaysia, 1971). In the first place, expenditure on roads, railways, airports and harbours made Malaysia a particularly attractive venue for foreign direct investment. Secondly, the diversification of the agricultural sector made Malaysia a little less vulnerable to downturns in world demand for natural rubber; when the price of that commodity fell, there was always the likelihood that palm oil, which was coming on line by the late 1960s, would be profitable. Furthermore, the early movement towards the cultivation of palm oil enabled Malaysia to establish a good share of the market for this product. Thirdly, the establishment of import substitution manufacturing contributed to the containment of the balance of payments deficit that existed until recent years. It also aided in the creation of at least some new job opportunities for an expanding, and increasingly-educated, population. Most importantly, however, the legislation enacted, and the industrial estates created to encourage import substitution manufacturing, served as "attractors" to world-market oriented manufacturing capital, which was seeking sites for off-shore investment after the late 1960s.

In the period 1957–1970, the GDP in Malaysia grew by approximately 5.5 percent per annum. This was a higher rate of growth than the target set by the United Nation for lesser developed countries. Agriculture continued to be the mainstay of the economy. In 1970, this sector contributed 32 percent to GDP and still employed nearly half (49.6 percent) of the labour force. Industrial manufacturing, however, was the fastest growing sector during the period under review. By 1970, manufacturing contributed 13.4 percent to GDP and employed 9.2 percent of the labour force (Malaysia, 1971, Table 2–5:31; Malaysia 1976, Table 2–1:12; Malaysia, 1977, Table 7.12:436). These were changes that the government policy-makers were aiming for. Essentially, however, this was developed on much the same trajectory as had been set during the period of direct colonial rule: the fundamental character of Malaysian society remained the same, nor had there been any particular attempts made to change it. The long-established fusions of ethnicity and class, ethnicity and economic function continued to exist. The corporate economy was still largely (62.1 percent) foreign owned. Malaysian Chinese interests continued to hold the highest local share of the economy (22.8 percent). Malays and other indigenous people and Malaysian Indians had a negligible participation in the ownership of the main means of production (1.5 and 0.9 percent respectively; Malaysia, 1971, Table 3–1:40). There was some change in the division of labour in the period 1957–1970 but most of the old associations of ethnicity and economic function still existed. (Compare, for instance, the data in Tables 12.1 and 12.3 which detail the labour force by industry and ethnicity at these two points in time. Tables 12.2 and 12.4, which show the ethnic structure of the labour force in 1957 and 1970, do not lend themselves to comparative analysis. An examination of their content will, however, help to illuminate this argument.)

Table 12.3: Percentage Distribution of the Employed Labour Force by Industry and Ethnicity, Peninsular Malaysia 1970

Industrial Sector	Malays	Chinese	Indians
Total Agriculture	68	22	10
• Agriculture, Forestry, Hunting and Fishing	81	17	1
• Agriculture Products Requiring Substantial Processing	57	26	17
Mining and Quarrying	24	67	8
Manufacturing	29	65	5
Construction	22	72	6
Utilities	48	18	32
Commerce	23	66	11
Transport etc.	42	40	17
Services	47	37	14
Not adequately described	51	38	10
Total	52	36	11

Notes: 1. Derived from Malaysia, 1977, Table 7.12(a):438.
 2. The columns do not total 100 percent because the category "Others" has been omitted.

Table 12.4: Percentage Distribution of the Employed Labour Force by Occupation and Ethnicity, Peninsular Malaysia, 1970

Occupational Category	Malays	Chinese	Indians
Professional, Technical and Related Workers	46	39	13
Administrative and Managerial Workers	23	65	8
Clerical and Related	36	48	15
Sales Workers	23	66	11
Service Workers	46	39	13
Agricultural etc. Workers	69	21	9
Production and Related and Transport and Labourers	34	55	11
Total Experienced Labour Force	52	36	11

Notes: 1. Derived from Malaysia, 1977, Table 7.15a:445.
2. The columns do not total 100 percent because the category "Others" has been omitted.

B. The New Economic Policy

Social inequalities generate discontent. In the Malaysian context, the overlap of ethnicity and class, as well as the existence of a marked fusion of ethnicity and formal social power (Weber, 1968) means that dissatisfactions that have their roots in a variety of social, economic and/or political causes are often expressed in ethnic terms. In May 1969, there was a major outbreak of inter-ethnic violence in Malaysia. Parliamentary rule was suspended and a "state of emergency" was declared. When parliamentary rule resumed, the government of the day introduced a New Economic Policy (NEP) under the Second Malaysia Plan, 1971–1975 (Malaysia, 1971). This Plan, which was initially specified to run until 1990, is one of the major internal factors associated with the social and economic transformation and development that has taken place in Malaysia in recent years.[2]

The NEP has two major aims. The first is to eliminate poverty, irrespective of race; the second is to restructure society so as to reduce the association of ethnicity and economic function noted above. The attainment of these goals is recognized as contingent upon a number of inter-related factors. Principal among these is a perceived need for ongoing economic development, both to finance the cost of the Policy as well as to ensure that the redistribution of resources does not involve the acquisition of assets already held by Malaysians. Secondly, there has been a recognition that the actors involved in this social interplay must also change; the Malays, who have been identified as the main disadvantaged group in society, must be "modernized."

A variety of means have been used to attain these goals. Insofar as economic growth is concerned, manufacturing has been identified as a major vehicle of developing and diversifying the economy, promoting industrialization and creating employment opportunities. In addition to giving support to the continuation of import-substitution manufacturing, the NEP also stresses the growth of resource-based and non-resource based manufacturing. A variety of investment incentives, including tax "holidays," labour and locational relief schemes have been established to encourage both foreign and local capital to invest in industries of these types. In addition to supporting the development of industrial manufacturing, and contrary to many other development plans, the NEP stresses that agriculture should not only be maintained but, as was the case during the immediate post-colonial period, this sector should continue to be diversified and upgraded. All other natural resources should likewise be fully exploited.

The NEP places great emphasis upon restructuring the corporate economy so as to reduce foreign ownership and increase local and Malay ownership and control. Specifically, the aim is that the corporate economy of the country should be 70 percent locally owned (including 40 percent owned by Malay and other indigenous people) by 1990. The Policy as implemented requires all new companies to be established along the lines of the equity provisions noted above, and existing companies above a certain size to restructure so as to meet these aims. Due to the economic and human resources available within Malaysia, the ongoing development of agriculture, mining and finance, property and business services were considered to be well within the limits of local financial and technological capabilities. Concerted efforts were thus made to acquire foreign assets in these sectors of the economy through a process of mergers and take-overs. Insofar as the development of manufacturing is concerned, however, more capital and technology resources seen to be needed than are available domestically. Foreign direct investment in this sector has thus been actively encouraged (Malaysia, 1971, 1976, 1986a).

Under the NEP, the main strategies employed to alter the human resource base of the country lay in the fields of education and the labour market. The structure of opportunities in the former area expanded, at the same time a quota system has been established to ensure that the Malays have full access to the school, college and university systems and access the full range of disciplines. Emphasis was placed upon increasing the number and type of job opportunities *per se*, as well as promoting the employment of Malays. The labour market is designed to change to employ Malays, in all industries and at every level of the occupational hierarchy, in numbers equal to their share of the population (Malaysia, 1971, 1976, 1986a).

External Factors: The New International Division of Labour

At the same time the NEP was being implemented, a major restructuring of the capitalist world economy was taking place. From the mid-1960s onwards, the cost of labour in the already developed OECD countries began to rise, and labour unrest became widespread. At the same time, a near revolution in transport and communications technology, in particular the development of containerized shipping, as well as changes in the product and process technology of many commodities, enabled many developed country manufacturing companies to relocate part or all of their production process "off-shore" in certain parts of the lesser developed world. Here they hoped to find more favourable production conditions than were available to them on their home grounds. Countries such as Malaysia were the recipients of large inflows of this foreign direct investment (Frobel *et al.*, 1980; O'Brien, 1987). What this meant is that at the very time Malaysian government policy emphasized the value of foreign direct investment and Western technology, manufacturing capital from the OECD was seeking to find countries like Malaysia able and willing to host their production facilities. This coincidence of a soundly based economic development strategy, the availability of international capital and technology and markets for the productive output has been the main reason why Malaysia has been able to move towards the NIC status.

A Brief Evaluation of the Economy Today

The aims of the NEP are inherently contradictory. During its course, policy-makers in Malaysia have at one and the same time been trying to: (i) attract foreign capital and; (ii) buy back the farm. In addition, the Policy's sponsorship of essentially one ethnic group, ultimately at the cost of educational, labour market and other opportunities for other groups in the society, has probably generated more tensions than it has resolved. Despite these issues, which are of critical importance but are not the subject of this chapter, the NEP was, by many standard measures, quite successful. In the two decades of its operation, Malaysia has moved from the status of a developing but essentially post-colonial economy and society, to a second-tier NIC. The defining features, under the influence of the NEP, are as follows:

(a) Very high rates of growth of GDP: despite a short period of negative growth during the global recession of the early 1980s, GDP in Malaysia has been growing at a rate considerably higher than that achieved in the OECD countries.

(b) The majority share of ownership of the corporate economy as a whole is now "locally" owned: the *Mid-Term Review of the Sixth Malaysia Plan 1991–1995* indicates that by 1990 Malaysians owned 74.9 percent share capital of limited companies in Malaysia, while the foreign share of ownership had been reduced to 25.1 percent (Malaysia, 1991, Chart 1–5:14).[3] The exception to this trend towards local ownership is the manufacturing sector. Overall, manufacturing conforms to the NEP requirement of 70 percent local, 30 percent foreign equity in limited companies. Some industries, however, especially high technology industries, evidence very high levels of foreign ownership and control (O'Brien, 1989a, 1989b).

(c) The foreign capital and associated technology that the NEP sought to attract and that was looking for favourable off-shore investment locales, have been instrumental in the development of an export-oriented, resource and non-resource based manufacturing sector. This exists alongside an import substitution producing sector. Thus the two together, but most especially the former, contribute much to job creation, to GDP and aid in the maintenance of a favourable balance of payments situation.

(d) Although agriculture and manufacturing are still too narrowly based to be able to avoid the consequences of fluctuations in global demand for principal products (most especially rubber and palm oil, semi-conductor devices and air-conditioning units) there was not only more economic growth but also a greater variety of sources than in the pre-NEP period. Both agriculture and manufacturing in Malaysia are strong at present and are forecast to be of great importance in the future.

The Human Resource Base

The estimated population of Malaysia in 1990 was 18 million people (Malaysia, 1991, Table 1–7:28).[4] Due to a combination of differing fertility trends among the ethnic groups and different means of enumeration, Malays and other indigenous people are estimated to now comprise 58.1 percent of the population and are expected to increase their share even more in coming years. Chinese are estimated to comprise 31.4 percent, Indians 9.9 percent. Both these groups are expected to hold slightly lower shares of the population in the future (Malaysia, 1986a, Table 4–1:129). The NEP has been instrumental in reshaping every aspect of life for this population. For some ethnic groups, the impact has been positive; for others, it has severely limited life chances, as shown below.

A. Educational Change

The population as a whole now receives more years of schooling and other forms of training, and is now exposed to a broader range of educational options and opportunities, than it ever has before. This does not mean that the system of education is now "egalitarian;" class differentiation in the quality of education persists. Nonetheless the school system is now much less stratified than it was in the past. Most of the changes that have taken place seem to have been of particular benefit to the Malays, as an ethnic group.

During the colonial period and the years up until 1970, schooling in the peninsula was conducted in four languages, i.e., Malay, Chinese, Tamil and English. Nearly all Malay schools were fully government funded as were some non-Malay medium schools. A great many other "private" schools received substantial state subsidies. The main defining features of the four types of schooling were that only the English schools, which were primarily available to the children of the elites of all ethnic backgrounds, had primary, secondary and tertiary levels, and interconnected with the "modern"[5] labour force. Chinese-language education interconnected with occupations in the sizeable Chinese-owned, controlled and operated sector of the economy. Tamil-medium schooling, of the most rudimentary kind, was the preserve of the children of estate workers, who would, in time, themselves become rubber tappers or weeders. Although some Malay children were educated in English, the majority attended vernacular schools at the primary level, which comprised the sum total of their formal education. Some Malays moved into the English language stream at the secondary level and became school teachers, or joined the public service.

Since colonial times, Malay education has been fully sponsored, and Malays have had good access to scholarships. The lack of science education in the rural areas, however, limited the secondary and higher education options available to these predominantly rural-dwelling people. This, in combination with certain Malay cultural practices, meant that even those who did continue their education beyond the secondary school level were more likely to enrol in diploma or generalist/Arts degree courses (which were the precursors of teaching or administrative work roles) than in those science and technology based fields of education that were linked to a broader range of occupational options and opportunities.

By the mid-1960s, the divisive implications of streaming, both as regards the labour market and nation building, began to be addressed by policy-makers, and were soon after translated into official practice. In 1970, all government schools, whatever their existing medium of instruction, began to teach their Year 1 class in the Bahasa Malaysia or "national language."[6] The national language expanded throughout the school system along with the 1970 Year 1 intake of students. By the early 1980s, and under the influence of the NEP, most university-level courses were taught in the Bahasa Malaysia medium of instruction, to students who had their entire schooling in that language. Since 1970 and under the NEP, the following has occurred:

(a) Places have been reserved for Malays within the schools, colleges and universities.[7]

(b) These Malays have had an advantage over the other ethnic groups in that their mother tongue has increasingly become the medium of instruction and certification within the system of education.

(c) Science and technology are promoted, both as means of "modernizing" the Malays as well as aiding Malaysia's independent development. Science-based subjects are taught in urban and rural areas, mainly in the Bahasa Malaysia medium.

(d) The combination of these factors is slowly helping to move Malays out of the "Diploma and Certificate/Arts and Education" syndrome and into the more (labour) marketable degree fields: by 1985, Malays comprised 52 percent of those studying for a science and technology-type degree in

Malaysia (Malaysia 1986b, Table 19–3:490–491, Table 19–4:493).

(e) Of theoretical and empirical importance is the fact that because the NEP has placed such emphasis upon ethnicity, it seems to have over-ridden many of the negative consequences of gender. An examination of gender variations in the impact of the NEP reveals that Malay women then seemed to have shared as much in these educational and labour market reforms as Malay men (O'Brien, 1980).

B. Changes in the Occupational Structure

During the colonial period, Malays comprised the bulk of the rural population. Most worked as semi-subsistence farmers on their own small plots of land, as fishermen and/or in craft-related occupations. These were activities associated with very low levels of cash income. The NEP's aim to restructure society involved the implementation of policies to move a great many of these low-level educated Malays off the rural farms, and into jobs ear-marked for them in the mainly urban based factories and the wage labouring system.[8]

As a consequence of an expanding and more diversified system of education, and a labour market that is evolving to employ Malays in all categories and at all levels, the ethnic structuration of the Malaysian labour force changed markedly in the years since Independence. An examination of the data in Tables 12.1 (see p. 286), 12.3 (see p. 289), 12.5 and 12.7 shows that in the period 1957 to 1990, the proportion of Malays among workers in the agriculture increased from 60 percent to 76 percent. This rise has occurred despite the massive movement of Malays from small-holder farming into employment in factories, shops and offices. During the period under review, the Malay share of employment in manufacturing rose from 20 to 50 percent, and there was a clear trend for an increase in the proportion of members of this ethnic group among workers in the service sector (i.e. wholesale and retail trade, in finance and insurance, government services). Sectoral employment patterns for Malaysian Chinese also changed. Their share of the agricultural workforce fell from 25 to 16 percent, indicating the avail-ability of off-farm employment opportunities. Their share of employment in the manufacturing sector fell from 72 to 37 percent, suggesting the availability of white-collar employment opportunities for the second generation. The Chinese share of employment in the service sector as a whole likewise declined.[9]

**Table 12.5: Percentage Distribution of the Employed Labour Force
by Industry and Ethnicity, Malaysia, 1980**

Industrial Sector	Malays	Chinese	Indians
Agriculture	73	16	10
Mining and Quarrying	34	55	11
Manufacturing	41	50	8
Construction	39	53	6
Utilities	67	10	23
Transport, Storage and Communication	53	35	12
Wholesale/Retail trade	37	55	7
Finance, Insurance etc.	37	55	7
Services	60	29	10
Total Employed	57	34	9

Notes: 1. Derived from Malaysia, 1986b, Table 6–6:41.
2. The columns do not total 100 percent because the category "Others" has been omitted.

**Table 12.6: Percentage Distribution of the Employed Labour Force
by Occupation and Ethnicity, Malaysia 1980**

Occupational Category	Malays	Chinese	Indians
Professional and Technical	54	34	10
Teachers and Nurses	61	31	8
Administrative and Managerial	29	64	5
Clerical	52	38	9
Sales	31	62	7
Services	55	33	10
Agricultural	74	17	9
Production	46	44	10
Total	57	34	9

Notes: 1. Derived from Malaysia, 1986b, Table 6–4:39.
2. The columns do not total 100 percent because the category "Others" has been omitted.

The fall in the Chinese share of non-agricultural employment is a consequence of the movement of Malays from small-holder farming into more
urban and industrial work roles, thus increasing their proportionate representation and decreasing the percentage and numeric share of Chinese
workers in these areas. Data on employment by occupation and ethnicity
suggest that the Chinese have not so much been squeezed out but have been

upwardly mobile within most occupational hierarchies — this at a time that government policy sponsored the labour market aspiration of the Malays.

In terms of changes in the occupational structure, an examination of the data in Tables 12.2 (see p. 287), 12.4 (see p. 290), 12.6 (see p. 297) and 12.8 show that the most notable changes in the period under review has been the movement towards a more equitable representation of the ethnic groups in the various occupational categories. There is still, however, a clear under-representation of Malays, and over-representation for Chinese, in the better paid, more prestigious work roles. This is apparent in the professions, where despite expanded educational opportunities, Malays are still con-centrated at the "assistant" and quasi-professional level. It is also apparent in administration and management and in sales fields. In the case of the former, Malays are well represented among government administrators but under-represented in the managerial field. For the Chinese, their long history of involvement in private enterprise, the maintenance to a certain extent of a Chinese corporate sector, and their greater experience leads to Malaysian Chinese being preferred as managers. The extent of Malaysian Chinese involvement in the ownership and control of wholesale and retail trade, and a Chinese preference for the employment of ethnic Chinese workers, despite the NEP, helps to explain their over-representation among sales workers.

Table 12.7: Percentage Distribution of the Employed Labour Force by Industry and Ethnicity, Malaysia, 1988

Industrial Sector	Malays	Chinese	Indians
Agriculture	75	15	9
Mining and Quarrying	37	52	4
Manufacturing	42	49	9
Construction	43	50	6
Utilities	72	12	15
Transport, Storage and Communication	52	34	13
Wholesale/Retail trade	35	58	7
Finance, Insurance etc.	43	42	13
Services	68	23	8
Total Employed	57	34	9

Notes: 1. Derived from Malaysia, 1989, Table 3–9:64–65.
2. The columns do not total 100 percent because the category "Others" has been omitted.

**Table 12.8: Percentage Distribution of the Employed Labour Force
by Occupation and Ethnicity, Malaysia 1988**

Occupational Category	Malays	Chinese	Indians
Professional and Technical	56	31	12
Administrative and Managerial	28	66	5
Clerical	55	36	9
Sales	37	58	6
Services	58	30	10
Agricultural	76	17	7
Production	46	43	11
Total	57	34	9

Notes: 1. Derived from Malaysia, 1989, Table 3–10:66.
2. The columns do not total 100 percent because the category "Others" has been omitted.

C. Other Demographic and Social Changes

The decade 1970–1980 was a period of rapid industrialization in Malaysia. The introduction of the NEP under the *Second Malaysia Plan 1971–1975* sought to bring about this change. As noted above, the introduction of this Policy coincided with an upsurge in the massive inflow of foreign capital into Malaysia's manufacturing sector as a result of global restructuring. Some of this foreign investment was directed towards labour-intensive industries such as garment production, assembly of electronic components and the chemical industry. As a consequence, job opportunities, especially in manufacturing, but also in construction and in services, expanded. People were now not just moving from rural to urban areas in search of work, many rural people were now actively being recruited by urban-based employers who had jobs waiting for them.[10] The data set down in the Tables above do not directly indicate all the changes that have taken place in Malaysia in recent times, but embedded within them is an indication of the diversity of the process of proletarianization. Looking behind the figures detailed above it can be seen how, in the period 1957 to 1990, a great many Malays from peasant/farming backgrounds moved into the wage labouring system in the urban, industrial environment and how other Malays moved into agricultural industry. These data can also inform us that the expansion of educational opportunities for Malays has enabled a shift into white-collar employment in the service sector. These data do not reveal gender differentiation within industry structures and occupational hierarchies. Changes in this regard have been staggering. To a certain extent, the proletarianization of the Malays is the story of the proletarianization of Malay females. Behind the data are indications that Malaysian Chinese from agricultural industry backgrounds have moved horizontally into urban manufacturing, while others have been upwardly mobile within the occupational hierarchy and moved into the service sector. The variations in these changes reflect not only ethnically based variations in the structure of opportunities in the country, but also class differences within the ethnic groups.

Table 12.9 provides such details as are available concerning changes in the labour force that have occurred as a consequence of the process of urbanization, industrialization and development. In the absence of a Census of Population in 1990, the *Sixth Malaysia Plan 1991–1995* provides relatively little information concerning the population. Data on interstate migration for the decade 1980 to 1990 are not available. Given the labour force information for this period, we would expect, however, that the next Census — whenever it might be held — will reveal that the decade 1980 to 1990 witnessed a wave of interstate migration at least equal to, if not greater, than that which took place in the period 1970 to 1980. Furthermore, given the nature of the changes taking place in rural Malaysia, we would expect a continuation of this trend in the period 1990 to 2000. The reasons for this are as follows.

First, the traditional semi-subsistence agriculture, forestry and fishing occupations that sustained the majority of the rural population are not the type of work roles that are attractive to young, increasingly well educated, men and women. Even if they came from a rural background, these are the type of people who are most likely to move into the towns and cities in search of work. Second, a great deal of the agricultural sector today is land and capital, rather than labour intensive (i.e. modern agriculture does not generate many jobs). What these changes imply is that by the end of this century, the towns and cities of Malaysia will be even larger than they are today. As this century draws to a close, we would expect to find that the proportion of self-employed people in the labour force will continue the decline, and that the number and proportion of male and female employees — although not necessarily the number and proportion of those employed — will continue to rise as it did in the period 1957 to 1980.

Table 12.9: Employment Status of the Working Population, Peninsular Malaysia 1957, 1970 and 1980, by Ethnicity (%)

Employment Status 1957	Malays	Chinese	Indians	Total
Employer	48.9	28.3	9.8	35.0
Own account worker	(66.1)	(28.8)	(4.1)	(100.0)
Unpaid family worker	14.1	4.2	0.5	8.3
	(80.0)	(17.8)	(0.9)	(100.0)
Employee	37.0	67.6	89.6	56.7
	(30.8)	(42.5)	(22.9)	(100.0)
In employment	100.0	100.0	100.0	100.0
	(47.3)	(35.7)	(14.5)	(100.0)
Employment Status 1970	**Malays**	**Chinese**	**Indians**	**Total**
Employer	42.2	26.7	15.0	33.8
Own account worker	(66.7)	(28.0)	(4.5)	(100.0)
Unpaid family worker	22.0	13.1	4.6	17.0
	(69.0)	(27.2)	(2.7)	(100.0)
Employee	35.8	60.1	80.4	49.1
	(39.0)	(43.3)	(16.7)	(100.0)
In employment	100.0	100.0	100.0	100.0
	(53.5)	(35.4)	(10.2)	(100.0)
Employment Status 1980	**Malays**	**Chinese**	**Indians**	**Total**
Employer	2.6	5.8	4.6	4.0
	(35.5)	(51.5)	(12.3)	(100.0)
Own Account worker	32.9	24.7	8.3	27.4
	(64.5)	(31.5)	(3.2)	(100.0)
Unpaid family worker	9.2	5.4	3.3	7.3
	(67.9)	(26.2)	(4.9)	(100.0)
Employee	55.2	64.1	83.8	61.4
	(48.3)	(36.5)	(14.6)	(100.0)
In employment	100.0	100.0	100.0	100.0
	(53.6)	(35.0)	(10.7)	(100.0)

Sources: Department of Statistics, Population Census 1957, 1970 and 1980. Reproduced from Malaysia, 1986b, Table 6–2:37. The columns do not total 100 percent due to the omission of the category "Others".

Into the 21st Century: The Likely Direction of Change

An understanding of historical processes is a prerequisite for any meaningful understanding of the present and of the likely direction of social change in the future. The foregoing analysis of Malaysia's recent past suggests that many of the changes that together led to a virtual transformation of Malaysia in the period 1970 to 1990 will continue in the future. This means that as the country moves through the 1990s into the 21st century, it can be expected to become even more urbanized, even more industrialized than it is at present. In the absence of any indices to the contrary, we might expect that the main defining features of the economy and society in coming years will be an amplification of what exists at present. This forecast is confirmed by the projections contained in the *Sixth Malaysia Plan 1991–1995* and the policy directives of the *Second Outline Perspective Plan 1991–2000*, which embodies the National Development Plan, the successor of the NEP (Malaysia, 1991).[11]

As noted, the major share of ownership of the corporate economy of Malaysia is now in the hands of Malaysian residents. In coming years, some slight move towards more Malaysian resident ownership can be expected, but not much more than exists in the present. In areas where Malaysian technology and know-how are sufficient, the trend towards restructuring of ownership and control will continue. However, access to advanced and generally foreign-owned technology, especially in the manufacturing sector, has been a critical element of Malaysia's industrialization programme. There is evidence that while the foreign owners of esoteric technology may be prepared to enter into some joint venture arrangements for production in Malaysia, they want at least majority ownership of the means of production and often full control (O'Brien, 1989a, 1989b). This is seen as necessary both to protect their interests, as well as to maximize the market potential of the products they own. This in turn means the continued presence of at least senior foreign managers in the manufacturing sector in Malaysia,[12] and the continued existence of a ceiling on the potential for local executives in certain areas of the economy.

Our examination of changes in sectoral contributions to GDP and to exports in the period 1970 to 1990 suggests that in coming years, manufacturing can be expected to continue its remarkable increase. This, in combination with the advantages Malaysia has to offer as an investment environment compared to other countries in the ASEAN region, suggests that it would not be unreasonable to expect that up to 35–40 percent of GDP will be generated by this sector by the first decade of the 21st century, and that manufactured products will continue to comprise the lion's share of export earnings.[13] Recent trends also indicate that agriculture can be expected to continue to be a major sector of the Malaysian economy and to be an important source of employment. Although many rubber plantations are being given over to the production of palm oil, this commodity will not disappear. Furthermore, the palm oil plantations developed in recent years will continue to bear fruit, and the palm oil lobby seems able to deal with the competition from US soya bean producers. It is even possible that crops such as tropical fruits, which are grown commercially, will become more important, as the dietary demands of people in the region change. Despite these factors, the relative significance of the agricultural sector is expected to continue to decline in future years.[14] The exploitation of oil and natural gas, which has been so important in the recent past, can be expected to continue to make a major contribution to the economy in future years. This natural resource sector, like the non-resource based sections of manufacturing, however, is heavily reliant upon foreign capital, foreign technology and, at the upper echelons, foreign personnel. Such activities generate revenue, but provide limited employment and training opportunities for Malaysian labour. As in all urbanizing and industrializing societies, the service sector in Malaysia can be expected to continue to expand, as an increasingly affluent population needs and expects more and better education, health and other facilities, and as the country becomes more complex and developed.

If the changes in the economy noted above eventuate, it will mean that employment opportunities in Malaysia will continue to change, but within the trajectory already set during the 1970s and 1980s. Any move towards the further development of heavy industry in Malaysia and/or the production of capital goods can be expected to slow down the rate of job creation in manufacturing and reduce job opportunities for women in this sector. To the extent that investment in the production of labour intensive consumer goods continues, however, job opportunities in manufacturing can be expected to grow as they have in the past, and up to a quarter of the labour force could be expected to be engaged in manufacturing-related work roles by the first decade of the 21st century. If agriculture continues to hold its own, the number of persons working in this area can be expected to increase in the years ahead but agriculture's share of total employment can be expected to continue to decline. Furthermore as time goes by, and in terms of internal characteristics, fewer and fewer of the workers in this sector will be self-employed smallholder farmers, more and more will be employees in the agricultural industry.

As regards the defining features of the Malaysian labour force in coming years, data on educational and training opportunities, as well as the nature of the labour forces in other urban-industrial societies, suggest that we might expect that the majority of persons in the labour force will be employees, rather than employers or self employed workers. Of those employed in the dominant economic sectors in Malaysia, that is, manufacturing and service industries, the majority will be semi-skilled blue collar or clerical workers respectively, the next largest category will be skilled blue collar workers and technicians and white-collar workers with computing and accounting skills. As noted, the supply of, and the demand for, such professionals as doctors, engineers, chemists, accountants and lawyers, etc., will continue to grow, but these positions will represent the peak of the hierarchical labour force pyramid.

Insofar as the ethnic composition of the labour force is concerned, the proportional representation of Malays, Chinese and Indians is most likely to occur first at the industry level, then next at the lower levels of the occupational hierarchies. Due to changes that have taken place within the system of education, and given the policy requirement of the appointment of Malays in all categories and at every level of the occupational hierarchies, the present trend towards ethnic balance throughout the labour force can be expected to continue. Given the educational and training prerequisites for entry into so many work roles, however, and the time such changes take, the achievement of ethnic equity at the middle and top tiers of the occupational hierarchies is a medium to long term process. Thus we would expect that even as the country moves into the 21st century, professional and managerial work roles will continue to be dominated by non-Malays. Insofar as women are concerned, the trend towards a more educated and more readily employable female labour force, briefly noted above, may also continue. We would expect this in the case of non-Malay women. If, however, Islamic fundamentalism becomes more widespread, limits on the education of Malay females, as well as barriers to their entering into work roles where they dominate men, can be expected.

NOTES

1. In 1957, the peninsula was known as the Federation of Malaya. In 1963, the Federation of Malaysia, comprising the peninsula, Singapore and the former British colonies of Sabah and Sarawak, was formed. In 1965, Singapore was expelled from the Federation and became an island Republic.

2. The NEP has been succeeded by the National Development Policy.
3. The NEP's aim of a corporate economy that is 70 percent locally owned, including 40 percent owned by Malay and other indigenous people, seems not to have achieved. In 1990, Malay individuals and trust agencies owned 18.3 percent of the share capital of limited companies in Malaysia, Chinese Malaysians owned 44.9 percent. Nominee companies held 8.4 percent (Malaysia, 1991, Chart 1–5:14).
4. A ten-year Census of Population, due to be held in 1990, was not conducted. Population projections are thus based upon data gathered at the time of the 1980 Census.
5. Following Weber (1968), the term "modern" labour force is used to connote, at least in its ideal form, a degree of rationality and universalism rather than particularism as regards appointments and promotions.
6. Bahasa Malaysia is essentially the Malay language.
7. There are only so many vacant positions in the colleges and universities, and the imposition of quotas means that many talented non-Malays are denied the education they could expect to achieve within a meritocracy. Many non-Malay families overcome this difficulty by sending their children overseas to study. For the rich, this is not a hardship. For others, these educational opportunities are bought at considerable cost to family resources. Although the NEP *aims* to redistribute resources and create a more equitable society, the quota system in education provides evidence of just one instance of enhanced ethnic inequality. Because the Policy *assumes* Malays are the main non-poor, it does not address the difficulties faced by disadvantaged Chinese and Indians in the society.
8. The NEP also aimed to encourage the movement of better-educated Malays (most of whom are already urban dwellers) away from a dependence upon public sector employment and into the offices and boardrooms of private sector corporations, which also came under instruction to employ Malays at all levels, in numbers proportionate to their share of the population. Those non-Malays who obtained any benefit from the Policy's ethnic-quota system do so purely by default; there was no direct policy requirement, nor active practice, of an ethnic distribution of opportunities whereby Chinese of Indian Malaysians were aided in obtaining access to jobs relative to their share of the population.
9. It should be noted that the data in Tables 12.1–12.4 are for Peninsular Malaysia, while those in Tables 12.5–12.8 are for the nation as a whole.
10. A great many of the interstate migrants at this time were Malay women, who, contrary to the experience of many other women in the development process, were actively recruited: that section of international manufacturing capital which rests in Malaysia saw female labour as particularly suited to the needs of the global production line there.
11. After a detailed analysis of the National Development Plan the author considers

that the NDP will continue to guide Malaysia's development on the trajectory set by the NEP. The main differences between the two policies seem to be: (i) some "softening" of the ethnicity-specific employment guidelines in the NDP and; (ii) a very considerable emphasis now given to the role of private, as opposed to state capital, within the development process.

12. In the case of companies that are majority Japanese owned and controlled (and the Japanese are now the main foreign investors in Malaysia) this will probably mean the continued presence of middle-level expatriate managers and technicians too.

13. The *Sixth Malaysia Plan 1991–1995* targets manufacturing to contribute 32.4 percent to GDP by 1995 (Malaysia, 1991, Table 1–2:20).

14. The *Sixth Malaysia Plan* indicates that agriculture's share of GDP will have fallen to 15.5 percent by 1995 (Malaysia, 1991, Table 1–2:20).

REFERENCES

Amin, S. (1976). *Unequal Development: An Essay on the Social Formations of Peripheral Capitalism*. Sussex: Harvester Press.

Frobel, F., J. Heinrichs, and O. Kreye (1980). *The New International Division of Labour*. Paris: Cambridge University Press, Cambridge and Editions de Maison des Sciences de l'homme.

Kay, G. (1975). *Development and Underdevelopment: A Marxist Analysis*. London: Macmillan Press.

Malaya, Federation of (1949). *A Report on the 1947 Census of Population*. London.

Malaya, Federation of, Department of Statistics (1960). *1957 Population Census of the Federation of Malaya, Report No. 14*. Kuala Lumpur.

Malaysia, Federation of (1971). *Second Malaysia Plan 1971–1975*. Kuala Lumpur.

——— (1976). *Third Malaysia Plan 1976–1980*. Kuala Lumpur.

——— (1977). *General Report, Population Census of Malaysia 1970*, Vol. 1. Kuala Lumpur.

Malaysia, Federation of, Ministry of Labour (1985). *Labour and Manpower Report 1983/84*. Kuala Lumpur.

Malaysia, Federation of (1986a). *Fifth Malaysia Plan 1986–1990*. Kuala Lumpur.

Malaysia, Federation of, Ministry of Labour (1986b). *Labour and Manpower Report 1984/85*. Kuala Lumpur.

Malaysia, Federation of (1989). *Mid Term Review of the Fifth Malaysia Plan 1986–1990*. Kuala Lumpur.

——— (1991). *Sixth Malaysia Plan 1991–1995*. Kuala Lumpur.

O'Brien, L. N. (1980). "Class, Sex and Ethnic Stratification in West Malaysia." Ph.D. dissertation, Department of Anthropology and Sociology, Monash University, Melbourne.

———— (1987). "Malaysian Women and the New International Division of Labour." In *Class, Ideology and Women in Asian Societies*, edited by G. Pearson and L. Manderson. Hong Kong: Asian Research Service, pp. 201–222.

———— (1989a). "The Relative Significance of Foreign Investment in the Manufacturing Sector in Malaysia." Paper presented to the Institute of Australian Geographers 23rd Annual Conference, Adelaide, 13–16 February.

———— (1989b). "Technology Transfer and the Skilling of Labour in the Manufacturing Sector in Malaysia." Paper presented to the Malaysia Society of the Asian Studies Association of Australia Sixth Colloquium, Sydney, 10–11 June.

Taylor, J. G. (1979). *From Modernisation to Modes of Production: A Critique of the Sociologies of Development and Underdevelopment*. London and Basingstoke: Macmillan.

Weber, M. (1968). *Economy and Society*. New Jersey: Bedminster Press.

CHAPTER THIRTEEN

Hong Kong's Business Future: The Impact of Canadian and Australian Business Migration Programmes

Alan Naṣh
Assistant Professor, Department of Geography, Concordia University, Montreal, Canada

Introduction

This chapter will examine the effect of business migration to Canada and Australia on Hong Kong. In order to provide a suitable context for this discussion and also to justify the focus of this study, it is necessary first to estimate the total volume of emigration from Hong Kong, and to consider its various destinations, before turning to the specific role of business emigration from Hong Kong to Canada and Australia and an evaluation of the effects of the "brain drain" on Hong Kong. This examination will conclude by exploring what solutions could be utilized in the face of the problems business migration programmes specifically and migration policies in general are producing, not only for Australia and Canada, but also for Hong Kong itself.

Total Emigration from Hong Kong

The present population of Hong Kong is 5.6 million, of which some 3.25 million have British passports (although their right to live in Britain was repealed in 1971 when British immigration laws were changed). Under the 1984 Sino-British Joint Declaration, Hong Kong will revert to the People's Republic of China on 1 July 1997. Hong Kong will then become a Special Administrative Region (SAR) of China. The Declaration states that Hong

Kong's existing capitalist system will remain unchanged for fifty years and that the existing legal system, social system and lifestyle of its residents will also be preserved. However, concerns over how China will handle the handover, especially in the light of the Tiananmen event of 4 June 1989 and recently demonstrated by the protracted negotiations between China and Britain over the new US$18.6 billion airport, have encouraged increasing numbers of people to leave Hong Kong (Chen, 1988:634, 670–672; Cannon, 1989:16–28; DeMont and Fennell, 1989:1–27; Phillips, 1989; Anon., 1991g).

It is, however, very difficult to get hard data on the numbers and types of people leaving Hong Kong. Data are not systematically released by the Hong Kong government;[1] foreign embassies in the colony are reluctant to comment on the number or characteristics of those applying for immigration because they are concerned not to embarrass the Chinese government. The only consistent available source is the "certificates of no criminal record" issued by the Hong Kong Police Department. These documents are required by most countries of destination before immigration visas can be issued. Data available for 1986/1987 show that the Police Department was issuing an average of 200 a day during that year. By the second half of 1989, an average of 6,200 a month were issued. However, such evidence cannot be used as a surrogate measure for the estimation of migration since many of those receiving these certificates do not emigrate (Lau, 1987:22–23; Levin, 1989; Skeldon, 1990–1991:505). Similarly, stat-istics for visas at foreign embassies and consulates in Hong Kong, while providing a guide to trends, cannot give firm data. Thus the number of visa petitions at the US Consulate in September 1989 was 233 percent higher than a year before, but it is known from Canadian evidence that only 10–15 percent of those obtaining application forms ever follow the process through, and only 1 percent of those applying for independent immigration status will get a visa (Skeldon, 1990–1991:505–506; Levin, 1989).

Our best guide, therefore, are periodic statements made on the issue by the Hong Kong government: although, as Kwong (1990) notes, even these must be treated with some caution because those who left Hong Kong as non-migrants (as students or tourists, for example) but who changed their immigration status on reaching their destinations are not recorded by the Hong Kong government's system. Thus, while Canada stated that it received 19,994 immigrants from the colony in 1989, Hong Kong itself only recorded an emigration of 16,400 to that country (Kwong, 1990:301; Skeldon, 1990–1991:504).

Hong Kong government data show that between 1976 and 1979 approximately 14,500 people emigrated from Hong Kong per year. As Table 13.1 indicates, between 1980 and 1984, this annual average had increased to 20,640. By 1985 this figure had risen to 22,300, by 1988 to 45,800, and by 1989 had officially reached 42,000 — somewhat short of the estimates of between 50,000 and 55,000 made by various recent commentators (Lau, 1987:22–25; Anon., 1989a; Buruma, 1990:41). Total emigration for 1990 stood at 62,000, an increase of 47.6 percent on the previous year, and the most recently available statistics, for 1991, indicate current emigration rates of 1,500 per week (of whom, approximately 450 went to Canada), figures that, if the rate held, would translate into 78,000 a year (Anon., 1990b; Bociurkiw, 1990), a view at variance with official government estimates of a figure stabilizing somewhere between 58,000 and 62,000 for the next few years (Kwong, 1990:301; Skeldon, 1990–1991:510).

It is, of course, not possible to measure the true extent of emigration from Hong Kong without taking rates of return migration into account. Estimates of these rates vary. The official Hong Kong government scenario, announced in May 1990, stated that by 1991 the territory would have filled 37

Table 13.1: Hong Kong Government Estimates of Emigration, 1980–1991

Year	Number of emigrants	Percentage annual change
1980	22,400	
1981	18,300	− 22.4
1982	20,300	+ 10.9
1983	19,800	− 2.5
1984	22,400	+ 13.1
1985	22,300	− 0.4
1986	19,000	− 14.8
1987	30,000	+ 57.9
1988	45,800	+ 52.7
1989	42,000	− 8.3
1990	62,000	+ 47.6
1991	58,000	− 3.2
Total, 1980–1991	382,300	−

Source: Skeldon, 1990–1991:502 (based on statistics from Government Secretariat, Hong Kong).

percent of its projected labour force requirement of 2.86 million workers from existing stock, 28 percent with local graduates, 29 percent with students returning from their studies overseas and 5 percent from returning migrants and new immigrants to Hong Kong. These two latter statistics indicate that fully 34 percent of Hong Kong's estimated labour force needs are based on people returning to the territory. Indeed they require that 79,880 overseas students return between 1989 and 1996 (or approximately 10,000 per year) and that 39,856 former Hong Kong residents return to the territory over the same period (or about 5,000 per year). Such figures necessitate a return ratio of 67.5 per 100 departing students and 9.3 per 100 emigrants, at current rates of emigration (Kwong, 1990:326).

In view of the importance of these assumptions, it is necessary briefly to review here the evidence concerning student and emigrant return rates. The latest available information indicates, first, that 19,168 students left Hong Kong in 1989 for studies abroad (24 percent to Australia, 26.6 percent to Canada, 25.3 percent to the USA and 23.7 percent to Britain); second, that the rate of departure is increasing — thus the number of student visas granted for these four countries per 100 Hong Kong students aged between 15 and 19 years old has risen by 1 percent per year in recent years; third, that almost as many students now leave Hong Kong to attend tertiary educational institutions abroad as stay to attend one of Hong Kong's seven tertiary institutions (some 8,000 per year); and, fourth, that the total number of students overseas is of the order of 40,000 (Kwong, 1990:322–323; Skeldon, 1990–1991:511).

Such numbers have interesting implications for the host countries, since some have argued that they eventually constitute a political lobby in Hong Kong that can put pressure on Australia, Canada and the USA (Mosher, 1991). With this in mind, it is worth noting the words of Barbara Mc-Dougall, then Canada's Minister of Employment and Immigration, who observed in a speech to the Canadian Chamber of Commerce in Hong Kong on 5 September 1990 that:

> We have about 15,000 Hong Kong students studying in our schools — more than a quarter of our total foreign student population. Already more than 70,000 university graduates in Hong Kong graduated from Canadian universities (McDougall, 1990).

Motives for studying abroad vary, and while the lack of sufficient places in tertiary education institutions in Hong Kong is one important factor, clearly the hope that the student may gain permanent residence abroad (and thereby be able to sponsor his or her family also to emigrate there) is another factor; although this is a difficult one to gauge since estimating its significance is bound up with the problem of estimating rates of return (Skeldon, 1990–1991:511; Hillen, 1991:4). Reflecting on the issue of return rates, Skeldon has argued that "the majority [of overseas students] will probably return to Hong Kong on completion of their studies" while Kwong states, "I believe that the government's projection of a two-thirds return rate was unrealistic" (Kwong, 1990:323; Skeldon, 1990–1991:512).

Evidence that the latter opinion may be closer to the truth may be found, first, in a 1990 Hong Kong Certificate of Education Examination survey of those in Form 5. Of 540 students, 421 responded and 43 percent of them declared that they wished to emigrate; second, in the fact that the average age of students departing for overseas is decreasing, as 1997 approaches — thus, by 1989 the majority of those leaving for Canada were aged between 14 and 16, and only 10 percent were going to enter undergraduate programmes; and, third, in the observation that the number of students overstaying their visas abroad is steadily increasing. For example, 300 Hong Kong students overstayed in the USA in 1985, 500 in 1987 and 1,200 in 1988 (Kwong, 1990: 327).

Return rates for Hong Kong emigrants are somewhat easier to gauge because of stronger evidence, and clearly indicate that the government's scenario is very optimistic. Thus, a poll conducted in June 1989 by Hong Kong's Institute of Personnel Management (IPM) found that the rate stood at only 8.2 returnees per 100 emigrants in 1987, and 8.5/100 in 1988. Indeed, only 10 percent of the 224 organizations polled reported any returnees and one senior civil servant observed "of those that left in the early 1980s that intended to live overseas, 10–15 percent returned … [but] not one … during the last few years has returned" (Kwong, 1990:326–327).

Overall return figures indicate that more than 35,000 Hong Kong emigrants have come back to Hong Kong after getting Canadian passports (Mosher, 1991:11–12), but one case — the recent career of a Hong Kong photographer — strongly cautions against too much optimism being built on this. He had emigrated to Canada and spent some seven years there before returning to Hong Kong in 1985, but when interviewed there in 1989 said that he now planned to return to Canada once more (Levin, 1989).

Others in a similar situation but having left their families in Canada to await their eventual return from Hong Kong, have been called "astronauts" and have generated considerable interest in the Canadian media (Simpson, 1991). One recent report has argued that "one-third of emigrants [to Canada] return to Hong Kong, many to lead the astronaut lifestyle," another that one street in Vancouver is now known as "Widow Street" because of the wives that are left there by the "astronauts" (Anon., 1991b; Murphy, 1991:24). However, the events of Tiananmen have now prompted many such astronauts to return to Canada rather than wait for 1997, or even after, as they had perhaps originally planned (Levin, 1989).

One indication of the size of this flow from Hong Kong's perspective is indicated by the 1989 IPM poll which found that 72 (or 58 percent) of 124 individuals interviewed who had returned to Hong Kong, usually because they could earn more in Hong Kong than overseas, said that they were planning to leave Hong Kong again before 1997 (Kwong, 1990:326; Skeldon, 1990–1991:522).

In other words, what this all means is that while gross emigration rates do exaggerate the losses to Hong Kong, the rates of return are low and severely compromise official government plans for the territory's future.

Destinations

Stephen Chang, in a recent paper, argued that Australia, Canada and the USA are the preferred destinations for emigrants from Hong Kong (Chang, 1987). Throughout the early to mid-1980s this would seem to be true, as Table 13.2 indicates, with Hong Kong emigration to these three countries running at approximately 20,000 to 23,000 per year, a total that accounts — allowing for the data problems mentioned above — for almost all of the annual emigration in these years from Hong Kong.[2]

It is important to note that this percentage still holds for the late 1980s because, although American figures remain around 10,000 per year, the recent rise in emigration from Hong Kong is matched by substantial rises in the number that Canada and Australia receive. Thus, Canada received 6,309 emigrants from Hong Kong in 1980 and 23,281 in 1988; Australia received 2,822 in 1980 and 7,942 in 1988 (Table 13.2).

Such increases are in themselves worthy of note because they have meant that the relative importance of the USA as a destination for Hong Kong migrants has declined considerably over the 1980s: the USA alone

Table 13.2: Hong Kong Emigrants to Canada, Australia and the USA

Year	Canada	Australia	USA	Total
		Number of Hong Kong Emigrants		
1970	4,509	n.a.	9,720	14,229**
1971	5,009	n.a.	7,960	12,969**
1972	6,297	715	10,916	17,928
1973	14,662	734	10,300	25,696
1974	12,704	1,130	10,700	24,534
1975	11,132	1,593	12,547	25,272
1976	10,725	1,302	16,950*	28,977
1977	6,371	1,633	12,272	20,276
1978	5,740	2,313	11,145	19,198
1979	5,966	1,836	16,838	24,640
1980	6,309	2,822	n.a.	9,131**
1981	6,451	1,960	n.a.	8,411**
1982	6,542	2,414	11,908	20,864
1983	6,710	2,756	12,525	21,991
1984	7,696	3,691	12,290	23,677
1985	7,380	5,136	10,975	23,491
1986	5,893	4,912	9,930	20,735
1987	16,170	5,140	8,785	30,095
1988	23,281	7,942	11,817	43,040
1989	19,994	9,998	12,236	42,228

Data are for immigrants to Canada, Australia and the USA, whose last place of previous residence was given as Hong Kong.

Notes: Canada: Landed immigrants in calendar year; data by country of last permanent residence.

Australia: Settler arrivals for the financial year 1 July to 30 June.

USA: Immigrants admitted in fiscal year 1 July to 30 June from 1970 to 1975 and from 1 October to 30 September from 1977 to 1989.

*   Includes transition quarter June–September in realigned year, 1976.

** Data total incomplete.

Sources: Skeldon, 1990–1991:504, based on the following sources:

Canada: Employment and Immigration Canada, *Annual Immigration Statistics*, Ottawa, various years.

Australia: Department of Immigration and Ethnic Affairs, Australian Immigration, *Consolidated Statistics*, No. 13, Canberra, 1982; Department of Immigration, Local Government and Ethnic Affairs, *Statistical Note 36: Asian Immigration*, Canberra, 1988; Bureau of Immigration Research, *Immigration Update*, December 1989.

USA: US Department of Justice, *Statistical Yearbooks of the Immigration and Naturalization Service*, Washington, D.C.

was responsible in 1979 for 68 percent of total movement to the three main countries of destination for emigration from Hong Kong (Canada, Australia and the USA), but by 1988 was only receiving 27 percent of the total. Australia, on the other hand, had seen an increase from 7.5 percent in 1979 to approximately 18.5 percent in 1988 and Canada's share had risen from 24 percent to 54 percent over the same period. Indeed, by 1988, emigration to Canada alone represented half of all emigration from Hong Kong (see p. 311 Table 13.1 and p. 315 Table 13.2).

The dominance of these three countries as destinations for migrants from Hong Kong should not, of course, obscure the fact that other countries have also served as destinations and, significantly, that their involvement is increasing as 1997 approaches. Thus, Mauritius, Fiji, Hungary, Portugal, Belize, Gambia and Singapore have all recently begun schemes that offer passports to Hong Kong residents and the consulates of countries as diverse as Iceland, Sri Lanka, Honduras and South Africa have received visa applications (Anon., 1989a; Bociurkiw, 1990; Skeldon, 1990–1991:517). Tonga, Tahiti, the Marshall Islands, Trinidad, South Africa and Bangladesh have even indicated that sufficient Hong Kong investment in their countries will secure citizenship (Murphy, 1991:24). However, as the following section will show, notwithstanding efforts by other countries, Australia, Canada and the USA have become the major attractions for the Hong Kong migrant.

Business Migration

Australia's and Canada's increasing significance in terms of emigration from Hong Kong has been coupled over the 1980s with the competitive development in these two countries of business migration programmes; this is a development, it is worth noting, that did not occur in the USA until 1990 (Hawkins, 1988:256; 1989:397; Nash, 1990; Anon., 1990a). Business migration has become one of the important driving forces of Hong Kong emigration to Canada and Australia over recent years; indeed, it would not be too much of an exaggeration to say that both these countries have tolerated the large increase of Hong Kong immigration in recent years because it brings with it entrepreneurs and investors. Certainly, it could be argued that business migration programmes in both countries have become increasingly tailored to meet the needs of the Hong Kong business person.

The Canadian business migration programme (which has been in operation since 1978) has three components: the "self-employed" (who are required to create their own employment), the "entrepreneur" (who must establish a business that hires at least one Canadian) and the "investor" (who must possess a minimum net personal worth of Cdn$500,000 and must commit at least Cdn$150,000 for a three year period to an investment that contributes to business development and job creation; a component only in operation since January 1986). Of these three, the entrepreneur component has comprised approximately 75 percent of all admissions made under the programme (Nash, 1988a:19–20). The Australian programme (which has been in operation since 1982) seeks those who will transfer to Australia assets of at least Aus$500,000 "for the purposes of engaging in a commercial enterprise of benefit to Australia" (Department of Immigration, Local Government and Ethnic Affairs 1987, Section 9.4.3).

The immediate results of these programmes can perhaps be best quickly sketched by considering some actual Canadian examples. Thus, in early 1991, developers announced a multi-million dollar spa and resort project for the town of Summerside in Prince Edward Island; a project specifically designed to attract Hong Kong investor immigrant funds and only the most recent of a series of such ventures spawned by the investor programme (Anon., 1991c). Earlier cases include the Saskatchewan Government Growth Fund Ltd. that hoped to raise Cdn$36 million in venture capital by offering Cdn$150,000 shares in the fund which, according to its prospectus, was a vehicle for foreigners to invest in business in the province "to facilitate their admission to Canada as permanent residents"; and, in Winnipeg, the Hotel Executive Centre (International II) Ltd. Partnership that hoped to raise Cdn$12.75 million to finance the construction of the Lakeview Airport Executive Centre, a hotel-office-shopping mall complex, by similarly seeking investor immigrant funds (Cu-Uy-Gam, 1989). One recent case, concerning the firm Carley of California (Hong Kong), illustrates how Hong Kong-based business is using the programme to provide a "safety-net" for their employees. This small electronics assembly company has given its manager a sufficient lump sum for her to qualify for Canada's investor immigrant programme in the hope that she will come back to Hong Kong or delay her departure from the territory (Murphy, 1991:24). Such examples, of course, have to be seen in the context of the overall flow of funds from Hong Kong to Canada; this flow includes not only massive investments, such as Li Ka-shing's Cdn$484 million investment in Calgary-based Husky Oil, but also more modest sums, such as the planned Hong Kong rescue of C & C Industries, once Canada's largest yacht builders (Critchley and Reguly, 1987; Fennell, 1987; Ross and Freeman, 1987; Anon., 1991a).

Data for these programmes show that business migration was responsible for 15 percent (4,760) of all Hong Kong immigration into Australia between 1982 and 1988, for 19 percent (or 7,574) of Hong Kong immigration into Canada over the years 1987 to 1988.[3] It is also worth noting that Hong Kong business migrants account for the majority of business migrants entering Canada and Australia under such programmes (see Table 13.3 for overall data on these programmes). Of the total number of entrepreneur and investor immigrants who arrived in Canada in 1988 (a figure of 4,437), those from Hong Kong accounted for 37 percent (or 1,633 cases). Of the total number of 1,864 business migrant visas issued in Australia between July 1988 and March 1989, Hong Kong cases accounted for 887, or 48 percent of the total.[4]

An impression of the economic impact on Hong Kong of such business

Table 13.3: The Impact of Business Immigration: Australia and Canada

Australia			Canada			
Year	Funds transferred (Aus$ million)	Cases	Year	Funds transferred (Cdn$ million)	Employment	Cases
1982/83	42.8	171	1979*	204.0	2,152	1,237
1983/84	143.6	379	1980*	360.0	2,621	1,558
1984/85	157.0	368	1981*	441.0	3,183	1,893
1985/86	242.1	456	1982*	667.0	4,220	2,040
1986/87	500.9	919	1983	843.0	4,597	1,982
1987/88	1,018.1	1,852	1984	817.0	8,271	2,094
1988/89**	1,529.6	2,481	1985	1,200.0	9,715	2,136
			1986	1,700.0	12,119	2,428
			1987	2,287.0	11,918	3,642
			1988**	3,371.0	14,781	4,437

Notes: * Data based on number of landings (remainder based on visas).
         ** Data are preliminary.

migration to Australia and Canada can be readily gained from the following statistics. During the three year period 1984 to 1986 Hong Kong entrepreneur migrants planned to create or retain 11,979 jobs in Canada; those arriving in 1988 alone planned to create or retain 8,654 jobs.[5] The available data suggest that the average number of jobs created per entrepreneur immigrant in Canada is between six and seven, evidence from New South Wales indicates an average of eight.[6]

Of more concern, perhaps, are the data on the movement of funds. Those Hong Kong business migrants who arrived in Canada between 1984 and 1986 intended to transfer a total of Cdn$1.5 billion into the country (a figure representing over half the total transferred under the programme); those who arrived in Canada in 1988 alone declared a total of Cdn$1.7 billion to be transferred to Canada.[7] Those Hong Kong migrants who entered Australia under its Business Migration Programme transferred Aus$276 million to Australia during the second half of 1987 and Aus$456 million between July 1988 and February 1989 (figures representing 83 percent and 45 percent respectively of the total funds transferred to Australia under this programme during these periods).[8]

These figures fall into sharper perspective when it is realized that, according to the best available government estimates for 1988, the total magnitude of funds leaving Hong Kong for Canada in that year was reckoned to be of the order of Cdn$2.5 billion, for Australia Aus$847 million. In other words, in 1988, business migration accounted for 68 percent of all Hong Kong funds moving into Canada and approximately 80 percent of those moving into Australia.[9]

More recent data are equally arresting. In 1989, the total amount of funds transferred to Canada by all migrants from Hong Kong in that year was Cdn$3.5 billion of which some Cdn$2.21 billion, or 63 percent, was to be transferred by the business migration component (Anon., 1990c; Ip, 1990; Skeldon, 1990–1991:507). Since it is estimated that the total dollar flow (including investments) from Hong Kong to Canada in 1989 was approximately Cdn$5 billion (Anon., 1990c), this means that business immigration from Hong Kong was responsible for 44 percent of the total flow of funds in that year, and overall immigration from Hong Kong for 70 percent.

Data for 1990 are still very preliminary, but the consensus points to a figure of approximately Cdn$4.0 billion as the amount estimated to be transferred by all emigrants from Hong Kong to Canada — certainly, such a figure is quoted in the official Canadian government briefing book used for Prime Minister Brian Mulroney's 1991 visit to Hong Kong (Bociurkiw, 1990; Anon., 1991e; Terry, 1991a, 1991b). If we assume that the proportion of this flow contributed by business migration remains the same as in 1989, this would mean that some Cdn$2.5 billion was transferred by business migrants to Canada from Hong Kong in 1990.

Turning to Australia, Kwong has estimated that the 900 business migrant families visaed in 1989/1990 transferred Aus$432 million to Australia in that fiscal year, a figure representing 84 percent of that transferred by all Hong Kong migrants in Australia in that year (a total of Aus$512 million) and he adds:

> How much Hong Kong money has been transferred abroad in the year 1989/90? An Australian banker attending an international conference on banking in Geneva forecast that Hong Kong migrants and investors would transfer at least 6,000 million Hong Kong Dollars (HKD) to Australia in 1990, and 24,000 million HKD to Canada in the same year…. In other words … 30,000 million HKD would be transferred to just *two* countries in a single year (Kwong, 1990:298; his emphasis).

Reflecting on these data, Kwong adds that:

> In the light of these estimates for Australia and Canada, it is plausible to reckon that the outflow to the rest of the world … would probably add up to a level at least matching the Geneva figures … for Australia and Canada; that is in an order of magnitude of HK$60 billion [US$8.108] worldwide for 1989. There is little evidence of abating of capital outflow. Signs pointing to an acceleration of the outflow abound (Ibid.:299).

An important series of caveats to these reflections is provided by Ronald Skeldon and it is worth quoting his comments at some length. He writes:

> there is little evidence to support the idea of a massive outflow of capital from Hong Kong. The data, far from adequate though they may be, suggest that up to 1983 there was a net capital inflow followed by a five-year period of a small but diminishing outflow until 1989, when there was indeed a net outflow of capital, almost certainly directly attributable to events in China. The capital that emigrants were taking with them was in any case completely overshadowed by investments made overseas by Hong Kong-based entrepreneurs and, until 1989, these outflows were "largely and possibly entirely, offset by a substantial inflow of foreign capital" (Hongkong Bank, *Economic Report*, April 1990). Although

Hong Kong capital as a whole is not being drained by the flows of emigrants, the amounts of capital available to migrants is hardly small (Skeldon, 1990–1991:509).

In support of these comments, it is worth noting, as examples, the continued active presence in Hong Kong of six of Canada's major banks and six of its insurance companies; indeed, 70 Canadian companies currently have subsidiaries or branches in Hong Kong and 400 are represented by distributors there (Anon., 1990d). More importantly, perhaps, a recent survey of 3,195 overseas companies based in the territory, conducted by Kong Kong's Industry Department, found that only twenty-nine companies had moved their regional headquarters from Hong Kong (Bociurkiw, 1990). The Japanese industrialist Kazuo Wada has recently moved the headquarters of his billion dollar international retail department store empire (numbering 120 stores worldwide) to Hong Kong, a move that has contributed to Japan's considerable ongoing investment in the territory. Current estimates suggest that direct investment by Japanese corporations in Hong Kong since 1982 total approximately US$8 billion (Hewett, 1990).

However, encouraging as these observations are, the facts remain that, as Skeldon himself observes, Hong Kong investment flows have experienced a net outflow since 1989 and that in order to counter this, as he notes it has in the recent past, Hong Kong must continue to attract ever-increasing influxes of foreign capital to be able to match, or exceed, the apparently ever-increasing volume of funds leaving with Hong Kong's emigrants. Whether this will be possible remains to be seen, but it is obvious that the challenge to Hong Kong has been made much more daunting because of the development of business migration programmes.

It would be inappropriate to conclude this examination without mentioning some of the major problems that have been encountered by business migration programmes in Canada and Australia and considering the problems business migration raises for Hong Kong.

As far as the evidence indicates, it appears that between 60 and 80 percent of all Hong Kong funds entering Canada and Australia are invested in real estate (Sheppard, 1988; Fennell, 1989:31; Anon., 1989b:15–16, 34). The city of Toronto, for example, is currently experiencing an investment in its real estate of over Cdn$1 billion a year from Hong Kong (Sheppard, 1988). Such large inflows of funds have fuelled a growing anti-immigration backlash in cities as Sydney and Vancouver (Totaro, 1988; Bayless, 1989;

Taylor, 1989); in the latter, for example, it is widely believed by public opinion that incoming Hong Kong money has been the cause of recent rapidly rising real estate prices (Ip, 1989).

The second major problem largely stems from the fact that business migrants are poorly monitored by the relevant authorities once they arrive in either Canada or Australia. Because of this, it has been difficult to discover whether business migrants have carried out their stated intentions or have fulfilled programme requirements. The long term effects of the programmes are particularly difficult to gauge because of this. Moreover, the lack of adequate monitoring has encouraged fraud by those who are not *bona fide* business people and has meant that it is very difficult to know how long funds transferred to Australia or Canada by business migrants have remained in these countries (Malarek, 1987:215–229; Cannon, 1989:224–225; DeMont and Fennell, 1989:106). Indeed, in an 24 April 1991 submission to the federal Public Accounts Committee, the Australian Federal Police said that it was "concerned that individuals are arriving in Australia under the business migration programme by using funds provided by organized crime," an opportunity provided to criminals (including known Chinese gangs in Hong Kong), the police believed, by inadequate monitoring of the programme (Taylor, 1991). Such fears have yet to be expressed concerning Canada's programme but the public has often vented its concerns over the possible entry of Triad members and other Chinese criminal elements into the country under Canada's immigration programmes (Dubro, 1991).

The final problem concerns the regional disparities produced by these programmes. Business migrants have focussed on the "have" areas of both Canada and Australia; they seldom settle in the "have not" areas (Nash, 1988b). Thus, in the Australian case, almost 40 percent of initial funds intended to be transferred to Australia by business migration programme migrants visaed between July 1988 and February 1989 went to New South Wales, a total of Aus$394 million. Only a total of 8 percent (or Aus$77.3 million) went to South Australia, Tasmania and the two territories.[10] Indeed, estimates show that 36 percent of all business migration to Australia goes to Greater Sydney and that little effect of this movement is felt even in large centres only 140 kilometres away.[11]

In the Canadian case, data show that while entrepreneur immigrants intended to create or retain over 14,000 jobs in Ontario between 1984 and 1986, those settling in Newfoundland intended to hire only three individuals. Ontario received 45 percent of the funds to be transferred during the same years, while Newfoundland received only 0.01 percent of the total. These effects are mirrored and compounded by an underlying metropolitan dominance so that 70 percent of all entrepreneur immimgrants to Canada are found in the three cities of Montreal, Toronto and Vancouver (Nash, 1988a:22–23; Islam, 1989:229–230).

Clearly, if the maximum benefit is to be obtained from these business migration programmes, greater thought must be given to their possible use in strategies of regional development and to the refinement of such programmes so that business migration may play a positive role in these development strategies. If geographers can discover how best to do this, that is, to encourage business migrants to locate where they are most needed, they will have made a significant contribution to the improvement of business migration programmes in both Australia and Canada.

As far as Hong Kong itself is concerned, business migration programmes are responsible for significant losses in both business people and funds to the territory. As estimates given earlier in this chapter suggest, during the year 1988/1989 alone, a total of 2,520 business people emigrated from Hong Kong to Canada and Australia, where they planned to create 15,750 jobs; those that had left during 1987/1988 indicated that they were transferring a total of HK$14.7 billion out of Hong Kong and those that left in 1989/1990 took approximately HK$15.64 billion. Such figures are estimates for only annual periods; clearly, the total loss to Hong Kong from the inception of such programmes to at least 1997 can only be guessed at, but must be of a considerable magnitude as we have already seen.

The Effects of the "Brain Drain" on Hong Kong

The effects of emigration upon Hong Kong have been the focus of some controversy among academics, journalists, government officials and business people; certainly, the evidence is not always as unambiguous as one might wish. Nevertheless, some convergences of opinion and areas of consensus are beginning to develop.

First, the effects of emigration upon the professions has received widespread popular attention. Thus as early as 1987, concerns were being voiced in Hong Kong over the loss of civil servants, bankers and other professionals that Hong Kong could ill afford to lose (Lau, 1987:22–25).

One commentator observed that "the brain drain is already so serious that people with special skills have to be paid more and more to stay on" (Buruma, 1990:46). According to one market research company, which concluded "20 percent of families may emigrate," a survey conducted in January 1988 showed that 14 percent of the 1.5 million families in Hong Kong had at least one family member with the right of abode in a foreign country, and another 7 percent had a least one member attempting to emigrate (Chen, 1988:675).

Other reports have argued that the pressures created by those desperate to join such an exodus have resulted in recent widespread allegations of corruption in Hong Kong concerning the sale of Panamanian passports, forged documents (including the sale of passports for the nonexistent Republic of Corterra) and the alleged bribery of Venezuelan, Hong Kong and New Zealand immigration officials; the media have also commented on the animosity that has been created as the bulk of Hong Kong's population, and especially its refugee communities, have discovered that no such special migration programmes have been created for them (Buruma, 1990:41, 46; Oziewicz, 1990; Skeldon, 1990–1991:514; Murphy, 1991:24).

A recent article in the prestigious American magazine, *The Atlantic Monthly*, argued that 98 percent of the colony's pharmacists, 85 percent of its surveyors, 80 percent of its accountants, 63 percent of the government's doctors and 50 percent of Hong Kong's veterinarians were planning to leave Hong Kong before 1997; the singer and actress Anita Mui was quoted as believing that 80 percent of Hong Kong's entertainment community will have left by this date (Murphy, 1991:22).

That such estimates are not exaggerated is clear from a comparison with the more sober and careful examination of the impact of emigration upon the professions conducted by Paul Kwong and summarized in Table 13.4 and Table 13.5 below. His data show that of Hong Kong's accountants, 66 percent of a group of 4,600 surveyed in late 1989 had applied for foreign passports and an additional 27 percent planned to emigrate; of the colony's pharmacists, 48 percent of an early 1990 survey already held foreign passports and a further 43 percent planned to emigrate (Table 13.4). Overall, the foremost summary of the situation is perhaps best provided by Hong Kong's Institute of Personnel Management (IPM). On the basis of a 1989 survey of its membership, IPM argued that approximately 50 percent of all

Table 13.4: The Impact of Emigration on the Professions

Profession	Impact
Accountants	66 percent have applied for foreign passports; 27 percent of the remainder plan to emigrate (survey of 4,600 conducted in late 1989).
Architects	52 percent have applied to immigrate; 24 percent intend to emigrate (survey of 1,026 members conducted in March 1990; 565 responded).
Bank staff	33 percent of managers who leave their jobs cite emigration as a cause; 20 percent of supervisors and secretaries; 8 percent (or 1,120) of staff.
Civil engineers	40 percent would emigrate within three years; 40 percent "probably would" emigrate within years (January 1990 survey of 760 expatriates in government; 548 responded).
Civil servants	1,500 of those who left the service 1988/1989 cited emigration as a cause; they comprised 14 percent of those leaving the service 1988/1989 (Acting Deputy Secretary, Civil Service).
Clergy	10 percent of the 800 Protestant clergy have already emigrated (Director, Hong Kong Christian Institute).
Computer programmers	20 percent will emigrate within five years. Vacancies estimated at 2,400 by 1990 (Vocational Training Council).
Doctors and nurses	70 percent of government doctors plan to emigrate (October 1990 survey of government doctors); 58 percent of all doctors plan to leave by 1997 (representative of medical constituency in the Legislative Council).
Educators	1,012 teachers and 184 lecturers & professors estimated to have emigrated in 1989; 7.7 teachers lost per school per year and 25 percent loss of faculty at The Chinese University of Hong Kong by 1995 due to emigration, quitting.
Engineering technicians & surveyors	70 percent would quit before 1997 to emigrate or change jobs (March 1990 survey of 1,700 in government; 500 responded).
Lawyers	60 percent would leave before 1997 (1989 survey of the 2,100 members of the Law Society of Hong Kong; 1,600 responded).
Pharmacists	48 percent already hold foreign passports; 43 percent plan to emigrate (January 1990 survey of 488; 209 responded).
Psychologists	20 percent have emigrated 1987–1989 and more are planning to leave (Hong Kong Psychological Association).
Radiographers	70 percent of Hong Kong's 380 radiographers had applied for overseas passports (early 1990 union survey).
Secretaries	90 percent of those who do not have the right of abode abroad plan to emigrate and of these, 57 percent have applied for immigration visas (January 1990 survey of 1,700 persons).
Social workers	14 percent (34) quit in 1989 in order to emigrate (late 1989 survey by Hong Kong Council of Social Services).

Source: Kwong, 1990:380–316.

Table 13.5: Emigrants from Hong Kong: Economically-active Population, 1987–1988, by Estimated Occupation

Occupation of emigrant	Emigrants, Number	1987–1988 Percentage
Professional and Technical	12,683	34.11
Nurses and midwives	2,224	5.98
Teachers	1,920	5.16
Engineers	1,898	5.10
System analysts & computer programmers	1,448	3.89
Accountants & auditors	1,326	3.57
Doctors & dentists	797	2.14
Architects & surveyors	493	1.32
Engineering technicians	351	0.94
Professors & lecturers	350	0.94
Artists & photographers	338	0.91
Other professional workers	253	0.68
Social workers & labour officers	217	0.58
Medical assistants	216	0.58
Lawyers & judges	195	0.52
Authors, editors, reporters	154	0.41
Members of religious orders	96	0.26
Musicians & actors	88	0.23
Marine & aircraft officers	70	0.19
Other technical workers	64	0.17
Librarians	43	0.12
Economists	43	0.12
Physical scientists	32	0.09
Medical science technicians	31	0.08
Athletic coaches	17	0.05
Physical science technicians	14	0.04
Medical scientists	5	0.01
Administrative & Managerial	5,915	15.91
General managers & production managers	5,875	15.80
Government administrators	40	0.11
Clerical & Related workers	4,843	13.03
Stenographers & typists	1,938	5.21
Other clerical workers	1,590	4.28
Bookkeepers & cashiers	1,076	2.89
Transport & communication workers	167	0.45
Government executive officers officials	72	0.19

**Table 13.5: Emigrants from Hong Kong: Economically-active Population,
1987–1988, by Estimated Occupation** (Cont'd)

Occupation of emigrant	Emigrants, Number	1987–1988 Percentage
Sales workers	4,663	12.54
Managers, wholesale & retail	3,703	9.96
Others sales workers	960	2.58
Service workers	3,841	10.33
Cooks & waiters	2,700	7.26
Other service workers	513	1.38
Protective service workers	437	1.18
Managers of hotels, restaurants & other establishments	191	0.51
Production & Transport workers	3,330	8.96
Garment makers	919	2.47
Other production workers	522	1.40
Foremen & supervisors	445	1.20
Drivers and sailors	430	1.16
Electrical and electronic workers	362	0.97
Construction workers	294	0.79
Machinery fitters	231	0.62
Food & beverage processors	107	0.29
Spinners & weavers	20	0.05
Other Occupation or Unclassifiable	1,905	5.12
Total, economically active emigrants	37,180	100.00

Notes: During the period 1987–1988, the following "economically inactive" persons also emigrated:

Students	21,682
Homemakers	11,149
Retirees	1,800
Others	3,185
Total	37,816

("Students" here are defined as holders of immigration visas who left Hong Kong together with their close kin; they are not those holding student visas).

These detailed occupation distributions by economic activity status have been estimated by Paul C. K. Kwong, Pak-wai Liu and Stephen L. W. Tang (1990) on the basis of the occupational profile data of Hong Kong emigrants to the major destination countries in 1987 and 1988.

Source: Kwong, 1990:303–306 (based on estimates reported in Paul C. K. Kwong, Pak-wai Liu and Stephen L. W. Tang, *The Functional Core of the Labour Force*. Hong Kong: Department of Sociology, The Chinese University of Hong Kong, 1990).

personnel managers, engineers and bankers would "probably" or "definitely" leave the colony by 1997 (Murphy, 1991:24). Indeed, Patrick Maule, the principal investigator of the IPM survey, remarked, in late 1989, that "the proportion of professionals wishing to emigrate could have reached 71 percent by now" (Kwong, 1990:326).

The current impact of such a loss of professionals is more disputed. The annual movement of professionals, managers, administrators and technicians from Hong Kong has represented approximately a quarter of the territory's total losses through emigration since 1987: the annual figures are 7,400, 11,200, 9,800 (estimate) and 14,500 (estimate) respectively. However Kwong has argued that such a figure of 24 percent — the official government estimate — gives a misleading picture of these losses for a number of reasons. First, he believes that the figures should more realistically be presented in terms of the numbers of families leaving. If this is done, Kwong estimates that in 1987, out of a total of 8,000 families, 5,000 were headed by professionals. In other words, the professionals in that year were responsible for 62 percent of total emigration from Hong Kong (Kwong, 1990:301–303).

Second, annual emigration statistics for the professions can be misleading if they are not compared with the total size of the professions in Hong Kong. Thus, Kwong argues, the total outflow of professional, administrative, managerial and technical workers in 1987 represented a loss or "depletion" of 2.7 percent of the territory's total population of such people according to the data derived from Hong Kong's 1986 Census, and in 1988 and 1989 represented an annual depletion of approximately 3.6 percent. Overall, these rates may seem low, indeed Skeldon has argued because of this that the effects of current rates of loss have been exaggerated. Thus, he notes, an IPM company survey of 1988 found that while annual weighted staff turnover in the colony was of the order of 27 percent, emigration was only responsible for 5 percent and only 1 percent of overall turnover in 1988 (Kwong, 1990:301–304; Skeldon, 1990–1991:509–510).

However, such an argument fails to recognize that for certain sub-groups within the economy the depletion rates are particularly marked. Thus, the 1988 IPM survey itself observes that finance, insurance, real estate, business and professional services witnessed a 2.2 percent overall turnover rate due to emigration in 1988 and cautioned that their data obscured the fact that most emigrants were concentrated in middle management positions, where the effects of their loss would be out of proportion to their number, and that certain sectors were experiencing problems due to emigration (Skeldon, 1990–1991: 509–510). Thus, calculations for the period 1987 to 1988 indicate depletion rates of 6.5 percent for Hong Kong's stock of general and production managers, 10 percent for engineers, 11 percent for nurses and midwives, 13 percent for lawyers, judges, doctors and dentists, 22 percent for accountants and auditors, and 35 percent for the colony's programmers and system analysts (Kwong, 1990:304, 307).

Third, and perhaps most important, although professional, administrative and managerial losses are portrayed as only a quarter of Hong Kong's emigration losses, they in fact represent 50 percent of the territory's annual emigration of "economically-active" people (see Table 13.5).[12] If this estimate is correct and such rates of emigration continue until 1997, then, as Skeldon has argued, "perhaps a quarter of a million of Hong Kong's best and brightest will depart before the Chinese takeover" (Skeldon, 1990–1991:510). Such a loss would certainly pose difficulties for the territory if Kwong and his associates are correct that the "functional core" of the Hong Kong labour force consisted of only 130,200 people in 1989 (Kwong, 1990:303; Kwong et al., 1990; Skeldon, 1990–1991:510). Skeldon, while disputing both the functioanl core thesis and its estimated size (arguing that there is no practical or theoretical basis to measure or justify a number "that is critical to normal business"), does nevertheless agree that such levels of emigration "could indeed have profound implications for Hong Kong's economy" (Skeldon, 1990–1991:510).

Indications of how profound the implications will be are already apparent from the present situation in the territory. Thus, commentators note that there is already a labour shortage in Hong Kong. In 1989 estimated job vacancies totalled 120,000 (or 3.6 percent of total employment); by 1990 the shortage had become so critical that the government introduced legislation to allow the importation of 14,700 foreign workers to fill key positions and to allow firms to recruit students from China. Indeed, it has been noted that without its growing employment of workers in Guangdong province of mainland China (estimated at between 1.0 and 2.5 million workers), the effects of such a labour shortage in Hong Kong itself would be far more accentuated (Bociurkiw, 1990; Skeldon, 1990–1991:501, 516). Recent reports also suggest that banks and hotels are beginning to experience difficulties in keeping staff; and that a shortage of pharmacists and teachers is developing and that Cathay Pacific has lost airline technicians to Quantas in Australia (Anon., 1991d).

Other commentators have drawn attention to the size of the current "brain drain" that present emigration levels have caused. Thus, Kwong has noted that 18.7 percent of all Hong Kong's emigrants in 1987 had degree-level education, a figure that has only marginally declined to stand at 15 percent for both 1988 and 1989, whereas by comparison only 3.5 percent of the general population have acquired this level of education. Assuming four years per degree, he estimates that the total human capital loss to the territory over the period 1987 to 1989 is 74,400 college years and comments that "added with the hundreds of thousands man [sic] -years of postgraduate working experience, the combined loss of *human capital* is staggering, much of it irreplaceable" (Kwong, 1990:303; his emphasis).

One series of responses to this loss has been in the work place itself. Thus, Peter Wong Hong-yuen, a member of the Legislative Council and a spokesperson for the accounting constituency notes that emigration has resulted in: increased staff turnover (by as much as 33 percent in one accounting firm); increased salaries (by as much as 27 percent for the accounting profession, twice the rate for other professions); declining quality and efficiency of service (because senior staff become overburdened and junior staff, who must be increasingly used for senior rank tasks, are inexperienced); and, ultimately, a declining satisfaction for employees — which itself contributes to their desire to emigrate (Kwong, 1990:309; Anon., 1991d).

A second series of reponses concerns overall economic growth itself. Thus, the Asian Development Bank in its comments on Hong Kong contained in the report *Asian Development Outlook for 1991* cautioned that "weak fixed investment growth and continued emigration of professionals and skilled workers have limited the capacity for an early return to the high growth rates experienced in the past" (Anon., 1991d). In the face of this, it is perhaps little wonder that some businesses are beginning to leave the territory, with increasing numbers leaving for destinations such as Bermuda, Singapore and, in the case of Cathay Pacific and the Royal Hong Kong Jockey Club, Australia, where these companies have moved their computing operations (Tierney, 1989; Bociurkiw, 1990; Murphy, 1991).

In general terms, what these findings appear to suggest is that at present rates of loss, and assuming no replacement, the territory almost certainly will be faced with the challenges of a grave shortage of key professional groups — if not well before 1997, then at least by the turn of the century. However, whether these rates will continue at such levels or whether they can be mitigated remains debatable. Skeldon has argued strongly that the effects of improved education policies and return migration may be sufficient to counter such depletion effects, although it has to be admitted that it is hard to envisage how this is possible at their current rates (Skeldon, 1990–1991:510).[13]

The Future

As far as Hong Kong's future is concerned, there are strong grounds to conclude that the situation can only continue to deteriorate. Thus, given current trends, both Canada's and Australia's intake of business immigrants from Hong Kong will continue to increase in size; indeed both countries have stated their continuing support for business migration programmes (McDougall, 1990). Moreover, emigration from Hong Kong will be further increased in future as other countries develop business and general migration programmes tailored for Hong Kong.

Thus, both the USA and the UK have recently announced their intention to join the competition for the wealthy and skilled Hong Kong emigrant. The numbers that they plan to admit (a global limit of 10,000 per year in the American case; 50,000 families *in toto* from Hong Kong in the British case) can only serve to exacerbate Hong Kong's difficulties (Buruma, 1990:46; Valeriano, 1991). Indeed, a number of M.P.s in a British House of Commons debate on the Thatcher government's plans specifically noted their concerns over the contribution such programmes would make to a brain drain from Hong Kong (BBC, 1989). In addition, Singapore has recently announced its intention to take 25,000 workers from the territory and the Americans, as part of a thoroughgoing 1990 revision of their immigration legislation, have raised the quota of visas to be allocated to Hong Kong residents from 3,000 to 25,000 per year by the end of 1994 and have extended the validity of these visas to between 10 and 15 years (Anon., 1990c; Skeldon, 1990–1991:517; Terry, 1991a).

Faced with such developments, it is little wonder that the projected emigration losses for Hong Kong from 1990 to 1991 have been given as between 550,000, the "optimistic" scenario, and 700,000, the "pessimistic" view (Kwong, 1990:301); and, that, in view of these estimates, a number of gloomy economic forecasts have been made. Thus Price Waterhouse has recently estimated that continued emigration from Hong Kong could reduce the territory's economic growth by 45 percent before 1997 (Skeldon, 1990–1991:501). The emigration of skilled labour may even, as other commentators have suggested, prevent the Hong Kong government reaching its forecast medium term GDP growth of 5.5 percent per year. Failure to meet such fiscal forecasts might result in the need to cut government spending, as in the early 1980s, a move that could easily jeopardize the new airport scheme (Bowring and Taylor, 1991:46–48).

It may be argued, of course, that such views and projections are predicated on misplaced apprehensions and pessimism about Hong Kong's situation after 1997. However, it is sobering to reflect that even if Hong Kong's long term economic future will be a secure and prosperous one under Chinese rule — as some commentators have argued it will be under the terms of the 1984 Sino-British agreement — the reality is that current opinion among many in Hong Kong is not to stay and find out. Thus, as even a recent optimistic newspaper report on Hong Kong's future was forced to admit:

> Although there is a generous guarantee of economic freedoms under Chinese rule for 50 years after 1997, this has not been enough to stop Hong Kong's intellectual lifeblood from draining away (Anon., 1990b).

The challenge Hong Kong now faces, therefore, is how to solve the many problems posed by such a drain of skills and resources.

It would be inhumane and illegal under international law to prevent emigration from the territory. However, it is not with such a response that the solution lies.

Moreover, existing government policies to combat the problem should continue: these have been styled "retain and retrain" in the case of those designed directly to combat the brain drain, and "new crew" in the case of those designed through education and overseas recruitment to replace those lost to Hong Kong (Kwong, 1990:329, 334). Indeed, the potential in this regard of the one major influx of population that Hong Kong has received — its refugee and illegal immigrant population of approximately 50,000 — should not be overlooked by the Hong Kong authorities (Anon., 1991f:36–38).

However, as the evidence abundantly indicates, these strategies alone are entirely inadequate. Thus, by February 1991, only 7 percent of those that were expected had applied for British citizenship, an important plank in the scheme to retain key workers in Hong Kong. This is evidently because of the lack of a Chinese commitment to recognize such arrangements after 1997 and the unattractiveness of the British economy relative to that of North America, thus effectively eliminating this approach as a solution (Winchester, 1991).[14]

Similarly, recruitment campaigns overseas have achieved little: the Hong Kong Social Welfare Department's 1989 campaign only resulted in seven Canadian applicants (only two of whom could come in 1990) whereas total vacancies totalled 593 posts; the government attempt to recruit up to 2,500 overseas workers in the same year resulted in only 900 arriving by February 1990 (Kwong, 1990:327); and, as we have seen, expanded tertiary education faces ever-increasing losses as students themselves go overseas.

Rather, the answer rests with those countries that have sought after Hong Kong's business emigrants; they must be persuaded to renounce the lure of what seems to be "easy money" and instead to demonstrate their faith in Hong Kong's continued economic future. The various business migration programmes that these countries have focussed on Hong Kong, by their very nature, do not do this. Hong Kong ought therefore to insist that they be abandoned, to be replaced by supportive economic policies and emigration programmes that are sensitive to the needs of Hong Kong rather than those of the USA, the UK, Canada or Australia.

ACKNOWLEDGEMENTS

I would like to express my thanks to Professor Yue-man Yeung for comments on an earlier draft of this paper; to David Frost, Michael Marsden, Jacqueline Anderson, Suzanne Mackenzie, Patricia Wiesinger, Alena Perout, and the staff at the Australian High Commission in Ottawa for their help in finding information; to Zeng Yang for translations; to Sherri Labour for data analysis; and, to the Social Science and Humanities Research Council of Canada for funding part of the work upon which this paper draws.

NOTES

1. "The Hong Kong Government does not produce statistics of people emigrating from Hong Kong, only statistics of people leaving from Hong Kong on Hong

Kong travel documents (many of whom would later return to Hong Kong), and of people returning to Hong Kong." (Personal Communication, Hong Kong Government Office, London, 13 October 1987; Ref. 541/3/2).

2. With reference to the statistics in this section, see also Lau, 1987:22; Australian Bureau of Statistics, 1987:7–8; Canada Employment and Immigration Commission 1984, 1986, 1987, 1988 and unpublished tabulations 29 September 1989.

3. Table 13.2; and unpublished tabulations, Australia: Department of Immigration, Local Government and Ethnic Affairs (Statistics Section), December 1988, (Business Migration Section) June 1989; Canada: Employment and Immigration Commission, 5 May 1988 and 6 June 1989.

4. Table 13.3; and unpublished tabulations, Canada: Department of External Affairs (MASENT database) 28 February 1989 and 1 March 1989; Australia: Department of Immigration, Local Government and Ethnic Affairs (Business Migration Section) June 1989.

5. The 1984–1986 statistics are derived from Nash 1987, Table 32; 1988 data are derived from Department of External Affairs (MASENT), unpublished tabulations, 28 February 1989 and 1 March 1989.

6. Canada: Nash 1988a, 21; Australia: unpublished tabulations, Department of Industrial Development and Decentralization (New South Wales) 18 February 1988 and June 1988.

7. See note 5.

8. Wu and Connell 1988; Department of Immigration, Local Government and Ethnic Affairs (MPMS/Business Migration Section), unpublished tabulations, April 1989.

9. The government sources are: David Lawrence, Special Advisor to the Canadian High Commission in Hong Kong (quoted in Ross and Freeman, 1987:36; Lau, 1987:23; see also National Film Board, 1989; Ip, 1990) and Australia's Foreign Investment Review Board (quoted in Walters, 1990:84 and in Anon., 1989b:15–16, 34); the latter are defined as "investment inflows by country (approvals basis)." It is worth adding here that when commenting on these totals in late 1990 (as contained in the conference summary of this paper), Canadian and Australian High Commission officials in Hong Kong stated that the total fund transfers were now actually much higher. In the Canadian case, it was argued to be "nearly double" the figure presented here (Macdonald, 1990). The discrepancy would appear to be simply due to the dates of the various estimates. Certainly, this must remain the explanation for the time being since, at the time of writing, the Australian High Commission in Hong Kong had not yet replied to a request to provide details with which to pursue this matter further.

10. Department of Immigration, Local Government and Ethnic Affairs (MPMS/Business Migration Section), unpublished tabulations, April 1989.

11. Personal Communication, Robert Salt (Senior Consultant, Business Migration Services), Department of Industrial Development and Decentralization (New South Wales), 18 February 1988 and 4 July 1989. (This department has subsequently changed its name to Business and Consumer Affairs).

12. The other half of the economically-active population are made up of clerical, sales, services and production workers. The remainder of Hong Kong's annual emigration flow, approximately 50 percent, are made up of the rather inappropriately named "economically-inactive:" students, homemakers and retirees (Kwong, 1990:303–306).

13. The issue of return migration has been discussed earlier in this paper. Numbers with tertiary-level education in Hong Kong have been increasing by approximately 10,000 per annum over the period 1986 to 1990 and may increase further as a result of increased government initiatives in the 1990s (Skeldon, 1990–1991:510).

14. It is also because of such fears over Chinese policy towards those who hold foreign passports in Hong Kong after 1997 — that China simply will not recognize their validity — that other attempts to pursuade people to remain in Hong Kong by providing them with the "safety-net" of a foreign passport are also likely to fail. Examples include Swiss, Italian, Belgian, French and German multinational corporations, who are reportedly "quietly" beginning to pressure their governments to grant residency to key Hong Kong employees (Murphy, 1991:24); and the Canadian Chamber of Commerce, which is currently studying the implications of Canadian passports being given to key Hong Kong residents who work for foreign-owned firms in Hong Kong (Skeldon, 1990–1991:514).

REFERENCES

Anon. (1989a). "Hong Kong Residents Scour World for Refuge." *The Globe and Mail* (Toronto), 23 September, A5.

———— (1989b). "Queensland Draws Immigrants to Australia's Gold Coast." *The Emigrant*, 1 (11), pp. 9–47

———— (1990a). "Hong Kong Immigrants." *The Globe and Mail* (Toronto), 7 November, A6.

———— (1990b). "Canadian Role Growing in Hong Kong Imports." *The Globe and Mail* (Toronto), 8 November, B25.

———— (1990c). "Optimism Breaches Massive Shadow Looming over Colony." *The Globe and Mail* (Toronto), 8 November, B25.

———— (1990d). "Hong Kong Beckons Red-tape Weary Business." *The Globe and Mail* (Toronto), 22 November, B24.

———— (1991a). "Sale of Yacht Maker C & C to Hong Kong Firm Likely." *The Globe and Mail* (Toronto), 19 February, B17.

———— (1991b). "Social Studies — Wordwatch: 'astronaut' " *The Globe and Mail* (Toronto), 15 March, A18.

———— (1991c). "Spa for Summerside." *The Globe and Mail* (Toronto), 9 April, B3.

———— (1991d). "Asian Economies Expected to Keep Performing Well." *The Globe and Mail* (Toronto), 24 April, B19.

———— (1991e). "Mulroney Blasts Critics of Japan." *The Globe and Mail* (Toronto), 21 May, A4.

———— (1991f). "Interview: Clinton Leeks, Hong Kong's Refugee Coordinator." *Refugees* (Geneva), June (86), pp. 36–38.

———— (1991g). "Hong Kong Airport Deal." *The Globe and Mail* (Toronto), 5 July, B2.

Australia. Australian Bureau of the Census (1987). *Overseas Arrivals and Departures*. Canberra: Australian Bureau of the Census (Catalogue No. 3404.0).

Australia. Department of Immigration, Local Government and Ethnic Affairs (1987, with subsequent updates). *Migrant Entry Handbook*. Canberra: Department of Immigration, Local Government and Ethnic Affairs.

Bayless, A. (1989). "Lotusland Grapples with an Ugly — and Costly — Backlash." *Financial Times* (Toronto), 10 July.

BBC. (1989). "Hong Kong Immigration Plan." British Broadcasting Corporation World Service Radio News (London), 20 December, 06:00 GMT.

Bociurkiw (1990). "Record Emigration Figures Belie Veneer of Calm." *The Globe and Mail* (Toronto), 27 November, B28.

Bowring, P. and M. Taylor (1991). "Bring on the Reserves: Hong Kong Faces Challenge of Mobilising Vast Assets." *Far Eastern Economic Review*, 4 April, pp. 46–48.

Buruma, Ian. (1990). "The Last Days of Hong Kong." *The New York Review of Books*, 12 April, pp. 41–46.

Canada Employment and Immigration Commission (1984). *1982 Immigration Statistics: Canada*. Ottawa: Ministry of Supply and Services.

———— (1986). *Immigration Statistics 1984: Canada*. Ottawa: Ministry of Supply and Services.

———— (1987). *Immigration Statistics 1985: Canada*. Ottawa: Ministry of Supply and Services.

———— (1988). *Immigration Statistics 1986: Canada*. Ottawa: Ministry of Supply and Services.

Cannon, M. (1989). *China Tide: The Revealing Story of the Hong Kong Exodus to Canada*. Toronto: Harper and Collins.

Chang, S. (1987). "Towards 1997: Apprehensions and Preparations in Hong Kong." Paper presented at the Canadian Association of Geographers (Ontario Division) Annual Meeting, 15 October, Windsor, Ontario.

Chen, A.H.Y. (1988). "The Development of Immigration Law and Policy: The Hong
    Kong Experience." *McGill Law Journal*, 33(4), pp. 631–675.
Crithchley, B and E. Reguly (1987). "Canada for Sale." *The Financial Post* (Toron-
    to), 16–22 March, p. 1.
Cu-Uy-Gam, M. (1989). "Immigrants Waiting to Bring Their Money into Canada."
    The Financial Post (Toronto), 3 July.
DeMont, J. and T. Fennell (1989). *Hong Kong Money: How Chinese Families and
    Fortunes are Changing Canada*. Toronto: Key Porter.
Dubro, R. (1991). "Shooting It out in Chinatown." *The Globe and Mail* (Toronto),
    5 March, A15.
Fennell, T. (1987). "Rich and Powerful." *Macleans* (Toronto), 17 August, pp. 24–27
——— (1989). "Fear in the Colony." *Macleans* (Toronto), 19 June.
Hawkins, F. (1988). *Canada and Immigration: Public Policy and Public Concern*,
    2nd edition. Kingston and Montreal: McGill–Queen's University Press.
——— (1989). *Critical Years in Immigration: Canada and Australia Compared*.
    Kingston and Montreal: McGill–Queen's University Press.
Hewett, G. (1990). "Japan Sees 1997 as Buy Opportunity." *The Globe and Mail*
    (Toronto), 27 November, B28.
Hillen, E. (1991). "Poor Big Rich Town." *Saturday Night* (Toronto), March,
    pp. 38–42.
Ip, G. (1989). "Immigration Debate Prompts Name-calling." *The Vancouver Sun*,
    26 May, B4.
——— (1990). "Immigrant Investor Plan Reviewed." *The Financial Post* (Toronto),
    7 August, pp. 1, 3.
Islam, N. (1989). "Canada's Immigration Policy: Compassion, Economic Necessity
    or Lifeboat Ethics?" *How Ottawa Spends 1989–90: The Buck Stops Where?*
    edited by K. A. Graham. Ottawa: Carleton University Press.
Kwong, P.C.K. (1990). "Emigration and Manpower Shortage." *The Other Hong
    Kong Report 1990*, edited by R.Y.C. Wong and J.Y.S. Cheng. Hong Kong: The
    Chinese University Press.
Kwong, P.C.K., Pak-wai Liu and S.L.W. Tang (1990). *The Functional Core of the
    Labour Force*. Hong Kong: Department of Sociology, The Chinese University
    of Hong Kong.
Lau, E. (1987). "On To Greener Pastures." *Far Eastern Economic Review*, 18 June,
    pp. 22–25
Levin, M. (1989). "Hong Kong Canadians Line up to Leave Colony." *Financial
    Times* (Toronto), 3 July, p. 10.
Macdonald, P. (1990). "Huge Loss to Territory in Migration." *Hong Kong Standard*,
    9 December.
Malarek, V. (1987). *Haven's Gate: Canada's Immigration Fiasco*. Toronto: Mac-
    millan of Canada.

McDougall, The Honourable Barbara (1990). Address by the Minister of Employment and Immigration to the Canadian Chamber of Commerce, Hong Kong, 5 September. Ottawa: Employment and Immigration (Public Affairs, Immigration).

Mosher, S. (1991). "Declaring an Interest: US and Canada Whom Concern over Territory's Future." *Far Eastern Economic Review*, 13 June, pp. 11–12.

Murphy, C. (1991). "Hong Kong: A Culture of Emigration." *The Atlantic Monthly*, April, pp. 20–26.

National Film Board (1989). *Who Gets In?* Montreal: National Film Board of Canada.

Nash, A. E. (1987). *The Economic Impact of the Entrepreneur Immigrant Programme.* Ottawa: The Institute for Research on Public Policy (Discussion Paper 87.B.1).

———— (1988a). "Our Enterprising Immigrants." *Policy Options*, 9 (10), pp. 19–23.

———— (1988b). "Entrepreneur Immigration in Canada and Australia: A Comparison." Paper presented at the International Geographic Union, 22 August, Sydney, Australia.

———— (1990). "The Need to Explain Immigration Policy: Canada and Australia have much in common — Including Reticence on This Issue." *Policy Options*, 11 (1), p. 36.

Oziewicz, S. (1990). "Canadian Diplomats Wary of Bribe Attempts." *The Globe and Mail* (Toronto), 7 December, A6.

Phillips, A. (1989). "Apprehension in Hong Kong." *Macleans* (Toronto), 19 June, p. 27.

Ross, A. and N. V. Freeman (1987). "The Richest Refugees." *Canadian Business*, May, pp. 32–42 & 95–100.

Sheppard, J. (1988). "For the Wealthy, Canada Has Two Prime Attractions." *The Ottawa Citizen*, 23 January, B6.

Simpson, J. (1991). "The Emigrants Are Lining up in Hong Kong and Looking to Canada." *The Globe and Mail* (Toronto), 19 June, A18.

Skeldon, R. (1990–1991). "Emigration and the Future of Hong Kong." *Pacific Affairs*, 63 (4), pp. 500–523

Taylor, P. (1989). "Hong Kong Yacht People Buy up Vancouver." *The Sunday Telegraph* (London), 4 June.

Taylor, L. (1991). "Police Fear Business Migration Crime Link." *The Australian*, 25 April, p. 2.

Terry, E. (1991a). "PM Upholds Hong Kong Distinctiveness." *The Globe and Mail* (Toronto), 23 May, A7.

———— (1991b). "Hong Kong Autonomy Essential for Entire Region, Mulroney Says." *The Globe and Mail* (Toronto), 25 May, A6.

———— (1991c). "PM's Message Fails to Impress." *The Globe and Mail* (Toronto), 27 May, A8.

Tierney, B. (1989). "China Puts Squeeze on Hong Kong." *The Ottawa Citizen*, 13 September, A9.

Totaro, P. (1988). "Anti-Australian Bbacklash Sweeps S-E Asia." *Sydney Morning Herald*, 23 August, p. 4.

Valeriano, L. (1991). "Green-card Law Means Business to Immigrants." *The Wall Street Journal*, 27 February, B1, B2

Walters, R. (1990). *Recent Developments in Asia Pacific Direct Investment*. Research and Discussion Paper 7. Canberra: Department of Foreign Affairs and Trade, Trade Strategy Branch.

Winchester, S. (1991). "Old Dart No Bullseye for Emigrants." *The Australian*, 15 April, p. 9

Wu, C. T. and J. Connell (1988). "Australia: Promised Land for Asia and the Pacific." Paper presented at the International Geographic Union, 22–25 August, Sydney, Australia.

Index